D0775904

MAKING GOVERNMENT WORK

MAKING GOVERNMENT WORK

A CONSERVATIVE AGENDA FOR THE STATES

FOREWORDS BY

NIKKI HALEY

AND

RONALD REAGAN

EDITED BY

TAN PARKER

REGNERY PUBLISHING
A Division of Salem Media Group

Copyright © 2020 by Tan Parker, Spaeth Communications, Inc., and Texas Public Policy Foundation
"Defending the Second Amendment" chapter copyright © 2020 by Chuck Norris
Foreword by Ronald Reagan reprinted with permission.

Care of: *Making Government Work*
901 Congress Ave.
Austin, Texas 78701

All rights reserved. No part of this publication may be reproduced or transmitted in any form or by any means electronic or mechanical, including photocopy, recording, or any information storage and retrieval system now known or to be invented, without permission in writing from the publisher, except by a reviewer who wishes to quote brief passages in connection with a review written for inclusion in a magazine, newspaper, website, or broadcast.

Scriptures taken from the Holy Bible, New International Version®, NIV®. Copyright © 1973, 1978, 1984, 2011 by Biblica, Inc.™ Used by permission of Zondervan. All rights reserved worldwide. www.zondervan.com The "NIV" and "New International Version" are trademarks registered in the United States Patent and Trademark Office by Biblica, Inc.™
Scripture quotations taken from the New American Standard Bible® (NASB), Copyright © 1960, 1962, 1963, 1968, 1971, 1972, 1973, 1975, 1977, 1995 by The Lockman Foundation. Used by permission. www.Lockman.org.
Scripture taken from the New King James Version®. Copyright © 1982 by Thomas Nelson. Used by permission. All rights reserved.

Regnery® is a registered trademark of Salem Communications Holding Corporation

ISBN: 978-1-68451-168-6
eISBN: 978-1-68451-175-4

Published in the United States by
Regnery Publishing
A Division of Salem Media Group
300 New Jersey Ave NW
Washington, DC 20001
www.Regnery.com

Manufactured in the United States of America

10 9 8 7 6 5 4 3 2

Books are available in quantity for promotional or premium use. For information on discounts and terms, please visit our website: www.Regnery.com.

This book is dedicated to the memory of Tex Lezar. Tex was one of the nation's greatest conservative legal minds of the century, a dedicated patriot and public servant, and most importantly, a wonderful husband and father and a man of deep faith. We thank him for his life of service to others and for constantly giving back to the state and nation that he loved. He is dearly missed by all who knew and loved him.

His life and legacy live on through his wife, Merrie, his wonderful children, and in the ideas and principles that he championed that are contained in the pages of this book. My hope is that he would think we did justice to his life's work.

This book is dedicated to the men and women of the United States Armed Forces, who have sacrificed their time, talents, and all too often their lives to advance and protect the cause of liberty. They have allowed this constitutional republic to flourish despite great challenges for over 240 years, and in so doing have cultivated the most economically prosperous, freedom-loving, compassionate, and generous nation the world has ever known.

Soldiers, Sailors, and Airmen of the Allied Expeditionary Force:

You are about to embark upon the Great Crusade, toward which we have striven these many months.

The eyes of the world are upon you. The hopes and prayers of liberty-loving people everywhere march with you.

In company with our brave Allies and brothers-in-arms on other Fronts you will bring about the destruction of the German war machine, the elimination of Nazi tyranny over oppressed peoples of Europe, and security for ourselves in a free world.

Your task will not be an easy one. Your enemy is well trained, well equipped, and battle-hardened. He will fight savagely.

But this is the year 1944. Much has happened since the Nazi triumphs of 1940–41. The United Nations have inflicted upon the Germans great defeats, in open battle, man-to-man. Our air offensive has seriously reduced their strength in the air and their capacity to wage war on the ground. Our Home Fronts have given us an overwhelming superiority in weapons and munitions of war, and placed at our disposal great reserves of trained fighting men. The tide has turned. The free men of the world are marching together to victory.

I have full confidence in your courage, devotion to duty, and skill in battle. We will accept nothing less than full victory.

Good Luck! And let us all beseech the blessing of Almighty God upon this great and noble undertaking.

General Dwight D. Eisenhower
June 6, 1944

Contents

Foreword

by Ronald Reagan, from the 1994 edition of
Making Government Work

During my time as Governor of California, I realized that the biggest problems we had regarding big government had to be solved in Washington, which was gradually but inexorably taking power from the states. We have now at least begun the process of returning to the states some of the powers they need to meet the needs of our citizens. That effort must be continued—and met—by new proposals for action by the states and localities. That is the purpose of this book, to provide A Conservative Agenda for the States.

I'm reminded of something that James Madison said in 1788: "Since the general civilization of mankind, I believe there are more instances of the abridgment of the freedom of the people by gradual and silent encroachment of those in power than by violent and sudden usurpations." His friend and neighbor, Thomas Jefferson, thought much the same way. "What has destroyed liberty and the rights of men in every government that has ever existed under the sun?" he asked. And he then answered: "The generalizing and concentrating of all cares and powers into one body."

As Governor of California, I experienced how the federal bureaucracy had its hand in everything and was "concentrating all cares and power into one body." Washington would establish a new program that the states were supposed to administer, then set so many rules and regulations that the state wasn't really administering it—you were just following orders from Washington. Most of these programs could not only be operated more effectively but also more economically with greater state and local discretion.

The federal government didn't create the states; the states created the federal government. Washington, ignoring principles of the Constitution, has, however, too frequently tried to turn the states into nothing more than administrative districts of the federal government. And the primrose path to federal control has, to a large extent, followed the lure of federal financial aid. From our schools to our farms, Washington bureaucrats have tried to dictate to Americans what they could or could not do. They have portrayed bureaucratic control as the price Americans must pay for federal aid from Washington. The money comes with strings that reach all the way back to the Potomac.

Usually with the best of intentions, Congress passes a new program, appropriates the money for it, then assigns bureaucrats in Washington to disperse the money. Almost always, the bureaucrats respond by telling states, cities, counties, and schools how to spend this money.

To use Madison's words, Washington usurped power from the states by the "gradual and silent encroachment of those in power." Federal handouts frequently went to the states for programs the states would not have chosen themselves. But they took the money because it was there; it seemed to be "free."

Over time, states and localities became so dependent on the money from Washington that, like junkies, they found it all but impossible to break the habit. Only after becoming addicted did they realize how pervasive the federal regulations were that came with the money.

As all this was going on, the federal government was taking an ever-increasing share of the nation's total tax revenues—making it more diffi-cult for states and local governments to raise money on their own. As a result, states and localities became even more the captives of federal money, federal dictates, and federal governments surrendered control of their own destiny to a faceless national government that claimed to know better how to solve the problems of a city or town than the people who lived there. And if local officials or their congressmen ever tried to end a program they didn't like or they thought was unproductive and wasteful, they discovered that the beneficiaries of the program and the bureaucrats who administered it had formed too tight an alliance to defeat. Once started, a federal program benefitting any group or special interest is virtually impossible to end and the costs go on forever.

We have strayed a great distance from our Founding Fathers' vision of America. They regarded the central government's responsibility as that of providing national security, protecting our democratic freedoms, and limiting the government's intrusion into our lives—in sum, the protection of life, liberty, and the pursuit of happiness. They never envisioned vast agencies in Washington telling our farmers what to plant, our teachers what to teach, our industries what to build. The Constitution they wrote established sovereign states, not administrative districts of the federal government. They believed in keeping government as close as possible to the people. If parents didn't like the way their schools were being run, they could throw out the Board of Education at the next election. But what could they do directly about the elite bureaucrats in the U.S. Department of Education who sent ultimatums into their children's classrooms regarding curriculum and textbooks?

As President I tried to do as much as I could to return responsibility to the states and localities. Today, the hottest area of public policy making is now back in the states, or as the former House Democratic whip Representative William H. Gray III has recently said, "I don't think the federal government will be the engine of major change in the 1990's." Somehow I believe that our Administration's emphasis on turning back to the states areas of responsibility that had been wrongfully preempted by the federal government has encouraged the states as problem solvers.

For the states to provide real solutions to the problems and challenges of the 90's and the 21st Century and beyond, state policymakers will need the benefit of research that is both practical and also reflects basic American principles—an emphasis on the individual, respect for private property, reliance upon government closest to the people, shared western values, and the dynamism of the free market.

For policymakers and interested citizens, this book should be the first stop on the road to turning the Tenth Amendment of the U.S. Constitution from a flabby invalid into a healthy and muscular individual. I know that in the days ahead I will frequently refer to *Making Government Work: A Conservative Agenda for the States* as my guide for state public policy. I urge all Americans to do likewise.

Foreword

by Nikki R. Haley

It's been more than twenty-five years since the first edition of this wonderful book. In the foreword he wrote at the time, President Ronald Reagan, just a few years out of the Oval Office, expressed his hope that states would "provide real solutions to the problems and challenges" of the future. He wrote those words in 1994. Now it's 2020. How have we done?

I think President Reagan would be proud.

The last two and a half decades have seen an incredible explosion of state-based leadership. From coast to coast, governors and state legislators have found new and creative ways to help their citizens thrive. They've stepped up in the wake of the September 11, 2001, terrorist attack, the 2008 economic collapse and the Great Recession that followed, and most recently, the coronavirus pandemic and the shocks that it caused. In good times and bad, state leaders have worked hard to do right by the people they represent.

Not only have states led the way on issue after issue, they have fought back against a federal government that is still too big, too bossy, and too bloated. The Constitution's system of federalism, which President Reagan did so much to renew, is very much alive in the twenty-first century. In his day, thanks to his actions, he was able to say that the "hottest area of public policy making is now back in the states." Fast-forward to our day, and state policy leadership continues to set the standard.

I had a front-row seat to a lot of the great state progress of recent years. In 2004, I was elected to the South Carolina House of Representatives, and in 2010, the people of South Carolina took a chance on me as their governor. It was my privilege to serve alongside some truly innovative, effective, and principled governors who were also elected that year—Rick Scott in Florida, Scott Walker in Wisconsin, Susana Martinez in New Mexico, and so many others. In the years that followed, America saw some of the most important state reforms in generations, many of them grounded in the ideas found in the first edition of this book.

For my part, I worked hard to make South Carolina a place where every family could thrive. From day one, I wanted to make it clear that government was there to serve the people, not the other way around. Good government requires remembering who you work for, so I had all state employees start answering the phones by saying, "It's a great day in South Carolina. How can I help you?" They hated it. The people loved it.

Growing up in a small family business, I knew that government can have your back, or it can stab you in the back. So I told my agencies that time is money, and if you were costing a person or business time, then you were costing them money, and that was no longer acceptable. We had every agency streamline things to set businesses up to succeed, not regulate them into failure.

I did my best to make sure South Carolina gave people enough support to find their best path. We reformed how our state spent money on education, helping poor and rural communities the most. We launched a job training program that prepared tens of thousands of students to get good-paying jobs and instituted a Second Chance program that helped thousands of inmates prepare for life on the other side of the fence. And we launched a program that moved more than thirty-five thousand South Carolinians from welfare to work, which was a 54 percent drop in the welfare caseload. Our success was based on my belief that when you give a person a job, you take care of a family.

What we were able to accomplish made South Carolina an even better place to live, work, and raise a family. And it made us one of the most competitive and attractive states in America. We attracted over $20 billion in new capital investment. We were number one in foreign capital investment and number one in export growth in our region. And only a generation after South Carolina was devastated by the collapse of the textile industry, our state was building airplanes by Boeing, cars by BMW, Mercedes-Benz, and Volvo, and we had five international tire companies.

I went from South Carolina to the United Nations, where as ambassador I saw how exceptional our constitutional system is. No other country on earth empowers states to experiment, innovate, and compete with each other to prove which one can give the American people the best shot at the best life. Every day I was in that job, my appreciation for America grew.

I also came to a deeper recognition of the many serious challenges we face, both at home and abroad. From the economy to education, from innovation to infrastructure, from cultural renewal to the defense of free speech, we need to take action to strengthen America for the next generation. The question is how we'll do this—and who will lead.

Given what needs to be done, it's no surprise that we're hearing renewed calls for Washington, D.C., to take a bigger role in American life. But this is as wrong today as it was when Ronald Reagan was governor of California. And we are right today to fight it as Reagan did as president of the United States. In the years ahead, governors and legislators need to be more assertive than ever in the defense of the states' constitutional role. And all of us who have served, now serve, or will serve in state government need to think creatively and courageously about how to solve the problems that confront our country.

Of course, the challenges of today are different from those of twenty-five years ago. But the principles that we need to overcome those challenges are the same. Personal freedom. Economic liberty. Equal justice. The rule of law. And above all, a deep belief in the American people. Our duty is also the same as it has always been: empower our fellow citizens to do what they do best and show the world what free people are capable of. That starts in the states, and the bigger their role, the brighter our future.

For anyone who wants to usher in that future and strengthen America at the all-important state level, this book is for you. It has an all-star lineup of contributors. Tan Parker has done a public service by taking on this project. It gives a new voice to the values at the heart of our country. It doesn't just need to be read, it needs to be put into practice. I'll do my part, and I'm confident that millions of Americans from all walks of life will join me.

God bless,
Nikki R. Haley

Preface

by Tan Parker

Serving in the Texas House of Representatives over the years, I have witnessed firsthand the impact that a state like Texas can have on the future direction of the nation. The Founders' belief that stronger states make for a stronger union is alive and well today in state capitols across the country.

The innovation and creativity generated in the states has unleashed public policy that is transforming lives, lifting people up out of poverty, educating our children in new ways, reducing crime, creating new levels of economic prosperity, improving the protection of our children, and driving medical innovation. Often legislation that originates in a particular state spreads from one state capitol to another before its potential adoption as federal policy. In this very real sense, the states are serving as laboratories for innovation and efficiency to help guide the nation.

Our accomplishments as states are not often talked about by citizens of this great nation because, candidly, they don't get the national attention they deserve on the evening news. As conservatives, we have lost our way when it comes to communicating the successes of extraordinary public policy breakthroughs throughout the states.

Why is this happening? Well, it's my belief that as conservatives we lost our storytelling tradition after the passing of President Ronald Reagan. One of President Reagan's unique gifts was the ability to distill complex policy and solutions in a widely understood manner. He was able to blend both his strong grasp of a particular subject and his humanity by pragmatically connecting policy to the hopes and aspirations of the American people. This is why he was known as "the Great Communicator." I was indeed very blessed as a young man to experience President Reagan's abilities firsthand. I was granted the honor of spending a day with him in which, with the greatest of skill, he seamlessly wove together stories from his life and presidency with major policy priorities and accomplishments. It became more evident to me than ever before that his storytelling ability was not only natural, but unparalleled.

As conservatives, we have incredible stories and successes to share about what we have achieved through the years on behalf of the citizens we are so fortunate to represent. However, we have not done a good enough job consistently articulating what these victories mean in tangible terms for the people of this country.

In this 2020 edition of *Making Government Work: A Conservative Agenda for the States*, twenty-six years after the original book's publication (led by my friend and mentor Tex Lezar), it's my aspiration and vision to share some of these stories of success from across the nation.

It's also my hope, beyond revitalizing President Reagan's storytelling tradition, to put forth a compelling blueprint for what we believe as conservatives on a wide range of public policy subjects that are critical to the future of the nation.

Another unique aspect of the states' power to drive high-quality public policy is the ability of legislators in many state capitals, including Texas's in particular, to engage with one another across party lines with civility. Historically, civil discourse has been one of the hallmarks of why we have been able to achieve so much as a diverse nation since our founding.

Today, we Americans have a very real concern that Washington will not be able to meet the challenges that lie ahead because of this lack of civility and respect for one another. This lack of civility has existed in Washington now for several decades.

It goes well beyond traditional politics. For example, with our sports championships at both the collegiate and professional levels, controversy surrounds teams that simply go to the White House for their accomplishment to be celebrated (a long-standing tradition). Often, teams or players skip out completely on what should be the honor of a lifetime, being recognized by their president and nation for a job well done.

This book's message is simple—we must accept one another in spite of our differences and agree to disagree without demonizing one another, striving to foster civility where possible for the good of our citizens and the future longevity of our nation.

As I conclude writing this book in April 2020, the United States is facing what is likely the greatest threat to public health and economic well-being in the nation's history: the COVID-19 pandemic. My prayer is that, as Americans, we will pull together regardless of our political differences and work together to solve the crisis in a manner worthy of our people and the greatest nation the world has ever known, as we have proven time and time again throughout our history.

I'm deeply grateful for the opportunity in life to have been mentored as a young man by Tex Lezar, who served as President Reagan's assistant U.S. attorney general, along with a host of additional remarkable career achievements including being editor of the original *Making Government Work: A Conservative Agenda for the States*, in 1994.

Tragically, Tex passed much too young in 2004. He truly was one of the greatest conservative legal minds of our time. His life and legacy live on through his wife Merrie Spaeth and their children. I wish to thank Merrie for her friendship, confidence in me, and for requesting that I lead the effort to create a 2020 version of *Making Government Work*. I also wish to thank the Texas Public Policy Foundation for its support of the original book in 1994 and for being a great partner again in 2020.

I'm most grateful to the incredible authors who have participated and shared their views in this 2020 edition. Thank you to all of you who believed in me and said yes to participating in this vision for creating a new conservative blueprint for the states and our nation.

A complete listing of those I wish to thank for their contributions can be found in the Acknowledgments portion of this book.

Finally, I wish to thank you, the reader, for taking the time to study *Making Government Work*. I hope you will find this book beneficial to your own journey and understanding of the topics addressed, topics which now challenge our states and nation.

For liberty,

Tan Parker

Acknowledgments

I'm most grateful for the extraordinary opportunity to lead and create the 2020 edition of *Making Government Work*.

It's been an incredible lifelong journey that led me to develop an updated version, and the process of constructing the book itself is certainly an experience I shall never forget.

This journey began for me as a young man. I had the distinct privilege as a nineteen-year-old college student to intern under Tex Lezar in his first race for Texas attorney general and to meet and work with his wonderful wife, Merrie Spaeth. Among many other remarkable career achievements, Merrie served President Reagan as his director of media relations. They were both so fabulous to me and took me in as a young college student at the University of Dallas. The education I received from them on so many levels was priceless!

Tex was an amazing man in so many ways. He served as a speechwriter for President Nixon, as President Reagan's assistant U.S. attorney general, as a member of the Federal Judiciary Advisory Group, and as a delegate to the United Nations International Conference on African Refugee Assistance. Immediately following his graduation from Yale, he was mentored by William F. Buckley, who solidified in him his lifelong conservative beliefs. Tex was one of the greatest conservative legal minds of the century. He believed passionately in limited government, the importance of adhering to a strict constructionist view of the U.S. Constitution, and the critical importance of the separation of powers. He also believed fervently in federalism and the importance of the Tenth Amendment in creating stronger states and therefore a stronger nation. He was also a man who loved his country deeply and was devoted to his family and his faith.

In 1994, Tex created the original *Making Government Work: A Conservative Agenda for the States*. The book was widely praised in conservative circles and offered a template for making the states stronger and more vibrant.

Tex was so good to me and always made time for my questions and to help me better understand the timeless principles of the separation of powers and the importance of states' rights and the Tenth Amendment.

The Lord called Tex home much too early in life, at just fifty-five. It was one of the great blessings in my life to have known him, to have worked with him, and to have been mentored by this great man who was so generous to me.

After Tex's passing, I continued my friendship with Merrie Spaeth throughout the years. She has been my trusted advisor and my communications and media consultant. I selected her to share her expertise with my Texas House Republican Caucus colleagues when I led the organization.

In 2019, Merrie approached me and asked that I pick up Tex's mantle and lead the creation of a 2020 version of *Making Government Work*. You can imagine my great surprise and emotion at being asked to do so. Words can't adequately express my gratitude for her confidence in me to embark on an endeavor so important to the nation and the legacy of her loving husband. I am so grateful for Merrie's tremendous support and active involvement with me in the creation of this book.

I want to thank Kevin Roberts, the executive director of the Texas Public Policy Foundation (TPPF), for his incredible support of this book as well. He has been a tremendous partner in this journey. TPPF has become one of the great conservative institutions in our nation, a critical pillar for protecting liberty and limited government.

I'm also very grateful to Brooke Rollins for her support of the book. She led the creation of the modern-day TPPF for many years as president of the organization before transitioning to the role of senior advisor to President Trump in the White House. Tex partnered with TPPF in 1994 on the original version of the book and also served as an early president of the organization, so I could not have asked for a better group of people to partner with in 2020.

Meaghan Klitch at Spaeth Communications did a wonderful job assisting me daily in this journey and I'm so thankful to her. I'm also very grateful to Roy Maynard for his professionalism and dedication to the project. I also wish to thank Trish Robinson, my chief of staff, who volunteered her time outside of her normal work commitments to support me in the creation of this book.

Many thanks to Brian Philips, Chuck DeVore, and Andrew Brown for their great contributions and Bridgett Wagner at the Heritage Foundation. Additionally, I wish to thank Tom Tradup, Nadine Maenza, John Polster, and Doug Deason for their wonderful support.

I want each of my individual authors to know how much I appreciate their time and contributions. I'm most grateful for their trust in me. This book would not have been possible without the tremendous commitment of each of the authors, who all worked tirelessly. They represent the best of America and I'm so grateful for their commitment to *Making Government Work*.

Author Listing:
House Majority Leader Dick Armey
Governor Jeb Bush
James Jay Carafano
Jacki Deason
Professor Richard J. Dougherty
Nicholas C. Drinkwater
Becky Norton Dunlop
Professor Robert P. George

Kathleen Hartnett White
Bob Hellman
Chad Hennings
Kathy Ireland
Lt. Governor Rebecca Kleefisch
Dr. Arthur B. Laffer
Tyson Langhofer
Marc Levin
Chuck Norris
Captain Scott O'Grady
Secretary Rick Perry
Vikrant Reddy
Senator Rick Santorum
Professor Bradley A. Smith
Merrie Spaeth
Dick Trabulsi
Grace-Marie Turner
Robert L. Woodson Sr.

Additionally, I wish to thank all of the participants who worked with Tex on the original version of *Making Government Work* in 1994 for the legacy they created.

I want to also share that all participants volunteered their time in the creation of this book and all proceeds generated from the sales will be donated, primarily to organizations that serve America's veterans.

Last but certainly not least, I wish to thank my wife, Beth, for her unwavering support and encouragement of me and my public service. She is my hero and inspiration in this life.

—Tan Parker

Federalism and the American Experiment: The Intention of the Constitution

by Professor Richard J. Dougherty

The drafting of the U.S. Constitution, which began on May 25, 1787, in the Pennsylvania State House and ended on September 17 of that year, is one of the greatest achievements in all of human history. The Constitutional Convention in Philadelphia created the framework for our nation. Once the ratification process was completed by each state, the Founders had created the most significant political document the world has ever known. The delegates to the convention in that summer of 1787 accomplished something unimaginable in just under four months. These Founders established the supreme law of the United States that has governed our nation beautifully for over 230 years. Our Founders established Federalism—the balance of power between the state governments and the federal government. The Founders also placed internal limits on government through the creation of the separation of powers and through the establishment of the Tenth Amendment, which guarantees states' rights. No one better understands or is able to more clearly explain our extraordinary founding documents than Professor Richard J. Dougherty, who is one of the leading constitutional scholars in the United States today. Throughout his career he has focused on constitutionalism and the principles of American politics, the presidency, and America's founding. He is the chairman of the Department of Politics and the director of the Center for Christianity and the Common Good at the University of Dallas (UD). I am very thankful to Dr. Dougherty for being such a wonderful teacher for me as a young man at UD and for accepting my invitation to write the historical context and framework for *Making Government Work*.

—Tan Parker

Contemporary debates about the proper scope and function of exercises of public power at the national level rightly often focus on issues such as the role of the federal bureaucracy, the separation of powers, executive overreach, and examples of judicial lawmaking from the bench. What these issues have in common is the way in which all the sectors of the federal government have undermined the legitimate role that state and local power were intended to play under our constitutional design.

Discussions of the proper role of state power regularly focus on distinctions between conservative and progressive views of policy and initiative, with conservatives typically being described as the more militant defenders of local power. But this is an outdated way of thinking of the question of federalism, as numerous policy issues have arisen that suggest a more robust interest in state and local power might in fact be used to forward more progressive causes, such as the legalization of marijuana and assisted suicide guidelines

For example, abortion, the most heavily debated of public policy and moral issues over the past half-century, is not so clearly understood along the older lines of thinking—there is certainly some concern among those favoring the right to abortion that a conservative Supreme Court might, for instance, simply ban the practice outright, perhaps by adopting the principle that the unborn child deserves protection as a person under the Fourteenth Amendment's "due process" clause.[1]

The importance of federalism, then, is not that it serves a particular political agenda. Rather, the issue is one of the structure and meaning of the fundamental institutions and operations of American government, intended as they are to serve the protection of the interest of liberty and the rights of American citizens. Undermining the intended form of the constitutional design serves as a direct threat to the protection of those rights and interests, and it thus behooves all parties to be concerned about the intervention of the heavy hand of the federal government in the lives of its citizens.

The increased role of the federal government in policy-making and enforcement has resulted in the proliferation of federal programs and agencies, many of which have virtually no accountability to the American citizenry. The proper solution to much of what concerns our society today is not to turn to bodies of unaccountable "experts" whose decisions about policy concerns are unconnected to the real interests of constituents. As always, the real solution to our very real problems is always more politics, not less politics.

THE FOUNDERS ON FEDERALISM

General dissatisfaction with the Articles of Confederation at the time of the American founding led to the call in 1786 for a convention to correct or improve the Articles, eventually leading to the convening of the Constitutional Convention in May 1787. The delegates to the convention quickly recognized the need to start over in the construction of a new arrangement, which resulted in the drafting and ratification of the Constitution in 1787 and 1788. One of the central questions was the role that the states would play in this arrangement.

Surely Publius saw the efforts of the states under the Articles of Confederation as ineffective, and he suggests in the *Federalist Papers* the cause of that incapacity. He describes in *Federalist* No. 15 what he considers the "great and radical vice" of the Articles, which is to be found in "the principle of LEGISLATION for STATES or GOVERNMENTS, in their CORPORATE or COLLECTIVE CAPACITIES, and as contradistinguished from the INDIVIDUALS of which they consist."[2] In other words, the federal or general government, to be effective, must have some capacity to pass laws directly affecting individual citizens and not be beholden to the individual states to carry out national policies. The states under the Articles were seen as too often dragging their feet on implementing those policies, or even through their open hostility to the general government as simply disdainful of the ends it was promoting.[3]

But for advocates of the Constitution, the fact that the general government would have more power did not mean this power would be unlimited. There was no question, in other words, that the state and local governments would maintain a good degree of authority. Publius in the *Federalist Papers* attempts to persuade the defenders of state authority that the Constitution maintains substantial state power:

> The proposed Constitution, so far from implying an abolition of the State governments, makes them constituent parts of the national sovereignty, by allowing them a direct representation in the Senate, and leaves in their possession certain exclusive and very important portions of sovereign power.[4]

One way in which Publius makes the point is to argue that the Constitution as proposed contains, in fact, a mixture of forms, such that it cannot be accurately described as simply national—meaning consolidating all power—nor simply federal, because it is both at the same time:

> The proposed Constitution, therefore, is, in strictness, neither a national nor a federal Constitution, but a composition of both. In its foundation it is federal, not national; in the sources from which the ordinary powers of the government are drawn, it is partly federal and partly national; in the operation of these powers, it is national, not federal; in the extent of them, again, it is federal, not national; and, finally, in the authoritative mode of introducing amendments, it is neither wholly federal nor wholly national.[5]

The Founders did not envision a federal government with unlimited power and reach that could or would commandeer all power unto itself or supplant the power of states exercising their legitimate authority. Because the Constitution does not empower the new government to exercise unlimited or unrestricted power, in Publius's view "the proposed Government cannot be deemed a national one; since its jurisdiction extends to certain enumerated objects only, and leaves to the several States a residuary and inviolable sovereignty over all other objects."[6] Understanding the limits of that crucial phrase, "certain enumerated objects," is central to acknowledging the Framers' design.

What are those enumerated objects? Publius gives us an account of what they would be in *Federalist* No. 56, rebutting the claim that the House of Representatives would be too small and that the members would thus not have sufficient knowledge of their constituents' needs and interests. Publius notes that representatives do not have to be aware of every particular need of the constituents since the federal government is not entrusted with addressing these matters comprehensively. "What are to be the objects of federal legislation?" he asks. "Those which are of most importance, and which seem most to require local knowledge, are commerce, taxation, and the militia."[7]

In other words, the government is not entrusted with care over the everyday activities of its citizens, and thus requires only limited local knowledge.[8] There would be no doubt, then, that from the Founders' point of view the individual states would continue to play a substantial role in the direction of public policy and enforcement of the law.

Indeed, in Publius's understanding the states would maintain their prominence, given their role in "the ordinary administration of criminal and civil justice," which activity he asserts is "of all others . . . the most powerful, most universal, and most attractive source of popular obedience and attachment."[9] There is a normal and natural attraction that people have for the bodies that are closer to them, especially when they see those bodies actively maintaining their liberty and security; it serves as the "great cement of society," in Publius's words.[10]

HISTORICAL DEVELOPMENTS

How, then, did the United States move from the founding-era conception of political liberty and federalism to the contemporary era, where the federal government's influence is so far felt in so many areas of American life?[11] There are numerous factors that contributed to that shift, including the political, economic, military, and social changes that have taken place over the course of the past centuries. But the crucial point to recognize is that they were almost all entirely a result of specific choices made at particular times in American history.

An examination of just one example among many such choices will be worthwhile—the regulation of interstate commerce as a mechanism for expanding federal influence.

Historically, there were two general principles that guided the regulation of commerce by the federal government. One principle was that Congress could only regulate matters that were directly connected to interstate commerce. The other was the recognition of the difference between manufacturing and trade.[12]

"Trade" was subject to federal regulation if it was trade across state lines, but "manufacturing" was generally understood to be by definition not interstate, and thus manufacturing could not be included in Congress's powers to regulate "commerce" among the states. Yet, these distinctions came to be rejected by both Congress and the Supreme Court in the New Deal era, opening the door for vast expansions of interstate regulation.

An understanding of the process of the expansion of the conception of commerce can be found in comparing two cases from the first half of the twentieth century, *Hammer v. Dagenhart*, decided in 1918, and *United States v. Darby Lumber Company*, decided in 1941. Both cases dealt with the issue of child labor laws, but came out quite differently on the merits.

In *Hammer*, the Supreme Court struck down a federal labor law (the Keating-Owen Child Labor Act of 1916) that sought to impose a national age limit on child labor.[13] Dagenhart sued on the grounds that Congress did not have the authority to regulate manufacturing, which was distinct from commerce, and the Court upheld his challenge to the law. Justice Day, writing for a divided Court, began by articulating a broad understanding of the American political order, specifically as it relates to the principle of federalism:

> The maintenance of the authority of the states over matters purely local is as essential to the preservation of our institutions as is the conservation of the supremacy of the federal power in all matters entrusted to the nation by the federal Constitution.[14]

The legitimate authority of Congress to regulate commerce "among the several States," granted in Article I, Section 8, of the Constitution, does not extend to regulating the manufacturing of goods; thus if there is going to be any such regulation it must be done by the states.[15] As Justice Day notes, in the early and important 1824 *Gibbons v. Ogden* case Chief Justice Marshall, in defining the extent and nature of the commerce power, said, "It is the power to regulate; that is, to prescribe the rule by which commerce is to be governed."[16] Day reads this to mean that Congress does not have the authority to prohibit or eliminate commerce—he says to "destroy" it—but only to prescribe the means by which or through which the commerce can move. Thus, he argues, any further regulation that might be exercised is left to the hands of the states:

> In interpreting the Constitution it must never be forgotten that the nation is made up of states to which are entrusted the powers of local government. And to them and to the people the powers not expressly delegated to the national government are reserved. The power of the states to regulate their purely internal affairs by such laws as seem wise to the local authority is inherent and has never been surrendered to the general government.[17]

Because the Court sees manufacturing as local, or as not interstate, it holds that Congress does not have the authority to regulate it, though it would have the authority to regulate commerce.

By 1941, though, the Court had shifted significantly in regard to the question of the extent of national power, as seen in a number of dramatic cases that arose in the previous decade. From the mid-1930s, the Court struck down major pieces of New Deal legislation, ruling that parts of the Agricultural Adjustment Act and the National Industrial Recovery Act were unconstitutional.[18] But by the early 1940s, following the death or retirement of a number of justices, a unanimous Court was vastly expanding its conception of allowable federal regulation.

An especially illuminating account of this expanded understanding can be found in the 1941 *Darby Lumber* case.[19] Here, in explicit contrast to the earlier *Hammer v. Dagenhart* ruling, the Court upheld a regulatory scheme imposed by the federal government on the manufacturing of goods, including wage and hour requirements. In doing so, the Court openly acknowledged that it was overruling *Hammer,* rejecting the limiting effect of what had been construed as commerce "among" the states:

> The power of Congress over interstate commerce is not confined to the regulation of commerce among the states. It extends to those activities intrastate which so affect interstate commerce or the exercise of the power of Congress over it as to make regulation of them appropriate means to the attainment of a legitimate end, the exercise of the granted power of Congress to regulate interstate commerce.[20]

This quite broad reading of the commerce power, which came to be definitive for the Court in subsequent decades, introduced a newly charged dynamic into the power exercised by Congress, with almost no limiting principle.[21]

The Court in *Darby* addressed the question of the relationship between the state and federal governments through an analysis of the Tenth Amendment, given its apparent limitation on the exercise of federal power: "The powers not delegated to the United States by the Constitution, nor prohibited by it to the States, are reserved to the States respectively, or to the people." The Tenth Amendment as construed by the Court here is read as follows:

The [Tenth] amendment states but a truism that all is retained which has not been surrendered. There is nothing in the history of its adoption to suggest that it was more than declaratory of the relationship between the national and state governments as it had been established by the Constitution before the amendment, or that its purpose was other than to allay fears that the new national government might seek to exercise powers not granted, and that the states might not be able to exercise fully their reserved powers.[22]

In short, the Court argued, there is no substantive meaning to the Tenth Amendment, as it but states a truism. Yet for the amendment to state a "truism," there must be something true about it; the Court's ruling here in *Darby* seems to significantly contradict that assertion.

The subsequent decades brought a marked expansion of federal authority in all kinds of areas, to more general questions than commerce, significantly affecting the way state legislatures were at liberty to exercise their powers.

For example, in 2005 the Supreme Court addressed an interesting and important case concerning the authority of states to pass laws promoting the interests of local businesses. The state of Michigan had passed a law favoring in-state wineries, allowing them to sell directly to consumers, but the law was struck down by the Court.[23] In *Granholm v. Heald*, the Court ruled that Michigan could not impose burdens on out-of-state shipments that it does not impose on in-state producers, while also holding that they do still retain some power of their own:

States have broad power to regulate liquor under Sec. 2 of the Twenty-first Amendment. This power, however, does not allow States to ban, or severely limit, the direct shipment of out-of-state wine while simultaneously authorizing direct shipment by in-state producers. If a State chooses to allow direct shipment of wine, it must do so on evenhanded terms. Without demonstrating the need for discrimination, New York and

Michigan have enacted regulations that disadvantage out-of-state wine producers. Under our Commerce Clause jurisprudence, these regulations cannot stand.[24]

Interestingly, the Court does not entirely eviscerate the claim of state power to regulate, only that in instances such as this it must be done in an "evenhanded" way. Yet, even here the state might be allowed to do so only if it "demonstrated" the need for such discrimination—that is, demonstrated that need to the Court.[25]

A MODEST PROPOSAL

The federal government is capable of some degree of flexibility, as can be clearly seen in an issue which has been much in the public eye over the past decades—insurance. There rightly has been much concern about the rising cost of insurance, especially health insurance, and a common suggestion for helping to ease the burden of such costs has been to allow people to buy health insurance across state lines. But you cannot at present purchase insurance coverage across state lines. How did it occur that this one area of economic activity has been cordoned off to be controlled by the states? As it turns out, there is an interesting and perhaps important background to the arrangement.[26]

Individual states began regulating insurance companies in the nineteenth century, and in a series of cases brought before the Supreme Court that state regulation was upheld as constitutional. The Court's acceptance of state regulation was based in part on the idea that the purchase of an insurance policy was not "commerce" in such a way that it would fall under Congress's authority to regulate it. For example, the Court in the *Paul v. Virginia* case in 1879 held that "[i]ssuing a policy of insurance is not a transaction of commerce. . . . These contracts are not articles of commerce in any proper meaning of the word."[27]

This position was adopted by the Courts and upheld in cases such as *New York Life Insurance Company v. Deer Lodge County* in 1912[28] until—unsurprisingly—the New Deal Court in 1944 overturned that series of opinions in *United States v. South-Eastern Underwriters Association.*[29] Justice Black, writing for a divided Court, allowed for the extension of the Sherman Antitrust Act to cover insurance carriers, and in the process stated what is undoubtedly true at this point:

> [T]he reasons given in support of the generalization that "the business of insurance is not commerce" and can never be conducted so as to constitute "Commerce among the States" are inconsistent with many decisions of this Court which have upheld federal statutes regulating interstate commerce under the Commerce Clause.[30]

Given where the Court had moved by 1944, there was no reason to anticipate that the Court would uphold its earlier decisions in this case.

But our interest in this case is a different one. What is most remarkable about the case is what happened in the aftermath of the ruling. In 1945, in response to the decision, Congress passed the McCarran-Ferguson Act, which established an arrangement whereby Congress would allow the states to continue to regulate the health insurance industry.[31] The law did provide that Congress could engage in such regulation, but only when it made clear that it was intending to do so. Absent that assertion of authority, states were free to regulate the activity and were held immune from falling under the aegis of antitrust regulations as well, as long as they did act to regulate the industry—in the absence of engaging in such regulation, the federal regulations would apply.[32]

This shows that there was nothing inevitable about the developments that led to the concentration of power in the hands of the federal government. That development was a voluntary choice, and one that did not have to turn out the way that it did in so many other areas of social and economic policy.

CONCLUSION

The foundational principles of the Constitution, in particular the separation of powers and federalism, are central to the sustained success of the American experiment, and yet are all too often jettisoned for immediate political advantage or for a lack of understanding just how crucial they are to the flourishing of the larger system.

Alexis de Tocqueville, writing in *Democracy in America* in the 1830s, famously attributed great significance to the role that New England townships played in American life, as they served as a kind of free school for the development of the principle of self-government. It was the existence of these active political communities that allowed him to conclude that the American Constitution was "the most perfect of all known federal constitutions," but one that could perhaps succeed only in America:

> Everything is conventional and artificial in such a government, and it can be suitable only for a people long habituated to directing its affairs by itself, and in which political science has descended to the last ranks of society. I never admired the good sense and the practical intelligence of the Americans more than in the manner by which they escape the innumerable difficulties to which their federal constitution gives rise.[33]

The core of that American system, Tocqueville asserts, is "the dogma of the sovereignty of the people," a principle which extends to the smallest circles of the community, even within the household. This dogma, he notes, holds that "Providence has given to each individual . . . the degree of reason necessary for him to be able to direct himself in things that interest him exclusively."[34] To take that exercise of reason away from him, which must result from the greater concentration of power in the hands of the general government, is to undermine the capacity for self-government that is crucial to the success of representative democracy.

The post–New Deal American government has grown dramatically in both size and scope, with the result that virtually no aspect of public life is unaffected by the rules, regulations, directives, guidelines, mandates, and funding supplied or imposed by the federal authorities. The resulting stress on the constitutional order is clear in a number of ways, including the significant difficulty we have with understanding the proper role of supervision over the large bureaucracy that has become part and parcel of that new arrangement.

An insightful articulation of that problem can be seen in the account of an early observer of that expansion, Robert Jackson, who served as attorney general under Franklin Roosevelt and was subsequently put on the Supreme Court by FDR. In a 1952 case, *Federal Trade Commission v. Ruberoid*, Justice Jackson described the difficulty of reconciling the rise of administrative agencies with the original constitutional structure, noting the problem even of categorizing them:

> Administrative agencies have been called quasi-legislative, quasi-executive or quasi-judicial, as the occasion required, in order to validate their functions within the separation-of-powers scheme of the Constitution. The mere retreat to the qualifying "quasi" is implicit with confession that all recognized classifications have broken down, and "quasi" is a smooth cover which we draw over our confusion as we might use a counterpane to conceal a disordered bed.[35]

Administrative agencies like the Federal Trade Commission routinely operate like governments within themselves, making, enforcing, and judging compliance with policies and procedures they originate. The danger they represent is in part in their operations, of course, but also in the very arrangement of powers manifested in them, operating as they do outside the contours of the Constitution's structure.

Retaining popular control over elected officials is made far more likely when the officials retain their own elected powers, do not cede them to unelected bureaucrats, and when their power as a whole is limited to the enumerated powers granted them under the Constitution. Both of these measures would result in the return of power to the hands of state and local officials, which would be a beneficial way of beginning to restore American liberty and protecting the rights and interests of American citizens.

Guidelines for Pro-Growth Tax Reform for the States

by Dr. Arthur B. Laffer
and Nicholas C. Drinkwater

If there is one subject that touches almost every aspect of our modern lives, it's the economy. Having a strong and robust economy at the state and federal levels provides opportunities to improve the quality of life for our citizens. A strong economy means plentiful jobs exist, inflation is in check and therefore buying power is maintained, consumers are buying goods and services, companies are investing not only in new plants and equipment but also in research and development, and citizens are saving for their retirements and confident in the future. Different schools of thought exist within the realm of economic policy. As conservatives, we believe in the importance of free markets and free enterprise itself. We believe in low average and marginal tax rates for individuals and for businesses in order to allow both to thrive. As a result of keeping the tax wedge low, individuals and businesses are able to make new investments, creating jobs and economic opportunity. For over five decades, Dr. Arthur B. Laffer has been one of the leading conservative economists in the United States, advising both individual states and the federal government on optimal economic policies and strategies. He is probably best known for his service and counsel to President Ronald Reagan, and he is also, of course, the creator of the famous "Laffer curve" that depicts the relationship between tax rates and tax revenues. Nicholas Drinkwater serves as chief operating officer of Laffer Associates and is one of the leading young economists in the nation. It's a tremendous blessing to have both participate and share directly with Americans their wisdom on how the states themselves and the nation as a whole can continuously strive to be economically vibrant.

—Tan Parker

INCENTIVES AND THE REASON FOR TAXATION

When drawing a road map for pro-growth tax reform for the states, the first step is to set the stage for tax reform by outlining the major economic concepts involved in state economies. There's nothing more practical than good theory. And like everything in economics, it all comes down to incentives.

THE FIFTY STATES AS LABORATORIES FOR POLICY EXPERIMENTS

The Commerce Clause of the U.S. Constitution prohibits excessive impediments to the free trade in goods, services, and even labor among the states of the United States. And under the Privileges and Immunities Clause, people are entitled to migrate and resettle into any state without limitation; they need only abide by the laws and regulations of their new home just as longtime residents do. State and local governments also have almost unlimited powers to tax, spend, regulate, and oversee as long as their voters choose to permit them to do so.

Given the trivial differences in language as spoken among the various states, the existence of a common currency, and the social customs of the various state populations, which all seem fairly similar, as well as the contiguous nature of all but two of our states, in-migration and out-migration are as painless and as costless as possible. The economic integration of the fifty states truly is as close to a perfect economic union as can be conceived. This remarkable integration between states over a long period of time affords us an enormous body of data to examine when trying to identify ideal structures of taxation. Anything that can be done by states has probably been done by some state at some time.

FIRST PRINCIPLE: INCENTIVES MATTER

There are two types of incentives—positive incentives, which incentivize people to do something, and negative incentives, which warn people what not to do. An example of a positive incentive is if you feed a dog, you know exactly where the dog will be at feeding time. Positive incentives play on people's self-interest as to what they want to do. Government subsidies and other spending are positive incentives to get people to do something they otherwise might not want to do, or at least do more of it.

Negative incentives, on the other hand, discourage people from doing something they otherwise might do. Using another analogy, the hot stove really doesn't care where your hand is so long as your hand is not on the hot stove.

Taxes are negative incentives. We tax cigarettes to discourage people from smoking. We tax speeders to get speeders to slow down. And why, you may ask, do we then tax people who earn income, employers who employ workers, investors who provide capital to the economy, and property owners who make our lives worth living? And the answer, which at times isn't so obvious, is that government (hopefully) does not tax incomes, employment, investments, and property to reduce incomes, lower employment, curtail investments, or shrink property values, but instead to raise the necessary proceeds to fund worthwhile government. But we all should know full well that reduced incomes, lowered employment, curtailed investments, and depressed property values are what those taxes will cause. The reason countries, states, counties, cities, towns, school districts, toll roads—and yes, even mosquito abatement districts—tax income, employment, investment, and property values should be to provide services that are of greater value to the citizens than the damages caused by the taxes themselves.

But what we also should know is if reported income is taxed, there are many ways not to report taxable income. People are ingenious. They will report less income, whether it's through less work, evasion, avoidance, moving to a less taxed location, or all of the above. People can change the volume of income, the timing of income, the location of income, and the composition of income. At 90 percent tax rates, it is worth nine times as much to reduce taxes by one dollar than it is to earn one more taxable dollar.

The state has many options as to how it can change incentives. It can tax, regulate, adjudicate, prohibit, or subsidize all sorts of things, but there are limits, as we shall see.

SECOND PRINCIPLE: BIG PICTURE, HOW TO LEVY TAXES

Recognizing the damaging effects taxes have on income, employment, investment, property values, and many other metrics of economic activity, we want to raise those requisite tax revenues in the least damaging fashion. Therefore, we want to have the lowest possible tax rate on the broadest possible tax base. We have a true flat tax to provide people with the fewest incentives to evade, avoid, or otherwise not report taxable income and to provide people with the fewest number of places where they can put their income to avoid taxation—simple, efficient, transparent, and fair.

There are a number of additional reasons for a low-rate, broad-based flat tax aside from minimizing disincentives to work, save, employ, and produce, as well as eliminating loopholes for would-be taxpayers to avoid paying their fair share. A low-rate, broad-based flat tax also greatly limits the ability of politicians and bureaucrats to pick winners and losers or generally to manipulate the economy.

Save for in a society of wishful thinkers and do-gooders, taxes are a system of enforced exactions that would-be taxpayers would just as soon not pay. Taxpayers' desire not to be taxed is balanced by government officials' desire to get their money. Both sides of this struggle for the money need to be reined in by clear-eyed, rational tax policy. Both too much taxation and too little taxation are, in the extreme, unattractive. Widely divergent tax rates and selective tax enforcement more likely reflect political selection than in-depth economic wisdom.

I know it's hard to imagine (just kidding), but government slush funds, ambiguous regulatory guidelines, and arcane tax codes are ripe hunting grounds for government corruption. Lawyers use complex, confusing tomes of tax laws to find unintended (or purposeful) glitches in the law that they can exploit for personal gain.

The more taxpayers there are and the more transparent tax codes are, the more difficult it is for lawyers, politicians, and bureaucrats to finagle excessive sums from producers and consumers. Excesses by government, when exposed, will be met with broad-based resistance. And the simpler the tax codes, the more obvious the excesses.

Likewise, a broad-based flat tax will more evenly spread the burden of taxation, thus removing the ability of government to gain unfair advantage by pitting one group of taxpayers/producers/consumers against any other group. Divide-and-conquer may win elections when tax codes are unjust, but such actions ultimately lead to a race to the bottom. A low-rate, broad-based flat tax is the best antidote to government corruption.

The most mobile factors—think people and their associated incomes—facing taxation are the most agile in their response to being taxed, while the least mobile factors—think the classic example in economics of railroad tracks—are far less able to dodge property assessors wanting to raise tax rates. But, with time, even railroad tracks, factories, and other large capital investments will migrate to greener pastures. It takes a long time to develop a capital stock and a long time to destroy that capital stock. But that time interval notwithstanding, excessive taxation will ultimately destroy all capital.

Take the example of a large state-of-the-art factory. If tax rates are dramatically increased on the factory as soon as it becomes operational, the factory won't necessarily shut its doors, but required maintenance will be delayed and planned expansions won't occur. Eventually, the technology becomes dated and the corporation finds it relatively unprofitable to continue operations when it could easily produce elsewhere in a more hospitable environment, maybe just a stone's throw away across a state border. Detroit (and Michigan more broadly) is perhaps the most striking example of this heavy industry migration phenomenon in the United States.

In 1967, Michigan imposed a state income tax, initially setting the highest rate at 2.6 percent, using federal adjusted gross income (AGI) as its tax base. The state's income tax rate peaked in 1983 at 6.35 percent and is now down to 4.25 percent. Even though a 4.25 percent maximum tax rate is a lot better than a 6.35 percent tax rate, those high historical tax rates have surely damaged Michigan's current economy. Who can really trust what the next state leadership will do once the precedent is set? Additionally, the state's corporate tax rate stands at 6 percent. These unwarranted, burdensome taxes on business have added greatly to Detroit and Michigan's decline. Once an economy starts failing, it's doubly difficult to reverse course.

In 1962, Detroit adopted an income tax of 1 percent for residents and 0.5 percent for non-resident income earners. In 1964, Detroit initiated a 1 percent corporate tax as well. The city's income tax stands at 2.4 percent today, and the corporate tax is 2 percent. Businesses that can locate outside Detroit do. As a boy, my parents used to take me to Detroit on vacation from our home in Cleveland, Ohio. Detroit in 1950 was the Paris of North America—the Detroit train station was an American Taj Mahal. In 1950, there were approximately 1.85 million Detroit residents. Today the population of Detroit would be lucky to top 700,000. The city is close to bankruptcy—again. You just can't balance a budget on the backs of people who either leave or are unemployed.

Figure 1
Population of Detroit, Michigan

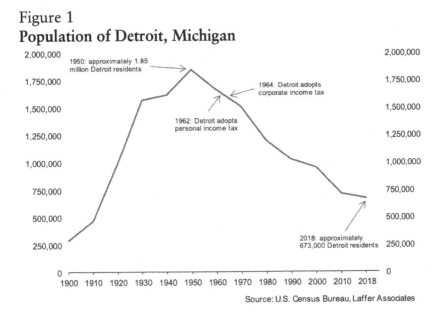

Source: U.S. Census Bureau, Laffer Associates

A great analogy for over-taxation and poverty: Imagine a boiler's heat is turned way up, its safety valves are shut off, and you tap the boiler every five minutes with a little brass tap hammer. By turning the boiler's heat way up and shutting off the safety valves, you have guaranteed the boiler will explode. By tapping the boiler every five minutes with a little brass tap hammer, you're guaranteed to be there when the explosion occurs. Such is the case with Detroit, and its bankruptcy will not be the last or the biggest. As difficult as it is to move seemingly immobile capital stock such as the Motor City's giant factories and production lines, poorly planned tax regimes put in place by greedy and shortsighted politicians have done just that.

THIRD PRINCIPLE:
HOW MUCH SHOULD WE TAX?

Governments are run by politicians who, by their very nature, tend to go far beyond appropriate levels of taxation and spending. They find it much easier to spend other people's money than to spend their own. But how do you determine the correct level of taxing and spending? Stated differently, what's the right size of government?

The theory behind the answer to the question of how much a government should spend is simple: governments should tax right up to the point where the harm done to the economy by the last dollar of taxation is just a smidgeon lower than the benefit to society by that last dollar spent by government. Any combination of taxation and spending less than that optimal point means government is too small, and any combination of taxation and spending greater than that optimal point means government is too large. It's that simple.

FOURTH PRINCIPLE:
THE MATH OF REDISTRIBUTION

Taxation and government spending are frequently forms of redistribution. Government redistributes income by taking income (the tax) from someone who earns more and giving the proceeds as a subsidy to someone who earns less. By taxing income from the person who earns more, that person's incentive to produce income declines, and he or she will produce (earn) less.

Also, as a result of giving the proceeds from the tax (the subsidy) to someone who earns less, that person will now have an alternative source of income other than working and therefore will work less. Any government attempt to redistribute income will reduce total income, and the larger the redistribution, the larger the decline. If government taxes people who work and pays people who don't work, don't be surprised if you find a lot of people not working.

THE INCOME TAX

The elephant in the room when it comes to state tax policy is the income tax. The state income tax is, after all, what drove me to leave my

Table 1: Metrics of the Eleven States That Adopted an Income Tax Post-1960 as a Percentage of the Thirty-Nine Remaining States

	First Year of the Tax	Maximum Tax Rate		Population			GSP			Total State and Local Tax Revenue		
		Initial	Current	5 Years Before	2018	% Change	5 Years Before	2018	% Change	5 Years Before	2016*	% Change
Connecticut	1991	1.50%	6.99%	1.8%	1.4%	-21.7%	2.4%	1.8%	-23.4%	2.4%	1.2%	-47.5%
New Jersey	1976	2.50%	10.75%	4.9%	3.5%	-28.6%	5.4%	4.2%	-22.5%	5.4%	3.1%	-43.5%
Ohio	1972	3.50%	5.00%	7.6%	4.6%	-38.9%	8.0%	4.5%	-43.8%	6.1%	3.5%	-43.1%
Rhode Island	1971	5.25%	5.99%	0.7%	0.4%	-38.3%	0.6%	0.4%	-36.3%	0.7%	0.3%	-46.7%
Pennsylvania	1971	2.30%	3.07%	8.5%	5.1%	-40.3%	8.5%	5.3%	-38.0%	7.7%	4.0%	-48.2%
Maine	1969	6.00%	7.15%	0.7%	0.5%	-28.2%	0.6%	0.4%	-25.9%	0.6%	0.4%	-37.6%
Illinois	1969	2.50%	4.95%	8.1%	5.1%	-37.4%	9.8%	5.8%	-41.2%	7.8%	3.8%	-51.0%
Nebraska	1968	2.60%	6.84%	1.1%	0.8%	-30.4%	1.0%	0.8%	-20.3%	0.9%	0.7%	-27.9%
Michigan	1967	2.00%	4.25%	6.3%	4.0%	-37.3%	7.9%	3.5%	-55.2%	6.6%	2.5%	-61.9%
Indiana	1963	2.00%	3.23%	3.8%	2.7%	-30.1%	3.8%	2.4%	-35.7%	3.4%	1.7%	-48.6%
West Virginia	1961	5.40%	6.50%	1.5%	0.7%	-53.5%	1.2%	0.5%	-56.5%	1.1%	0.5%	-53.3%

* Latest year for which data are available. Source: Bureau of Economic Analysis, U.S. Census Bureau

beloved California and set course in 2006 for zero-earned-income-tax Tennessee. Leaving California was not easy—I had called it home for four years during my graduate studies at Stanford and then for three decades while a University of Southern California professor and later chairman of my research firm Laffer Associates. But I made the right choice by leaving California. As added confirmation that I made the right choice to move to Tennessee, I was able to buy my home in Nashville with my first year's tax savings.

There are currently nine states without an "earned" income tax.[1] Of the forty-one states with earned income taxes, top marginal state income tax rates range from low rates such as North Dakota's 2.9 percent top rate and Pennsylvania's flat rate of 3.07 percent to as high as California's 13.3 percent top rate.

Common sense and in-your-face data show that income taxes have a large detrimental effect on economic growth and prosperity. The effects are universally felt. Table 1 contains a comparison of each of the eleven states that adopted an income tax after 1960 with the other thirty-nine states. Each of the eleven states' performances since adopting an income tax have been bad, and some have been disastrous. Just take a look at the table above and draw your own conclusions.

COLLATERAL DAMAGE IN ADDITION TO ACTUAL INCOME TAXES COLLECTED

Tax rates and tax bases aren't the only relevant topics when discussing state and local income taxes—the number of taxing jurisdictions also matters. Each taxing jurisdiction requires a certain amount of fixed costs that have to be in place before the first dollar of taxes can be collected. These are costs (tax inspectors, collectors, filing costs, and so on) to maintaining the system, and a great deal of government and tax reporting inefficiency is introduced when there are many competing tax jurisdictions. The worst income tax structure I know is in Ohio, where there are some 1,440 separate income tax jurisdictions. Each jurisdiction's tax indirectly impacts the other tax jurisdictions, resulting in total taxes that are way too high. This is called an "agency" problem. The people who tax are not the same people who bear the costs. The right to tax should be given to only one authority, and that authority must be fully accountable to the people who are taxed.

What is the answer for dealing with states and their local governments that have run wild with excessive income taxes? Look to Missouri: Missouri Proposition A was a 2010 ballot measure that repealed the authority of all cities to use earnings taxes to fund their budgets. The only two cities in Missouri allowed to keep their earnings taxes are St. Louis and Kansas City. The measure also required those voters in cities that currently have an earnings tax to approve continuation of the tax at an election held every five years thereafter. If the voters in the city vote out the earnings tax, it must be phased out over ten years and cannot be revived. The measure prohibited any city from adding a new earnings tax to fund its budget. Proposition A passed 68.4 percent to 31.6 percent by a vote of the citizens.

THE PROPERTY TAX

Property taxes are typically assessed at the local level to provide services to the communities paying the taxes, and their tax rates vary widely. Property tax rates are high in Connecticut compared to the rest of the U.S. Connecticut's property tax revenue collections per adult are the third highest of all fifty states ($3,642 as opposed to the national average of $1,908 using 2016 Census Data).

Effective property tax rates in Connecticut's 169 municipalities range from as low as 0.8 percent to as high as 5.2 percent, with an average effective tax rate of 2.2 percent. Figure 2 shows Hartford, Connecticut, to be the prime offender when it comes to excessive property tax rates, followed closely by Waterbury and Bridgeport.

Figure 2
Connecticut Effective Property Tax Rates, 2017
(166 of 169 municipalities)

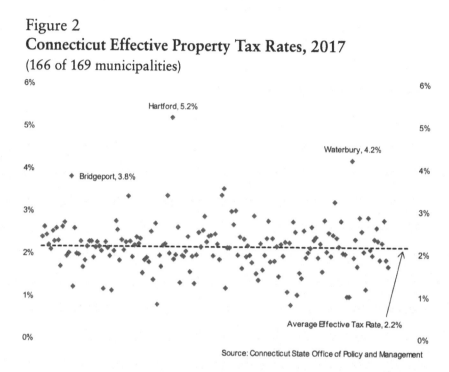

Source: Connecticut State Office of Policy and Management

A story from the *Hartford Courant* in July 2019 perfectly captures the tragedy that looms in the state as a result of the unbridled levies: ". . . D'Aprile didn't own D&D's old Hartford quarters at 276 Franklin Ave.—his father actually does—he was still responsible for paying real estate and personal property taxes. At its peak, he owed $54,000 a year to the city." He bought "a smaller property less than 4 miles away in Wethersfield, where he'd eventually relocate his entire business and 38 employees. Since opening the Wethersfield location on Wolcott Hill Road in 2014, sales are up 35 percent, D'Aprile said. Just as important, he's paying less than a quarter of the property taxes—$12,000 annually—than he did in Hartford."[2]

The *Hartford Courant* article goes on to say that the effective property tax rate for a commercial landlord in Hartford is higher than what New York City, Boston, and Chicago landlords face, and the services provided to property owners are inferior. As a result, the all-transactions housing price index for the Hartford–East Hartford–Middletown, Connecticut, Metropolitan Statistical Area (MSA) has grown at less than half the rate of that of the rest of the United States since 1988.

Illinois has a similar problem of an equal order of magnitude. In 1968, a year before Illinois adopted the income tax, Illinois's local property tax share of GSP was 2.8 percent, twenty-seventh highest in the nation, and was one-tenth of a percentage point lower than the rest of the United States' unweighted average (excluding Illinois) of 2.9 percent. In 2016, however, Illinois's local property tax share of GSP was ranked seventh highest in the U.S. at 3.4 percent, compared to the unweighted average of 2.5 percent, and the state has a big income tax it adopted in 1969.

Illinois communities operating under "home rule" law do not have limitations on property taxes. The local jurisdiction can do whatever it wants regarding property taxes. In Illinois, "home rule" automatically applies to communities with over twenty-five thousand residents. Communities under twenty-five thousand residents can vote to implement "home rule" by means of a referendum. Since 2017, at least nineteen separate localities in Illinois have tried to become "home rule" communities. Eighteen of those campaigns failed because voters didn't trust that their taxes would be kept under control.[3]

To further illustrate the mess that huge numbers of jurisdictions can cause, just read this quotation from my study of Kentucky regarding only Louisville-Jefferson County, Kentucky, with its 105 property tax jurisdictions:

> First, all qualifying inventory in Louisville-Jefferson County is subject to state inventory taxation. At the county level, motor vehicles held for sale, manufacturers' raw materials are exempt from taxation by statute as they are in all local jurisdictions, but manufacturers finished goods and merchants inventory, are subject to taxation at a rate of 98.2 cents per $100 market value. Two school districts operate in Louisville-Jefferson County and both levy taxes on merchant's inventories (at rates

of 98.2 cents and 71 cents per $100 of market value)—so long as the inventories are not considered Goods-In-Transit (GIT), which are exempt from city, county and school district taxation. Of the 21 special districts in Louisville-Jefferson County, 19 tax merchant's inventory and 18 tax inventory Goods-In-Transit (GIT) at varying rates (Note that Goods-In-Transit are exempt from all tax jurisdictions except special districts—of which 776 with the authority to tax were active in Kentucky in 2012, making Goods-In-Transit (GIT) subject to taxation across much of Kentucky).[4] Considering that revenues from taxes in these special districts are devoted to provision of ambulance services, fire department services, garbage collection and parks services, and assuming businesses operating in Louisville-Jefferson County have access to most or all of these services, those businesses would be subject to inventory taxes in several special tax jurisdictions. Of the 81 city-level districts that tax inventory in Louisville-Jefferson County, four tax merchant's inventory.

Kentucky taxes tangible personal property at varying rates depending on the type of property. For example, raw materials are taxed at a state rate of $0.05 per $100 valuation and are exempt from local taxation.[5] Manufacturing machinery is taxed at a rate of $0.15 per $100 valuation at the state level and is exempt from taxation at the local level.[6] Business furniture and computer equipment is taxed at a rate of $0.45 per $100 value at the state level and is not exempt from local tangible property tax taxation. According to Kentucky's Cabinet for Economic Development, aggregate local tax rates for tangible property taxes vary, "averaging $0.45 per $100 of assessed market value among the 120 counties [the total number of counties in Kentucky] and $0.2863 per $100 of value in the 299 cities that levy the tax."[7] According to the Kentucky Department of Revenue, the weighted average state and local tangible property tax rate is $0.64 cents per $100 of assessed market value.[8]

Just imagine what it would be like to be a first-time business owner trying to navigate this mess—there's almost no possible way for you to be compliant, despite your best intentions.

If Connecticut, Illinois, and Kentucky are glaring examples of how not to impose property taxes, California and the property tax system set up through Proposition 13 in 1978 is the road map to good property tax policies.

California's unexpected success with property taxes is a direct consequence of California's landmark constitutional amendment of June 1978, referred to as Proposition 13, which passed in a landslide vote of 65 percent to 35 percent.[9] This constitutional amendment restricted property taxes on a specific piece of property in California to never exceed 1 percent of that property's true market value and to never increase by more than 2 percent per year unless the property is sold. When sold, the new basis of a property for tax purposes is the market price at which it sold. Figure 3 shows exactly what happened after the passage of Proposition 13.

Figure 3
Excess State and Local Tax Burden vs. Excess Unemployment: California vs. United States
(annual, 1963–1990)

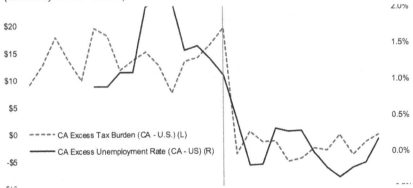

The important takeaway from Figure 3 is that prior to Prop 13, California's tax burden was way above the U.S. average, and it dropped almost instantly to the national average when Prop 13 passed. Almost hand in glove, California's unemployment rate went from way above the national average down to the national average. Taxes matter.

In spite of Proposition 13, California's property taxes as a share of personal income are still fairly high, in large part because of the enormous historical rise in property values in California relative to the rest of the nation. California's unusually low property tax rates are especially beneficial for California home values, as they offer a relative tax shelter in an otherwise high-tax state. Low or tax-exempt activities always flourish in high-tax environments.

THE SALES TAX

For states that already implement a sales tax, the recipe for success is just the same as for any tax structure: low rates with broad bases always do the least harm to economic growth. The political problem with the sales tax is all of the exemptions, exclusions, and deductions. In my adopted home state of Tennessee, where the overall tax burden is the lowest in the nation, the sales tax is the workhorse revenue source for government. Sales tax revenues are more durable and easier to predict than income taxes, and the tax base can be simple to define (at least before the politicians get involved). If the collection mechanisms are already in place for retailers to remit sales taxes, it's about as efficient a tax as a state can employ.

Alaska, Delaware, Montana, Oregon, and New Hampshire are states without state sales taxes. Despite the potential efficiencies of a sales tax for collecting revenue, it just wouldn't make sense to implement a whole new tax structure in these states when they can instead focus on improving the efficiency of tax structures they already have in place.

The most stunning example of bad sales tax policy I've encountered is Missouri's rat's nest of counterproductive sales tax rates, sales tax jurisdictions, and taxing authorities. Along with co-authors Rex and Jeanne Sinquefield, we took a deep dive into Missouri's tax structure and were shocked by what we found. There are 8,458 stackable sales tax rates whose varying overlapping geographies are combined into 2,331 sales tax jurisdictions that use their powers to tax in order to raise funds for all sorts of purposes.[10] There is an average of 4.63 stacked tax rates per jurisdiction, and there are 2,154 separate taxing entities. This number of 2,331 sales tax jurisdictions in the Show-Me State is not only the highest in the nation, but is growing rapidly. But other states are not immune.

Missouri's sales tax structure was one of the most arcane, grotesque, and complicated tax structures we had ever seen and an open invitation to tax evaders and government corruption. The below paragraphs are quoted directly from a 2017 white paper written by the former director of the department of revenue in the state of Missouri, Joel Walters. In brackets, we updated his data. We quote Walters's paper directly because we couldn't have written it better:

> While the sales tax is simple in concept, in practice it is one of the most complex state taxes. More than 200 exemptions or exclusions currently riddle Missouri's sales and use tax base. Most exemption costs are not tracked by the Department of Revenue. However, in Fiscal Year 2016, Missouri saw total state revenue losses of $4.5 million for the textbook sales and use tax exemption and $55.8 million for one of many manufacturing exemptions. . . .
>
> Currently, Missouri does little to limit the nearly 2,300 [2,331 today][11] local sales tax jurisdictions that complicate the state's overall sales tax environment. . . .
>
> In October 2012, Missouri had 16 taxing jurisdictions with a combined state and local sales tax rate of more than 10%. In June 2017 Missouri had 53 [there are currently 126 as of January 2018][12] taxing jurisdictions with combined state and local sales tax rate of more than 10%. . . .[13]

Not only can there be any number of separate taxing authorities in each sales tax jurisdiction, but there are also a number of different sales tax rates for different products in each and every one of these sales tax jurisdictions. On a very broad level, there's a general sales tax rate, a general use tax rate, a food sales tax rate, a food use tax rate, a domestic utility tax rate, and, of course, a manufacturing exempt sales tax rate. Other rates which we believe exist as well would be for school books, religious items, farm equipment, land sales, medicine, services, business to business, and on, and on, and on.

In addition to all of these smaller taxing authorities, the state component of the sales tax is 4.225 percent, which applies equally to all locations but does not apply equally to all forms of sales. The state's component of sales taxes varies depending on which specific goods are being bought or sold. Food, for example, is taxed at a lower rate than other products, and all sorts of products are exempted from the state's sales tax altogether. There are even sales tax credits.

These exemptions, exclusions, credits, and less-taxed sales make for an uneven playing field for businesses in Missouri. And this uneven playing field causes all sorts of distortions and inefficiencies in the marketplace. Estimates at present put the value of exempted items at something close to 53 percent of all personal consumption expenditures on goods and services.[14]

Missouri has over two hundred sales tax exemptions.[15] For example, most services in Missouri are exempt from sales and use tax, and the fourth amendment to Missouri's constitution prohibits the expansion of any state and local sales or use tax to any services not taxed as of January 1, 2015.

These exemptions not only make for distortions and inefficiencies, but they also represent lost revenues to the state and therefore higher sales tax rates on the sales of products that are taxed. And just so no one misses the point: higher sales tax rates than absolutely necessary mean less sales, more tax shifting, more tax evasion, more official corruption, more sales outmigration, less output, less prosperity, and less employment. High sales tax rates are a major concern for Missouri.

GIFT AND ESTATE TAXES

In November 2011, I wrote a detailed analysis of the Tennessee gift and estate tax.[16] The figures are almost a decade old, but the concepts are timeless. By the way, we were successful, and the state eliminated its gift and estate tax over the objections of several prominent politicians.

Tennessee's gift and estate tax is the poster boy for bad tax policy. Tennessee is one of only 19 states with a separate estate tax and one of only 2 states with a gift tax.[17] Tennessee has the single lowest exemptions for both its estate tax and its gift tax. Tennessee's economy has way underperformed other right-to-work states and other states with no earned income tax, low corporate taxes, and low overall tax burdens. And, for what has Tennessee made this sacrifice? Tennessee collects less than 1% of its tax revenue from its gift and estate tax according to the U.S. Census Bureau.[18]

To show how people really do respond to incentives, a comparison between Florida and Tennessee is especially poignant. Both states have no earned income tax, are right-to-work states and have low tax burdens and are generally pro-growth and pro-business. Yet, Tennessee has the highest gift tax and estate tax in the nation, and Florida has neither.

In 2010 Florida had almost twice as many federal estates filed per 100,000 population than Tennessee, and the average size of Florida's federal estate was $7,403,172 while Tennessee's was $4,441,685. Doesn't this just say it all?

Potential gift and estate tax payers expend effort and money to avoid the tax. Many leave the state in anticipation of Tennessee's death tax taking with them jobs, spending, investments, and entrepreneurial skills. Once gone, they are loath to come back. Potential immigrants to Tennessee are also put off by Tennessee's extreme gift and estate tax.

The average taxable estate in Tennessee is consistently smaller than the U.S. average. In 2010 the average size of a federal estate filed in Tennessee was almost 25% smaller than the U.S. average federal estate, or $1,350,000 less. And, in Tennessee there were over 20% less federal estates filed per 100,000 population than the U.S. average. People really do leave Tennessee because of Tennessee's gift and estate tax— and they leave in droves.

Quite simply, Tennessee's gift and estate tax is the single greatest reason why wealthy people don't want to live in Tennessee. Many leave the state and few move into Tennessee. They take all their jobs, entrepreneurship, spending, homes and wealth with them. This is the single greatest detriment to Tennessee's growth and Tennessee's ability to raise sufficient tax revenues. If Tennessee's gift and estate tax were repealed or greatly reduced Tennessee's state tax revenues would increase, not decrease.

FIFTH PRINCIPLE: HIGH TAX RATES AND NARROW TAX BASES PUNISH HONESTY AND REWARD CHEATING

High tax rates on narrow tax bases are also inherently unfair and capricious. Those who eschew the tricks and gimmicks of tax lawyers, accountants, and political lobbyists bear the full damaging brunt of the tax law, while those who skirt the fringes of our tax codes never pay.

A Commonsense Guide for the States: The Texas Model

by Secretary Rick Perry

When reflecting on the greatness of America and its promise for all of its people, one state in particular stands out for its rugged individualism, boldness, can-do spirit, boundless opportunities, entrepreneurial drive, and unmatched freedom and liberty. That state is Texas. Texas is the second-largest state in the nation geographically, has the second-largest population in the country, and has the second-largest economy in the United States. In fact, it has the tenth-largest economy in the world. The incredible economic growth and prosperity that Texas has experienced is often referenced in magazines and newspapers across the country. No one better understands or has been more influential in the success of Texas in recent decades than Rick Perry. As the longest-serving governor in Texas history, he was instrumental in expanding and promoting the Texas Model of controlling taxes and spending, implementing sensible regulation when necessary, investing in the workforce, and enacting lawsuit reform. Rick Perry also served America most recently as our nation's fourteenth secretary of energy. I'm most grateful to him for his friendship over the years, working with him as a Texas legislator, for his participation in *Making Government Work,* and for providing an opportunity for more

51

Americans to better understand the success of Texas and read firsthand his beliefs and views on optimal public policy.

—Tan Parker

On December 21, 2000, I stood at the podium in the Texas Senate chamber to take the oath of office as the forty-seventh governor of Texas.[1] My predecessor—and friend—George W. Bush looked on; he had recently resigned as governor so he could serve as president of the United States.

He had governed with civility and compassion. He led by uniting and including. And he left us with an enduring legacy that reminds me of the famous words of another Texas legend, Sam Houston, who once said, "Do right, and risk consequences."

Under then governor Bush's leadership, our economic prosperity had transformed Texas into a haven of opportunity, a place where vivid dreams and bold ideas awaited their realization.

My goal was not merely to celebrate that progress, but to advance it, to extend opportunity to more of our citizens, and to do so with the help of every willing Texan without regard to party politics or political ideology.

I pledged to Texans a government built on the virtues of our people—a government that was open and honest, that realized its limits but performed important duties effectively.

Eventually, we called that vision the Texas Model. It is no secret formula—though you might say it is a magical formula. You might simply call it common sense. That model is low taxes, smart regulations, fair courts, and educational excellence.[2] Every state in America can do what Texas has done. They just have to be willing to do the right thing—and risk the political consequences.

Yet for America—and Texas—December 2000 was not without its economic challenges. Texas had enjoyed thirteen straight years of job growth, but like the rest of the country, was facing a softer economy, driven by rising interest rates and a weakening global economic outlook.[3]

It was by no means a hard-candy Christmas, but in the second half of 2000, consumer spending was down. Yet there was good news, too. Employment growth in Texas topped 3.7 percent (compared to a national rate of 1.6 percent), and our exports were surging.[4]

"Texas exports to Mexico, which make up about half the total, surged nearly 31 percent in the first three quarters over the same period in 1999," the Dallas Fed reported. "Texas exports to Asia improved dramatically over 1999, increasing more than 50 percent in the first three quarters of 2000."[5]

Rising oil prices are both a blessing and a challenge for Texans; by December 2000, crude prices had tripled from their 1998 levels. This meant more jobs, but also higher gas prices for Texas families.

The economic outlook was mostly positive, according to the Dallas Fed; moderated growth could be expected, though high oil prices and booming exports could act as a buffer for the Texas economy. This forecast was made, we should note, in the Federal Reserve Bank of Dallas's *Southwest Economy*, dated March/April 2001.[6]

9/11 AND THE DOT-COM CRISIS

I will never forget that morning of September 11, 2001. Four terrorist attacks, separate but coordinated, killed nearly three thousand Americans. We lost so many good Americans—mothers, fathers, and even children.

I was less than a year into my fourteen years as governor, and I remember watching the towers fall on television and thinking the world had changed. Islamic terrorists had been at war with us for decades. That morning, we realized we were at war with them.

9/11 would transform our country. It would send our heroes to far-flung areas of the globe to stamp out this threat, leading to several thousand giving their lives and many more returning scarred and wounded. Every American would experience a transformation, characterized by longer security lines and more rigorous security practices;

but beyond new inconveniences, we would see the country come together, united across religious, racial, and ethnic lines because of our love of country.

The cost of 9/11 would be felt not only in the great tragedy of lives lost, but in the form of economic challenges. Eventually, the attacks of September 11 would directly cost the U.S. economy $2 trillion by some estimates.[7] Indirectly, the costs were even higher.[8]

At the same time, Texas—where the microchip was invented[9]—was not immune from the effects of the dot-com crash. October 9, 2002, was the day of reckoning for the dot-coms; the technology-laden NASDAQ lost nearly 80 percent of its value.[10]

Across the country, as the *Houston Chronicle* reported, "Billions of dollars simply…evaporated."[11] And Austin was hit hard.[12] According to the Dallas Fed, Austin's "manufacturing sector lost almost 28,000 jobs from the end of 2000 through December 2003, shrinking in importance from 12.3 percent of total employment to 8.7 percent."[13]

But from both crises, Texas emerged both resilient and resolute.

Knowing we faced an uncertain economy, we felt the focus of government should not be on finding new revenue sources, but on encouraging revenue generators like small and start-up businesses and encouraging existing employers to expand in or relocate to Texas, creating jobs throughout our economy.

We knew it would not be easy. We found out just how hard it was going to be in January 2003, when Texas comptroller Carole Keeton Strayhorn told the legislature we were facing a shortfall of nearly $10 billion in the next biennium.[14]

The pressure was on to raise taxes. But I—along with other Texas leaders—knew we had to resist the cycle of raising taxes, spending money, and then finding we needed to raise taxes again. If higher taxes ensure sufficient revenue, then why did California face a $35 billion gap in its own budgetary cycle that year? Over the long term, tax hikes do not alleviate economic and budgetary problems. They exacerbate them.

Showing fiscal discipline is not easy. Sometimes it requires saying no to worthwhile programs. Sometimes it requires accepting reductions in your own favored initiatives. I did my part; in my State of the State address that year, I provided the legislature with $9 billion in suggested cuts. Lawmakers accepted some of those ideas and rejected others.

And by the end of the session, we kept our promises. We balanced the budget. We cut spending, we drew down our rainy-day fund—at an appropriate time, in an appropriate manner—and we leveraged federal dollars to ensure that Texans' needs were met. We increased our spending on education, on the health of poor Texans, and on infrastructure.[15] And we did it all without raising taxes.

Texas's fiscal restraint helped fuel its economic recovery. This was aided by our increasingly diversified economy. "Texas' economy is more closely tied to that of the United States than it once was, with oil and gas accounting for about 7 percent of the economy today, versus about 20 percent in 1981," *Southwest Economy* reported in March/April 2004.[16]

Most telling, though, was how the Dallas Fed closed its summary of the state's recovery: "In addition, Texas has an attractive combination of low costs and favorable government policies that will continue to attract workers and firms to the state in the long run."[17]

Those factors—which we began referring to as the Texas Model— were key to how the state fared in the Great Recession of 2008.

MEDICAL MALPRACTICE REFORM

Another key accomplishment of the 78th Texas Legislature in 2003 was medical malpractice reform. For years, medical liability lawsuits had been driving physicians out of Texas. In addition to sky-high malpractice insurance premiums and ruinous judgments, doctors found they were forced to practice "defensive medicine"—a kind of medicine designed to ensure the wellness of malpractice insurance firms, not patients.[18]

But then we passed House Bill 4, the most sweeping lawsuit reform measure in the nation (up to that time). By capping non-economic damages and providing greater protections for many of our hospitals that provide charity care, we were able to lower malpractice insurance rates and keep doctors, nurses, and hospitals doing what they do best: providing health care to Texans in need.

And it is worth pointing out that Texans wrongfully harmed by an act of malpractice can still recover all economic damages, such as all medical bills and lost wages. And if a jury unanimously agrees, harmed Texans can also recover punitive damages in addition to economic and non-economic damages.[19]

Fifteen years later, the Texas Medical Association (TMA) celebrated the anniversary of this life-changing—and life-giving—legislation. "Two decades ago, physicians might call the Texas Medical Association in tears because they had lost their medical liability coverage and no one else would insure them," TMA's Joey Berlin wrote in 2016.[20] "Now, insurance rates are at staggering lows, and dozens of companies are competing for the doctors' business.... The TMA-backed tort reforms that went into effect 15 years ago this month changed all that, and proponents say physicians and patients alike are in better shape because of it."

Tort reform (medical malpractice reform is a component of this) is an important part of the Texas Model—and any model for a successful state. It is also an issue with bipartisan support: 90 percent of the Senate voted in favor of HB 4, as did 76 percent of the Texas House.

THE SHALE REVOLUTION

In 2005, no one could have predicted the Shale Revolution, or its world-shaking effects. Petroleum imports to the United States peaked in September 2006, with 455,595 barrels imported in that thirty-day period.[21]

But American expertise and ingenuity were already at work, refining methods for extracting oil and gas once thought unreachable, particularly in shale formations. Fourteen years later, in September 2019, our total imports were down to 290,150 barrels. The U.S. is on its way to being truly energy independent.[22] And that fact is changing the world's geopolitical landscape and strengthening the United States.[23]

Through horizontal drilling and hydraulic fracturing, U.S. oil companies opened up vast fields, from the Permian to the Bakken to the Eagle Ford shale formations. Even the Haynesville shale, in East Texas and Louisiana, is undergoing a revival as an important source of natural gas close to the LNG export facilities on the Gulf Coast.[24]

And as Kathleen Hartnett White, also a contributor to this edition of *Making Government Work*, wrote for the Texas Public Policy Foundation in 2018, the Shale Revolution couldn't have happened anywhere else.

"Instead of nationally owned oil companies, cartels, and multinational corporations, the shale revolution is the work of small to medium-sized energy companies in the only country in the world that recognizes private property rights in subsurface minerals," she wrote.[25]

Former Texas Railroad Commission chairman Barry Smitherman agrees—and says Texas policies helped make the Shale Revolution happen.

"It would be wrong to say that government caused these advances in natural gas and oil production. However, government leaders do play an important role," he wrote in 2016.[26] "They can prioritize and facilitate, or conversely, present obstacles and cause delay. Several states, for example, have placed moratoria on fracking, thereby denying all parties—industry, mineral interest owners, tax paying citizens and hard-working Americans within those states—remuneration and great jobs."

As fracking techniques improved and drilling increased, the Texas Railroad Commission (which regulates oil and gas in the state) needed additional resources just to keep up. We responded.

"The result? From 2011 through 2014, the RRC permitted more than 92,000 wells," Smitherman notes. "In the peak year 2014, almost 100 drilling permits were issued every working day, and the average time from permit filing to approval was a matter of days, rather than weeks or months."[27]

MORE REFORMS

Throughout my tenure, the Texas legislature worked with me to reform government. In the 79th Texas Legislature (2005), we promised we would lower property taxes, further reform medical malpractice laws, and—despite tough economic times—that we would not raise the price of government in order to balance the budget. And we delivered on each one of those promises.

Lower property taxes, more lawsuit reforms to keep doctors practicing medicine, and increased investments in job creation, public education, and vital transportation projects meant that Texas had a stronger foundation for a prosperous future. And because we had the discipline to rebuild the budget from scratch, examining every cent we spent and restraining the growth of government, we balanced our budget without new taxes—unlike many other states.

At the same time, we invested $1.1 billion in new funds into vital health care programs for the most vulnerable Texans, as well as an additional $1.2 billion for public education.[28]

EDUCATION EQUALS WORKFORCE

Some states measure success based on educational inputs. Money put into teacher pay. Money poured into the classroom. These are, of course, important. But in Texas we were always focused on outputs. What does our money buy?

We were never going to rank the highest in teacher pay in a state with a lower cost of living. The same can be said of overall education funding. But we switched the focus. We led the way in setting high standards, creating strong accountability, and measuring what students learned through assessment.

In 2010, *Education Week* gave Texas an "A" for standards, assessments, and accountability. Student performance had already been on the rise. ACT scores increased in all four subjects from 2007 to 2011.

Our goal was for every student to graduate career- or college-ready. That started with ensuring more students graduated, period. We succeeded wildly in this regard. When I took office on December 21, 2000, our dropout rate was abysmal. By 2009, Texas ranked seventh in a twenty-six-state comparison of states reporting four-year on-time graduation rates. In 2010, our on-time graduation rate was 84.3 percent.

Achievement crossed key demographic groups. In 2009, our eighth-grade Hispanic and African American students had the seventh- and eighth-highest scores on the NAEP Science test, scoring eight or more points higher than the national average. We tied Massachusetts for the best math scores among eighth-grade African American students nationwide, while their Hispanic and Anglo peers finished fourth in the nation.

These were important achievements in their own regard, but important for another reason: in order to provide a skilled workforce to a growing economy, we needed to ensure a high school diploma in Texas meant something. And during our tenure, it increasingly meant a Texas graduate was prepared for a good job in the changing economy. Even combined with a low tax burden and fair regulatory scheme, all the tort reform in the world only means so much if your future workers are not prepared for the jobs of the future. But we met that great economic need.

RECESSION AND RECOVERY

According to economists, the Great Recession started for the United States in the fourth quarter of 2007.[29] It turned out to be the longest recession since the Great Depression. The unemployment rate went from just 5 percent in December 2007 to a peak of 10 percent in October 2009. Foreclosures rose (nationwide, some 9 million families lost their homes)[30] and spirits fell. The federal government responded with the American Recovery and Reinvestment Act, a $787 billion stimulus bill (it would later be revised to $831 billion[31]).

Texas, however, was having a different experience than most of the rest of the nation. Yes, many Texans were hurting, with friends, neighbors, and family members losing their jobs. But, overall, the downturn failed to take root in Texas like it did in most of the rest of the country.

This was the case from the beginning of the Great Recession. During the first year of the Great Recession, from October 2007 through October 2008, 500,000 jobs were lost in the rest of the United States while Texas was creating 250,000 new ones.[32] The trend continued from 2008 through 2011, with Texas adding almost 184,000 jobs while the other states bled more than 5.1 million jobs.

At the time, we knew that our state's economy was better suited to weather the economic downturn than just about any other state. But we did not know how clearly Texas stood apart. From 2001 to 2011, Texas added 1.2 million new jobs during the same period that the United States (without Texas) lost 713,000 jobs. Our state actually kept the U.S. economy afloat. The Texas Model begat the Texas Miracle.

Of course, many on the left did not like getting their fake economics refuted in real time. Paul Krugman, for instance, complained, "So what you need to know is that the Texas miracle is a myth, and more broadly that Texan experience offers no useful lessons on how to restore national full employment."[33]

About the same time Krugman was writing, an unlikely source refuted his attack on Texas. In 2011, while the crisis was still ongoing, Derek Thompson in *The Atlantic* summed it up nicely.

"Texanomics is well-suited to a recession stemming from a financial crisis," he wrote.[34] "When consumers' balance sheets are hurting, they seek out low cost-of-living. That's Texas. When companies don't have access to credit, they hire cheaper labor. Texas again. When young couples look to start a family, they're drawn to affordable housing, nice weather, and industries that hire: Energy and aerospace in Houston, health care and military in San Antonio, tech and education in Austin, and communications and more energy in Dallas."

Of course, we cannot take credit for the weather; we must thank God for that. But housing and business climate—public policy plays a big part in those. Smart regulations encourage people to build, whether it is new homes or new businesses.

Texas also cannot take credit for the oil and gas wealth under our feet. Yet other states have mineral wealth like ours, and they fared far worse in the recession than Texas did. Governors and legislators in California, New York, and elsewhere enacted policies that discouraged exploration and drilling.[35] Their citizens paid the price.

We had set the stage for weathering the Great Recession with our refusal to raise taxes in 2003 and instead stick with the Texas Model. As the Dallas Fed had pointed out previously, the Texas economy was diversifying, and our manufacturing base was strong. I told the Dallas Regional Chamber near the beginning of the downturn, "I am convinced that the strength of our workforce, the health of our business climate, and the freeing effect of our low taxes will carry us through this tough time."[36] I pledged to double down on the fiscal restraint and regulatory reform that would help us weather the worst of that storm and lead the way to recovery.

The same choices we faced in 2003 once again faced us as the 82nd Legislature opened in 2011. Faced with calls for more spending, I called for many of the same things I had previously called for.[37] I called for balancing the budget by making tough choices instead of by raising taxes. I called for government to work leaner and smarter. I called for reforming eminent domain laws and abolishing local "sanctuary city" ordinances. I reminded lawmakers of the faith placed in us by Texas voters.

We did our job; we entered the next biennium with a much better economic outlook and, oddly enough, even more demands for additional spending.[38]

The best thing we could do for our economy, for employers, employees, and our state was to provide some tax relief. When Texans keep more of their own money, they invest it, they start new businesses, they educate their children, and they blaze new trails.

Following the close of the 83rd Texas Legislature, I announced I would not seek another term as governor. I expressed my deep appreciation to the Texans who had placed such trust in me, and I reflected on what we all had achieved together.

We created the strongest economy in the nation. We balanced budgets while prioritizing critical infrastructure, including water, roads, and public schools, all to encourage economic growth. We passed sweeping lawsuit reforms that allowed thousands of doctors to improve access to health care. Our civil justice reforms protected jobs and investment, ensuring the courthouse is reserved for legitimate disputes.

Working with legislative leaders, I signed seven balanced state budgets, restrained spending in lean times, and invested more in necessary services when our economy was strongest. We stopped all major tax hikes and kept the overall Texas tax burden among the lowest in the country. We cut property tax rates, reformed the franchise tax, and provided tax relief to small businesses. We stood strong against unwise policies from Washington that would bust the bank, policies that came with strings attached and a large cost down the road, things like an unwise expansion of unemployment insurance or an unsustainable expansion of the Medicaid program.

And while many were (and still are) lamenting the skyrocketing cost of college and the crushing burden of student debt, we created the Texas Affordable Baccalaureate Degree Program. In 2011, I called on Texas public universities to find a way to offer a degree for no more than $10,000. Texas educators rose to that challenge, and in 2013, seven students signed up for affordable degrees at Texas A&M-Commerce and South Texas College. In 2016, enrollment was 300 students, with 121 graduates.[39]

WHAT WORKS

Today, Texas remains at the top of the economic heap. And the reason is clear: the Texas Model—low taxes, smart regulations, and fair courts. We focus on economic opportunity for all, not equal outcomes for everyone. Texas works because we have less government and more liberty. We have built a pathway to prosperity through innovation and ingenuity.

Of course, Texas continues to have its detractors. Yet through the Great Recession, and even through the Great Oil Bust of 2015 (which came after my time at the helm of the Lone Star State), Texas led the nation in job creation.[40] The Texas Miracle is no myth; it's a documented fact.

What works in Texas? The Texas Model. But again, it is not exclusive to Texas. In fact, we actually did not come up with it. It is really just a restatement of the American Dream, built off of the principles enshrined in our founding documents, including those self-evident truths "that all men are created equal, that they are endowed by their Creator with certain inalienable rights, that among these are life, liberty and the pursuit of happiness."

Economist Vance Ginn points out that other states should take notice. "The sooner other states adopt and adapt that model, the better they will be able to meet economic challenges and propel America towards greater prosperity," he wrote in 2016.[41]

What I said in my first inaugural address is still true today. The lesson I have learned is that a government that attempts to do all things for all people does few things well. The larger government grows, the smaller the circle of our freedoms. We limit government so that opportunity is unlimited. Where government should play a role, it must do so with clarity and purpose. When economies soften, the burden should not be on taxpayers to pay more, but on government to spend less.

If we abide by these principles, we can make government work—again.

Making American Health Care Great: A Conservative Agenda for States to Create Innovative Health Care Markets

by Senator Rick Santorum and Grace-Marie Turner

No policy area in America is more complex or more personal than health care. Protecting the health and well-being of our families is a top priority for us all. As Americans, we are blessed with the greatest medical practitioners and most innovative technologies in the world, but hidebound government programs and endless bureaucratic red tape hinder the innovative solutions desperately needed to make sure everyone can access the health care they need and have insurance coverage that is affordable. Throughout his incredible career, former U.S. senator Rick Santorum has been an advocate for commonsense health care reform in this country and has most recently advised President Trump and his administration and leaders in Congress on the best path forward to reform the system, utilizing a free market approach that engages the states. His approach is also based on his passionate belief in the sanctity of every human life. Grace-Marie Turner, president of the Galen Institute, has spent her entire career advancing ideas to reform our health care system based on the timeless ideals of individual freedom, competition, and consumer choice. I am very thankful that they accepted my invitation to participate in *Making Government Work*. Together they have put forth an incredibly compelling and timely path forward for the nation that all Americans should read.

—Tan Parker

A LOOK BACK: HOW WE GOT HERE

The modern debate over health reform began in Pennsylvania in 1991. Harris Wofford was a self-proclaimed liberal Democrat running against Republican Richard Thornburgh in a special election called to fill the unexpired term of U.S. Senator John Heinz, who tragically died in a plane crash that spring.[1]

Wofford talked about health insurance in his campaign speeches, but economic issues were center stage.

Early polls showed Thornburgh with a whopping 47 percent lead, but Wofford gained steadily during the campaign by stressing the economy and calling for sweeping health care reform. Wofford won the election and concluded that his victory represented not only a referendum on taxes and the economy but a call for national health insurance.[2]

The themes resonated with voters ready to focus on domestic issues after the end of the Cold War and the collapse of the Soviet Union. Health care and the economy would be key themes in Mr. Clinton's presidential campaign in 1992. It was no coincidence that Democratic political strategist James Carville advised both the Clinton and Wofford campaigns. With thirty-five million uninsured Americans in 1992, health care reform became a rallying cry—something that Democrats had long believed government should and could fix.

THE LEFT PUSHES FOR A GOVERNMENT-RUN SYSTEM

In September 1992, candidate Bill Clinton delivered his campaign's main health care speech at the headquarters of Merck & Co. in New Jersey. That November, Clinton won an upset victory over incumbent President Bush.

Like Wofford, President Clinton and his advisors attributed their victory largely to their advocacy of health care reform, and the new president appointed his wife to take the lead in developing the legislation.

But the 1,342-page ClintonCare bill that was produced overreached with its complexity, penalties, and government intrusion, and never came up for a vote even though Democrats had big majorities in both houses of Congress.

Democrats did not give up, though, and health care reform was set to take center stage in the political debate for years to come. A number of health care delivery reform bills subsequently became law with bipartisan support: creation of the State Children's Health Insurance Program (CHIP) in 1996 and enactment of the Health Insurance Portability and Accountability Act of 1997, both of which were signed into law by President Clinton.

The next major health care reform legislation was the Medicare Modernization Act of 2003, signed into law by President George W. Bush, which created Health Savings Accounts along with a new Medicare Advantage program and a prescription drug benefit for seniors.

But the Left was determined to return to its push for "universal coverage." A health policy advisor to both the Clinton and Obama administrations, Princeton University professor Paul Starr, explains why:

> Whoever provides medical care or pays the costs of illness stands to gain the gratitude and good will of the sick and their families. The prospect of these good-will returns to the investment in health care creates a powerful motive for governments and other institutions to intervene in the economics of medicine. Political leaders since Bismarck seeking to strengthen the state or to advance their own or their party's interests have used insurance against the costs of sickness as a means of turning benevolence to power.[3]

OBAMACARE AND ITS IMPACT

In 2008, Democrats prepared to take the dive again, believing they had a mandate for health care reform after the election of Senator Barack Obama to the presidency in 2008. Democrats once again held strong majorities in Congress, and a bill to become known as "Obamacare" squeaked through the Senate on a snowy Christmas Eve in 2009. By March 2010, it was headed to the House floor for a final vote.

Thousands of citizens had marched to the U.S. Capitol hoping to stop passage of the massive health care overhaul bill that many saw as a violation of health and economic freedom.[4] House Speaker Nancy Pelosi passed the demonstrators that afternoon as she and her entourage of Democratic committee chairmen linked arms and marched from the House office buildings to the Capitol across the street. She carried an oversized gavel across the Capitol grounds to signal her determination and confidence that the bill would pass.

Democrats gave speech after speech on the House floor that evening promising that the bill would finally achieve their vaunted goal of universal coverage. But U.S. Representative Paul Ryan warned in his floor speech that Obamacare was a test of the larger vision of our country.[5]

"America is not just a nationality," he said. "America is an idea. It's the most pro-human idea ever designed by mankind. Our founders got it right when they wrote in the Declaration of Independence that our rights come from nature and nature's God—not from government."

But, he warned, "We are fast approaching a tipping point where more Americans depend on the federal government than on themselves for their livelihoods—a point where we, the American people, trade in our commitment and our concern for our individual liberties in exchange for government benefits and dependencies. . . . Today marks a major turning point in American history."

Just before 11:00 p.m., on a fateful Sunday, March 21, 2010, Pelosi slammed down the gavel as Congress passed the sweeping health care overhaul bill. Obamacare would become the law of the land when the president signed it into law two days later.

But it soon was clear that the bill, which supporters ironically called the "Affordable Care Act," was an overly complicated system that required dozens of repairs and has still failed to meet its promises. At least twenty-eight million people are still uninsured, and millions struggle to afford premiums and deductibles.

Small businesses were forced to restructure their workforces to avoid the unaffordable health insurance mandate, primarily by eliminating the entry-level jobs that new workers need to get their start in the workforce.

Millions of people soon found the plans they had and preferred were cancelled because they did not comply with the plethora of Obamacare rules and mandates. *Politico* deemed President Obama's promises that "if you like your plan you can keep your plan" and "if you like your doctor you can keep your doctor" the "Lie of the Year" in 2013.[6]

And so much for his promise that the average American family would save $2,500 a year in health insurance premiums. Premiums more than doubled in the first four years after the bill's passage, and deductibles have soared even though networks of available doctors and hospitals have narrowed.

Through seven years of court battles, elections, and the emergence of new movements, the fervor to repeal and replace Obamacare stayed in the forefront of the nation's political debate—until the fall of 2017, when, with one thumbs down vote, the late Senator John McCain stopped Republican efforts to advance legislation that would offer the American people more sensible solutions.

WHERE ARE WE NOW?

Another twenty million Americans now are trapped and dependent on government for their health coverage through expansion of Medicaid and subsidized insurance through the Obamacare exchanges. Opposition to Obamacare has softened as more and more people have become dependent on the massive taxpayer subsidies that help them afford their increasingly expensive health insurance.

The Left's goal of incrementally expanding government control over health care is succeeding. More than seventy-five million people are now enrolled in Medicaid, the federal-state program for the poor; sixty million seniors and disabled people are on Medicare; and millions more are on CHIP, veterans' health care, the Indian Health Service, TriCare for active and retired military, and other government programs.

In a paper for the American Enterprise Institute, Wharton School professor Mark Pauly explains that the federal government plays a controlling role in our health sector. Pauly details how the federal government shapes an even larger share of spending than the portion it finances directly.[7] He finds the share of "government-affected" spending in 2016 totaled nearly 80 percent—"not leaving much in the unfettered, market-based category."

The federal government finances nearly 55 percent of all "explicit and implicit" health spending, he reports—from Medicare, the federal share of Medicaid, and ACA subsidies to very generous tax preferences for employer-sponsored health insurance. But the federal government controls even more through regulations and mandates on other allegedly private plans. Consumers also have little control over health spending since nearly 90 percent of all health costs are financed through some form of third-party payment.[8]

The more government gets involved, the more the providers throughout the health sector are forced to respond to legislative and regulatory demands rather than to the needs and preferences of patients. Some now contend that the mess can only be solved by even more government involvement.

The growing presence of government is the main contributor to frustrations the American people have with our health sector. Unlimited taxpayer spending on health care entitlements continues to put upward pressure on prices while restricting options for consumers to find more affordable coverage.

Government officials, not consumers, increasingly determine what services can or must be covered, how much will be paid, and who is eligible to both deliver and receive these services. Third-party payment systems and the resulting lack of price and benefit transparency lead to significant disruptions in the market. Consumers are at the bottom of the health care totem pole.

Americans are understandably frustrated, and they want change. Millions remain uninsured, and coverage and care cost too much. Many are simply priced out of the market for health insurance. The costs of premiums and deductibles can be prohibitive, especially for those who do not get subsidies.

One father in Virginia trying to provide coverage for his family faced premiums of $4,000 a month for an Obamacare policy.[9] Many face deductibles of $8,000 or more—an amount they must pay before insurance kicks in.

Even those with insurance can face thousands of dollars in "surprise billings," and out-of-pocket costs can be so high that many say they might as well be uninsured.

The Affordable Care Act significantly disrupted the individual health insurance market. Average premiums more than doubled between 2013 and 2017 and increased another 27 percent in 2018, according to the Centers for Medicare and Medicaid Services. People in more than half of U.S. counties had a "choice" of only one insurer in the individual market in 2018. These rising premium costs and limited choices led many people who were not eligible for subsidies to drop out of the insurance market. Between 2016 and 2017, enrollment by people who did not qualify for health insurance subsidies declined by 20 percent nationally and by more than 40 percent in six states.[10]

Those on public programs are often frustrated as well. Many Medicaid recipients struggle to find physicians who can afford to take the program's low payment rates, and they can find it especially difficult to get appointments with specialists for more serious health problems.

People are hurting, and they feel powerless against this system. Health care has become a very big and lucrative business. Many patients feel they are simply cogs in the $3.6 trillion health sector with little power to impact choices of care or coverage—or even find out before they get care what it is going to cost them. Independent physicians are selling their practices to hospitals, and some hospital systems have become virtual oligopolies, setting prices and giving health plans and purchasers little choice but to pay inflated prices.

These and other frustrations have generated interest in a bold plan that promises universal coverage for all patients, with no premiums, copayments, or deductibles, and the ability to choose any provider or hospital they want.

But it is hard to see how consumers would be more empowered when dealing with a single government payer. In a country that values diversity, will one program with one list of benefits and one set of rules work for everyone? How will total government control over our health sector lead to lower costs and more choices?

While many people say they long for the simplicity a government-run system would offer, everything we know about government programs tells us it will lead to more bureaucracy, fewer choices, and higher costs.

TRUMP ADMINISTRATION ADVANCES CHOICE AND COMPETITION

While many on the left accuse the Trump administration of sabotaging Obamacare, the administration actually has taken important steps to improve the market and expand the choices of coverage.[11] The Trump administration is offering new options through its regulatory authority. One example is Association Health Plans (AHPs). The administration created options for smaller- and medium-sized firms to provide more options of more affordable health coverage to their employees by allowing them to band together through various associations.

There have been some criticisms that these plans might not offer the same protections as ACA-compliant plans. But a study shows that they offer benefits comparable to plans offered by large firms, and they haven't tried to discriminate against patients with pre-existing conditions, an analysis by Kev Coleman, a former analyst at the insurance information website HealthPocket, found.[12] "We're not seeing skinny plans," he said.

The *Washington Post* reported that "[c]hambers of commerce and trade associations have launched more than two dozen of these 'association health plans' in thirteen states in the seven months since the Labor Department finalized new rules making it easier for small businesses to band together to buy health coverage in the same way large employers do. And there are initial signs the plans are offering generous benefits and premiums lower than can be found in the Obamacare marketplaces."[13]

AHPs, however, are on hold because of the Left's legal challenges to the AHP regulation. Congressional action is needed to codify the rule.

Short-Term Limited Duration Plans (STLDs) are another innovation from the Trump administration, which finalized in 2018 a rule to expand access to short-term, limited-duration plans to give Americans access to health insurance coverage that does not have to comply with all of the expensive Obamacare rules and mandates. The Obama administration had limited these policies to three months of coverage and had prohibited their renewal. Under the new Trump administration rule, these plans now can be offered for up to 364 days and renewed for up to 36 months, subject to state regulation.

Short-term plans are helpful to people with gaps in employment,[14] to early retirees who no longer have employer-sponsored health insurance and need bridge coverage before they qualify for Medicare, to people between jobs, young people who no longer have coverage from their parents and are working in the gig economy, people who are leaving the workforce temporarily to attend school or training programs, and entrepreneurs starting new businesses. Premiums for short-term health plans are typically less than half those of ACA plans.

The administration's rule actually improved consumer protections. Under the Obama administration's previous 2016 rule, people could lose their coverage after three months if they acquired a medical condition during the three-month period, because the policies could not be renewed. By extending the contract period, people can be protected for up to three years.

Because the plans are not required to cover the comprehensive list of benefits required by the ACA, consumer education is important in understanding how they differ from ACA-compliant plans. But the plans are much more affordable and can be a lifeline for those unable to afford Obamacare-compliant policies.

One single father told us he had to drop his ACA coverage because it was too expensive, but he bought a less expensive short-term plan to make sure his two sons had coverage. Some months later, one son was diagnosed with leukemia. So far, the plan has paid more than $170,000 in benefits for the boy's treatment. The father said the short-term plan truly has been a lifeline.

An estimated 1.7 million people who would otherwise be uninsured are expected to enroll in STLD plans.[15] Unfortunately, several states have passed legislation to limit their residents' access to STLD plans, but in so doing, they are denying them what may be their only realistic option for coverage.[16]

A White House report on "Deregulating Health Insurance Markets: Value to Market Participants"[17] provides important data showing the positive impact of this consumer-friendly health policy change. Economists estimate that STLDs would produce a marginal social benefit of $80 billion over ten years.

While some say that STLD plans are "junk" insurance that sabotages the ACA, this report provides solid evidence that consumers will benefit, both in expanded coverage and lower costs. The Trump administration believes this policy option, together with other deregulatory reforms, will generate benefits to Americans that are worth an estimated $450 billion over the next ten years.

Next, there are new Health Reimbursement Arrangements. The Trump administration issued a rule to enhance employer and employee options through Health Reimbursement Arrangements (HRAs), originally created by the Bush administration to give employers more options in their benefit offerings.

In a 2017 executive order, President Trump directed administration officials to "increase the usability of HRAs, to expand employers' ability to offer HRAs to their employees, and to allow HRAs to be used in conjunction with nongroup coverage."[18]

The rule allows employers to fund an account that employees can use to purchase a compliant health plan outside the workplace. This is an especially important option for smaller firms that don't have the money or administrative capacity to run a full-fledged health benefit program. HRAs provide a new option for small employers to provide a tax-free benefit to workers without the overhead costs of bigger competitors and to give employees the option of portable coverage with the same tax benefits as larger companies.

States are also innovating. States have much more experience than the federal government in overseeing health insurance markets and have greater flexibility to meet the needs of their residents.

One part of the ACA—Section 1332—provides an option for State Innovation Waivers that allow states to reallocate existing resources in ways they believe would provide better care for their residents, including those with pre-existing conditions.

States that have used early waiver authority to create risk-mitigation programs have seen, in many cases, dramatic results with no new federal spending. They are employing various risk-mitigation strategies to finance coverage for those with high health costs—repurposing federal money to pay medical bills for residents in poorer health.

By separately subsidizing those with the highest health costs through high risk pools, reinsurance programs, and so on, they can lower premiums for individual health insurance for others. And by lowering premiums, more healthy people are enrolling in this more affordable coverage.

The Galen Institute's Doug Badger and Heritage scholar Ed Haislmaier explain, "Several states have successfully used a waiver to change market conditions sufficiently that premiums fell for individual health insurance while still protecting the ability of people with high health care costs to access care."[19] The waivers are helping states to better manage the costs of patients with chronic and pre-existing conditions without driving up premiums throughout the market.

According to the paper, "States repurpose a portion of federal money that would otherwise have been paid to insurers as premium subsidies, supplement this federal money with non-federal sources, and then use the resulting pool of money to pay medical claims for policyholders who incur high medical bills. Since this process would reduce premiums, it also would reduce federal premium subsidies, making it budget neutral to the federal government."

They report that after the waiver reform in Alaska, for example, premiums for the lowest-cost Bronze plans plunged by 39 percent in 2018. Premiums for the highest-cost Bronze plans fell by 20 percent. In Minnesota, the third state with an approved waiver, premiums dropped in both 2018 and 2019. Average premiums for ACA coverage in 2019 were lower for every Minnesota insurer than they were in 2017.

Four other states have had waivers approved for 2019: Maryland, Maine, New Jersey, and Wisconsin.[20] Badger found in 2019 that premiums in states that adopted Section 1332 waivers "fell by nearly 7.5 percent, while premiums in the other 44 states under Obamacare rose by more than 3 percent."[21]

The administration is doing all it can through its regulatory authority to improve health insurance options for consumers.

THE LEFT'S NEW PUSH FOR SINGLE-PAYER

Meanwhile, the Left is continuing its push to expand government control over the U.S. health sector. Health reform clearly is a major issue in the 2020 presidential debate, as various Democratic candidates called for Medicare for All, Medicare for Some, Medicare for All if you want it, and the "public option," all of which lead to the same place.

This is a dangerous path that will erode the quality of care, restrict access to medical treatment, and put government bureaucrats in charge of life-and-death decisions.

And these plans would disadvantage the most vulnerable. Because just 5 percent of the population accounts for more than half of U.S. health care spending,[22] those who are sickest with the greatest health needs are most disadvantaged when the health system is stressed for resources and stretched to capacity, as too often happens in countries with a government-controlled health system. Political leaders inevitably work to make sure the great majority of their constituents are somewhat satisfied with the system, even if it means restricting access to services to the small minority with the most expensive needs.

This path would restrict access to care. The Fraser Institute in Canada devotes considerable time and resources to tracking waiting lists for Canadians seeking care.[23] In "Waiting Your Turn: Wait Times for Health Care in Canada, 2018," it finds that the median wait time for medically necessary treatment in Canada was 19.8 weeks. The wait is considerably longer for some specialty services.

We regularly see articles in British papers about patients stuck in ambulances for hours waiting for an opening to a hospital emergency room.[24] And once patients are admitted, they can be warehoused in hallways for days, with some dying before a hospital bed becomes available.[25]

Sally Pipes of the Pacific Research Institute, who was born and raised in Canada, writes that Britain's version of Medicare for All is struggling with long waits for care.[26] "The [National Health Service] routinely denies patients access to treatment. More than half of NHS Clinical Commissioning Groups, which plan and commission health services[27] within their local regions, are rationing cataract surgery. They call it a procedure of 'limited clinical value.'[28] It's hard to see how a surgery that can prevent blindness is of limited clinical value," she writes.

Nearly a quarter of a million British patients have been waiting more than six months to receive planned medical treatment from the National Health Service, according to a recent report from the Royal College of Surgeons.[29] More than thirty-six thousand have been in treatment queues for nine months or more.[30]

THE DANGERS OF MEDICARE FOR ALL

Most plans advocated by the Left involve dramatically cutting payments to doctors and hospitals. They would assign Medicare rates to hospitals with payment rates that are roughly 40 percent lower than commercial rates, while physicians would be reimbursed at rates that are 30 percent lower than those paid by private insurers. These payment reductions would gradually grow larger over time for both.

Medicare actuaries have warned that if Medicare payment rates contained in current law were extended to all care, many providers would face "negative margins." That could mean that many physician practices and hospitals would be forced to close or significantly cut back on services. Some anticipate the new program would look more like "mandatory Medicaid" as a result.[31]

A new report from the Association of American Medical Colleges finds that, even under our current health system, the U.S. will see a shortage of up to nearly 120,000 physicians by 2030.[32] The demand for physicians is expected to grow faster than the supply, and rural areas will be hit especially hard, according to the report.[33] The Left's proposed payment cuts would likely exacerbate this trend as more physicians close their practices or otherwise withdraw because of the payment reductions.

The list of problems with government-run health systems goes on and on. It would be a disaster for the American health care system, destroying innovation and consumer choice, and ultimately impacting the quality of care that Americans value.

THE TRUTH ABOUT GOVERNMENT-RUN HEALTH SYSTEMS

The allure of this promise of "free" health care has seemed compelling on the political circuit, but the reality of living under government-controlled health systems is a very different story.

Here is the truth about Canada's government-paid health care system. Canada's emergency rooms are packed, the Daily Signal reports.[34] In the province of Quebec, wait times average over four hours, leading many patients to just give up, go home, and hope for the best. The publication explains:

- Seeing a specialist can take a shockingly long time. One doctor in Ontario called in a referral for a neurologist and was told there was a four-and-a-half year waiting list.
- A sixteen-year-old boy in British Columbia waited three years for an urgent surgery, during which his condition worsened and he was left paraplegic. One Montreal man finally got the call for his long-delayed urgent surgery—but it came two months after he had died.
- Canadians have found a way to escape the rationing, the long waits, and substandard equipment. They go to the United States.

It's no better in the United Kingdom, which just "celebrated" the seventieth anniversary of its government-run health care system.

From long waits to outdated care and shoddy, aging technology, the British pay a high price for their "free" health care, Sally Pipes explains in her new book.[35] A native of Canada, she provides great detail about the painful realities of the wait times, substandard care, and even horror stories in single-payer systems. The latest medicines are rationed or not available at all, with the government making a decision based upon what it believes your life is worth. A fifty-year-old single mother of three who lives in Wales was denied a liver transplant. The best reason she can find: she had missed an appointment six years earlier at a hospital 120 miles from her home. "Can they just let me die?" she pleaded.

The stories of bureaucratic intrusion into health care decisions gained national attention with Charlie Gard, born in 2016 with a rare disorder that causes muscle weakness and respiratory failure. A neurologist in New York City had an experimental treatment he thought could work and his parents wanted to give it a try, Pipes reports in her book. But the British government decided it was time to stop little Charlie's life support. "In the United Kingdom, it's up to the courts—not doctors and patients—to decide how to treat a sick child and decide when to cut off life support."

Leaders from Pope Francis to President Trump tried to intervene on behalf of Charlie in the ensuing court battles. But they, and little Charlie and his family, lost. He died on July 28, 2017.

SLOWER ROADS TO SINGLE-PAYER

The popularity of Medicare for All has waned as people realize the real costs, including losing their current private health insurance, but there have been calls from the Left for "smaller" reforms.

Some have suggested that the movement to a federal single-payer system can start with state-based programs. But Colorado and Vermont recently failed in their attempts to implement statewide single-payer systems.

Colorado voters rejected a single-payer initiative in 2016 by a four-to-one margin, with residents especially concerned about the high taxes that would be required to finance it and about losing their current coverage to the uncertainties of the new system.

Vermont officials worked feverishly to design a single-payer system but found that the costs of the program would be prohibitive and that the higher taxes required would seriously damage the state's economy.

Others, including former vice president Joe Biden, call for creating a national "public option" government insurance plan to compete with private insurers. We have recent experience with a similar program—Consumer Oriented and Operated Plans, or co-ops.[36] The ACA initially set aside $6 billion to fund these entities, but Congress continued to cut back funding as members saw the programs collapsing. The co-ops were founded on the idealistic belief that new entities could create new health insurance companies that would be "member-driven, service-oriented, and would not have to answer to shareholders or turn a profit."

But the twenty-three co-ops that were created had significant start-up costs, no experiential data upon which to set premiums, usually had to pay extra to lease physician and hospital networks, and had few people in the companies and none on their boards with insurance experience. The idealism has quickly faded.

Only a few co-ops remain,[37] and they are being closely watched by regulators after so many failures have wasted federal tax dollars and forced millions of people out of their co-op plans, leaving them scrambling to find new coverage.

Still others suggest a Medicare buy-in approach. But that also leads to a slippery slope of government managing an ever larger share of health coverage and adding even more costs to the Medicare program.

It is hard to see what problem Medicare buy-in would solve. If early retirees were able to buy into the Medicare program and pay their full share, the cost would be an estimated $1,111 per person.[38] For many, that would be prohibitively expensive, possibly requiring yet another federal program to provide taxpayer-financed subsidies. In the ACA exchanges, a fifty-year-old pays an average premium of $668 for a Silver plan; for a sixty-year-old, it's $723. Exchange coverage is cheaper, even without subsidies.

PRICE TRANSPARENCY TO BATTLE FRAUD

Price transparency is a crucial element of reform. "Greater transparency in health care pricing will help employers to offer better payment structures for their employees and give employees and other consumers more tools to get better value in health spending," according to Galen senior fellow Brian Blase.[39] "Price transparency should also give employers the ability to monitor insurer effectiveness and eliminate counterproductive middlemen, and more visibility in pricing will put pressure on high-cost providers to lower prices."

Blase reports that consumers who used a New Hampshire price website prior to medical imaging visits saved 36 percent off the original cost of the test. "This shows that policy changes to encourage greater consumerism can produce significant benefits to employers, employees, and patients—enhancing their ability to obtain greater value from their health spending."

While some are skeptical about consumers' ability or willingness to utilize price transparency tools, he says transparency can have four key beneficial impacts: "1) Better informed consumers and patients; 2) Better informed employers that help workers shop for value; 3) Improved ability for employers to monitor insurer effectiveness and eliminate counterproductive middlemen; 4) Public pressure on high-cost providers."

Transparency is important all around, including in how taxpayer dollars are being spent. Blase has also written about the misguided incentives in the current Medicaid program that are promulgating misuse of funds.[40] Based upon an analysis of government data, he and colleague Aaron Yelowitz of the Mercatus Center found that the ACA's Medicaid expansion "appears to have more than tripled the amount of improper spending in the program. 20 percent or more of Medicaid spending in 2019—an amount likely to exceed $75 billion—is improper. Before Obamacare, the Medicaid improper-payment rate was 6 percent."

Since states view the Medicaid expansion as a cash cow, they have generally failed to conduct proper eligibility reviews, Blase and Yelowitz find. "One federal audit by the Health and Human Services Department's inspector general found that more than half of sampled enrollees in California's Medicaid program were either improperly enrolled or potentially improperly enrolled."[41]

They advise federal officials to address the problem to protect "those who are truly eligible and most need Medicaid, as well as to the nation's taxpayers. They should start by requiring eligibility redeterminations in areas where the problem is most severe and by recouping funds improperly claimed by states."

THE HEALTH CARE CHOICES PROPOSAL

The solution is not more government involvement in our health sector, but energizing the forces that deliver better care and services and lower costs through the rest of the economy. That requires a federalist approach to problem solving.

A group called the Health Policy Consensus Group has developed a plan to increase choices, lower costs, and expand access to health care and coverage. We have been working with a large group of colleagues in the Consensus Group to develop this new generation of patient-centered health policy recommendations. The plan, called the Health Care Choices Proposal, would move power away from Washington bureaucrats and ultimately put it in the hands of doctors and patients.

The Health Policy Consensus Group is made up of more than one hundred state and national health policy experts, along with members and leaders of grassroots organizations from around the country who are determined to give Americans relief from the high costs and restricted choices that Obamacare has imposed. "We know health reform is needed, but for too long, conservatives have battled over the right solution—whether to provide tax credits, tax deductions, or some combination to help people afford health coverage," according to Yuval Levin of the Ethics and Public Policy Center, one of the leaders in the effort.

The Health Care Choices plan moves on from that battle to a health reform initiative based on our system of government that devolves power to the states. Rather than having an all-powerful, deficit-spending federal government pulling the strings, it would empower states to create a more vibrant market for health coverage, giving consumers more choices of more affordable coverage while providing better protections for those with serious health conditions.

At the launch event for the plan in 2018, I (Rick) explained my passion for advancing patient-centered health reform. It stems partly from my experience with my daughter, Isabella, who was born with a genetic disorder called Trisomy 18. Half of babies born with Trisomy 18 die in the first three months of life, and most do not live beyond one year. But we had just celebrated Bella's tenth birthday. We have been able to get sufficient medical care in the United States, and because of the health care she

THERE ARE IMPORTANT GOALS FOR HEALTH REFORM:

- Everyone should be able to access the health care they need
- Coverage and care should be affordable, including for those with chronic medical conditions
- A variety of options should be available to account for the vastly different preferences of individuals and families
- People should be able to see the physicians and other providers of their choice
- Federal tax and spending policy should not advantage some types of coverage over other types
- Choice and competition should be maximized in order to foster innovation and drive price declines and quality improvements
- The most vulnerable, including the unborn and those at the end of life, must be protected

has been able to receive we have the miracle of this beautiful child.

I fight every day to make sure that children like Bella will have the freedom to get the health care they need without the government interference that tragically happens in countries with government-controlled health care systems that can block access to care, as in the cases of Charlie Gard[42] and Alfie Evans.[43]

Unlike Obamacare, the Consensus Group's Health Care Choices plan devotes dedicated resources to help finance care for those with expensive health care needs, including those with pre-existing conditions. In contrast, Obamacare puts these patients in the same pools with everyone else, without extra subsidies. This has driven up premiums to the point that healthy people are being driven out of the market.

Also at the launch event for the Health Care Choices plan, former governor Phil Bryant of Mississippi expressed strong support for policies that would allow states to provide real choices of affordable coverage for their citizens.[44] "The best government is the government closest to the people," he said. "This plan represents a grassroots, commonsense effort that a majority of the American people will gladly welcome."

State senator Bryce Reeves of Virginia told the group that putting more people on Obamacare is not the answer. He read an email from a constituent who said his health insurance now costs more than his mortgage. "What am I supposed to do for my family?" the man asked him.

"So now, my constituents have to choose between having a roof over their heads or having protection against huge medical bills? This is unacceptable," he said, adding that the Consensus Group's plan offers a much better choice. "We all have to get engaged to turn the tide."

U.S. Senator Lindsey Graham of South Carolina says the plan was "created by grassroots groups committed to lowering health care costs and increasing choices for people across the United States. . . . This idea—returning money and control to the states and localities—has been used before with great success when we reformed welfare. It freed states from the grips of a Washington-knows-best bureaucracy and allowed for innovation and cutting-edge reforms."

Obamacare has led to millions of people becoming dependent on government subsidies for their increasingly expensive insurance. A transition is needed to make sure they do not lose their coverage as states rebuild health insurance markets that were broken by Obamacare. Clearly, the federal government is not capable of micromanaging a market as personal and local as health care.

No one is saying that consumers should be asked whether they want an MRI or a cheaper X-ray if they are wheeled into an emergency room after an accident. But most are more than capable of making decisions about the type of health insurance they want to have for these and other needs for medical care.

The experience with Obamacare shows the importance of turning away from greater and greater centralization of power in Washington over health care. We have seen what leads from government, not consumers, deciding what benefits must be covered by health insurance, with even Catholic nuns being directed to provide employees access to birth control and abortion in abject violation of their religious beliefs. The U.S.

Supreme Court had to intervene to stop the intrusion, but the Left will not give up and is back in court again over the issue.

Concentrating power over health care decisions puts trillions of dollars under the control of political leaders and government regulators. And centralization in Washington opens the door for even more consolidation among industry players—hospitals, physician practices, and so on. These bigger players increasingly cater to the federal government's directives and demands, not to those of consumers.

We believe power must be devolved to consumers by funneling more flexibility and resources to the states, which have decades of experience in overseeing health insurance markets and are closer to understanding the needs of their citizens and the resources available in their states.

The Health Care Choices Proposal would give states much greater flexibility and resources to help their small group and individual markets heal from the assault of Obamacare, giving them new incentives to revive competition and give people more choices of coverage they can afford. The actual bill would, of course, contain additional provisions, including grant allocation formulas, transition funding, and likely enhancements to Health Savings Accounts.

The money that the federal government currently sends to insurance companies under Obamacare would be repurposed and sent to the states in the form of grants they can use to stabilize their health insurance markets and to provide assistance to those with lower incomes and to the sick and needy.

An analysis by the Center for Health and Economy has shown that the Health Care Choices plan would reduce average premiums for individual health insurance coverage by one-third while keeping coverage numbers at least level.[45] By encouraging healthy people to remain covered, insurance pools are healthier, and resources can be directed to help those with greater health needs.

Legislative action is needed to unleash the innovation and energy that are pent up in our health sector. The Health Care Choices Proposal is focused on healing states' individual and small group health insurance markets that have been so damaged by the ACA. Our plan would provide states with resources to assist people who need help in purchasing health insurance, especially those with pre-existing conditions, and empower states with new flexibility to create more affordable options for coverage.

The Health Care Choices plan would start by repealing the ACA's expansion of Medicaid to childless, non-disabled, working-age adults and its entitlements to individual health insurance subsidies that have doubled the cost of coverage and priced millions of people out of their individual policies.

These resources would be redirected as grants to the states, coupled with new incentives, so they can better meet the needs of their citizens. States would use the grants to provide assistance to those with low incomes and high health costs and also to stabilize their individual and small group health insurance markets.

To ensure that people have more choices of care and coverage and that the vulnerable are protected, states must ensure that:

- At least 50 percent of the grant goes toward supporting people's purchase of private health coverage
- At least 50 percent goes to provide coverage for low-income people (the two categories will overlap)
- A portion of the grant goes to offset the costs of high-risk patients to make sure they get the care they need so they do not drive up premiums for everyone else in the market
- Anyone eligible for financial assistance under the grant, CHIP, or Medicaid can take the value of their premium assistance to purchase the private plan of their choice
- The grant would be distributed through the Children's Health Insurance Program, which provides protections against taxpayer money being used to fund abortions

Obamacare requirements on essential health benefits, single risk pools, minimum loss ratio requirements, and the 3:1 age ratio would not apply in states receiving federal allotments.

Nullifying these mandates, along with providing new flexibility to the states, would reduce premiums, allow fairer premium variation and, in combination with risk mitigation, assure that the sick get the coverage they need without charging the healthy unfairly high premiums.

Funds to finance the formula grants would be based upon spending, as of a fixed date, on ACA subsidies (both tax credits and cost-sharing reduction payments) plus current and projected Medicaid expansion funds.

The Health Care Choices plan contains many other provisions to lower costs and enhance access to modern coverage arrangements, such as Health Savings Accounts, plus ways to create much greater price transparency so newly empowered consumers can get better value in their health spending.

We believe the Health Care Choices Proposal would give states more power to make sure their healthy residents can get and keep affordable health coverage and their most vulnerable citizens have better options for care.[46]

JANET: BETTER CARE AND COVERAGE BEFORE OBAMACARE

A woman with serious health problems provided a testimonial about why further reforms are needed.[47] Janet reported to us:

> In 1999, I was diagnosed with Hepatitis C, which made me ineligible for insurance [denied for pre-existing conditions]. I live in Colorado, and they had a high-risk pool that covered people like me. I applied for that and was accepted.
>
> My premiums in 2010 were $275/month with a total out of pocket of $2,500. [While I was on] this plan, my liver

failed, and I needed a liver transplant. It was approved without a question. My $600,000 transplant was covered 100 percent with a $2,500 out of pocket maximum!

When Obamacare went into effect, Colorado's high-risk pool was closed.

I was forced into the regular marketplace that everyone was telling me was a good thing because I couldn't get denied. I think my first year on that policy, my premiums were in the $450 range—which I thought was not too terrible, but still more than I had been paying.

The thing I noticed from the start was that instead of full coverage, almost everything I needed was denied, which threw me into the world of having to appeal (sometimes several times) to get the basic care I needed.

Since then, my premiums skyrocketed. In 2017, I paid $735 a month with total out-of-pocket costs of $5,500. In 2018, my premiums went up to $1,100 a month with a deductible of $6,300. Once I hit that mark, I'm covered 80 percent.

Further, none of my anti-rejection meds are on the formulary of my insurance. If I could not afford them, my body would most certainly reject my liver, causing another liver transplant that would not be covered 100 percent.

I don't get any [tax] credits from the government to reduce my premiums. Those of us who are self-employed but make more than the threshold for tax credits wind up footing the whole bill ourselves. I have to spend $19,500 before my insurance pays anything, and it doesn't cover all my prescription costs. My old plan was almost a third of what I have to pay now.

I have many friends and work associates in the same boat as me. Many of them are doing without insurance and are betting that they won't need more than what they can afford to pay out of pocket. I cannot do that, because if something happened and I needed another transplant, it would bankrupt my family.

Janet has coverage for pre-existing conditions, but her access to care is inferior to the state high-risk pool coverage she had before, and the cost of her coverage is much higher.

The current system is not working for Janet and others like her who cannot receive the care they need.

A NEW APPROACH TO HEALTH REFORM

We believe that if resources are redirected to the states and coupled with new incentives, states will better meet the needs of their citizens with more flexible programs and more focused assistance for those who most need help.

The plan is to get the federal government out of the business of micromanaging our health care. It has created tens of thousands of pages of rules and regulations in its clumsy and misguided effort to overhaul the individual health insurance market. It has driven up costs, reduced choices, and made it harder for sick people to get care—all while giving a blank check from taxpayers to health insurers, hospitals, and other big health care businesses.

Health care is too local and personal for a one-size-fits-all approach to work. Health reform should be about your care and your coverage to put you and your doctor in control of your health care decisions.

Religious Liberty and the Human Good

by Professor Robert P. George

Of all the freedoms we are so blessed to have in America, the right to religious freedom is at the top of the list for most Americans. No one in the country understands better—or is able to articulate as well—the origin and underlying foundation of religious freedom than Robert George. Professor George has been leading the discussion on major topics such as religious freedom in this nation for almost four decades. He has had an extraordinary career and has long been someone I greatly admire. With his appointment to the U.S. Commission on International Religious Freedom in 2012, Professor George has had the opportunity to shape opinion and policy regarding religious freedom not just in the United States, but around the world. I am blessed that he chose to participate in this new version of *Making Government Work*.
—Tan Parker

Writing from a jail cell in Birmingham, Alabama, Dr. Martin Luther King Jr. anticipated a challenge to the moral goodness of the acts of civil disobedience that landed him behind bars. He anticipated his critics asking: How can you, Dr. King, engage in willful law-breaking, when you yourself had stressed the importance of obedience to law in demanding that officials of the southern states conform to the Supreme Court's desegregation ruling in the case of *Brown v. Board of Education*?

Let us examine King's response to the challenge:

> The answer lies in the fact that there are two types of laws: just and unjust. I would be the first to advocate obeying just laws. One has not only a legal but a moral responsibility to obey just laws. Conversely, one has a moral responsibility to disobey unjust laws. I would agree with St. Augustine that "an unjust law is no law at all."
>
> Now, what is the difference between the two? How does one determine whether a law is just or unjust?
>
> A just law is a man-made code that squares with the moral law or the law of God. An unjust law is a code that is out of harmony with the moral law. To put it in the terms of St. Thomas Aquinas: An unjust law is a human law that is not rooted in eternal law and natural law.
>
> Any law that uplifts human personality is just. Any law that degrades human personality is unjust. All segregation statutes are unjust because segregation distorts the soul and damages the personality. It gives the segregator a false sense of superiority and the segregated a false sense of inferiority.[1]

So, just laws elevate and ennoble the human personality, or what King in other contexts referred to as the human spirit; unjust laws debase and degrade it. Now, his point about the morality or immorality of laws is a good reminder that what is true of what is sometimes called "personal morality" is also true of "political morality." The choices and actions of political institutions at every level, like the choices and actions of individuals, can be right or wrong, morally good or morally bad. They can be in line with human well-being and fulfillment in all of its manifold dimensions; or they can fail, in any of a range of ways, to respect the integral flourishing of human persons.

In many cases of the failure of laws, policies, and institutions to fulfill the requirements of morality, we speak intelligibly and rightly of a violation of human rights. This is particularly true where the failure is properly characterized as an injustice—failing to honor people's equal worth and dignity, failing to give them, or even actively denying them, what they are due.

But, contrary to the teaching of the late John Rawls and the extraordinarily influential stream of contemporary liberal thought of which he was the leading exponent, I wish to suggest that good is prior to right and, indeed, to rights.[2]

Here is what I mean: To be sure, human rights, including the right to religious liberty, are among the moral principles that demand respect from all of us, including governments and international institutions (which are morally bound not only to respect human rights but also to protect them). To respect people, to respect their dignity, is to, among other things, honor their rights, including, to be sure, the right that we are gathered today to lift up to our fellow citizens and defend, the right to religious freedom.

Like all moral principles, however, human rights (including the right to religious liberty) are shaped, and given content, by the human goods they protect. Rights, like other moral principles, are intelligible as rational, action-guiding principles because they are entailments and, at some level, specifications of the integral directiveness or prescriptivity of principles of practical reason that direct our choosing toward what is humanly fulfilling and enriching (or, as Dr. King would say, uplifting) and away from what is contrary to our well-being as the kind of creatures we are—namely, human persons.

And so, for example, it matters to the identification and defense of the right to life—a right violated not only when the death of another is sought as one's end or as a means to one's end, but also in cases in which someone's death is foreseen and accepted unfairly as a side effect of one's action in pursuit of an end—that human life is no mere instrumental good, but is an intrinsic aspect of the good of human persons and an integral dimension of our overall flourishing.[3] And it matters to the identification and defense of the right to religious liberty that religion is yet another irreducible aspect of human well-being and fulfillment—a basic human good.[4]

But what is religion?

In its fullest and most robust sense, religion is the human person's being in right relation to the divine—the more-than-merely-human source or sources, if there be such, of meaning and value. Of course, even the greatest among us in the things of the spirit fall short of perfection in various ways; but in the ideal of perfect religion, the person would understand as comprehensively and deeply as possible the body of truths about spiritual things, and would fully order his or her life, and share in the life of a community of faith that is ordered, in line with those truths. In the perfect realization of the good of religion, one would achieve the relationship that the divine—say God himself, assuming for a moment the truth of monotheism—wishes us to have with him.

Of course, different traditions of faith have different views of what constitutes religion in its fullest and most robust sense. There are different doctrines, different scriptures, different structures of authority, different ideas of what is true about spiritual things and what it means to be in proper relationship to the more-than-merely-human sources of meaning and value that different traditions understand as divinity.[5]

For my part, I believe that reason has a very large role to play for each of us in deciding where spiritual truth most robustly is to be found. And by reason here, I mean not only our capacity for practical reasoning and moral judgment, but also our capacities for understanding and evaluating claims of all sorts: logical, historical, scientific, and so forth.

But one need not agree with me about this in order to affirm with me that there is a distinct basic human good of religion—a good that is uniquely architectonic in shaping one's pursuit of and participation in all the basic human goods—and that one begins to realize and participate in this good from the moment one begins the quest to understand the more-than-merely-human sources of meaning and value and to live authentically by ordering one's life in line with one's best judgments of the truth in religious matters.

If I am right, then the existential raising of religious questions, the honest identification of answers, and the fulfilling of what one sincerely believes to be one's duties in the light of those answers are all parts of the human good of religion—a good whose pursuit is an indispensable feature of the comprehensive flourishing of a human being. If I am right, then man is, as Seamus Hasson puts it, intrinsically and by nature a religious being—homo religiosus, to borrow a concept, or at least a couple of words of Latin, from Eliade—and the flourishing of man's spiritual life is integral to his all-around well-being and fulfillment.

But if that is true, then respect for a person's well-being, or more simply respect for the person, demands respect for his or her flourishing as a seeker of religious truth and as a man or woman who lives in line with his best judgments of what is true in spiritual matters. And that, in turn, requires respect for his or her liberty in the religious quest—the quest to understand religious truth and order one's life in line with it. Because faith of any type, including religious faith, cannot be authentic—it cannot be faith—unless it is free. Respect for the person—that is to say, respect for his or her dignity as a free and rational creature—requires respect for his or her religious liberty.

That is why it makes sense, from the point of view of reason, and not merely from the point of view of the revealed teaching of a particular faith—though many faiths proclaim the right to religious freedom on theological and not merely philosophical grounds—to understand religious freedom as a fundamental human right.

Interestingly and tragically, in times past, and even in some places today, regard for persons' spiritual well-being has been the premise, and motivating factor, for denying religious liberty or conceiving of it in a cramped and restricted way. Before the Catholic Church embraced the robust conception of religious freedom that honors the civil right to give public witness and expression to sincere religious views (even when erroneous) in the document *Dignitatis Humanae* of the Second Vatican Council, some Catholics rejected the idea of a right to religious freedom on the theory that "only the truth has rights." The idea was that the state, under favoring conditions, should not only publicly identify itself with Catholicism as the true faith, but forbid religious advocacy or proselytizing that could lead people into religious error and apostasy.

The mistake here was not in the premise: religion is a great human good, and the truer the religion the better for the fulfillment of the believer. That is true. The mistake, rather, was in the supposition made by some that the good of religion was not being advanced or participated in outside the context of the one true faith, and that it could be reliably protected and advanced by placing civil restrictions enforceable by agencies of the state on the advocacy of religious ideas.

In rejecting this supposition, Catholicism did not embrace the idea that error has rights; they noticed, rather, that people have rights, and they have rights even when they are in error.[6] And among those rights integral to authentic religion as a fundamental and irreducible aspect of the human good is the right to express and even advocate in line with one's sense of one's conscientious obligations, what one believes to be true about spiritual matters, even if one's beliefs are, in one way or another, less than fully sound, and, indeed, even if they are false.[7]

Now, the Catholic Church does not have a monopoly on the natural-law reasoning by which I am today explicating and defending the human right to religious liberty.[8] But the Church does have a deep commitment to such reasoning and a long experience with it. And in *Dignitatis Humanae*, the Fathers of the Second Vatican Council present a natural-law argument for religious freedom—indeed they begin by presenting a natural-law argument before supplementing it with arguments appealing to the authority of God's revelation in sacred scripture.

So let me ask you to linger with me a bit longer over the key Catholic texts so that I can illustrate by the teachings of an actual faith how religious leaders and believers, and not just statesmen concerned to craft national or international policy in circumstances of religious pluralism, can incorporate into their understanding of the basic human right to religious liberty principles and arguments available to all men and women of sincerity and goodwill by virtue of what Professor Rawls once referred to as "our common human reason."[9]

Of course, from the point of view of any believer, irrespective of his or her particular tradition of faith, the further away one gets from the truth of faith in all its dimensions, the less fulfillment is available. But that does not mean that even a primitive and superstition-laden faith is utterly devoid of value or that there is no right to religious liberty for people who practice such a faith. Nor does it mean that atheists have no right to religious freedom. The fundamentals of respect for the good of religion require that civil authority respect (and, in appropriate ways, even nurture) conditions or circumstances in which people can engage in the sincere religious quest and live lives of authenticity reflecting their best judgments as to the truth of spiritual matters.

To compel an atheist to perform acts that are premised on theistic beliefs that he cannot, in good conscience, share, is to deny him the fundamental bit of the good of religion that is his, namely, living with honesty and integrity in line with his best judgments about ultimate reality. Coercing him to perform religious acts does him no good, since faith really must be free, and dishonors his dignity as a free and rational person. The violation of liberty is worse than futile.

Of course, there are limits to the freedom that must be respected for the sake of the good of religion and the dignity of the human person as a being whose integral fulfillment includes the spiritual quest and the ordering of one's life in line with one's best judgment as to what spiritual truth requires.

Gross evil—even grave injustice—can be committed by sincere people for the sake of religion. Unspeakable wrongs can be done by people seeking sincerely to get right with God or the gods or their conception of ultimate reality, whatever it is. The presumption in favor of respecting liberty must, for the sake of the human good and the dignity of human persons as free and rational creatures—creatures who, according to Judaism and Christianity, are made in the very image and likeness of God—be powerful and broad. But it is not unlimited. Even the great end of getting right with God cannot justify a morally bad means, even for the sincere believer.

I do not doubt the sincerity of the Aztecs in practicing human sacrifice, or the sincerity of those in the history of various traditions of faith who used coercion and even torture in the cause of what they believed was religiously required. But these things are deeply wrong and need not (and should not) be tolerated in the name of religious freedom. To suppose otherwise is to back oneself into the awkward position of supposing that violations of religious freedom (and other injustices of equal gravity) must be respected for the sake of religious freedom.

Still, to overcome the powerful and broad presumption in favor of religious liberty, to be justified in requiring the believer to do something contrary to his faith or forbidding the believer to do something his faith requires, political authority must meet a heavy burden. The legal test in the United States under the Religious Freedom Restoration Act is one way of capturing the presumption and burden. To justify a law that bears negatively on religious freedom, even a neutral law of general applicability must be supported by a compelling state interest and represent the least restrictive or intrusive means of protecting or serving that interest.

We can debate, as a matter of American constitutional law or as a matter of policy, whether it is, or should be, up to courts or legislators to decide when exemptions to general, neutral laws should be granted for the sake of religious freedom, or to determine when the presumption in favor of religious freedom has been overcome; but the substantive matter of what religious freedom demands from those who exercise the levers of state power should be something on which reasonable people of goodwill across the religious and political spectrums should agree—precisely because it is a matter capable of being settled by our common human reason.

Three Cheers for the Electoral College

by Professor Bradley A. Smith

In recent years there has been much discussion about the role of the Electoral College in electing the president and vice president of the United States. The establishment of the Electoral College dates back to the founders of our nation, when they initially drafted the United States Constitution. I asked Professor Bradley Smith to write on this important topic because he is one of the leading experts in the nation on the importance of the Electoral College. He also served as a former commissioner, vice chairman, and chairman of the Federal Election Commission. I believe more Americans need to better understand the wisdom of our Founding Fathers in creating the Electoral College, and no one is better suited to share that message with Americans than Professor Smith.

—Tan Parker

INTRODUCTION

One would be hard-pressed to name a provision of the Constitution that gets less respect than the Electoral College. A 2019 Gallup poll found respondents supported a constitutional amendment to abolish the College in favor of direct popular election of the president by a 55 to 43 percent margin. But that is actually good news for the College. Prior to 2016, support for direct popular election in a Gallup poll had never fallen below 58 percent, reaching a peak at 80 percent in 1968. Over a thousand constitutional amendments have been proposed to alter or abolish the College. But passing a constitutional amendment is hard work, and so the College has survived.

Supporters of direct popular election have now come up with a scheme to end-run the difficult amendment process. Called "National Popular Vote" (or "NPV"), it calls for states to join an interstate compact. Signatory states would agree not to award their electoral votes to the winner of the popular vote in their state, but to the winner of the aggregated popular vote across the fifty states and the District of Columbia. The compact would become effective once states comprising an Electoral College majority—that is, 270 or more Electoral College votes—sign on, thus guaranteeing that the candidate with the most popular votes would win the presidency. As of the close of 2019, 16 states with 196 Electoral College votes had joined the NPV compact.

It would be a shame if, just as popular understanding of and support in the polls for the Electoral College is growing, we altered our system for electing presidents through constitutional chicanery. The Electoral College is an important part of our constitutional plan of government and offers practical benefits in administering elections and preventing fraud. Furthermore, the NPV plan to forgo a constitutional amendment is of doubtful constitutionality, and NPV promises to create a litigation, constitutional, and political crisis dwarfing that seen in the Florida recounts of 2000.

THE ELECTORAL COLLEGE, POPULAR VOTE, AND THE CONSTITUTION

Critics of the Electoral College focus blindly on the fact that the College may not always elect the winner of the "popular vote." Here they misunderstand the very notion of a national popular vote and ignore other important constitutional values that the College serves.

THERE IS NO "NATIONAL POPULAR VOTE" FOR PRESIDENT

Electoral College critics offer a simple and superficially appealing claim: nationwide popular vote totals should always determine the winner of the presidency. In fact, that usually happens with the Electoral College. Of forty-eight presidential elections since 1828, the first year for which we have meaningful national totals for the popular vote, there have been just four elections in which the Electoral College winner did not win the popular vote—1876, 1888, 2000, and 2016. NPV would remedy these "misfires" by declaring the candidate with the most popular votes from the fifty states to be the winner of the presidential election, even if that winner received far less than a majority of the total votes.

The first of many problems with NPV is that we don't actually have a national popular vote. The states differ in how long they keep their polls open, in whether or not they allow "straight ticket" voting, whether convicted felons can vote, whether to count write-in votes, and the ease with which third-party and independent candidates can qualify for the ballot.

California allows "ballot harvesting," in which organized workers from parties and interest groups collect absentee ballots from voters and return them to a polling place or election office. Most states do not, seeing the practice as ripe for fraud. Thirty-two states require voters to register in advance, with varying rules on who can register and how and when one must vote, but seventeen states allow Election Day voter registration, and North Dakota doesn't require voter registration at all. Oregon and Washington conduct their elections by mail; most states still think it better if most voters go to the polls. Some states have early voting, of various durations, and others have none.

All of these practices are determined by local preferences and needs, and all of them can affect voter turnout—and hence, local election results. In short, there is really no "national popular vote," because the rules vary across the country as to who votes, when they vote, and how they vote. Simply aggregating the votes from fifty-one different jurisdictions using a variety of rules does not yield a true "national popular vote."

Even more importantly, candidates campaign to win the Electoral College vote. Were candidates trying to rack up popular vote pluralities, they would quit campaigning in small towns and rural areas, or in competitive states such as Michigan, Pennsylvania, and New Hampshire, and focus their energies on urban centers and on jacking up the vote in their partisan stronghold states.

Furthermore, aggregated popular vote totals are routinely within the margin of error. For example, in 2000, Al Gore won the aggregated popular vote by approximately 540,000 votes. But more than three times that number of ballots were thrown out nationwide as a result of voter error.[1]

So simply aggregating the popular vote from elections in fifty states and the District of Columbia into one total does not give us a true "national popular vote." But this objection merely begs the question: Why not abolish the Electoral College, establish a single, national system for voting, and use the popular vote to elect the president? Before answering this question, some international perspective may be in order.

IN MOST ADVANCED DEMOCRACIES, IT IS POSSIBLE TO BE ELECTED TO THE TOP OFFICE WITHOUT WINNING THE NATIONAL POPULAR VOTE

Erwin Chemerinsky, the dean of the University of California, Berkeley, Law School, claims, "The U.S. is . . . the only country in the world where the candidate who loses the popular vote can be chosen president."[2] But that is not true, at least not if we substitute "head of government" (thereby including "Prime Minister" or "Premier") for "president." In fact, Chemerinsky's statement is almost the exact opposite of the truth—most advanced democracies permit a candidate to become head of the government without winning the popular vote.

In October 2019, Canadian prime minister Justin Trudeau was reelected despite his Liberal Party winning just 33 percent of the popular vote to the Conservative's 34.4 percent. In 2009, Benjamin Netanyahu was elected Israel's prime minister despite finishing second in the popular vote. The United Kingdom, Sweden, Norway, Germany, Italy, Japan, Australia, New Zealand, and India have also all had recent elections in which the party that won the popular vote was not elected head of the government. In Sweden, Germany, Norway, and Italy, this happened because of coalitions formed after the election, but elsewhere candidates won the office even while losing the popular vote—in some cases after losing the popular vote by an outright majority.

It is simply not true that the United States is unique in sometimes choosing the second-place finisher to head the government. Of course, all of these countries have parliamentary systems, but that does not change the fact that each allows the head of government to be elected without winning the popular vote. The United States is in tune with most developed democracies in recognizing that, while popular vote matters tremendously, it is not the only criterion for a legitimate government.

This brings us to the correct question: Can we defend a system in which, in four of forty-eight elections, the winner of the popular vote has not been elected president? The reasons may differ, but for the United States, as for these other countries, the answer is clearly yes.

THE ELECTORAL COLLEGE IS ONE OF MANY CONSTITUTIONAL PROVISIONS AND POLITICAL NORMS INTENDED TO ENSURE WISE, ENDURING MAJORITIES WHILE SECURING THE RIGHTS OF MINORITIES

The United States is founded on the idea that the people—not some king or the sitting government—are sovereign. The Declaration of Independence proclaimed—contrary to all established political systems of the time—that "Governments . . . deriv[e] their just powers from the consent of the governed." The signers of the Declaration made clear that they signed only as agents "of the good People of these Colonies." In 1787, "in order to form a more perfect union," we adopted a new Constitution. The new Constitution was ratified not by state legislatures, but by conventions elected specifically for that purpose—by "we the People of the United States." But while legitimacy rested on popular consent, crude majoritarianism was never the design or intent of the people.

Our Constitution is democratic, but with numerous checks and balances to ensure enduring majorities, moderation, and respect for minority rights and desires. These include separation of powers into three supportive but independent branches, a national government of enumerated powers, a bicameral legislature, staggered elections, presidential veto power, and federalism. Even then, the people only ratified the Constitution after assurances that further checks on the majority would be added to it. These additional checks became the Bill of Rights.

Our national legislative design also rejects raw majoritarianism. Not only do states have equal representation in the Senate, but in the House of Representatives each state, no matter how small, is guaranteed at least one congressional representative. It is possible for a party to gain a House majority without winning a plurality of the aggregated national vote for House candidates (as happened in 2012), and thus to elect the Speaker, who is second in line to the presidency. If the Electoral College is illegitimate simply because on rare occasions it yields counter-majoritarian results, so are the Senate, the House, and even the Bill of Rights.

In fact, the Electoral College is part of our rich constitutional fabric. It allows for rare departures from straight plurality election in order to implement other values equally important to Americans—including a guarantee that a president can only be elected with broad popular support. Like many other features of the Constitution, while the Electoral College may sometimes contribute to counter-majoritarian results, its benefits lie elsewhere.

THE ELECTORAL COLLEGE ENSURES THAT THE PRESIDENT WILL BE ELECTED WITH SUBSTANTIAL POPULAR SUPPORT

Though not required by the Constitution, since 1836 every state (except for South Carolina until the Civil War) has used a popular election to choose its presidential electors. With just two exceptions—Nebraska and Maine—states award all of their electoral votes to the popular vote winner of the state. This makes it impossible to win the Electoral College without winning a substantial portion of the national aggregated popular vote. Only one winning candidate has been elected with less than 40 percent of the aggregate popular vote—Abraham Lincoln, who received 39.6 percent of the aggregated popular vote in 1860, enough to beat his nearest competitor by over 10 percentage points.

In the four elections in which the Electoral College winner did not win the aggregate popular vote (1876, 1888, 2000, and 2016), the successful candidate averaged 47.4 percent of the aggregated popular vote. Seven times the popular vote winner has received less than 47.4 percent of the aggregate popular vote; five times he has received less than Trump's 45.9 percent; and in seventeen presidential elections the popular vote winner received less than 50 percent of the aggregated popular vote. In other words, on the rare occasions when the Electoral College does not coincide with the aggregated popular vote, the winner of the Electoral College has still received popular support roughly equivalent to or better than more than a third of those elected president while winning the aggregate popular vote.

Under a national popular vote, candidates would need neither a popular nor an Electoral College majority—just more votes than anyone else. Thus, a candidate could win with as little as 25 or 30 percent of the vote, and we should expect to see such elections.

Some have suggested that this could be solved by a runoff election in which, if no candidate gained a majority of the popular vote (or perhaps some lower threshold, such as 40 or 45 percent), the top two finishers would face off in a second round. NPV, however, cannot provide for this—a constitutional amendment, which NPV is designed to avoid, would be necessary. Even if the Constitution were amended to provide for a runoff, we would likely see numerous candidates in the first round. Candidates would have an incentive to stay in, in the hopes of winning 20 to 30 percent and making the runoff, or if not finishing in the top two, putting themselves in position to strike a bargain for their support in the runoff. Extreme candidates of the Right and Left who have dedicated followers totaling some 25 to 30 percent of the election but are disliked by everyone else would frequently end up in the runoff.

This has happened in France's recent elections with the far-right National Rally, founded by Holocaust denier Jean-Marie Le Pen. So while a direct popular vote may assure a plurality winner, it does so at the cost of creating winners who regularly have far less total popular support than is the norm under the Electoral College.

THE ELECTORAL COLLEGE ENSURES THAT THE PRESIDENT IS ELECTED BY A BROAD CROSS SECTION OF AMERICA

As important as the Electoral College is in ensuring that a candidate has significant popular support, it is even more important in shaping how candidates create their voter coalitions. The Electoral College requires a candidate to run national campaigns across regions of the country.

States have always been, and were intended to be, key building blocks of American government. Congressmen and senators are elected by states. There is a reason why St. Louis, Missouri, and East Saint Louis, Illinois, or Kansas City, Missouri, and Kansas City, Kansas, are always in different congressional districts, and it is because these neighboring cities are located in different states. This element of federalism serves an important purpose by ensuring that all parts of the country—specifically all states—are represented in the national legislature.

The Electoral College serves the same purpose in the executive branch. In a country as large and diverse as the United States, it is essential that the president has substantial support across many sections of the country and not win simply due to overwhelming support in one region. In 2000, for example, George Bush narrowly won the Electoral College, while Al Gore narrowly won the popular vote. But Gore's plurality support was concentrated in a small number of areas, while Bush's spanned the country. Bush won almost 80 percent of the nation's counties and thirty states.

The nation cannot be governed by amassing large majorities in just a few states. It is no accident that the only other democracies that span a continent—Canada and Australia—also have systems in which a candidate can become prime minister without winning the total popular vote by winning a large share of the popular vote across the country. In fact, this has happened recently in both countries: Australia in 1990 and 1998; Canada in 1979 and 2019.

Only three times has a candidate won the Electoral College vote without winning the popular vote in a majority of states. In 1880, James Garfield and Winfield Hancock each won nineteen states, with Garfield carrying the Electoral College while winning the aggregate popular vote by a razor-thin 48.3 percent to 48.2 percent. In 1960, Richard Nixon won twenty-six states to John Kennedy's twenty-four, but Kennedy narrowly won the aggregate popular vote victory (49.7 percent to 49.6 percent) and the Electoral College majority (303–219). And in 1976, Jimmy Carter also won just twenty-four states, but edged Gerald Ford with 50.1 percent of the aggregated popular vote and a 297–240 margin in the Electoral College.

In short, not only does a candidate need substantial popular support to win the Electoral College, but that support must span many regions of the country. Even the most "sectional" of our presidential winners, Abraham Lincoln in 1860, was more of a national candidate than his competitors. Lincoln won nothing south of the Mason-Dixon Line, but he won New England, the Midwest, the prairie, and the West Coast—he won states from Maine to California. The second-place finisher, John Breckinridge, won only in the South.

Popular vote advocates argue that in any presidential election many individual states are not competitive. For example, in 2016, only seventeen states were won by less than ten points. But those states were a diverse bunch. They included states from New England (Maine, New Hampshire), the Mid-Atlantic (Pennsylvania), the south (Virginia, Florida), the industrial Midwest (Michigan, Ohio, Wisconsin, Minnesota), and the west (Nevada, Colorado). There were big states (Florida, Texas) and small states (Maine, Nevada). They included three of the eight states with the largest percentage of an African American population (Georgia, North Carolina, Virginia), and four of the five with the largest percentage of a Hispanic population (New Mexico, Texas, Arizona, and Nevada).

Yet they also included three of the five states with the highest percentage of a white population (Iowa, Maine, New Hampshire). They included states with heavily unionized work forces (Michigan, Minnesota), and states with some of the lowest unionization rates (Texas, Georgia, Virginia, North Carolina). They included manufacturing states (Ohio, Michigan), and states with very little manufacturing (Nevada, New Mexico). They included high tax states, such as Minnesota and Iowa, and low tax states, such as Florida and New Hampshire. To win the Electoral College, a candidate must appeal to a wide array of geographic, economic, and social interests.

To increase their chances of winning the Electoral College, candidates must find ways to boost their appeal to voters in states different from those where they are already strong. In a direct popular vote, however, the candidate can increase the odds of winning simply by doubling down on the states and demographics already in his corner.

In a country as large and diverse as the United States, it matters not only that a candidate has popular support, it matters how a winning coalition is assembled. The Electoral College solves that problem at the same time that it ensures that the winner will have a high level of popular support.

THE ELECTORAL COLLEGE IMPROVES ELECTORAL ADMINISTRATION AND REDUCES POSSIBILITIES FOR VOTER SUPPRESSION AND FRAUD

As we have seen, a meaningful national popular vote would require a nationwide, uniform set of rules. This would affect not only presidential elections, but elections for state and local offices that are typically held simultaneously. One benefit of having fifty separate state elections is that states can tailor their procedures for the needs and preferences of the local electorate, geography, and culture.

The Electoral College also provides a benefit that the Founders never considered: it cordons off voter suppression and fraud, limiting their effects on the national government. This is clearly seen in the presidential elections of 1876 and 1888. In each, the Democratic candidate narrowly won the popular vote, but lost in the Electoral College. However, the Democrats' popular vote margins were fueled by massive voter fraud and suppression throughout the Deep South. This fraud included ballot box stuffing, intimidation, and even the horrors of violence against African Americans and other Republican voters. This gave Democratic nominees Samuel Tilden and Grover Cleveland (themselves honorable men) huge popular vote majorities in the Deep South and provided for narrow victory margins in the national aggregated popular vote. However, it didn't help them win. For example, Cleveland won South Carolina with over 82 percent of the official vote count. But winning South Carolina with 82 percent was no more valuable in the Electoral College than winning with 52 percent—much of the fraud and intimidation had no effect on the outcome of the presidential race. In both 1876 and 1888, one could fairly say that the Electoral College more truly represented public opinion than the national popular vote totals.

Today, the state-by-state nature of American presidential elections still makes it harder to steal elections. Someone trying to win through fraud or suppression must predict, in advance, where stolen votes will matter. That is no easy feat, but when it can be done, it is likely that others—the opposing candidate, good government groups, and honest authorities—will have made the same observation, and that area will be closely watched. Without the Electoral College, however, a vote stolen in any part of the country can affect the national outcome—even if that vote was easy to steal.

As Electoral College scholars Tara Ross and Robert Hardaway note, "[D]ishonest individuals would only have to succeed once, or maybe a handful of times, in any random American precinct. Meanwhile, anti-fraud forces would need to play defense in every corner of the country."[3]

Even absent fraud and voter suppression, a national popular vote would provide a strong incentive for states under partisan control to race to the bottom. States will increase the odds of their preferred candidate winning the national popular vote by removing barriers to fraud for desired voters and increasing barriers to voting for undesired voters. The Electoral College limits the incentives for such shenanigans.

Relatedly, the Electoral College avoids the possibility of large-scale national recounts. Many Americans will recall the chaos surrounding the 2000 recount in Florida. With a national popular vote, every state would have a strong incentive to conduct recounts in any close election. Even states in which the election was not close might seek recounts because their vote totals would affect the national outcome. Using the standards most states use for recounts at the state level, at least five presidential elections would have triggered nationwide recounts under a popular vote system. A Florida-type conflict in which the whole country was up for recount would be politically catastrophic.

NATIONAL POPULAR VOTE—A LITIGATION AND CONSTITUTIONAL NIGHTMARE

The Electoral College can only be abolished by constitutional amendment, which is extremely difficult. For that very reason, NPV seeks to end-run the amendment process through an interstate compact.

Under NPV, states would agree to award their electors to the winner of the aggregated national popular vote totals. Since these states would comprise a majority of Electoral College votes, this would guarantee that the winner of the aggregated popular vote would win the election.

This sounds easy enough, but in fact NPV is the worst of all worlds, a litigation and constitutional nightmare waiting to happen.

The Constitution prohibits states from entering into interstate compacts without congressional approval. The Supreme Court has interpreted this requirement to apply only when a compact would increase the power of states at the expense of the federal government. NPV backers say they will not submit the measure to Congress.

The NPV compact, however, should require congressional approval. NPV is an avowed effort to alter the constitutional system for electing the president, substituting direct popular vote for the state-by-state system in the Constitution. The federal government surely can claim an interest in preserving the constitutional system. Moreover, the Constitution provides that if no candidate wins a majority in the Electoral College, the election goes to the House of Representatives. NPV removes that role for the House. This, too, should require federal approval.

Even if courts were to hold that congressional approval was not necessary, or if it were given, NPV is likely unconstitutional. First, the Constitution provides, "Each State shall appoint [electors], in such Manner as the Legislature thereof may direct." This gives the legislature broad authority, but it does not authorize it to delegate the appointment to someone else. Just as the president cannot delegate the decision to sign or veto a bill to someone else, a legislature cannot delegate away its power to select electors to someone else, whether that be the pope, the president of France, or the voters of other states.[4]

Second, NPV effectively alters the constitutional mechanism of presidential election without going through the amendment process required by Article V. Does Article II—giving states the power to appoint electors—trump Article V, the amendment process, which guarantees every state a say in whether an amendment passes? NPV backers say it does, but it's not clear courts will agree.

Additionally, NPV creates one national electorate, but leaves in place fifty-one sets of state election laws, which, as we have seen, differ in important ways. The effect is to treat voters differently, based on their place of residence. But in *Bush v. Gore*, the case deciding the 2000 Florida recount, the Supreme Court held that under the Equal Protection Clause of the Fourteenth Amendment states may not treat voters in the same election differently. This problem is exacerbated in a close race. NPV makes no provisions for a nationwide recount. Individual states, meanwhile, have different rules for recounts, so if the popular vote is close, some might choose to recount while others might not. If only some states conducted a recount in that situation, or states used different rules, it would appear to violate the Constitution—yet there is no provision in NPV to coordinate a national recount.

All of these issues would likely be litigated, and such litigation would occur under the tight time pressure and partisan passions of a close election.

But it gets worse. Suppose that a Republican presidential candidate wins, or is poised to win, the popular vote, but not an Electoral College majority. In that scenario, there will be overwhelming political pressure in heavily Democratic signatory states, such as California and New York, to withdraw from the compact. NPV purports to address this problem by forbidding states to withdraw after July 20 in a presidential election year. The problem is that Article II of the Constitution gives state legislatures the power to decide how the presidential electors are selected, with no temporal limitation: state legislatures retain the power to change the presidential election process in their state at any time before the electors vote, even after the popular vote in November.

If, as NPV backers claim, Article II trumps Article V of the Constitution, it certainly trumps an interstate compact. So the anti-withdrawal provision is unconstitutional and unenforceable. At an absolute minimum, we will likely see litigation the first time this happens—again, litigation under the time pressure of a constitutional deadline for submitting electors and the partisan pressure of a hotly contested election.

Finally, it is not clear that the states can command their electors to vote against the will of the voters in the state's presidential election. In 2019, the U.S. Court of Appeals for the Tenth Circuit held that a state cannot prohibit a presidential elector from casting a vote for a candidate other than the one to whom the elector is pledged. Although there have been a few "faithless" electors over the years, they have never mattered to the result. But given the enormous pressure we would expect to see placed on electors to ignore the compact and vote in accordance with the voters of their state, faithless electors may well become a real problem under NPV. This, too, would be a probable source of litigation.

There is a reason it is hard to amend the Constitution. The framers wanted to prevent rash or ill-conceived changes to our fundamental governing document. NPV illustrates their wisdom. The plan makes no provision for recounts in a close race. Its supporters blithely wave away serious constitutional issues and ignore the litigation chaos that is likely to ensue the first time (and perhaps every time) that the aggregate popular vote goes against the Electoral College vote. Its supporters seem not to have considered the effect that NPV is likely to have on the states, such as increasing incentives for fraud, voter suppression, and manipulation of the ballot. They have given little thought to the effects it would have on candidate campaigns—more regional campaigns, more campaigning in large population centers, more appealing to the base vote in party strongholds rather than attempting to bring new states into play. The possibility that candidates might be elected with far less than 40 percent of the vote is not discussed.

In summary, the NPV plan is a careless effort in pursuit of an extra-constitutional remedy that ignores why we have an Electoral College in the first place and would damage the important constitutional values the College promotes.

CONCLUSION

Americans take a certain relish in criticizing our government and our presidents—often with good reason. Yet what country has prospered more over the past two hundred years? What other country can produce a line of chief executives to match Washington, Jefferson, Lincoln, Teddy Roosevelt, Coolidge, FDR, Truman, Ike, and Reagan? The late political scientist Walter Berns, dean of Electoral College scholars, once noted, "In all the years I have been engaged in this issue, I have yet to encounter a critic of the Electoral College who argues that a president chosen directly by the people is likely to be a better president."

The Electoral College is not an anti-democratic anomaly, but an integral part of our complex, nuanced constitutional fabric. As Alexander Hamilton said, the Electoral College may not be "perfect," but it is, as he also noted, "excellent," and it has served our country well.

Labor Unions and the Public Sector

by Lieutenant Governor Rebecca Kleefisch

The role of labor unions in this country dates back to our founding. As conservatives, we believe that unions have the right to exist and have historically provided benefit to American workers. There is a great distinction, however, between public sector unions and private sector unions. Public sector unions negotiate for higher wages utilizing taxpayer dollars. It's also a conservative belief that there should be room for individual decision-making. Members of public sector unions should have the fundamental right to determine whether they want dues automatically deducted from their paychecks. The decision should reside with the individual, not the union. Often, public sector union members disagree with the political positions and funding of specific political causes made by union leadership utilizing their contributions. There is no better example in modern history of the fight to balance a state budget and protect the needs of taxpayers from the fiscally reckless demands of public sector unions than in Wisconsin. This challenge was met head-on by my good friend, the former lieutenant governor of Wisconsin, Rebecca Kleefisch. She is one of the brightest, most charismatic, and highly capable Republican leaders in the nation today. More Americans need to know and read her story, and I am most grateful that she accepted my invitation to participate in *Making Government Work*.

—Tan Parker

Labor unions in America have a purpose. In the private sector, they can allow a group of employees to present a strong bargaining bloc to an employer to seek a larger share of a company's revenue, in the form of higher pay and benefits. In the event that they demand too much, however, a company may lose its competitiveness and risk going out of business.

With public sector labor unions—government employees—the calculus is totally different. Unlike unions in the private sector, unionized government employees can select their employers by funding the campaigns of favored politicians or, if unsuccessful at election time, threaten or otherwise induce elected officials into favoring their view. If government unions seek more pay and benefits than their employer can afford, unions see it as no problem—taxes can always be raised, money borrowed, or programs cut to meet the terms of the new collective bargaining agreement.

How elected officials in a state interact with public sector unions has emerged as a significant factor in whether a state thrives and attracts jobs or spirals down in a series of tax hikes. The neighboring states of Wisconsin and Illinois offer a stark comparison.

As ballooning liability for its public employee pensions became a pressing problem for Illinois in 2011, its governor raised income taxes to pay for the promises of politicians who had been fueled by the campaign cash of the public employee unions for decades. This tax increase merely confirmed a bizarre reality of politics: union members' dues often went to fund Democratic campaigns. When the Democrats won their races, they were the ones sitting across the bargaining table from their donors in order to negotiate how much taxpayers would pay them to perform their union jobs.

But more on Illinois later, as it would play an unexpected role in Wisconsin's struggle with powerful government workers' unions.

In Wisconsin as well, government unions had taxpayers paying much bigger chunks for union members' retirement accounts and health insurance than employers did in the private sector. It used to be that a government job would often mean a trade-off: a lower salary for better job security, higher retirement income, and more benefits. Eventually, unions won a higher salary as well, making government employment superior to that in the private sector in every respect.

By 2007, Wisconsin taxpayers were on the hook for $1.3 billion to support government employee pension systems, with the amount expected to rise every year—and that was before the onset of the recession.[1] The mounting fiscal imbalance was one of the contributing factors in the election of Governor Scott Walker and me in 2010.

By 2009, in Madison, our state's capital, at least seven bus drivers were making more than $100,000 per year, with one pulling in $159,258.[2]

In Wausau, a northern community, the union had stepped in to forbid the use of volunteer school crossing guards because they believed that work should be done by paid union workers.[3]

In southern Wisconsin's Racine County, the union filed a complaint called a grievance against county decision-makers who hired contractors to haul snow in a crippling blizzard. They thought the snow should have frozen there until the government union workers could get there, commuters be damned.[4]

In Milwaukee, a woman who won a statewide honor as "Outstanding New Teacher of the Year" was fired because she had the least seniority, a metric that mattered more than quality in the union teaching contract.[5]

Even the Milwaukee mayor's wife complained openly in a local magazine that she was let go from her K–12 education job because she had not racked up the seniority points.

In cases like these, the union bosses had negotiated the best deal for government workers who wanted to stay at a job for a long time and make lots of money. But the negotiations had steered so far from fiscal responsibility and common sense that taxpayers were beginning to cry foul.

In school districts, hiring practices flew in the face of logic, protecting the most senior teachers even if they were not the best. If you were a newly hired teacher and you were awesome, but there were budget cuts, you were the first on the chopping block because the union had bargained for it to be that way.

Most school districts weren't even allowed to shop around for the best deal on health insurance, either.[6] Despite this being a huge cost driver, health insurance was often negotiated at that same tilted bargaining table—everything seemed to tip toward the union, away from the taxpayers.

In state government, workers were contributing very little toward their health insurance premiums. In one of the most shocking results of collective bargaining, many union workers had taxpayers paying the employer contribution of their retirement funds—and the employee share! As more taxpayers got wind of the government union benefits, a sense of indignation filled an electorate appalled by working hard all day to pull in less than those whose paychecks they funded.

Even union members were not unanimously in love with the system. I heard stories from government workers about how the unions were protecting those who simply wanted to get by in their day jobs and retire well. Unions provided no incentive for excellence and even blocked incentives from the employer seeking to reward those going above and beyond. In some cases, the unions claimed to protect people from going above and beyond.

Bizarrely, the unions considered what I had been raised to think of as making efforts to get ahead and succeed as exploitive overwork. Those who wanted to excel were stymied by unions sponsoring mediocrity. And this celebration of the status quo was on track to eventually bankrupt our kids.

States cannot declare bankruptcy like municipalities can. While many feigned shock at Detroit's 2013 bankruptcy, most Michigan government insiders and economic development professionals I talked to predicted it. Detroit was on a crash course to insolvency and was the perfect example of how union bosses and politicians collaborate to wreck governments.

Years ago, I went back to Detroit to see what Wisconsin's own star city, Milwaukee, could learn from the recovery attempts being made by community activists and honest public servants. I was born in Pontiac, Michigan. Detroit was home to my dad's biggest accounts and it was where he taught me how to sell envelopes. He had a boxy red Volvo and one of the world's first "car phones." The phone was black and the size of about ten iPads stacked on top of each other. It weighed a ton, but I was proud that Dad had one. He was great at relationship-building and he loved his product; you could tell both from the back slaps and wide smiles he got when he walked through a customer's door. Detroit needed a lot of envelopes, and I was sure that Dad's boxes, covered in tiny envelopes of every sort, would always be in every stockroom in Motown. And then came the internet.

Adaptability is the hallmark of many successful companies, but in the envelope business, company after company folded, unable to diversify fast enough. Even the best salesman could not convince America that communication required paper, and that paper needed envelopes. About the same time, Dad began to worry about the Milwaukee plant's unionizing. There was rumbling that some of the workers wanted to organize, and Dad was worried that it would happen right as the envelope industry was under assault by competition from the internet. As profit margins slid, the workers wanted more. I remember the tension in Dad's face. We rarely saw it, but we knew that money was a worry and that the envelope business was not as dependable as it once was. The plant threatening to unionize made a deep impression on me.

Twenty-five years later, the threats to the bottom line were the same, but the players were very different. This was not a family-owned envelope company; union demands were threatening the solvency of an entire state. Wisconsin had a $3.6 billion deficit that Governor Walker and I had promised to fix without raising taxes, and our pension promises and health insurance costs were looming.

The budget bottom line that the unions were threatening was a line made not from profit, but hard-earned money taken from taxpayers. As budget pressure grew from Wisconsin's legacy costs, so did the pile of evidence that the union bosses had been taking advantage of the people who paid the bills.

Something had to be done to correct this systematic, costly, and unfair union overreach.

The night the governor privately introduced his plan to fix it, our cabinet was attentive and quiet. I sat to the governor's left, as I always did. Keith Gilkes, as chief of staff, reviewed the preparations he viewed as necessary to address the likely union response. Each cabinet secretary should be prepared to function with full responsibility and accountability, despite expectations that some of their workers would walk off the job. They predicted picketers.

But when Keith said that we should be prepared for mass protests, I thought he was being melodramatic. Why would adults, public servants at that, stomp off the job because they had been asked to contribute to their pensions and health insurance like their private sector, tax-paying employers? It seemed absurd. I thought the very suggestion was insulting to our coworkers. Perhaps they would be angry about the changes to collective bargaining. The plan would eliminate most of it, with collective bargaining remaining on wages, which could only be bargained for up to the Consumer Price Index.

If union members wanted more than that, taxpayers would have to approve it. Perhaps the unions would be angry that they would have to adapt their financial planning—just as their fellow Wisconsinites who had coped through the recession had. Perhaps, but they would certainly understand the logic. Everyone but government had just gone through a recession. They had futures they wanted secured too, right?

Having only worked in the private sector, I thought the changes were reasonable and that my friends with years of government experience were underestimating the logic and maturity of government workers. Usually, I counted my lack of time in government as an asset. Only two months into the job, it revealed my naïveté. My colleagues with years of government under their belts were about to be unilaterally right.

The next day was Valentine's Day, and I was in my Capitol office. I was called upstairs. I was not surprised. Already people had joked that I had been up and down the stairs separating the governor's and lieutenant governor's offices more times in the first week than the previous lieutenant governor had been in eight years. It was through no fault of her own. My predecessor did not have as warm a relationship with the previous governor.

The governor's office was literally above mine, and through the chief of staff's door is the governor's conference room. The night before, it had been ringed by cabinet secretaries in our explanatory meeting. Today, it was set up for a press conference. I would not be expected to speak, just to stand by the governor as he rolled out the plan. The secretary of the department of administration would flank the governor on the right; I was to stand at the left. We entered together and I was surprised by the amount of media. It was as if they anticipated the size of the story. The lights were bright, and the governor stood behind a podium using his hands to frankly explain the situation we faced and how we would fix it. The biggest political story of the year had been launched.

The workers were forbidden by law to strike, so they struck their blows by calling in sick and spending endless hours at the Capitol. Tens of thousands of protesters assembled in the marble halls within days of the announcement that our $3.6 billion deficit would be closed in part by asking our employees to make a 5.8 percent contribution (about the national average) toward their own retirement accounts, make a 12.6 percent contribution for health insurance (about half the national average at the time), and accept the changes to collective bargaining. The collective bargaining changes were necessary because that was the process that had led to politicians of both parties over-promising pay and benefits, digging a big hole in our budget that had taxpayers on the hook.

At first, it was just a wave of University of Wisconsin-Madison teaching assistants, students, and occasional professors. Many of these folks went out of their way to solidify crusty old stereotypes about college campus liberals: there were '60s and '70s songs, grungy yarn caps, lots of drums, and ridiculously inflammatory signs. Eventually the hubbub grew. As media cameras collected from across the nation and the protestors realized how much attention they were getting, there was no end to the made-for-TV anger. Michael Moore came. Jesse Jackson came. UW Medical doctors wrote fake medical excuses for any protestor who needed an excused absence from work because "Scott Walker made them sick." It was a gross abuse of our democratic process, taxpayers' patience, and our beautiful Capitol.

Eventually the governor began to get death threats that extended to his family and me. Perhaps because the threats came only weeks after the horrific shooting of Arizona congresswoman Gabrielle Giffords, the governor ordered protection for his family and for me. When I was at work, he reasoned, I should be protected. I had a couple of stalkers in my previous career as a news anchor, and so death threats did not startle me the way they might have someone else. I was still grateful for his concern. The protestors made it impossible to walk to my office the normal way. They had set up a headquarters of sorts right outside my desk window. I am sure it was by design that they piled up sleeping rolls, pillows, blankets, and bags directly in my view. I am sure they were hopeful that the governor would one day peer out the window right above mine and reconsider the whole thing.

Because I would have caused a ruckus simply by walking into work, a special branch of the Wisconsin State Patrol assigned to keep us safe would get me in and out of my office undetected. The car would pull into an underground parking garage across the street from the Capitol and pull up to an unmarked entrance to a tunnel. There, I would hop out and scoot through the door to a waiting tugger, a quiet little vehicle like the ones they use to get people to their flights in large airports. Down the long tunnel were signs taped to the walls noting different police and sheriffs' departments. Under the signs stood big black piles of shields and helmets, batons and boxes: riot gear. The entire tunnel was a lineup of riot gear. As the tugger whizzed past the ominous queue, I always held my scarf across my nose and mouth.

Unfortunately, it was about this time that I also began a struggle with a more serious battle: cancer. While the air was not freezing, the speed of the little vehicle always brought on that chemo side-effect paralysis. If I had had any idea of what to expect from being lieutenant governor, I am pretty sure this medical challenge would not have been it.

My husband, Joel, a state representative, was on Wisconsin's Joint Finance Committee. It is one of the most powerful legislative committees in America because it approves spending in our state. It is made up of half assembly representatives and half state senators, and it is normally quite an honor to serve. Joel's "honor," though, came during the most tumultuous time in Wisconsin's political history, and he knew he would have to take a statewide tumult tour before it was over. The schedule was grueling, and it boiled over into my calendar.

When Joel did his statewide Joint Finance listening tour, my staff had to schedule me to meet the school bus each day he was gone. During those times, I read and wrote emails and made calls from home after 4:00 p.m. on the days he was traveling. Gaps were filled by my long-suffering mother or our dear Carly, a physical therapy grad student who patiently taught our girls the basics of tennis (with Dora and Barbie rackets). After I put the kids to bed, calls from Joel put our home-life circus in perspective. Joel's tales from the road were disturbing.

While the Capitol was overrun with protestors, those who could not make it to Madison seemed to find a way to testify before the travelers of the Joint Finance Committee. Joel told me the hearings were crammed with people dressed in zombie costumes. Inexplicably, there was also an Abraham Lincoln, a Tweety Bird, and a pig. The hearings were marathons because the committee's Republican majority wanted to make sure that they gave everyone a fair chance to be heard.

Joel said the members were shouted down as they entered, exited, or spoke. People screamed at them, cried to them, and exclaimed that the Republicans hated children. It wore on Joel, especially the stuff about hating children. Pro-life to the core and the son of two educators, Joel takes special pride in fatherhood. If you ask him his proudest accomplishment, he will never mention a trophy buck or Emmy nomination. He will always say how proud he is to be Dad to his girls. Joel loves his children and has authored bill after bill to protect them and all kids. The protestors were not fighting fair.

At the Capitol, Democrats were not either. To prevent a vote on the reform legislation, all fourteen Senate Democrats left—just got up and left the building. They knew that in order to vote on a bill that deals with money, the Senate had to have a quorum; at least nineteen people needed to be there. To reach the nineteen-senator threshold, at least one Democrat would have to be present. If they all ran away together, they figured they could prevent a vote. In a comic twist, they sought refuge in the state with the supersized unfunded pension liability and mega tax hikes, Illinois.

When a Tea Party cameraman finally spotted them, they were in my old stomping grounds, Rockford, where I began my career as a news anchor. As a cub reporter, I covered many a meeting at Rockford's Clock Tower Resort, where the Senate Democrats had set up shop. But this news story had national consequences. And the senators who had holed up at the Clock Tower were not only postponing the inevitable vote of the majority to enact reforms, but they were practically painting their self-portraits next to "political theater" in the dictionary.

But this act was about to get more dramatic. The reforms needed to be passed and signed because they were a necessary component of our budget repair bill. This particular budget repair bill would come to be known as Act 10. Without that fully working component, the state's ability to pay its bills would grind to a halt. Wisconsin is required by law to pass a balanced budget, but when less tax money comes in and spending stays the same or goes over budget, we end up with a deficit.

The previous administration had left us with one of those, and we needed to refinance some bills or else we would have to lay off state employees to pay our bills. If those Democrats did not come back and vote, the very workers they claimed to be protecting—1,500 of them—would be laid off. I told Sean Hannity this on February 22, eight days after the bill was introduced and six days after the Democrats had left the building.

> HANNITY: All right. So, is it going to come down to—first of all, has anybody found these guys? Are they still at the Best Western? And is it going to come down to having to lay off 1,500 people?
> KLEEFISCH: Well, I sure hope not. And I know that these senators, the missing fourteen, have been found. They have been located. They've been talking to the media nonstop while they are taking this taxpayer-funded vacation. Because every single day they are out of town, Sean, they are costing the taxpayers a collective $1,915 in salaries, on top of that, health benefits. And now they are using their vacation to fundraise out of state. We think that this is a very poor example to set when democracy has not come to a screeching halt in Madison. In fact, democracy continues, just without them. The Senate was in session today and they were passing legislation. And so we urge the missing fourteen to come back to work because we know that we have the votes in both the Senate and in the Assembly. We are hoping to avoid those layoffs.
> But Governor Walker has warned; he has said over and over again, that if this does not pass, and Friday is drop dead date for us—because we have $165 million that we need to refinance on Friday—if this does not happen, we will be seeing massive layoffs in the state of Wisconsin.

You do not really understand how God has prepared you for your battles until you are in them. Sometimes you do not even appreciate it until after you have laid down your weapons. Almost immediately, though, I was thankful for the fact that I had spent a career in TV news. There were far too many media requests for the governor to do alone. I took the overflow, but the media schedule, in addition to regular work, took its toll. I began to lose more hair due to the chemotherapy for my cancer.

Frequently I would get up for a hit on a morning show and end the day after the girls were asleep, doing another live East Coast interview. Only once did I have to make the trek to Chicago for a live shot. I liked to go to the Fox studio in Chicago because Chicago offers opportunities to do economic development work, but this day I had to ask my kind state patrol sergeant to make a couple of pit stops. (Chemo does weird things to your body.) Mercifully, most times people were accommodating about live shots.

Once a satellite truck even came to my house because I had already put the kids to bed. Of course, I do not for a moment suspect it was out of empathy. Journalists need their stories. No one was willing to be scooped by another news outlet by not having another installment of *As Wisconsin Turns*. The Democrats at the Capitol and union rabble-rousers were relishing their starring roles.

That was especially true of the Democrat fourteen who ran away from their state senate jobs. On March 4, more than two weeks after they had left, state senator Lena Taylor told Greta Van Susteren, "We're not going home today and we're not going home, you know, tomorrow that I'm aware of. But what I will tell you is this. We need to go home because the governor has gone from his budget repair bill to—you know, from a war on workers to a war on the people."

But because they had not come home to vote on behalf of the people for whom they claimed to fight, the layoff notices went out. And the runaway senators did not even seem to care that these government workers would have thirty days before they potentially lost their jobs. That same night, I told Greta Van Susteren, "These 1,500 layoffs will not be necessary if this budget repair bill passes. I should say when this budget repair bill passes because as soon as the Democrat fourteen return, we will be able to pass this budget repair bill in the state senate."

While the senators stayed out of state, the Capitol turned into a pulsing, heaving mass of humanity. Law enforcement now allowed the protestors to camp inside the Capitol, and my husband Joel had to step over protestors, sometimes two to a sleeping bag, just to use the restroom during extraordinarily long floor debates. On the ground floor, where the lieutenant governor's office is, they set up folding picnic and card tables to hand out mini shampoos so people could wash in the public restrooms. They passed out fresh underwear for those in need. There were crockpots and crockpots of stew, which added to the odor of the place. There were the omnipresent placards, and those without signs to hoist sometimes brought drums to bang to keep the beat of the protestors' favorite chant, "This is what democracy looks like! This is what democracy looks like!"

It actually did not look anything like a representative democracy. Our form of democracy allows for the voices of the people to be heard. The protestors just wanted their own voices heard. Everyone else they angrily drowned out. This is what anarchy and lawlessness looked like. During the most heated time, my friend, then a state senator, now Congressman Glenn Grothman, walked outside only to be surrounded by an angry mob. It was all caught on camera, and watching the video makes me think of *Lord of the Flies*. The protestors screamed in his face and pressed in on him until he could not escape. It is scary to watch. He was rescued by eccentric Democratic state representative Brett Hulsey, who urged the crowd to back off, explaining that, though they had differences of opinion, Grothman was his friend. It is the only time during the video you can stop holding your breath.

Hulsey was there because he was a state representative. Senator Grothman still had no colleagues on the Democratic side of the state senate chamber. Though the governor's chief of staff and the deputy chief of staff were trying to negotiate a path for the Democrats to return, the senators sat in Illinois.

Finally, a conference committee, led by State Senate Majority Leader Scott Fitzgerald, broke the impasse. In a decisive, swift move, Republicans broke the collective bargaining changes away from the rest of the bill, effectively separating it into one bill with fiscal impact and one bill, the one changing collective bargaining, without. The state senate convened and voted on the controversial collective bargaining changes. With no collective bargaining bill to block anymore, the senate Democrats came back. It had been three weeks.

The assembly quickly followed with its own vote. (Just like in Congress, the versions of the bills voted on must be the same.) Members had voted on Act 10, the most controversial bill in Wisconsin in living memory. For Joel, it had been a harrowing night. After the longest debate in Wisconsin Assembly history, the clerk finally called the roll, and the Republican members braced for whatever was to come. The Speaker of the Assembly had been told by police that the members' safety could no longer be guaranteed. When the votes registered on the tote board, the gallery and the floor erupted. Democrats, clad in fluorescent orange matching T-shirts, began chanting, "Shame!" Some even threw things as Joel and his colleagues marched quickly out of the chambers and were spirited away through the tunnels and onto buses so they could not be hurt by out-of-control protesters.

Democrats and unions began talking almost immediately about recall elections. The drama and hurt that had bubbled to the surface during Act 10's debate and passage had not yet felt the salve of budgetary savings. We were confident, though, in Act 10's intended effects. We asked for reasonable contributions to retirement accounts and health insurance. And we asked for smart changes to the process that had given the budget trouble in the first place—collective bargaining. Once the new law had a chance to work, the people would start saving money, and even our opponents would see the merits of the idea.

And today, Democratic governor Tony Evers never seriously considers changes to what is known as Act 10. It has saved hundreds of government workers' jobs because employees are paid a justifiable wage and benefits package, and it has saved taxpayers more than $5.3 billion. It is truly a lesson for America.

There were many lessons learned in Wisconsin, as well as in other states that saw public employee union reforms.

The first is that total pay and benefits, including deferred compensation in the form of a pension and healthcare benefits, must be both fully understood by all parties—the public, the workers, and lawmakers—and must be sustainable and reasonable. The challenge with pension promises is that support and votes can be won today with huge out-year costs on future generations of taxpayers and the lawmakers who represent them.

Second is the importance of communication with the public. Government unions are strong and can speak with a unified voice. It takes a concerted effort, combined with political courage, to break through and communicate your message clearly to the public.

The final lesson is that unions represent only themselves—not the taxpayers and certainly not the "children." And, frequently, unions represent their highly paid senior leadership at the expense of rank-and-file workers, especially those with little seniority. We should try to connect with these younger, dissatisfied union members. Many of them are motivated by public service and quickly become disillusioned by the union and its protection of those without the drive to continuously improve.

Remember, if something cannot go on forever, it will not go on forever—someone or some group of people will be the first to see that problem and fix it. Have courage to be that person!

Our Energy Future

by Jacki Deason

When it comes to the importance of economic security for America, energy independence has always been a top priority. Through a combination of bold, innovative technologies and entrepreneurial spirit—coupled with intelligent state public policies and, more recently, strong federal policy leadership from the Trump administration—the dream of energy independence for America has been achieved. No one better articulates this than Jacki Deason, who is one of the most knowledgeable experts in the nation on energy policy. Her career stretches from Capitol Hill to her *Jacki Daily Show* radio program to advising those who work at the highest level to promote American energy independence. As such, I thought more Americans needed to hear her insightful views.

—Tan Parker

INTRODUCTION

The countries of the world occupy an ever changing, broad spectrum of the "haves and have nots." While the ideas of a culture or country are what ultimately determine which end of the spectrum it will occupy (capitalism versus communism, or a culture of personal responsibility versus entitlement, and so on), one undeniable, signature trait of every country in the "have" category is access to affordable, abundant, reliable energy—primarily fossil fuels. It is this access that helped determine the outcome of the last two world wars and underpins much of the geopolitics and warfare of the last half-century.[1] General James Jones, the former national security advisor to President Barack Obama who served as commander of NATO's military forces, has described "energy scarcity" as a "potent" weapon, with energy security being a primary function of NATO.[2]

Fortunately for the United States, this century finds us more energy-rich than ever before, with the "Shale Revolution" making us the top producer of oil and natural gas on earth.[3] The U.S. nuclear industry generates more nuclear-sourced electricity than all other countries,[4] and we have more coal reserves than any other country on earth.[5] We are also blessed with some of the best renewable energy potential. U.S. hydro-electric production has produced reliable, renewable energy for decades. While the wind and solar sectors of our power system remain in single-digit percentages, we are positioned to harness both when advanced storage technology is available, given the U.S. wind corridor and "sun belt."

Currently, domestic U.S. energy production is the cornerstone of our energy and economic security. Before, we were dependent on OPEC and others for our petroleum. But U.S. crude oil imports from OPEC are down nearly 75 percent from the past decade.[6]

In addition to powering the world's top economy and counterbalancing hostile regimes, our energy production has the ability to reduce the federal trade deficit and make an enormous dent in the ever increasing $23 trillion U.S. national debt,[7] with as much as $50 trillion in reserves alone waiting to be tapped.[8] One would be hard-pressed to find a viable, competing plan for addressing the national debt—an existential issue mostly cast to the wayside by lawmakers.

The United States is newly emerged as an energy superpower, largely due to the Shale Revolution, a phenomenon that has only occurred in the U.S., even though many countries are rich in shale rock hydrocarbons. There are at least two reasons for our unique success:

1. **People trump government**: In America, minerals such as oil and gas are owned by the people, not the king or the government. This is in sharp contrast to the petro-states of OPEC and even democratic countries like Norway. U.S. oil and gas, and much of our other energy resources, are owned by millions of landowners, private and institutional investors, pension funds, and other private entities.

2. **States trump the federal government**: Energy production is regulated in large part by the fifty state governments, a decentralized model that diffuses power closer to the people who own the minerals and means of production, and who therefore have a strong incentive to bring resources to market. Again, this contrasts with dictatorships whose fortunes rise and fall with the judgment of the powerful few.

STATE POLICY BROUGHT US OUT OF THE GREAT RECESSION

It is no accident that the near-tripling of U.S. oil and gas production this century happened on state and private lands, not federal lands. The politics of the federal government restricted energy production on federal lands, but this was not an obstacle for the state governments, which permitted the energy sector to roll full speed ahead. Thanks to state policy, the U.S. became the number one oil and gas producer and the energy sector grew 40 percent after the recession, while the rest of the economy remained stagnant at less than 1 percent growth.[9] Since energy (including electricity, transportation fuels, and petrochemicals) is the foundational input into all other businesses, one could persuasively argue that it was state policy's permitting robust energy production that brought the U.S. out of the Great Recession.[10]

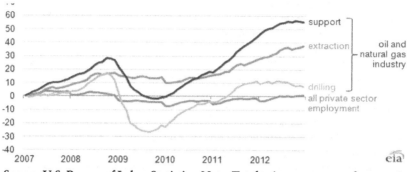

Source: U.S. Bureau of Labor Statistics. *Note: Total private sector employment is non-government employment, as derived from the Quarterly Census of Employment and Wages.*

Perhaps just as impressive is the benefit of the Shale Revolution to every American household and business in the form of saved costs, which are of far greater benefit than piecemeal handouts like $600 stimulus checks from the TARP program, for example. The graph below equates to an annual $2,500 savings for a family of four because of money saved on energy bills and lower gasoline prices, all thanks to the American Shale Revolution. These benefits disproportionately help those in the lower-income brackets, who spend a far greater share of their income on energy costs:

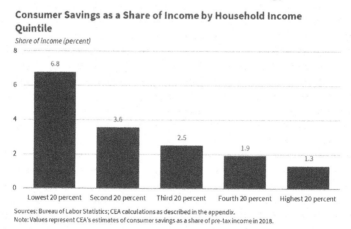

Source: White House. https://www.whitehouse.gov/wp-content/uploads/2019/10/The-Value-of-U.S.-Energy-Innovation-and-Policies-Supporting-the-Shale-Revolution.pdf.

The above graph is from a federal report that focuses on the varying approaches of state policies and highlights the states that stifle energy innovation and infrastructure, such as New York, a state whose citizens pay $233 more for energy each year due to poor state policy choices.

Who decides how much energy we will produce? Individuals are limited primarily by state—not federal—policies. While OPEC countries gather in Vienna to decide production quotas, the United States is unique in that it is chiefly the private sector and the millions of Americans that own and develop oil, gas, and other energy sources who determine exactly how much energy we will produce. Perhaps ironically, then, the resultant energy-based counterbalance the U.S. can wield against Russia and other petro-states, such as the OPEC countries, is a market-based, decentralized model. Absolutely no one is placing a call to the U.S. president or congressmen to ask their views on how much oil to pump, and American energy producers would take great umbrage if U.S. leaders even tried to tell them how to run their operations.

Energy can be a powerful foreign policy tool. The American people and fifty state governments play a primary role. The United States has never had a national energy policy. In fact, the U.S. did not have a Department of Energy until 1977, and most would agree that it would be more properly named the Department of Nuclear Energy, since it leaves the regulation of other energy sources primarily to others—mostly the states.

If state policy remains sound, then robust energy production can continue, and the days of deploying more than half a million Americans at a time to potentially spill their blood securing a foreign energy supply are likely over. Some of the most successful and prescient energy experts, such as shale pioneer Harold Hamm, believe the United States can become largely energy independent as early as 2022.[11] If not energy independent, we can certainly become "energy secure," either producing sufficient energy for ourselves or at least continuing to rely on friendly nations such as Canada and Mexico for our energy imports, rather than unstable, hostile regimes.[12]

In a book titled *Making Government Work*, a chapter devoted to energy seems almost counterintuitive. What has worked is not government, but the private sector, albeit with state regulators providing appropriate oversight. This dynamic has made the United States among the top industrialized countries in economic growth and energy production.[13] The states have a responsibility to continue the policies that have worked.

OUR ENERGY MIX TODAY AND THROUGH 2040 IS APPROXIMATELY 80 PERCENT FOSSIL FUELS

Any intelligent discussion of wise energy policy must begin by acknowledging one truth that very few are admitting, at least of late: fossil fuels are here to stay. We are not running out of them. They will not be "kept in the ground" (or if they are, they will simply come out of the ground in some other location on earth . . . but we will not use less). They are overwhelmingly the source that will supply our electricity, transportation, and petrochemicals, enabling modern life, health care, sanitation, and all that the "digital age" entails. The U.S. Energy Information Administration and the International Energy Agency confirm that the United States and the rest of the world will run on at least 70 percent fossil fuels between now and 2040.

PETROCHEMICALS

In all the media attention devoted to an anticipated "transition" from traditional fuels to renewable energy, one under-examined issue is the exploding use of petrochemicals. Petrochemicals are chemicals synthesized from hydrocarbons (such as oil and natural gas) that are used to create everything from pharmaceuticals to electronics, plastics, vinyl, most clothing (polyester, nylon, spandex), cosmetics, additives and preservatives found in food and vaccines, and those items necessary for modern sanitation.

Because petrochemicals are literally created from the chemical building blocks of oil and natural gas, they cannot be replaced by a transition to renewable energy sources in the electricity markets. Renewable energy such as hydroelectric energy, biomass, and wind or solar energy can replace some small percentage of natural gas or coal for electricity generation, but the electrons generated from these sources cannot displace hydrocarbons in the manufacturing of petrochemicals.

ECONOMIC GROWTH AND A CLEAN ENVIRONMENT

One of the greatest stories of the last fifty years that remains largely untold is the emergence of the United States as an energy superpower while it simultaneously reduced air pollution by almost 70 percent[14]—all while growing the economy by a whopping 275 percent![15]

The American story debunks the wildly proliferated myth that economic growth and environmental leadership are somehow at odds. As of 2019, the U.S. is the world's top oil, gas, coal, and nuclear energy producer.[16] At the same time, the U.S. has reduced federally regulated air pollutants by an average of 73 percent since 1980: lead by 99.2 percent,[17] sulfur dioxide by 89.6 percent, carbon monoxide by 84.2 percent, nitrogen dioxide by 60.4 percent, and ozone by 32.1 percent.[18] And while carbon dioxide is not a federally regulated pollutant—it is a greenhouse gas, but not a pollutant—the U.S. also holds the distinction of eliminating a higher percentage of carbon emissions than any country on earth.[19] All this while growing our population by over 120 million[20] and driving more than 3.2 trillion miles annually, up nearly 200 percent since 1970.[21]

As this graph from the U.S. Environmental Protection Agency (EPA) shows, for nearly fifty years America's economy, population, and energy usage has increased while pollution has decreased.[22]

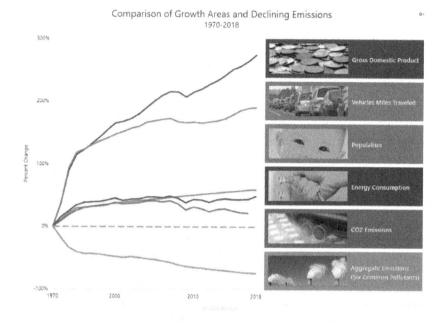

Comparison of Growth Areas and Declining Emissions
1970-2018

Most importantly, when it comes to eliminating the deadliest of all air pollution—fine particulate matter, or "PM 2.5"—the United States is one of the cleanest countries on earth, outperforming China by a factor of ten (and in some regions, a factor of twenty) and all major European economies, as shown in the graph below.[23]

One of the most important unheralded stories of the American environment is that our air is the safest it has been in one hundred years.[24]

Countries that criticize U.S. environmental performance at international conferences often cannot even begin to compete with American standards for clean air, clean water, or reduced emissions. Perhaps this is why the United States continues its tradition of abstaining from international environmental pacts like the Kyoto Protocol[25] and the Paris Climate Agreement,[26] while at the same time being among the few countries that actually honor the goals of those agreements.[27] There can be no justification for subordinating one's sovereignty to an international body whose members hardly know how to clean their own air, much less anyone else's. It is worth mentioning that the U.S. Constitution provides firm safeguards against the bartering away of our sovereignty, but a full discussion of that topic is beyond the scope of this chapter.

Members of the press find it fashionable to criticize the U.S. for allegedly abdicating leadership on environmental issues, but this is at odds with reality. We should all challenge them to find another country that has a gross domestic product (GDP) anywhere comparable to ours with a better environmental record.[28] Only island nations with a fraction of U.S. economic activity have better particulate matter (PM) levels than the U.S., with the exception of southern California, which finds itself on the receiving end of wind currents that export particulate matter from Asia.[29] And as with other measures of performance, we see improvement over time, with the U.S. now cleaning up Superfund sites at ten times the rate of the past decade.[30]

If there is one fact that drives our critics wild, it is that hydraulic fracturing (or "fracking") is our real "Clean Power Plan."[31] Because the surge in our supply of fracked natural gas has caused its price to plunge, natural gas has become the cheapest and largest feeder into U.S. electric grids, causing carbon dioxide emissions to plummet. The U.S. free market, state policy, and the resultant fracked natural gas have reduced our emissions far more than the European Union's "Cap-and-Trade" system[32] and the Obama administration's trumpeted "Clean Power Plan" and Renewable Fuel Standards. The numbers do not lie:

Annual Greenhouse Gas Emission Reductions from Shale Innovation and Major Environmental Policies

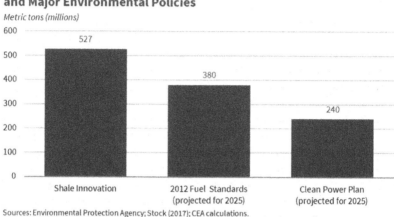

Sources: Environmental Protection Agency; Stock (2017); CEA calculations.
Note: The Fuel Standards refer to the 2012 Light-Duty Vehicle Greenhouse Gas Emissions and Corporate Average Fuel Economy Standards, which applied to the 2017-2025 years.

When considering GDP and population size, few nations can begin to compete with the American record on economic and environmental outcomes. The United States is the only highly populated nation in the world to meet the World Health Organization's PM standards. Rather than enduring criticism at world forums, the U.S. leadership should challenge America's critics to match our levels for eliminating this deadly air pollution.

Making government work where energy policy is concerned means that we continue policies that have improved the American economy, encouraged energy independence and energy security, and delivered impressive environmental outcomes.

The American model is a marvel, and the envy of the world.

WHAT AMERICA DOES RIGHT: PRESERVING FEDERALISM

Though we have sometimes veered from the proper balance of federalism, one of the best examples of the country's determination to right its course was the monumental and bold policy choice to replace the 2014 "Clean Power Plan" with the 2019 "ACE Rule."

The 2014 Clean Power Plan (CPP) was the most sweeping, unconstitutional power grab in EPA history. It promised an unimpressive .018 degrees Celsius reduction in global temperature over time, supplanted state regulation with federal regulation, and required $7.2 billion from American taxpayers—annually.[33] This promised reduction in global temperature was, of course, based on unrealistic assumptions that other countries would not cancel out American efforts. It should be noted that the total volume of carbon dioxide emission reductions by 2030 under the CPP is emitted by China in less than two weeks.[34]

Quickly, twenty-eight states and many trade associations challenged the CPP. The U.S. Supreme Court took the unprecedented step of staying the implementation of the administrative rule until it had full judicial review, saving the U.S. economy from a devastating blow and preserving—for the moment—the separation of powers and federalism required by the Constitution.[35] Regulation of electricity markets is the province of the fifty states. Congress had not delegated to the EPA the authority to regulate human-induced emissions of carbon dioxide. In fact, Congress promptly disapproved the CPP under the Congressional Review Act.[36] The CPP would have done great damage to the Constitution, the economy, and American wealth, all in exchange for speculative benefit to the climate.

Thankfully, the Affordable Clean Energy Rule (or "ACE Rule") replaced the CPP in August 2019. The ACE Rule restores the previous federalism balance by empowering the fifty states to control their energy markets and by relying on technology to solve environmental issues. The ACE Rule improves the New Source Review (NSR) program of the Clean Air Act (a program requiring installation of pollution control technology for industrial facilities) by ending nonsensical government deterrence to power plan efficiency, the most cost-effective way to improve environmental performance.[37]

While the ACE Rule is a step in the right direction, some experts believe the government should go further and extend the protections of the Clean Air Act to all regulated sources of emissions.[38]

POLICIES FOSTERING ENTREPRENEURSHIP AND INNOVATION

The U.S. remains one of the most innovative economies in the world.[39] For this reason, we are the only country on earth to experience a Shale Revolution in oil and gas production—despite shale being plentiful throughout the world. Specifically, it was the innovation of hydraulic fracturing (fracking) combined with advancements in horizontal drilling that unlocked the resources inside shale rock, making the U.S. the top producer of oil and gas on earth.[40] As President Barack Obama bragged, we are now "the Saudi Arabia" of natural gas, and we have, since that declaration, also become the Saudi Arabia of oil . . . and we already were the top country in coal, and arguably nuclear energy.[41]

Shale-driven innovation in oil and gas production led to an eight-fold increase in the production of natural gas and a nineteen-fold increase in our production of oil. The increased supply reduced our natural gas prices (the primary feeder into our electric grid and electricity costs) by 63 percent and the global price of oil by 10 percent, reducing gasoline costs dramatically.[42]

Government had almost nothing to do with these breakthroughs. It was innovation and investment by the private sector that perfected these techniques over a period of decades. Innovation in fracking fluid "cocktails," big data, 4D seismic imagery, improved drill bits, and countless other oil field improvements brought us to where we are today. The incentive for these innovations was simple: profits. The pioneers of the Shale Revolution are billionaires. This is how America works.

What government must do to continue the momentum is protect intellectual property, enforce contracts, and, above all, avoid draconian regulations that destroy incentives to innovate and prosper.

POLICIES FOR THE STATES GOING FORWARD

In a country as large and diverse as ours, one should use caution when recommending anything resembling a one-size-fits-all policy for the fifty states. Constitutionally and otherwise, the states have the legal right to govern themselves, and most have a track record of success (and the legal "right to be wrong" even where they do not have a record of success). Our country spans many time zones, geological zones, climate zones, and cultures. What works in one state might not work in another.

Still, there are some state-based trends across the country that are worthy of commentary and recognition.

AVOIDING PREMATURE EXPERIMENTS WITH WIND AND SOLAR ENERGY: IN 2020, "100 PERCENT RENEWABLE" IS NOT DO-ABLE

Most Americans agree that we should have an "all of the above" energy strategy. After the 1973 Arab oil embargo, Americans understand that energy is the lifeblood of the economy and that energy security and diversification is nearly always a smart strategy. All energy is good energy. But not all energy is created equal. Traditional energy sources are affordable and reliable, while newer energy sources remain relatively expensive and unreliable.

Despite tens of billions of dollars invested in wind and solar energy by federal, state, and local governments, Wall Street, and a small army of private investors,[43] the energy mix of the United States remains mostly unchanged from the last century.[44] According to the U.S. Energy Information Administration, 80 percent of our country's energy consumption continues to be powered by fossil fuels in 2018.[45]

An endless drumbeat of headlines proclaim that renewables make up an ever increasing share of our energy mix. Discussion of renewable energy can be terribly convoluted and misleading because the term generally connotes wind and solar. Most Americans would be shocked to learn, however, that the majority of our "renewable" energy is decades-old, tried-and-true hydroelectric and biomass energy—and some environmentalists even count nuclear energy[46]—not the wind and solar energy into which taxpayers and ratepayers have lately poured billions of dollars.[47] While it is true that renewable energy sources accounted for

11 percent of our energy consumption, only 2.42 percent (graphed below as 22 percent of 11 percent) of that energy was from wind, and less than 1 percent (graphed below as 8 percent of 11 percent) was solar.

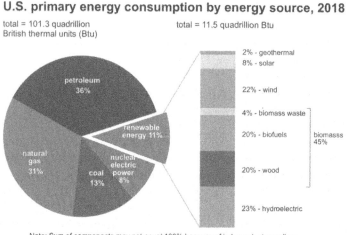

U.S. primary energy consumption by energy source, 2018

total = 101.3 quadrillion British thermal units (Btu)   total = 11.5 quadrillion Btu

- petroleum 36%
- natural gas 31%
- coal 13%
- nuclear electric power 8%
- renewable energy 11%

- 2% - geothermal
- 8% - solar
- 22% - wind
- 4% - biomass waste ⎤
- 20% - biofuels ⎬ biomasss 45%
- 20% - wood ⎦
- 23% - hydroelectric

Note: Sum of components may not equal 100% because of independent rounding.
Source: U.S. Energy Information Administration, *Monthly Energy Review*, Table 1.3 and 10.1, April 2019, preliminary data
eia

Given the enormous government funding and public relations campaigns for renewables, most Americans believe that wind and solar energy are the centerpiece of our energy future.[48] The production tax credit will cost at least an additional $48 billion before it fully phases out as currently scheduled.[49] Many states have adopted Renewable Portfolio Standards (RPSs) that distort competitive energy markets, requiring electricity providers to buy a minimum percentage of renewable energy by a certain date, creating a built-in market, regardless of price, reliability, or even feasibility. Likewise, cities across America are making the "100 Percent Renewable" pledge, leading their populations to believe that the city will operate on wind or solar energy exclusively, forgoing fossil fuels and nuclear energy. Taxpayers are told that the switch to renewables will save money and be more environmentally friendly.

These claims are misleading. The best illustration is the nation's number one wind energy producer: Texas.

In addition to producing more oil than any other state, Texas also produces more wind energy than any other. The state is part of the U.S. "wind corridor," which stretches from the Canadian border with North Dakota to the Mexican border near El Paso.[50] Massive federal and state incentives accelerated the build-out of wind farms years ahead of projections, but the costs of those are rarely mentioned when it comes to production price. Unfortunately, most wind farms are located far from the population centers they must serve, increasing transmission costs that reduce or negate any price savings. In fact, Texans paid another $6.8 billion through the creation of Competitive Renewable Energy Zones (CREZs) to add infrastructure to connect the West Texas wind farms to the large Texas cities in the east.[51]

THE ILLUSION OF A GREEN JOBS BOOM

On top of these incentives, Texas state law allows for property tax breaks for renewable developers.[52] In exchange, developers must create ten to twenty-five jobs, depending on location. The reality is that 50 percent of the tax agreements grant waivers to eliminate the job creation requirement, and 87 percent of all waivers go to wind developers.[53] This is just one way that estimates of new "green" jobs are dramatically exaggerated. Jobs initially projected from these tax incentives and all the added tax revenue and GDP from those jobs are largely illusory. Meanwhile, the cost to Texans was another $7.1 billion.

And what is the track record of renewables and electric vehicles producing "green jobs" nationwide? The world may never know, since the federal Bureau of Labor Statistics stopped tracking green jobs in 2013, as did California in 2010 despite a 2008 California state law that requires an annual report from the Green Collar Jobs Council to the legislature.[54] California stopped tracking "green jobs" because of difficulty distinguishing new green jobs from those that already existed in established industries.

"Green jobs" numbers are further masked with methodologies that include jobs in nuclear energy, hydropower, and ethanol. Sure, these are renewable energy sources, but these industries have been around for decades with existing workforces and are not what most information consumers have in mind when politicians boast of "green jobs" created from what is supposed to be an all-new energy transition. Moreover, these energy sources are often fiercely opposed by environmentalists who tout "green jobs."

Even so, our state and local governments have poured billions into the so-called "green" economy, and they are only getting started. After such generous government gifting, one might surmise that wind energy must be price-competitive, and many wind operators make bold claims that their rates are "at parity" with fossil fuels (when the subsidies, free transmission infrastructure, and other freebies are factored in, of course).

Texas adopted a Renewable Portfolio Standard (RPS) to require ten thousand megawatts of renewable energy by 2025. Because of handsome financial incentives from the state and federal government, Texas wind farms met the target for installed capacity in 2010, a full fifteen years ahead of schedule. RPS subsidies from taxpayers move to wind power generators through Renewable Energy Credits (RECs) to the tune of $560 million—so far.[55]

While it might seem that state incentives are the reason Texas is the top state in wind energy, this theory seems disproved by the fact that wind energy development came to a halt when the federal credits expired, even though the Texas RPS remained in force. The obvious implication is that wind power production prices were not competitive at all, and that federal "free money" seems to be the only reason wind power exploded in the first place. It could not sustain itself in even the "semi-free market" with lavish state incentives. This experience should prompt new skepticism when wind energy proponents claim their business is part of a "free market solution" to our energy challenges.

Despite the costs, cities have plunged headlong into "100 Percent Renewable" pledges.

CASE STUDY: GEORGETOWN, TEXAS

The poster child for unwise energy policy is Georgetown, Texas.[56] This city finds itself in one of the cheapest and most competitive energy markets on earth, deep in America's top energy-producing state. If there is one problem Georgetown didn't have, it was expensive energy.

So how did city leaders sell the notion to citizens of Georgetown that a vote to go "100 percent renewable" meant they could look forward to lower energy costs? Perhaps it was the $1 million grant that former New York City mayor Michael Bloomberg gave Georgetown for this experiment that gave the people confidence to proceed.

What transpired was decidedly less impressive. The truth is that the city continued to draw its electricity from the same grid as before, which is primarily coal- and natural gas–powered.

As is true for the rest of us, only a sliver of Georgetown's total energy mix comes from wind and solar. The city's energy costs rose dramatically, with each household experiencing an increase in energy costs. The people of Georgetown soon began clamoring for a way out of this "deal," and Bloomberg terminated the grant after the first tranche of funding "in response to local concern . . . that now is not the proper time to move forward with the project," rather than continue what one council member labeled "doing experiment[s]."[57] So, the people of Georgetown burn just as much coal as they did the day before they went 100 percent renewable, but now their ratepayers get to pay more than their share for renewable subsidies. This is what "100 percent renewable" really means.[58]

Don't be Georgetown, Texas.

With wind and solar energy, the key word is storage. Our best innovators have yet to find a way to store wind or solar energy in a cost-effective way so that consumers can draw down stores of renewable energy when the wind does not blow intensely or the sun does not shine consistently. An added problem is that wind and solar are optimal in areas far from the largest population centers, where the energy is needed. Current technology makes transmission over vast distances difficult and costly.

We should not underestimate the potential for American innovation to provide solutions for these obstacles. But until that time, wind and solar cannot power our economy no matter how many subsidies and incentives we throw at them.[59]

As of 2019, despite tens of billions of dollars invested by our government in wind and solar, on top of private investment, they still only supply 3.3 percent of the American energy mix. Had it not been for subsidies, they would supply even less.

It could perhaps be argued that, by virtue of our geography, no country on earth is positioned to eventually take advantage of renewable energy as well as the United States. The U.S. wind corridor stretching from North Dakota to southern Texas is an ideal location for wind energy capture, and the U.S. Mojave Desert boasts of the most intense solar energy on earth. Yet we still have not found a way to make renewables more than 11 percent of our energy supply. Given the limits of today's technology, there is no realistic scenario in which we can run our country on 100 percent renewable energy. Those who claim otherwise are likely relying on several false assumptions.

The first is to refer to installed renewable energy "capacity" for electricity generation as a meaningful reference point for renewable energy contributions to our lives. Glowing headlines about milestones in "capacity" create in the mind of the listener the idea that capacity is interchangeable as a benchmark for the amount of renewable energy we are consuming.

Capacity and consumption are two very different measurements that should not be confused, yet some journalists seem to work overtime to use them interchangeably, thus confusing the public's understanding.

What capacity means depends on whether one is referencing generation capacity (energy that can actually be produced) or installed capacity (energy that could be produced under hypothetical, ideal conditions that do not exist in nature, such as where the sun shines around the clock or where the wind blows incessantly at a brisk rate of speed).[60] The difference averages about 66 percent. Beware of the messengers who do not specify which "capacity" they reference, because installed capacity is the amount of energy that could be potentially produced by wind turbines or solar panels assuming that the wind blows at a brisk rate of speed or that the sun shines intensely.

Of course, it is impossible for most points on earth to experience endless high intensity wind or sunlight twenty-four hours a day, seven days a week. It would, however, be a perfectly true statement that the wind turbine or solar panel can—theoretically—produce energy incessantly at these high rates—until they age out. It just would never happen. Therefore, capacity can be a confusing measurement. For example, wind farms generate about 31.1 percent of their installed capacity in Texas, the state with the most wind installation—not to mention some of the most favorable natural conditions.[61]

Finally, few analysts factor in the hidden costs of renewables' intermittency: the necessity of twenty-four-hour backup with either fossil fuels or nuclear energy.[62] In fact, one wonders if most commentators even know that renewables require backup. Because wind and solar are inherently intermittent, there must always be a form of backup energy that can supply what wind and solar cannot—in an instant. Most often, this is a natural gas plant that must idle in wait, the same as a car at a red light. This constant idling is not cheap, and these costs are rarely factored into the costs of renewables. These costs are not borne by the investors or operators of renewable companies, but by the rate-paying consumers and taxpayers. In Texas, backup generation and other grid-related costs are approximately another $1.82 billion per year.

Wind and solar energy enthusiasts will note that both are constantly improving and have become less expensive over time. As one example, the costs of manufacturing solar panels have decreased in some instances by 90 percent.[63] That is great news for the taxpayers and ratepayers who are forced to underwrite the business. But the necessary implication is that the investment poured into solar panels in the last decade was foolish, considering what the money could produce for an equal investment in today's solar panels. Will we say the same ten years from now? The best days for wind and solar energy are in the future.

We should learn from Germany, a country that went headlong into primitive solar technology at the turn of the century, quadrupling German energy bills and leaving the country no choice but to import American coal and Russian natural gas to address the shortfalls primitive renewable technology caused.[64]

TREATING ALL ENERGY SOURCES EQUALLY

Wind and solar energy producers claim that they are competitive in the free market and "at parity" with their competition, so there is no need for perpetuating special treatment that has so far shown so little success in gaining market share for these businesses.

- Ending preferential tax treatment: States should treat wind and solar developers the same as every other business or property owner for tax purposes.[65] In many states, oil and natural gas producers must pay a "severance" or "separation" tax, which is literally a tax on the production of the minerals. In the state of Texas, the separation tax brings in over $13 billion annually for the state, with nearly $2 billion going to local school districts.[66] In addition to eliminating tax breaks that apply to renewables only, solar and wind energy producers should be taxed the same as fossil fuels, with a tax levied for each unit of energy produced.
- Eliminating subsidies: With wind and solar energy producers claiming to have achieved price "parity" with fossil fuels and nuclear energy, it is time to end state (and federal) subsidies to these industries. When the technology is ready for wider deployment, there will be plenty of investment capital prepared for the opportunity.
- A voluntary Renewable Portfolio Standard (RPS): States should make RPS compliance voluntary. At this point, there is a niche in the marketplace for wind and solar energy. Some wealthier communities desire to pay more for renewable energy because they prefer it to traditional fuels. That should be their choice.

- Transparency: States should require wind and solar energy producers to shoulder the costs they add to grid operation, discussed above. This includes managing the direct billing and collection for these additional costs through the private sector—rather than obscuring the true costs through Americans' tax bills, with the government acting as the middleman who collects taxes and then parses out subsidies. This reform would provide the energy market with greater transparency.

ENCOURAGING THE BUILD-OUT OF ENERGY INFRASTRUCTURE

State policy-makers must recognize that oil and gas will remain the dominant source of American energy until at least 2040.[67] The United States has about a one-hundred-year supply of natural gas and more than fifty years for oil at current levels of production and technology,[68] and we cannot continue to progress economically or geopolitically without more pipelines, refineries, LNG export terminals, and other energy infrastructure.

Pipelines are often held up by state-level environmental obstruction, and this obstruction is based on the false premise that pipelines are unsafe or environmentally unfriendly. The question is, compared to what? What other energy source can replace the 90 percent (or more) share of oil in the transportation sector, the near 40 percent share of natural gas in our electricity mix, or the role of both in the petrochemical industry? None. Once policy-makers understand that the U.S. will continue to rely on oil and natural gas for our energy supply, that we will not "keep it in the ground," then the value of permitting pipelines becomes obvious.

Pipelines are essential for our current distribution networks and will remain so for the foreseeable future. Crude oil can move by pipeline, rail, or truck. If activists succeed in blocking pipelines, then crude will be moved by rail or by truck, or imported from foreign producers, but we will not consume less. Pipelines are the safest and the most "green" of these options. Rail moves hazardous materials from point A to point B safely 99.997 percent of the time, and pipelines are a full 50 percent safer than rail.[69] As a general rule, American energy production is far more regulated, clean, and green than that imported from foreign dictatorships like the OPEC nations.

There are over 2.4 million miles of pipeline in the United States, and most of it has been in place for decades.[70] Americans rely on the oil and gas in these pipelines all day, every day, and chances are that if you have spent your life on the Eastern Seaboard or in the population centers of Texas, you have pipelines beneath your feet right now, and have had all of your life.

Pipelines have the smallest "carbon footprint," with rail having eight times the carbon footprint of pipelines, and trucks having many times more.[71] The reason is obvious: pipelines move the resource in one direction, while trains and trucks must move the resource and then travel the same distance back to the source to pick up another load. Plus, trains and trucks are enormously heavy, and just powering them from place to place is expensive and polluting before the resource is even loaded.

CASE STUDY: NEW YORK

One natural gas supplier, National Grid, is having to turn away twenty thousand new customers after New York State authorities turned down permits for the twenty-three-mile Williams Pipeline that would run from Pennsylvania and New Jersey to Rockaway Beach. The Department of Environmental Conservation has twice denied permits for the pipeline project and has another year to consider National Grid's reapplication, despite the company's repeated warnings that delaying the project would result in a service moratorium.

National Grid claims that its existing system is at total capacity, and adding new customers would jeopardize service to existing clients. The company bemoaned its 2,600 applications for new or expanded service in Brooklyn, Queens, and Long Island that cannot be processed without the new capacity that the pipeline would bring.[72]

Predictably, the project has been the target of opposition by environmental groups. But in the long term, such pipeline protests may be short-lived. Given New York's fracking ban, it must rely on other states for increased supply and add fuel transportation costs that will fall on ratepayers. Meanwhile, thousands of businesses and homeowners have few alternatives as the moratorium continues.

CONSERVATIVES VERSUS CONSERVATIVES: DIVIDED OVER THE USE OF EMINENT DOMAIN FOR PIPELINES

Conservatives have voiced legitimate concern about the abuse of eminent domain to build pipelines. The conservative principle of protecting private property appears from afar to collide with the conservative impulse to favor the free market in the development of fossil fuels.

Though federal and state constitutions require "just compensation" for any taking of land, compensation may not be "just" in every instance. This is a serious problem, but not with the law itself. Courts can and have supplied the remedy for abuse or neglect of the compensation requirement.

Having less legitimacy are the arguments that the landowner should be able to refuse truly just compensation since a pipeline is a "private concern" built by a private company, as opposed to being for public use. The debate is dramatically oversimplified as a powerful, private, corporate pipeline company versus a small, outgunned rancher or farmer.

While there are privately owned pipelines moving the private owner's resources only, the type of pipeline we see in eminent domain cases is typically that of a "common carrier." A common carrier pipeline is defined in most states as one that serves the public by transporting a product, such as oil or natural gas, for customers who retain ownership or who sell it to parties other than the carrier.[73] Literally, oil or gas owned by potentially thousands of individuals, companies, or investors can pass through the common carrier pipeline to refineries and then to market. Nearly all American individuals and businesses purchase product moved through common carrier pipelines, whether it is electricity from natural gas, transportation fuel derived from oil, or hydrocarbons (oil and natural gas) for petrochemicals, such as those used to make electronics or pharmaceuticals.

Therefore, common carrier pipelines, though constructed by private companies, are comparable to public highways, because they move the private property of thousands of mineral rights owners and royalty owners (those who have a property interest in the oil or natural gas) to market, where public utilities, universities, schools, hospitals, businesses, and private individuals purchase this energy for their most essential needs. In the state of Texas alone, there are millions of royalty owners (sellers) and millions of energy consumers (buyers) whose interests are served on both ends of common carrier pipelines. Common carriers truly serve a public use.

The United States is unique in that the people own the oil and natural gas beneath our soil, rather than the government. These mineral rights owners and royalty owners will never be able to exercise their property rights—selling their oil and gas—unless there is infrastructure, specifically pipelines, to transport the resource to market. An estimated 50 percent of U.S. natural gas is considered "stranded," meaning that the owners of this resource cannot sell their property because there is no pipeline or other means to get the gas to market. Eminent domain can solve part of this problem. Therefore, the eminent domain debate is not simply about big business versus farmer. It is about potentially thousands of mineral rights owners (and the market their product powers) versus the individual landowner.

Even if we confine an analysis to just the government (public) benefit of common carrier pipelines in a single state, the revenues are staggering. The University of Texas System receives about $1 billion annually in royalty-related distributions from oil and natural gas produced on lands it owns.[74] Texas school districts receive approximately a half-billion dollars annually in payments from oil and gas production, while the state's multi-billion-dollar "rainy day fund" is mostly comprised of oil and gas "severance" tax payments.[75] Without pipelines, the state would have to rely on only rail or truck to move its resources, and only a tiny fraction of these revenues would be realized.

Public utilities nationwide rely about 40 percent on natural gas to operate, without which the economy grinds to a halt. One would be hard-pressed to find a single American who does not rely each day on electricity, transportation fuel, or petrochemicals that make up our pharmaceuticals, electronics, clothing, heating and cooling, and cooking fuel. None of this is possible without oil and natural gas, and most use of oil and natural gas is not possible without the pipelines that bring it to market.[76]

Importantly, if the landowner "loses" in an eminent domain challenge, the not-so-dismal result is that the landowner is paid just compensation and is deprived the use of the property only as long as it takes to lay the pipe. The "taking" or displacement of the property owner is therefore limited and temporary. The pipeline company places the pipeline three to four feet beneath the ground (below plough depth), restores the surface, and then the landowner is free to use the property again, subject to the limited maintenance requirements of the pipeline operator. Major cities are built atop some of the country's most extensive pipeline matrices.

All the same, states can and should reinforce private property rights in eminent domain disputes:

- Ensure judicial review of administrative decisions, so that the private property owner can make a case with proper due process before an objective third-party tribunal: "Protection of private property rights . . . cannot be charged to the same people who seek to take those rights away."[77]
- Pass statutes to provide mandatory dissemination of a Landowner Bill of Rights, as is done in the state of Texas, explaining the due process rights of every landowner, such

as rights to just compensation, an administrative hearing, and judicial review.[78]

- Level the playing field between what could be unequal bargaining positions by shifting the burden of proof in eminent domain cases to the condemner.

CONCLUSION

America is working. The past half-century shows that "making government work" for sound energy policy means preserving the constitutional order. Our system of federalism, empowering state governments to play a primary role in energy production and policy, has been key to the emergence of the country as an energy superpower in the twenty-first century, regardless of political fluctuation across presidential administrations or Congresses in Washington, D.C. Once again, the governance model put in place by our Founders—long before the advent of the modern energy economy—proves itself sufficient for the continuing advancement of our nation across the centuries in an ever-changing world.

God's Green Earth

*by Becky Norton Dunlop
and Kathleen Hartnett White*

No subject seems to be more frequently discussed in the media than the environment. As Americans, we all love enjoying the great outdoors, our beautiful national parks, lakes, rivers, and streams. We also care deeply about protecting the health and well-being of our children and future generations and want to protect our resources for them. As the father of a daughter with asthma, I take issues surrounding air quality extremely seriously, as do most Americans. At the same time, we must balance our objectives of protecting the environment with our ability to have a healthy and productive economy to provide for the needs of our citizens. The wonderful news is that we can do both simultaneously with the right leadership and public policy. No two individuals in the country have a better understanding of these issues and the role the states can play than Becky Norton Dunlop and Kathleen Hartnett White, both of whom have led environmental policy decisions as conservatives. Becky is the Heritage Foundation's Ronald Reagan Distinguished Fellow. She served President Reagan in numerous senior roles, including special assistant to the president and director of his cabinet office and as deputy undersecretary of the Interior Department. She later went on to be secretary of natural resources in Virginia along with a host of other amazing career accomplishments. Kathleen is the director of the Armstrong Center for Energy & the Environment and a distinguished senior fellow-in-residence at the Texas Public Policy Foundation (TPPF). She served for many years as the chairwoman and commissioner of the Texas Commission on Environmental Quality (TCEQ) under previous governor Rick Perry and as then governor George W. Bush's appointee to the Texas Water Development Board. I am grateful that more Americans will have the opportunity to learn from their expertise on this most critical subject facing our nation.

—Tan Parker

Since President Richard Nixon issued an executive order creating the Environmental Protection Agency fifty years ago, Americans have lived by the same federal environmental policies. In reality, the EPA has served as more of a political solution than an advocate of helpful environmental policy. At this point, the concept of the environment reflects more of an ideological movement to secure government control over land use, big industry, and water. Conservatives reject this enormous power grab by big government and therefore are accused by statists of being against the environment. Nothing could be further from the truth. From the beginning, the EPA did not offer hands-on policies to regulate the environment.

As articulated in the first major environmental law, known as the National Environmental Policy Act (NEPA), the stated purpose of environmental policy is to protect the quality of the air, water, and land for the wise use of America's natural resources and for protecting the health and safety of each human individual. It is conservatives who still adhere to this view; our principles contend that "a policy cannot be good for the environment if it is bad for people." In a world where many strive to make public policy confusing and based on situational ethics, natural resource and environmental policy is guided by tried-and-true principles that not only work, but make progress in this area much less complicated.

CONSERVATIVE GOVERNANCE BENEFITS PEOPLE AND NATURE

Americans care about the quality and condition of the natural resources around them. They care, too, about their families and way of life, and sometimes feel that government values the flora and fauna more than it values the people for whom it is supposed to work. This too often is true. The value of people comes way behind grizzly bears and endangered species. Conservatives believe government officials should govern by a set of principles that will allow people, and their needs and way of life, and nature to be respected at the same time. The principles outlined here do allow people to prosper. Our natural resources can be managed in ways benefiting people while improving the quality and condition of the environment for generations to come. Conservatives who are elected or appointed to public office never forget they are public servants, and they care about the people they represent and their children and grandchildren. The principles that work for liberty and our natural resources are known as the American Conservation Ethic.

There are eight principles we will share that work to the advantage of our citizens and our resources:

1. People are our most important, unique, and precious resource.
2. Renewable natural resources are resilient and dynamic and respond positively to wise management.
3. Private property protections and free markets provide the most promising new opportunities for environmental improvements.
4. Efforts to reduce, control, and remediate pollution should achieve real environmental benefits.
5. As we accumulate scientific and technological knowledge, we learn how to get more from less.
6. Management of natural resources should be conducted on a site- and situation-specific basis.

7. Science should be employed to guide public policy.
8. The most successful environmental policies emanate from liberty.

You might think that these sound like common sense and assume that everyone will agree with them. Well, as with everything, the devil is in the details. You will find many who find reasons to oppose each of these principles when applied as written. Let us take them one by one and see how they can be applied.

PEOPLE ARE OUR MOST IMPORTANT, UNIQUE, AND PRECIOUS RESOURCE

All environmental laws and regulations should consider how they benefit people. They cannot be good for the environment if they are bad for people. After all, every human person is inherently more important and valuable than any other resource. Our intention with natural resource policy should be to improve human well-being. Furthermore, it is human beings who manage these resources. Policymakers should and can easily be advocates and champions for engaging all citizens in the good stewardship and improvement of our natural resources and environment.

As secretary of natural resources for Virginia, it was a pleasure for me (Becky) to enlist our citizens to care for Virginia's environment. I had the privilege of working with volunteer clubs, classroom teachers, and students of all ages, from the "Daisies" to college classes in science. I was also fortunate to stand alongside professionals who worked with resources in business and industry. We had thousands of citizens eager to demonstrate their commitment to being good stewards and improving our natural environment. Each spring we celebrated Spring Spruce-Up by repairing, replanting, and renewing after winter. And in the fall of each year, we led the Fall River

Renaissance, focusing efforts on improving a body of water in our community. Sure, there were the historically active environmental groups engaged, but Governor George Allen and I were eager and pleased to recognize the many thousands of Virginians participating in these stewardship activities, given a little encouragement and some positive recognition. We all had fun, learned more about the resources in our communities, and improved the quality and condition of our environment.

Policy-makers seeking to lead in environmental improvement must look beyond just environmental advocacy groups and look to all our citizens, who care about their families, neighborhoods, communities, jobs, and economic growth as well as the environment. A growing economy and an improving environment go hand in hand. And importantly, people contribute to both and appreciate the benefits of both. In other words, look for ways to involve lots of various citizens in efforts to improve the environment in their community.

RENEWABLE NATURAL RESOURCES ARE RESILIENT AND DYNAMIC AND RESPOND POSITIVELY TO WISE MANAGEMENT

Some would have us believe that all our natural resources are static and diminishing, that people only destroy natural resources, and that economic growth and development can only damage and harm our resources. This is a false narrative. It encourages fearmongering and a misunderstanding of the very essence of natural resources.

We know that resources can be impacted negatively by human activity and most certainly by natural events. Volcanos, hurricanes, cyclones, and tornados can emit far more particles and chemicals than any human activity. While some human activity can degrade air quality, it is an obvious fact that air quality can be improved through both natural circumstances and the benefits of human invention and ingenuity.

Savvy resource directors and government executives know that by offering scientific information about the nature of a problem and encouraging the development and usage of appropriate and affordable solutions, businesses and communities will seek ways in which they can contribute to improving these dynamic and resilient resources.

In Virginia, during my tenure as the natural resources secretary, my agencies focused on improving water quality in our streams and rivers by emphasizing the benefits to communities of the very existence of these resources. We also worked cooperatively with them to identify locations of impaired water quality. This was called our "Tributary Plan," and it was created based on public hearings and meetings with local government officials and citizens across the state.

The state, in an appropriate government activity, doubled the number of monitoring sites in Virginia's rivers and streams in order to have a quicker and more defined picture of any water quality issues a community might face. This might include agriculture run-off or industry point sources. Many government activities were also found to have deleterious impacts on water quality. Minor disruptions in maintenance proved to be a primary contributor to unwanted discharge from wastewater treatment plants. This discharge could have significant impact in that immediate area. Once identified and restored, however, the rivers quickly recovered.

Interestingly, the drinking water treatment plant and the wastewater treatment plant for Washington, D.C., are among the two worst polluters in the country, a fact conveniently ignored by the Washington governing elites and the federal EPA, which has direct oversight over these facilities. Nonetheless, the Potomac River's water quality can recover even from harmful impacts brought about by these two major polluting facilities. This recovery can happen quickly enough. Yet the local D.C. and federal government would rather take the few measures to improve the management of the facilities than invest in necessary upgrades that would eliminate the pollution being created.

Forests, soil, flora, and fauna all have shown themselves to be dynamic, resilient, and very responsive to wise management.

PRIVATE PROPERTY PROTECTIONS AND FREE MARKETS PROVIDE THE MOST PROMISING NEW OPPORTUNITIES FOR ENVIRONMENTAL IMPROVEMENTS

It is uncontested that ownership inspires stewardship. This is especially true with regard to our natural resources. When one owns and perhaps makes a living from natural resources, one is eager to maintain and even improve the quality and condition of these resources. Farmers seek ways to keep soil healthy to ensure greater quality of crops to harvest. The free market has provided numerous innovations to assist them in this goal. One example is the development of laser-guided equipment that allows the farmer to apply the exact amount of nutrients, pesticides, fungicides, or other needed inputs to the soil to maximize yield while limiting costly applications to exactly what is necessary for healthy crops and healthy soil.

Owners of forest lands manage their forests to minimize or eliminate pest infestations and fires while maximizing the growth of desired species for harvest and economic benefits. The free market system has developed technologies that use virtually every part of a tree, from the main trunk for beams and planks of every size, veneers, and engineered decorative beams, to chipped wood, bark, and sawdust for applications from plywood and chipwood sheets to mulch and plastic lumber.

Property owners using and managing water resources have benefitted from market technologies that minimize the use of water and develop options for re-use, such as gray water uses. One California city is recycling wastewater into drinking water using technologies developed in the marketplace.

Homeowners demonstrate their increased care and management of natural resources that surround their homes and neighborhoods. Interestingly, the federal government is shown to be the least responsible manager of natural resources.

We have mentioned just a few ways in which the free market has provided innovations that allow us to improve mankind's use of and management of natural resources. There are countless other innovations and resource leaders that do citizens a great service by finding, highlighting, and using every opportunity to clear the way for resource use and further innovation.

EFFORTS TO REDUCE, CONTROL, AND REMEDIATE POLLUTION SHOULD ACHIEVE REAL ENVIRONMENTAL BENEFITS

Reducing pollution is common sense. Actions speak louder than words, and many people and groups spend time, intellect, and treasure to seek new laws, additional litigation, more regulation, and financial support that do not achieve any real environmental benefits. Instead, they argue that their words will eventually result in actions that, counter to their claims, actually have no direct impact on the quality or condition of the natural resources but make them feel good and generate more money for them to continue their ineffective but emotionally satisfying pastime: forcing people to follow their prescriptive dictates.

The bottom line is that actions on the ground and in the field can measurably reduce negative impacts on the environment. Every action should be judged by what the measurable impact will be and just how quickly it can occur. Innovative and free people can solve problems. Every government leader should ask, "Can we measure the timing as well as the impact on our natural resources and environment regarding the actions being considered?"

In Virginia, the goal of our administration was to have our professionals work with citizens to reduce livestock impacts on streams and rivers by using on-the-ground assistance. This allowed landowners to fence off bodies of water or to plant streamside plantings that could benefit water quality by reducing runoff to the streams.

AS WE ACCUMULATE SCIENTIFIC AND TECHNOLOGICAL KNOWLEDGE, WE LEARN HOW TO GET MORE FROM LESS

Better equipment technology requiring reduced acreage to produce crops, the use of GPS for application of inputs like fertilizer and pesticides, improved varieties of crops that increase yield, and more sophisticated irrigation systems are but a few examples of technological innovation. Fracking and horizontal drilling also allow us to capture more oil and gas with a smaller footprint, fewer wells, and lower costs for extraction, resulting in available, affordable fuel to power economic growth.

The source of the extraordinary rise in U.S. energy production has been the shale boom, an American technological revolution that has unlocked previously inaccessible oceans of oil and natural gas. Combined with competitive markets, economic freedom, and property rights, the shale gale is a mighty force. Through hydraulic fracturing, horizontal drilling, seismic imaging, and deep data geophysical analytics, U.S. producers cracked the shale energy code and are transforming the world's energy markets.

During this process, President Donald Trump became the leader of the world's energy superpower. Through the combination of entrepreneurship and intelligent state and federal polices, we have seen great success. Now the Democrats want to quash the consumption of oil and gas and ban the use of innovative technologies.

Innovation has also occurred in other areas of our society, such as improved methods of managing garbage and refuse resulting in less land used for landfills and better management of solid waste in landfills, which reduce the chances for pollutants to negatively impact land, water, or air.

One of the most unique examples of this occurs at Texas Disposal Systems, located between San Antonio and Austin. Here is a waste management company with a business model and enough property to develop diverse, waste-oriented sites with a range of uses and re-uses. Such uses include a sizeable but relatively obscure site for burying waste, another site for handling different recyclables, and a beautiful park-like site dedicated to different species, from giraffes to swans to rhinos. The wildlife is housed in safari-like settings to address the needs of individual species. Managing wildlife in a safari-like setting preserves important species and provides educational opportunities for citizens. Working with certified zoos and other education-oriented wildlife facilities enhances the multiple goals of the site.

Texas Disposal Systems has a business model that benefits our resources, environment, and economic growth. It would be a huge benefit if state and local tax policy across the United States encouraged this type of resource management.

Another example of the compatibility of environment and innovation is in the Houston–Gulf Coast region. For decades, few could imagine this region would ever attain the National Ambient Air Quality Standard for ozone. The warm, sunny climate along the Texas Gulf Coast is a perfect recipe for the formation of ozone.

Against the odds, Texas did attain the national standard in 2010. Texas prevailed through the coordinated effort of local authorities, universities, and an innovative State Implementation Plan developed by my (Kathleen's) team at the Texas Commission on Environmental Quality. The EPA's response to this victory in Texas? The agency immediately raised the standard, making it impossible for Texas to remain in attainment.

In Texas, the source of these unprecedented environmental improvements was not the heavy hand of command and control governance. It was technological innovations and efficiencies in the private sector. Whether proposed by engineers or small local governments, these improvements were not the work of EPA's command and control, but of proud individuals fixing a problem.

MANAGEMENT OF NATURAL RESOURCES SHOULD BE CONDUCTED ON A SITE- AND SITUATION-SPECIFIC BASIS

Managing natural resources and our environment cannot be a one-size-fits-all prescription. That does not work and is not logical. Logic and scientific knowledge confirm that many factors contribute to how resources should be managed. For years, the environmental gurus and radicals have insisted upon one-size-fits-all policies executed by the federal bureaucracy. Conservatives reject that notion for several reasons.

Look at the United States to see the differences in topography, weather patterns, and land uses. We also have fifty individual states, each of which elects a governor and state legislature with the intent that these officials will guide the direction of state management with the best interests, needs, and resources of the citizens in mind. This would most certainly include natural resources and environmental policy. I live in Virginia. We have mountains, valleys, rolling hills, flat lands, pastures, ocean front, many rivers and streams, towns, cities, and the enormous population center of the greater Washington, D.C., area. Weather patterns vary from region to region in our state. Each region is different enough that environmental impacts have unique causes and the differences require different solutions—that is, if you want to have scientifically based, cost-effective solutions that are understood and accepted by the citizenry.

On a national level, tailpipe emissions are no longer the main contributor to air pollution. Differences in and among states show a wide variation, but the trend for the majority of states is declining tailpipe emissions.

The second example is impact on water quality. Again, the impact in Northern Virginia is primarily wastewater treatment facilities and runoff from suburban lawns and pavement. In the Shenandoah Valley, more likely sources that impact water quality would be septic systems and pasturelands filled with farm animals. Add to this the differences in the size of the rivers impacted and their flow rate, and one can recognize the starkly different circumstances in each region. These are the kinds of issues facing state resource managers, and each requires different solutions that consider all the various elements impacting the resources, the likely duration of the impact, and the needs and resources of the local communities.

The fifty-year history of environmental policy has many achievements, but it is also a highly contentious history, including federal and state authorities, activist organizations, businesses, and homeowners. All too often, the health and safety of human beings is excluded from official environmental protection.

SCIENCE SHOULD BE EMPLOYED TO GUIDE PUBLIC POLICY

The advance of science in our society has undeniably improved most aspects of our lives. Scientific observation and measurement enable us to understand facts about the world. Science, however, must be understood as a tool.

Environmental public policy must be based on science, but not science alone. Surely, science must be taken into account, into very high account. And it must be true science that is considered, not political science, or politicized science, or pseudo-science. The science that must be taken into account must be real, empirical, peer-reviewed, proven science that is based on the scientific method.

And it must be considered as one of many tools to guide public policy. Elected officials are chosen to represent people, their families, their dreams and aspirations, and to help enable them to meet their own needs. The values of these people, these constituents, if you will, must also be taken into consideration. The ability of a community to deal effectively with environmental policy must be considered. In other words, solutions must use sound science, but other considerations must play a part in determining proper public policy.

THE MOST SUCCESSFUL ENVIRONMENTAL POLICIES EMANATE FROM LIBERTY

Finally, liberty is the single guiding principle that organizes all other values, principles, and ultimately policies that our various levels of government create. It provides the driving, creative, and energizing force behind our society. As technology improves, as knowledge improves, and as we personally improve, we seek to free ourselves from limitations.

We seek clever innovations to free ourselves from oppressive problems. Throughout human history, liberty has allowed men and women to turn their environment into something usable. American history is rich with a culture of frontier cultivation, pioneers who explored the land and worked with it to achieve their own prosperity. They took the barren land and made it produce. They took the mountains and made them passable. They took the cold wilderness and made it breathe warmth. They took deserts and made them bloom.

These pioneers were liberated by this land of liberty to turn America into something previously unseen in the world: A land with amber waves of grain, planted by American farmers. Purple mountain majesties made passable by Americans seeking their destiny, by miners seeking their fortune. Fruited plains cultivated by American settlers building a homestead. Without liberty, our environment would be at the mercy of the tyranny of government, like so many other countries in this world. Tyranny arises without ordered liberty.

Government bureaucracies would pick winners and losers and dictate the way in which a business would operate, much as occurred in the Soviet Union. Liberty frees us to pursue life and happiness to the best of our ability. Liberty has guided the growth of human prosperity. It has guided American principles and it must guide natural resources policy.

The most wonderful part of serving the people of this great country in any role dealing with natural resources is that, if you believe the truth that our resources can be improved and managed for the betterment of mankind, if you believe that people respond to leadership grounded in truth, then you can joyfully and with integrity champion these principles and know that the truth represented in them will serve the people well and expand liberty, and that a growing economy and an improving environment go hand in hand.

Choosing the Best for Our Children

by Governor Jeb Bush

There is no public policy subject more important to America's political and economic future than the education of our children. Jeb Bush served as the forty-third governor of Florida and led the most successful effort in the nation to provide better educational options to parents and students with his school choice initiative. I was greatly honored that Governor Bush accepted my invitation to participate in *Making Government Work*. Although I am personally blessed to represent and work with some of the finest public school systems in Texas, many children in this country are not so lucky and are trapped in under-performing schools, finding themselves in a never-ending cycle of poverty and welfare dependency due to a lack of educational achievement. I think you will agree with me that no one in the country has a better story to tell on this important subject than Governor Jeb Bush.

—Tan Parker

When I was running for governor of Florida in 1998, I visited more than 250 public schools. I met so many children—full of energy and anxious to learn, representing the future of our state and country.

But the student I'll never forget was a high school senior. He had struggled to pass an eighth-grade-level test. One of the questions that stumped him was this: If a baseball game starts at noon and lasts three and a half hours, what time will it end?

My heart broke for this young man. He certainly had more than enough smarts to answer the question. What he lacked was the knowledge to answer it. After spending twelve years in our state's classrooms, he had never been taught at even that basic level. We had failed him. The system moved on, and he got left behind.

I vowed we would do better, that we would ensure that every precious child in our classrooms mattered and their success was prioritized.

I am telling that quick story to remind us all what education is about. It's not about politicians. It's not about administrators, bureaucrats, and principals. It's not about teachers or unions.

It's about kids, about the next generation of Americans who are going to inherit this incredible country—ready or not. If they are not ready, that is on us. And never have the stakes been higher. The upcoming generation faces challenges far greater than those my generation faced.

As technology advances and machines perform tasks with greater speed and increasing sophistication, change is accelerating like the *Starship Enterprise* hitting warp speed. Keeping up is hard to do, which makes this both the most exciting of times and also the most unsettling. Nowhere is this truer than in the workplace, where the battle of human versus automation is in full swing.

A study by McKinsey & Company, a worldwide management consulting firm, says that 45 percent of today's jobs could be automated with today's technology.[1]

There is a robot that can flip hamburgers, a robot that can bend over and pick up packages, and a robot that can clean windows. Robots have established themselves inside factories and soon will be doing so on the roads, driving everything from ride-share cars in the city to semitrucks on the highway.

The increasing automation of lower-skilled jobs has always been a given. But now we have computers that can beat world chess champions, read mammograms, translate languages, explore space, create music, and run the table in no-limit Texas Hold'em poker tournaments.

In other words, more and more, they can outperform us in ever more complex tasks. And that means white-collar jobs will be on the chopping block, too.

Even politicians aren't safe. An article by the World Economic Forum explores whether we would be better off if our leaders were replaced with artificial intelligence.[2] One survey shows a quarter of Europeans think we would.[3] Sometimes I can't blame them for thinking that.

What comes next has become almost impossible to predict. The unknown brings fear. But it also brings opportunities we can't yet imagine. Look at history. When automobiles replaced horses, this displaced the blacksmiths and saddlemakers. But how many more jobs—from mechanics to assembly line workers to road builders—came from the transition?

Remember when typewriters dominated offices with their familiar clickity-clack? And then came the word processors, which in turn were replaced by computer networks. How many offices in the 1960s had an IT department? As old jobs disappear, new jobs will replace them—jobs we haven't even contemplated yet. Who could have known only a few short years ago there would be a demand for app developers and cloud computing specialists?

Today's knowledge economy requires the ability to adapt, to continuously learn, to keep pace with new trends and technology, to become the master of machines rather than their victim.

To prepare, strong foundations must be laid early and built upon.

This is the challenge confronting our education system. And whether it meets that challenge will determine the success of the next generation and America's leadership role in the twenty-first century. Other nations understand this, which is why we see students in China, Singapore, South Korea, and Vietnam making strong gains on international assessments in science and math.

But while other nations up their game, academic progress in the United States has stagnated. We confront a world that is moving at dizzying speed with an education system that plods along at a nineteenth-century pace. We are preparing for a Digital Age future with an education model mired in an Industrial Age past.

Can you imagine if the modern military trained its recruits with sabers and muskets in boot camp to prepare for battlefields dominated by smart weapons and robotics?

In an economy that demands knowledge and skills, only about a third of high school graduates are prepared for college-level reading and math.[4] Because of that, remediation courses have become a staple in community colleges and universities.

Nor are we preparing enough students for high-paying technical careers, be they in construction, manufacturing, mechanics, or health care. A survey by ManpowerGroup in 2018 showed almost half of employers were having trouble finding skilled workers.[5]

We have job openings, and we have people looking for jobs. But separating the two is a wide and deep chasm of knowledge and skills.

To stay competitive, some of our biggest employers have started re-education initiatives for their existing employees, trying to update them with new skills. Amazon most recently joined their ranks, planning to spend $700 million on efforts to retrain one-third of its workforce.[6]

Corporate America isn't alone in confronting this. A 2012 report prepared for the Council on Foreign Relations by former secretary of state Condoleezza Rice and Joel Klein, former chancellor of the New York City Department of Education, found that the K–12 education system was "falling short" in preparing enough students for military service and for dealing with the next generation of threats, including the looming cyber battlefield.[7]

"For all Americans who care about the country's future, these results are of grave concern," the report noted. "The United States will not be able to keep pace—much less lead—globally unless it moves to fix the problems it has allowed to fester for too long."

America's vast network of education bureaucracies is not designed to accomplish the mission assigned it today. That's not an opinion. It's an objective analysis of the results they are producing.

New approaches must be considered. We arrived at this conclusion in Florida in 1999 and embarked on an unprecedented effort to reform the education system, an effort that continues to this day.

What we created in Florida is unrecognizable from what existed twenty years ago, in structure, expectations, and results. Let me briefly take you back in time to the pre-reform years to give you a better understanding of the issues we confronted and how we addressed them. We didn't simply pull reforms out of a hat—they were specifically targeted to address failings in the system.

In 1999, Florida had a richly deserved reputation for operating one of the worst public school systems in the country.

Results from high-quality tests administered as part of the National Assessment of Educational Progress (NAEP) revealed almost half of our fourth graders could not even read at a basic level. About 60 percent of low-income and minority students were unable to do so.

Children who are not capable readers by fourth grade are four times more likely to drop out of school. We were setting up these children, at a painfully young age, to fail in life. Given the statistical link between illiteracy and delinquency, it was like we had built a pipeline from our schools to the juvenile justice system.[8]

Governor after governor undertook reform efforts, dating back to the 1970s. Nothing worked because the solutions left the existing system intact. You cannot work within the system to fix a problem when the system itself is the problem.

We were in desperate need of bold solutions. So we structured them around two basic principles: accountability and school choice.

Our school districts operated as many across the country still do. They were monopolies, assigning students to schools without regard for the quality of the schools or the wishes of the parents.

More affluent parents had an advantage because they could purchase homes in neighborhoods with the highest-performing public schools or enroll their children in private schools.

The school districts understood this, of course. They had to compete for these students and therefore gave them preferential treatment in terms of resources, quality staff, and rigorous curricula.

School choice is a controversial term. But it has always existed for those with the means to afford it. Low-income families had no recourse but to accept the dictates of the bureaucracy. When you are without power, you are without a seat at the table. Schools in poor neighborhoods often lacked resources and academic rigor and disproportionately had less experienced and lower-performing teachers.

Imagine being a parent and dropping your child off every morning at a school you knew was failing him or her—and being powerless to do anything about it.

The purpose of public education should be to serve students. But like other states, Florida had that backwards. The captive population of children ensured a constant stream of funding for the bureaucracy and paychecks for the adults. But there was no reciprocity, because the adults did not guarantee the children a quality education.

Student success was optional. Failure was an accepted alternative. When large government bureaucracies don't have to do something, expecting that they will amounts to wishful thinking.

Prior to the 1990s, much of this failure went unmeasured, undocumented, and unreported to parents and the public. Academic standards and assessments were woefully inadequate, putting us in the dark as to how well our students were being prepared for graduation.

Students who had a great teacher, one who inspired them and set expectations high, hit the jackpot. Students who did not were out of luck.

Florida had literally thousands of academic standards at the time. Social promotion became the norm because moving struggling kids along was the path of least resistance.

And so a third grader who could not read was passed on to the fourth grade. The fourth-grade teacher in turn would pass the student into fifth grade—and so on and so forth. This turned schools into dropout factories, because there comes a time when a student just can't escape not being able to read the textbooks.

Too many adults in the system expected the children to fail based on where they came from or what they looked like. Kids are very astute and take their cues from adults.

As my brother, President George W. Bush, put it in a speech to the NAACP in 2000: "No child in America should be segregated by low expectations, imprisoned by illiteracy, abandoned to frustration and the darkness of self-doubt."[9]

The overarching theme of our reforms in Florida was that each and every child would be accounted for and that his success or failure would matter.

This required measuring academic progress, because what gets measured gets done. The measurement occurred on annual tests calibrated to reflect the expectations for mastering the standards set for each grade level. These tests filtered out the subjectivity of teachers and the variations in grading from classroom to classroom, presenting us with an objective picture of student achievement.

Most importantly, we made the results matter by holding schools accountable for the performance of students. We graded schools in the same way they graded students—on an A–F scale. This seemingly simple tool produced tremendous results.

Failure thrives in dark corners. It doesn't do so well when you turn the light on. Our grading system was designed to be a blinding spotlight.

The results came quickly. Schools that for decades had quietly failed one generation of students after the next were exposed. Long ignored, they found themselves on the front pages of newspapers, highlighted by the letter F.

School districts responded with new administrators and teachers. These schools received more resources. We provided reading specialists to work with students and teachers.

The turnaround was swift. In only a few short years, we saw pictures of students and teachers from once-failing schools celebrating A grades. Scores began rising on state tests, and this success was validated by the National Assessment of Educational Progress (NAEP) results.

In 1998, Florida's fourth graders were almost a grade level behind the national average. By 2003, they were ahead of the national average, with the biggest improvements made by our most disadvantaged students.[10]

As the data began to trend upward, we did not rest on our laurels. We elevated performance standards and expected more.

The schools often complained. Just when they had grown comfortable with the achievement levels expected of them, we raised the bar, and their grades dropped. But it had the intended effect. Teachers and students adjusted to the higher expectations, and school grades rebounded.

We put a laser focus on early-grade literacy. Students who struggled with reading were identified early so personalized intervention could begin with reading specialists. We provided multiple ways for the students to demonstrate they were prepared for fourth grade. If not, they received another year of intensive support in third grade. We forced the schools to prioritize their success, and, as expected, reading scores rose and retentions decreased.

Good education results require a smart investment of education funds. We directed money to where it would do the most good rather than just shoveling it into the bureaucracy like coal into a furnace. We let results be our guide.

For example, we wanted to ensure all students had access to advanced coursework, not just the high performers in more affluent schools. To accomplish this, we offered bonuses to teachers whose students successfully passed Advanced Placement (AP) classes, demonstrated by earning a three or higher on the AP test. The bonus was bigger for teachers in traditionally disadvantaged schools.

We incentivized schools by including AP success in the high school grading formula. We paid for the cost of the tests, lifting that burden from families and ensuring that as many students as possible could participate.

And the result: Florida became a leader in the number of high school graduates successfully completing an AP course. In 2018, Florida graduates had the third-highest AP success rate in the nation.[11]

To quote from a Floridapolitics.com story: "Florida demonstrated one of the best improvements in the country. According to the College Board report, Florida's high school graduates passage rates on the AP exams improved by 0.9 percent in 2018 compared with 2017, and was 12.4 percent better than the class of 2008. That ten-year progress was third most impressive in the country, behind only Massachusetts and Rhode Island."[12]

The idea of Florida being a leader in high achievement, of being mentioned in the same sentence as Massachusetts, would have been laughable back in the 1990s. And now it is expected.

Our students didn't suddenly get a whole lot smarter. Our teachers didn't suddenly get a whole lot better. We didn't have massive increases in education spending. We simply implemented commonsense policies, held firm against pushback, and built upon what was working.

Taxpayers in Florida are now getting a significantly better return as their investment in education produces significantly better results for students, families, and the state.

Accountability was a key tool in shaping our success. But the biggest game changer for parents was Florida's embrace of school choice.

It's important to note, again, that there has always been school choice—it simply has been limited to families with sufficient income to afford private schools or neighborhoods with high-performing public schools. Nobody complained about that. But when we began extending choice options to lower-income parents, the howls of protest began and union attorneys rushed to stop them.

If you want to see the power that teacher union money exerts in the political process, look at how quickly supposedly progressive politicians act to disempower the very constituents they supposedly champion.

When parents have choice, they have power. It makes school districts compete for them. And they do so by upping the quality of their product.

We also opened the door to charter schools. We tried to give poor kids stuck in habitually failing schools options to go to better schools. But the teachers' union and its political allies ended that program after seven years in a legal challenge.

Undeterred, we began the Florida Tax Credit Scholarship Program, which gave low-income children access to private schools. We set up the McKay Scholarship Program, allowing the parents of students with disabilities to choose the public or private school that best meets their needs, regardless of household income.

We became a national leader in online education by establishing Florida Virtual School, which serves public, private, and home education students. We allowed public school students to cross attendance boundaries.

In effect, we moved to democratize school choice. School districts responded with their own robust choice programs, particularly magnet schools that specialize in any number of fields including art, music, science, digital media, engineering, construction, aviation, international studies, criminal justice, and so on.

Forty-six percent of Florida's students have attended a school of choice.[13]

Every time we expand choice, parents embrace the options given them. More than 300,000 students attended charter schools in 2018, more than triple the number from 2006. There are about 100,000 students enrolled in Florida Tax Credit Scholarship schools. More than 31,000 students with disabilities are enrolled in McKay Scholarship schools.

A new choice option for students with disabilities, the Gardiner Scholarship Program, has expanded to 12,000 participants. There would be even more with increased funding. Gardiner directly funds parents so they can customize their children's education, pulling money out of their accounts to pay for private school tuition, tutoring, online education, home education, curriculum, therapy, and so on. It is the nation's largest Education Scholarship Account program.

Florida has not stopped there. Recent new programs include Reading Scholarship Accounts, with $500 for tutoring and other support available to students in grades 3–5 who are enrolled in a public school and scored below grade level on the state English language arts assessment in the prior school year.

Hope Scholarships provide any K–12 student enrolled in a public school who has been subjected to bullying or other incidents at the school with the opportunity to transfer to another public school with capacity or to enroll in an approved private school. And the Family Empowerment Scholarship will offer choice in education to 40,000 low- and middle-income students over its first four years of implementation.

None of this has come without a fight.

The Florida Education Association tries to block educational opportunity at every turn, unleashing its lobbyists and lawyers and emptying its war chest into political campaigns. It led a legal challenge in 2014 to abolish the Florida Tax Credit Scholarship Program. Think of that—they were willing to throw 100,000 of our most disadvantaged children out of schools chosen by their parents.

Dr. Martin Luther King III led 10,000 parents and other program supporters in a Tallahassee march opposing the union's efforts. "Ultimately, if the courts have to decide, the courts will be on the side of justice," Dr. King said during his keynote address. "Because this is about justice. This is about freedom. The freedom to choose what's best for your family and your child most importantly."[14]

Dr. King proved an astute prognosticator. In January 2017, the Florida Supreme Court dismissed the lawsuit. The scholarship program continues, with ongoing proposals to increase funding so scholarships are available to more children.

The importance of choice only grows with the increasing diversity of our student population. Florida has a minority-majority population. Our classrooms contain about 40 percent white students. Almost 60 percent of students qualify for the free or reduced-price lunch program. In my hometown of Miami, 20 percent of students are English language learners.

To shove these children into a one-size-fits-all education model and expect them all to learn in the same way, at the same speed, in the same subjects is simply not realistic. It's like putting a thousand kids on a track and expecting them all to run a mile at the same pace.

We have engineered an education system based on averages—the average amount of material students can learn in an average amount of time.

How does this play out in, say, a geometry class?

Students who have a knack for geometry get bored at the pace of the class, while kids who struggle with the subject can't keep up. Rather than schools accommodating children, the children must accommodate the schools.

And when they can't, they are labeled failures.

There is a wonderful young woman I've had the pleasure of getting to know named Denisha Merriweather. She failed third grade twice in her Jacksonville school. She got into fights. She was labeled a troublemaker and had resigned herself to dropping out.

Her godmother heard of the Florida Tax Credit Scholarship Program and, as a last resort, used it to enroll her in a small, Christian school. There, the teachers set entirely different expectations for her. They pushed her academically. They expected her to go to college.

"The atmosphere at my new school was unlike anything I have experienced before," she wrote in an op-ed for the *Tampa Tribune*. "I was expected to make honor roll and everybody celebrated when eventually I did. People believed I could do it, so I started believing it too. Learning became fun. Knowledge became a gift."[15]

Denisha went on to earn her graduate degree in social work at the University of South Florida. She has become a passionate, outspoken, and compelling advocate for school choice.

When you look at her case, you must wonder: How many more Denishas are out there? How many lives have been spent in poverty and dependency that could have had a much different outcome had we put them in the right educational setting?

Denisha is a story of individual success. But in her story is a bigger story—that of our nation's success. Go into a classroom in Florida, in Texas, in California—and there you will see the future of our nation. We need these children to succeed if America is to succeed. The world is too competitive a place to be leaving vast swaths of our nation's potential on the sidelines.

Because of our reforms, Florida's statewide graduation rate has increased 26.9 percentage points since 2003, despite increasingly rigorous academic requirements.

African American fourth graders have advanced two and a half grade levels on NAEP reading tests since 1998—progress that is double the national average. If our Hispanic fourth graders could form their own state, they would rank thirteenth nationally in reading.

Florida has long been one of the nation's leaders in academic gains by students with disabilities. The reason is that we made their progress count in school accountability formulas.

The last round of NAEP results, released in 2017, were a disappointment nationally, with reading and math scores stagnant or declining in most states. Florida was one of only three states to show improvement in fourth- and eighth-grade reading and math, with gains also made by students of color, low-income students, students with disabilities, and students still learning English.

In commenting on these results, Peggy Carr, from the National Center for Education Statistics, said: "Something very good is happening in Florida. Florida needs to be commended."[16]

We continue to move forward aggressively.

Preparing for success in today's economy means dispensing with the notion of high school diplomas as a goal for the K–12 system. These diplomas carry little currency in a job market that now demands more.

High school must become a transitory step to college or a meaningful career. Florida has fully embraced this concept.

We promote dual enrollment, so high school students can earn college credits—and hopefully even A.A. degrees one day—along with their diplomas. This saves parents a considerable amount of money and ensures that students are college-ready. Tying these goals to school accountability formulas has created a strong incentive for schools to participate.

In 2007, Florida lawmakers passed the Career and Professional Education Act to provide partnerships between the business community and educators, helping students prepare for meaningful careers while still in high school.

Students are earning industry certifications in information technology, health sciences, and more. They are training for high-demand fields such as auto mechanics, HVAC mechanics, transmission specialists, and so on.

At the Professional and Technical High School in Osceola, students take their academic courses at the school, then go next door to earn industry certifications at the Technical Education Center Osceola for careers ranging from pharmacy techs and electricians to digital designers and chefs. Students working on HVAC certifications sometimes earn internships at the school district.

Given the high cost of technical education, the savings for families are tremendous. So is the boost to Florida's economy, because we have created an education pipeline for high-demand jobs.

In 2008, Florida students had earned fewer than 1,000 industry certifications. That number has grown to about 140,000.[17]

This is the advantage of having a well-thought-out accountability formula in place. As time goes by and new strategies emerge to advance student success, you can tweak the formula to achieve desired results. It allows us to fast-track change in Florida, because every school strives to be an A school.

I am proud of what we have accomplished in Florida—and proud that so many other states have incorporated many of our reforms and have seen student achievement rise as a result.

But progress is not coming fast enough, given the challenges I laid out at the beginning of this chapter.

We need to fast-track reform.

After spending what seems to be three lifetimes in the reform movement, my conclusion is this: the best way to effect change is by moving toward complete local control of education decisions.

When I say local, I don't mean school districts. I mean local in the purest sense—parental control.

Parents should be able to choose the educational setting that best fits their child from a broad marketplace of options. State and local funding should follow the student.

A parent might decide simply to send her child to the neighborhood public school. Or perhaps there's a charter school that focuses on science or technology that's a better fit. Or a small faith-based school that provides more individual attention.

For gifted students, there could be the Stanford Online School, founded by Stanford University.

Or perhaps families could create a customized plan. For example, a student could spend the morning at a traditional public school, where she runs on the track team and plays in the band. She takes an online course in music theory from Juilliard. She studies Chinese in a Florida Virtual School class. And she has a math tutor to help with calculus.

It may be that a company like Amazon, tired of spending so much money on retraining employees, decides to get ahead of the curve and invest in K–12 education, offering classes in areas where they are experiencing shortages. This opens more job pipelines in high school.

There would be full transparency so parents could make informed decisions. The measuring stick would be ensuring a strong foundation in the early grades, with a laser-like focus on literacy. There should be a natural progression into quality college and career pathways that give students options on how to move forward.

We have to redefine the concept of public education. It should not be viewed as allegiance to bureaucracies but rather allegiance to student success. How that is achieved, whether it is through a traditional public school or through an alternative pathway, should be of secondary concern.

As U.S. Senator Ben Sasse from the state of Nebraska puts it, education should be the goal and schooling the vehicle.[18] And there should be many vehicles.

Such a system would spur innovation and efficiency, because that's what always happens when you create a new marketplace. It would be more agile and flexible, allowing faster pivots to keep up in today's world of rapid change.

It would be a marketplace built around parental empowerment and student success.

Education Scholarship Accounts are the tool that can facilitate this transition. They fund families to pursue the best options for their children instead of funding bureaucracies to dictate what those options will be.

We can get there. Our nation has a history of innovating and finding solutions when confronted with a challenge. What we need is the bold, big-picture vision to set us on our way.

That vision is not going to come from the federal government. It is not going to come from school districts and unions, which have demonstrated quite clearly that their priority is self-interest.

Leadership is going to have to come from the states—from our laboratories of democracy. We need governors and legislators with the political courage to tackle the status quo.

It is time to redefine the concept of public education as the education of children with public dollars. The single goal is their success. We should be agnostic as to where that success occurs—a traditional public school, charter school, private school, virtual school, home school, or some other provider.

Florida's Gardiner Scholarships are a version of this approach, although limited to students with disabilities. What the program is showing us is that when given more leeway to customize their children's education, parents come up with unique and innovative ideas.

Parents aren't perfect decision-makers. But when it comes to their children, history has taught us that they are the best decision-makers.

It's time we recognize that as we debate the future of education.

Restoring Public Universities as the Marketplace of Ideas

by Tyson Langhofer

"If liberty means anything at all, it means the right to tell people what they do not want to hear."

—*George Orwell*

The right to free speech in this country is a sacred freedom dating back to December 15, 1791, when the First Amendment was originally adopted. The ability to freely express and debate ideas and deeply held beliefs is an essential part of maintaining our democracy. Nowhere is it more important to protect the right to free speech than on the campuses of our nation's colleges and universities. In recent years, attacks on free speech have all too often occurred on campuses around the country. Individual states are now being called upon to address this very real threat to liberty itself. Tyson Langhofer is one of America's best conservative lawyers and is on the front lines of this fight every day and has devoted his career to defending campus free speech. I'm very grateful for his participation in *Making Government Work* and for the opportunity for more Americans to read his thoughts on this critical topic.

—Tan Parker

I grew up in the 1980s. It was a decade defined by excess. It featured hair bands like Poison, whose most famous anthem was "Nothin' but a Good Time," and artists like Madonna, known as the Material Girl.

189

But it was also an era defined by a shared, cultural understanding of and appreciation for freedom.

At the time, most Americans understood that they could indulge their passions, even to the point of excess, only because America provided them the freedom to do so. Although there were vast disagreements on many of the political issues that still divide us today, most Americans had a healthy respect for the fundamental freedoms that America provided: freedom to work, freedom to speak, freedom to worship, and freedom to vote.

This is largely because the Cold War between the U.S. and the U.S.S.R. was still being waged. For those of us who grew up in that era, there was a real and palpable fear of the Soviet Union. The battle lines were clearly drawn.

America was good; the Soviet Union was bad. Capitalism was good. Communism and socialism were bad. The freedom to speak and worship was good. Censorship and propaganda were bad.

Pop culture illustrated the clash of these two worldviews through movies such as *Red Dawn* and *Rocky IV*. *Rocky IV* pitted Rocky against Ivan Drago, a giant Russian, chemically enhanced by steroids. The lead song on the soundtrack was "Living in America" by the Godfather of Soul, James Brown. That song perfectly encapsulates the feeling of most Americans at that time—America was better than other countries because of its freedom.

Even the Beastie Boys recognized the importance of freedom with their famous '80s anthem "(You Gotta) Fight for Your Right (To Party)."

Much has changed in the last thirty-five years. The United States won the Cold War. The Soviet Union dissolved. And the U.S. is now the world's last remaining superpower. Those are good things. That said, without the constant threat of being attacked by a communist regime, many of the next generation of Americans never developed an appreciation for what differentiates us from other countries—our freedom.

So unlike my generation, which was focused on fighting for the very important right to party, today's generation finds itself debating a far weightier, and far more fundamental, right—the right to repartee. (See what I did there?)

On most college campuses, students are finding that they cannot engage in free and open dialogue with their fellow students on important political topics such as immigration, criminal justice reform, Second Amendment rights, same-sex marriage, transgenderism, terrorism, abortion, health care, women's rights, or economic policy. Students avoid these topics because they are afraid that if they express their views, other students will shout them down or label them as racists, bigots, homophobes, Islamophobes, transphobes, or misogynists—just for holding a different opinion.

Today's college students are driven by a sense of justice. This is beneficial to the extent that it drives them to work toward eradicating poverty, human trafficking, racism, sexism, and other such societal ills. But it has also created problems, because not everyone has the same understanding of what constitutes justice in every situation.

These differing views have led to inevitable conflicts. Often it leads to one or both sides calling for the other side to be censored or silenced because its views are allegedly hateful, demeaning, derogatory, or bigoted. In other words, many in our society today believe that some views must be silenced for the sake of justice.

At the Alliance Defending Freedom's Center for Academic Freedom, we defend the First Amendment rights of students and faculty at public universities so that everyone can freely participate in the marketplace of ideas.

In my experience, when young Americans picture going to college, they imagine being inspired by great minds and pursuing truth so that they can solve big problems. Unfortunately, students attending college today are more likely to experience censorship and suppression than free thought on campus. Young people who express viewpoints that are not in line with the prevailing progressive orthodoxy find themselves silenced. Across America, university administrators, faculty, and students are working every day to shut down views they dislike.

A few recent examples show the scope of the problem. In 2017, ADF represented a Students for Life group at Colorado State University in a lawsuit against school officials challenging a program known as the Diversity Grant.[1] The program was "designed to support programs that enhance the educational and cultural aspects of the university community and raise the awareness of differing perspectives." To further that purpose, the school gave grants to student groups to bring speakers to campus to speak on different topics.

Sounds great, right? And it would have been if the school applied the policy in a nondiscriminatory manner. Students for Life applied for a grant to bring a pro-life speaker to campus—a viewpoint rarely, if ever, presented on the campus. Even though the Diversity Grant's stated purpose is to "raise the awareness of differing perspectives," the university denied the request because it said the speaker was "not entirely unbiased on the topic of abortion." Not all listeners, it said, "would necessarily feel affirmed" in attending the event.

The university's reasoning is silly—not to mention unconstitutional. Of course the pro-life speaker is not unbiased on the topic of abortion. The purpose of the program is to provide a differing perspective, not an unbiased perspective. As for making students feel affirmed, that goes against the purpose of the program: to expose students to differing perspectives that may make them uncomfortable.

After the school denied Students for Life's application, the students sued. The school agreed to modify its policies so that funds were allocated to student groups in a viewpoint-neutral manner.

This is not an isolated incident. Bernadette Tasy and her Students for Life group at Fresno State University received an even more hostile reception to their pro-life speech. The group received permission to chalk life-affirming messages on the sidewalks of the campus, including the phone number for pregnancy centers that provide resources to pregnant women so that they understand they have choices other than abortion. Shortly after writing the messages, Bernadette witnessed a few students erasing them. When Bernadette questioned them, the students said Professor Gregory Thatcher had instructed his class to wipe out the messages.

Then she encountered Professor Thatcher himself. The exchange, which she captured on video, is at once horrifying and comical. Professor Thatcher explains that he and his students are wiping out the messages because he (mistakenly) believes that, "Free speech is free speech in the free speech area. It's a pretty simple concept, okay? This does not constitute a free speech area." When Bernadette informs him that the university approved the messages, Professor Thatcher begins wiping out one of the messages and says, "You had permission to put it down. I have permission to get rid of it. This is our part of free speech."

Professor Thatcher's ignorance (and arrogance) is appalling. He (wrongly) accuses Bernadette of violating university policy by exercising her free speech in a non–free speech area. Without a whiff of irony, he justifies his actions by saying that he is simply exercising his free speech. Recognizing this absurdity, Bernadette responds: "But, you're exercising your free speech in a non–free speech area." (Touché.) Unmoved and unwilling to be bound by such outmoded Western ideals as reason and logic, Professor Thatcher densely retorts: "College campuses are not free speech areas. Do you understand? Obviously you don't understand."

Bernadette promptly disabused Professor Thatcher of his misunderstanding of the First Amendment by filing a federal lawsuit. Soon after, Professor Thatcher agreed to pay damages and a large sum in attorneys' fees, and the court entered an order forbidding him from interfering with any of the students' future activities on campus. [2]

This problem is not limited to secular, public universities. In 2017, a group of students ran into trouble for expressing a Catholic view of marriage and sexuality at Georgetown University—the oldest Catholic and Jesuit institution of higher learning in the country.

Love Saxa, a recognized student group at Georgetown, exists "to promote healthy relationships on campus through cultivating a proper understanding of sex, gender, marriage, and family among Georgetown students." To promote this message, Love Saxa's president, Amelia

Irvine, published an op-ed titled "Confessions of a College Virgin" in *The Hoya*, Georgetown's student newspaper. The article explained Love Saxa's dedication to "healthy relationships and sexual integrity" and its stances on premarital sex, sexual complementarity, and same-sex marriage—none of which fit into the current progressive paradigm.

This led to outrage. In a complaint filed with the university through its internal grievance process, a student issued a blistering critique of Love Saxa's "violent ... dehumanizing ... hateful, and . . . dangerous" "rhetoric." The complaint, which incorporates testimony from other students, labels the group's views as "archaic," "cissexist," "homophobic," "transphobic," "queerphobic," "oppressive," "dehumanizing," "hateful," and "dangerous." The student was clear that she wanted the group silenced, writing, "What I'm asking for is for Love Saxa to no longer be recognized by the University."

The Hoya's editorial board likewise published a response to Irvine's "Confessions," imploring the student activities commission to "defund intolerance." As a result of this complaint, the students had to undergo a four-hour interrogation by the SAC. Thankfully, the SAC agreed not to derecognize the group.

What is driving these actions? Why are educated people who would describe themselves as liberal, tolerant, and open-minded acting in such intolerant, illiberal, and close-minded ways? The drastic increase in calls for censorship appears to be driven by two factors: first, the rise of two dangerous and pervasive fallacies; and second, the rise of victimhood culture.

FALLACY #1: SPEECH IS VIOLENCE

The first fallacy is that "speech is violence." The people promoting this view are not arguing that speech is metaphorically like violence. They are arguing that it is actual violence. By equating speech with violence, this argument encourages those who oppose certain speech to use actual, physical violence to oppose that speech, rather than combating ideas with better ideas. Unfortunately, this is not some fringe ideology that is being pushed by a bunch of ignorant, uneducated activists. This belief is widespread in the academic community among both faculty and students.

In July 2017, Lisa Feldman Barrett, a respected professor of psychology and emotion researcher at Northeastern University, published an essay on this topic in the *New York Times* in which she sought to explain the logic underlying the belief that speech is violence. Barrett made the following assertion: "If words can cause stress, and if prolonged stress can cause physical harm, then it seems that speech—at least certain types of speech—can be a form of violence."[3]

Barrett argues that if words can cause stress, and stress causes harm, then words are a form of violence because they cause harm. But this idea is false. In *The Coddling of the American Mind*, the authors take Barrett's argument and swap out "words" for other actions that cause stress such as "breaking up with your girlfriend" or "giving students a lot of homework."[4] Both actions can cause stress, and stress can cause harm, so both can cause harm (but not necessarily). But this does not mean that breaking up with your girlfriend or giving students lots of homework are violent acts.

Unfortunately, Barrett's fallacy has caught on quickly, and the consequences are everywhere. When students are taught that speech is violence, they begin to believe that engaging in actual violence to prevent certain speech is justified as self-defense. Several days after the riots at UC Berkeley in 2017, the leading student newspaper published a series of five op-eds under the theme "Violence as Self-Defense." One of the essays justified the violence: "Asking people to maintain peaceful dialogue with those who legitimately do not think their lives matter is a violent act."[5]

This statement attacks the basis of a liberal society. Liberalism is defined as "a political or social philosophy advocating the freedom of the individual, parliamentary systems of government, nonviolent modification of political, social, or economic institutions to ensure unrestricted development in all spheres of human endeavor, and governmental guarantees of individual rights and civil liberties."[6]

In other words, liberalism assumes that there is a nonviolent method to modify our political, social, or economic institutions. There are only two ways to modify these institutions: through speech (that is, rhetorical persuasion), or violence (that is, physical force). Yet those who conflate speech with violence assert that there is no nonviolent way to modify those institutions.

What many adherents to this philosophy fail to comprehend is that if words are equivalent to violence, and thus actual physical violence is justified in responding to pure speech, then civil society as we know it will no longer exist. If we as a free people can no longer advocate for change in society through the spoken word—even offensive words—then the only option left to enact change is through violence. As the recent incident at UC Berkeley and those at other campuses have shown, that is not an attractive option.

This is the reason that one of America's core founding principles was broad free speech protections. Supreme Court justice Louis Brandeis wrote, "Those who won our independence believed that the final end of the state was to make men free to develop their faculties . . . . They valued liberty as an end and as a means." The principle that liberty is both a means and an end in itself is the key insight of American self-government. It is quite literally the premise of the Declaration of Independence: "We hold these truths to be self-evident, that all men are created equal, that they are endowed by their Creator with certain unalienable Rights, that among these are Life, Liberty and the pursuit of Happiness.—That to secure these rights, Governments are instituted among Men . . . ."

Free speech is an end because it is a part of the liberty that the government exists to protect. It would be the duty of the government to protect free speech even if it accomplished nothing. It is a sphere of freedom that we are supposed to be able to enjoy. This principle finds its highest expression in *West Virginia Board of Education v. Barnette*, where the Court said, "If there is any fixed star in our constitutional constellation, it is that no official, high or petty, can prescribe what shall be orthodox in politics, nationalism, religion, or other matters of opinion or force citizens to confess by word or act their faith therein." Simply being a free person requires free speech, including freedom to speak or not to speak.

Free speech is a means because it must exist for the government to protect liberty at all. Even without the First Amendment, the need for free speech would be obvious, since a representative democracy could never exist without freedom to discuss policies and candidates openly.

Without free speech, our Constitution would bear all the ironies of the "people's republics" around the world that are neither republics nor governed by the people. And, for speech to fulfill its function, it must apply to everyone. The moment the group in power gets to silence those not in power, no one actually has free speech, because this really means that all speech is subject to the whims of power.

The choice is freedom for everyone or freedom for no one. As Chief Justice Roberts wrote, "The whole point of the First Amendment is to protect individual speech that the majority might prefer to restrict, or that legislators or judges might not view as useful to the democratic process." The answer to speech we do not like is not coercion, it's freedom: "However pernicious an opinion may seem, we depend for its correction not on the conscience of judges and juries but on the competition of other ideas." The worse an idea is, the easier it is to correct with good ideas.

This is why it is alarming to see some conservative lawmakers and commentators responding to censorship or de-platforming by advocating for more censorship. As conservatives, it is vital that we remain true to America's founding principles. We must resist the urge to react to the suppression of speech that we like by engaging in the same behavior. If we are going to protect free speech for everyone, we need to preserve it both as an end and as a means. If we stop thinking about free speech as something that the government should protect for its own sake, the only reason left to protect it will be that it does something that we think is useful. But our definition of "useful" will ultimately rest on our political judgments and preferences. This would carry us to the same place at which most of the public universities have already arrived.

FALLACY #2: JUSTICE CAN BE ACHIEVED APART FROM THE TRUTH

The second fallacy is that justice can be achieved apart from the truth, that justice and truth are separate. Some even argue that truth can thwart justice. This could not be further from, well, the truth. Justice and truth are inextricably linked.

This fact is recognized throughout history by a diverse group of people.

Mahatma Gandhi, leader of India's campaign for independence, said: "Truth never damages a cause that is just." Joseph Joubert, an eighteenth-century French philosopher, said, "Justice is the truth in action." Ravi Zacharias, a Christian apologist, said, "Justice is the handmaiden of truth, and when truth dies, justice is buried with it." Even Louis Farrakhan, leader of the Nation of Islam (who has said many other things that are not true), understands this basic reality. He said: "There really can be no peace without justice. There can be no justice without truth. And there can be no truth, unless someone rises up to tell you the truth."

These individuals are all very different. They lived in different countries, are of different religions, different political beliefs, some are still alive, and some lived more than one hundred years ago. Yet they all recognize this universal principle: justice cannot be achieved apart from the truth. We must first arrive at truth. Then, and only then, will we know what outcome is just.

Historically, virtually everyone in the Western world agreed that the highest purpose or mission of a university was the search for truth. In fact, Yale's motto, inscribed on its crest and engraved in stone on the arch leading to its old campus, is "Lux et Veritas," or "Light and Truth." Harvard's crest says simply "Veritas"—"Truth." In other words, the purpose of the university is to understand the world as it is.

Yet over the last three decades, that purpose has come under a sustained attack. Many administrators, faculty, and students now argue that the purpose of the university is not to understand the world, but to change the world through social justice.

Jonathan Haidt, a professor at New York University and an esteemed social psychologist, has written extensively on these two competing views of the purpose of a university.[7] According to Haidt, these two views are mutually exclusive. A university must choose one or the other. Haidt explains that when social justice seeks to ensure equal treatment for all individuals, then it is compatible with the university's mission to pursue truth. But when social justice seeks to ensure equal outcomes for all individuals regardless of differences or other relevant factors, then it is not actually justice, and is incompatible with the university's mission to pursue truth because truth is inseparable from justice.

The University of Louisville provides a recent example of the harm that results from a university pursuing a warped view of social justice instead of truth. For sixteen years, Dr. Allan Josephson was the chief of the university's division of child and adolescent psychiatry and psychology. From 2014 to 2016, Dr. Josephson received perfect marks on his reviews.

In the fall of 2017, Dr. Josephson participated in a panel discussion at the Heritage Foundation, in which he expressed concern about current recommended treatments for children experiencing gender dysphoria. His remarks angered a few of his colleagues, who then learned he had served as an expert witness addressing similar issues. They demanded that the university take disciplinary action. Within a few weeks, the university demoted him to the role of a junior faculty member. Soon after, the school refused to renew his contract, effectively firing him. Dr. Josephson retained ADF to file a federal lawsuit against officials at the university, challenging his termination. The lawsuit is still pending.[8]

In an article in *Clinical Psychiatry News*, two psychiatry professors at the University of California, San Diego, discussed how Dr. Josephson's firing could adversely affect the practice of psychiatry and patient outcomes. The professors begin by noting that Dr. Josephson's views were mainstream to many practitioners just a few years ago. More importantly, "[T]here is no large body of scientific evidence that has been generated to confirm that [Dr. Josephson] is promoting an unscientific perspective that should rightly be ostracized by the medical community." To the contrary, "[S]ome evidence suggests that some medical approaches to gender dysphoria have not always ameliorated the distress found in some patients."

The professors concluded, "If psychiatry chooses to produce or dismiss psychiatric diagnoses based on the inherent political inconvenience of said diagnoses, rather than their scientific and medical basis, the entire field will rightly be called into question."[9]

In other words, if psychiatry rejects truth in favor of some misguided idea of justice, the whole field of science will collapse.

THE RISE OF VICTIMHOOD CULTURE

The second factor contributing to the rise in censorship and shoutdowns on college campuses is the rise of victimhood culture. Bradley Campbell, professor of sociology at California State University, Los Angeles, and Jason Manning, professor of sociology at West Virginia University, have conducted extensive studies to determine the causes of the recent upheaval on college campuses. They have published their findings in various papers, including an article in Quillette titled "Purity and Tolerance: The Contradictory Morality of College Campuses."[10]

Professors Campbell and Manning argue that the rise in alleged microaggressions and the demand for safe spaces, trigger warnings, and speaker boycotts and cancellations are all manifestations of victimhood culture—a morality in which people display high sensitivity to slight conflicts by portraying themselves as weak and appealing to authorities. In victimhood culture, those who successfully identify as victims or allies of victims gain a kind of moral status.

Victimhood culture thrives on modern college campuses because of the presence of three factors: cultural diversity, social equality, and stable authority. Uniformity of thought counterbalances diversity of race, ethnicity, and gender expression.

Overdiversity—an increase in diversity such as the expression of a new idea or contact between two previously separate cultural groups—is a potent source of conflict. But so too is underdiversity—any decrease in diversity or any attempt to decrease it through the suppression of a cultural expression or group. Minor acts of underdiversity include ethnic or religious slights and slurs, while more extreme acts include enforced conformity and genocide.

The current university environment is a toxic blend of overdiversity and underdiversity. Increasing fragmentation based on identity (racial, sexual, gender, and so on) is endlessly combined with a lack of ideological diversity. In this tense environment, any increase in ideological diversity creates conflict. This environment leads students to develop unhealthy moral dependency on university administrators and hypersensitivity to perceived slights—exactly the results we would expect to find where there are high levels of diversity, equality, and stable authority.

Although these structural and moral conditions are present to some extent throughout much of American society, they predominate on university campuses. The lack of ideological diversity on college campuses is much more pronounced than in the larger culture. Only 12 percent of faculty members on public university campuses identify as politically conservative—far fewer than in the general population. Conservatives are even less represented in the humanities and social sciences, where many faculty members openly identify as activists seeking to advance left-wing political views through their work as scholars and teachers. As one would expect, this unified bloc reacts to those with differing views like inquisitors reacting to heresy.

The reaction to minority political views is most harsh in the sectors of academia with the least diversity, because uniformity of thought breeds intolerance of disagreement.[11] Thus, victimhood culture is more extreme on college campuses than elsewhere—for now.

THE CHOICE: FREE SPEECH OR CENSORSHIP

Faced with the spread of these two fallacies and the rise of victimhood culture, public universities had to make a choice—either reaffirm their mission of pursuing truth by promoting a robust culture of free speech and rejecting calls to suppress unpopular views, or discard their mission and give in to the demands for suppression. Unfortunately, most universities have chosen the latter.[12]

There are five primary varieties of policies that universities use to suppress speech.

SPEECH ZONE/PRIOR PERMISSION

Many universities censor or suppress speech by requiring students to obtain prior permission from university officials before speaking or handing out literature anywhere on campus. Some go even further by prohibiting students from speaking on campus except in a tiny area (that is, a speech zone), and many even require prior permission before using the speech zones. Nearly all these policies contain no objective criteria telling university officials when to approve or deny a student's request to speak, so universities often compound the problem by granting officials discretion in making approvals or denials. University officials can use this discretion to suppress speech they dislike and promote speech they like.

The Supreme Court has consistently invalidated these types of policies as violating the First Amendment. It has said, "[A] government regulation that allows arbitrary application is inherently inconsistent with [the First Amendment] because such discretion has the potential for becoming a means of suppressing a particular point of view" (*Forsyth Cty. v. Nationalist Movement*, 505 U.S. 123, 130, 1992).

The First Amendment was designed to protect against the suppression of minority or disfavored views by government officials. The notion that a college student must obtain permission from a university official before peacefully speaking with other students in an open, outdoor area of campus clearly violates the rights protected by that amendment.

College officials at Kellogg Community College (KCC) in Michigan recently demonstrated the peril (and lunacy) of these policies. In 2016, Michelle Gregoire, a student at KCC, and a few of her friends were on a large outdoor walkway of campus passing out copies of the U.S. Constitution and speaking to other students about starting a chapter of Young Americans for Liberty. Shortly after, college officials ordered the group to stop talking with other students because they had not obtained permission before speaking as required by school policy.

The group politely informed school officials that the First Amendment (contained in the Constitution that they were passing out) is the only permission slip they need to speak on a sidewalk on a public college campus. Undeterred, campus police arrested three members of the group for trespassing. They were handcuffed and remained in jail for seven hours before being released. After ADF filed a federal lawsuit on their behalf, all criminal charges were dismissed and the college agreed to modify its policies to ensure that all students can speak freely on campus without obtaining prior permission from college officials.

SPEECH CODES

Another common policy that university officials use to censor speech is a speech code. A speech code is a policy that bans or punishes speech expressing viewpoints that university officials or other students subjectively classify as uncivil, disrespectful, derogatory, hurtful, or demeaning. Certainly, as citizens in a democratic society with a wide diversity of views, we should all strive to communicate in a civil and respectful manner.

At the same time, a "bedrock principle underlying the First Amendment . . . is that the government may not prohibit the expression of an idea simply because society finds the idea itself offensive or disagreeable" (*Texas v. Johnson*, 491 U.S. 397, 414, 1989). Without this principle the First Amendment would be meaningless, because the only speech that needs protecting is speech expressing views that others may find offensive. Sadly, all too often today, university officials mainly employ speech codes to shut down students who express mainstream religious or conservative views because those views have become increasingly unpopular on today's college campuses.

This is what happened to Chike Uzuegbunam, a student at Georgia Gwinnett College. In 2016, Chike was sharing his Christian faith with his fellow students by leafleting and conversing outdoors on campus. College officials stopped him for violating their speech zone policy. They told Chike that if he wanted to talk with other students, he must do so in one of the school's two tiny speech zones—one patio and one sidewalk comprising less than 0.0015 percent of campus. Chike complied and later reserved one of the speech zones.

But college officials stopped him yet again, saying that because someone had complained, his speech constituted "disorderly conduct." Under the college's speech code, "disorderly conduct" included anything that "disturbs the peace and/or comfort of person(s)." After Chike retained ADF to file a federal lawsuit, the college revised its policies to eliminate the speech code and allow students to speak outdoors without prior permission.

FREEDOM OF ASSOCIATION

The Supreme Court has consistently recognized that college campuses are supposed to be a "marketplace of ideas," such as in *Healy v. James*, 408 U.S. 169, 180 (1972). A critical component of that marketplace, especially on large public university campuses that may number tens of thousands of students, is student organizations. Students supportive of an ideological, cultural, political, or religious cause seek out others with that common interest and join together to amplify their voices. And the First Amendment protects their right to do so.

Recognizing this, most universities maintain policies to facilitate the recognition of student organizations. Officially recognized student organizations receive benefits that unofficial groups do not, including the ability to reserve meeting spaces, receive funding from mandatory student activity fees, and invite speakers to campus.

Regrettably, many universities selectively enforce these policies to suppress certain views by denying recognition to groups that espouse conservative or religious views, especially groups that require their leaders, members, or both to agree to a statement of belief as a condition of leadership or membership.

Universities argue that allowing a student group to limit its leaders or members to those who share the group's beliefs would violate federal law or school policy forbidding the university from discriminating against certain protected classes. This argument misinterprets both federal law and nondiscrimination policies. Worse, it disregards students' First Amendment rights to associate around shared beliefs.

It is true that various federal laws prohibit a public university from discriminating against students based on race, sex, or religion. And most public universities maintain a nondiscrimination policy prohibiting the university from engaging in such discrimination. But these laws and policies apply only to the university's actions. They do not restrict the private actions of individual students. In fact, they cannot restrict those actions, because the First Amendment forbids it.

The reasoning for this constitutional protection is simple. Groups express their views through their leaders. Private associations must be able to decide who leads and speaks for them. The Supreme Court recognizes that this protection is especially important for religious groups. "A religious body's control over [those who will serve as an embodiment of its message] is an essential component of its freedom to speak in its own voice, both to its own members and to the outside world"

(*Hosanna-Tabor Evangelical Lutheran Church & Sch. v. E.E.O.C.*, 565 U.S. 171, 201, 2012) (Alito, J., joined by Kagan, J., concurring).

Unfortunately, religious student groups (primarily Christian groups) are the most frequent victim of universities' discriminatory decisions to deny official recognition.

The University of Colorado, Colorado Springs, is a perfect example. For three years, a group of students sought to form a Ratio Christi chapter at their school. Ratio Christi seeks to defend the Christian faith and explain how the Bible applies to various current cultural, ethical, and political issues. Any student can attend its events. Any student of any faith can become a member of Ratio Christi, as long as the group's purpose is supported. But Ratio Christi requires that those who lead the Christian organization share its religious beliefs. As a result, the university repeatedly denied it registered status, limiting its access to funding, meeting and event space, and administrative support.

Even worse, the university treated Ratio Christi differently than other groups. For example, non-religious groups are allowed to select members who support their purposes. The university allows fraternities that admit only men and sororities that admit only women to continue as registered student organizations, despite the university's policy against "discriminating based on sex." After Ratio Christi retained ADF and filed suit, the school agreed to recognize the group and modify its student recognition policies to allow groups to choose leaders that share the groups' beliefs.

DENIAL OF EQUAL ACCESS

Universities also routinely enforce policies that impose restrictions or deny a student group equal access to resources on campus because of the viewpoints expressed by the group or the group's invited speaker.

Schools impose these restrictions in many ways, including (1) charging security fees because the school considers the group's views controversial, or other students suggest they will protest or disrupt the event,

(2) denying the group's ability to reserve a venue, or relegating the event to a less desirable or less accessible venue, (3) limiting the size of the audience because of concerns that other students will disrupt the event, (4) denying a group's request to bring a certain speaker to campus because the school considers the speaker's views to be controversial, and (5) allowing other students or faculty to disrupt or obstruct a group's validly scheduled event.

In 2016, officials at California State University, Los Angeles, employed several of these restrictions to shut down a speech by Ben Shapiro. Young Americans for Freedom (YAF), a recognized student group on campus, invited Shapiro to campus to discuss free speech in higher education. But just one week before the event, the university informed YAF that it would have to pay security fees of $621.50 because Shapiro's "topics and views are controversial."

Four days later, the university's president told YAF that he was canceling the event, saying it would be "best for our campus community." When YAF went forward with the event as planned, hundreds of protestors—aided by professors and faculty of the university—flooded the university's student union and physically blocked access to the theater where Shapiro was speaking. Although the mob created unsafe conditions and violated many university policies and state and city laws, the president ordered university police not to interfere with the protestors' actions.

As a result, more than a hundred students and members of the community were prevented from attending Shapiro's lecture. After ADF filed a federal lawsuit on behalf of Shapiro and the student group, the university agreed to revoke its security fee policy and enforce its other policies in a viewpoint-neutral manner.

STUDENT ACTIVITY FEES

Another common method universities use to suppress or censor student speech is through unfair allocation of student activity fees. A student activity fee is a mandatory fee charged on top of tuition to fund expressive activities of students and student organizations. In *Board of Regents of the University of Wisconsin System v. Southworth*, the Supreme Court ruled that a public university may only impose a mandatory activity fee to fund student speech if it does not discriminate based on viewpoint when allocating the fees to the students.

A student activity fee policy is not viewpoint-neutral unless it contains an exhaustive list of objective criteria that must be used to evaluate requests for funds. These objective criteria prevent school officials from only allocating funds to their favored views.

Virtually every public university in America imposes a mandatory student activity fee. Universities collect and allocate hundreds of millions of dollars in such fees annually. Regrettably, almost no university employs a viewpoint-neutral policy. Not surprisingly, without the protection of a policy requiring viewpoint-neutrality, schools allocate nearly all student fees to student groups expressing liberal or progressive views. At the same time, schools shut out student groups expressing conservative or religious views, or give them pennies on the dollar.

Until February 2020, this was the situation for students at California State University. The Cal State System is the largest public university system in the nation, with twenty-three campuses throughout California and nearly 500,000 students. Cal State collects more than $50 million in student activity fees annually. In 2016, the university denied Students for Life, a recognized student group, a $500 grant to bring a pro-life speaker to campus at CSU–San Marcos. After doing some research, the group learned that in the 2016–2017 academic year, the Gender Equity Center and the LGBQTA Pride Center received almost $300,000 to fund their activities. Yet, in that same year, all other one hundred student groups combined received less than $6,000 for their activities. In other words, two groups received fifty-seven times more than all other one hundred student groups combined. That is the definition of discriminatory.

In 2017, ADF attorneys representing Students for Life filed a federal lawsuit challenging the university's discriminatory funding policies. In

August 2019, a federal court struck down the policy, describing it as a system of "back room deliberations." As a result of the court's ruling and the post-judgment settlement, the chancellor of the university agreed to require all twenty-three campuses to review and revise their funding policies to comply with the Constitution's viewpoint-neutrality requirement.

THE SOLUTION

While most colleges and universities pay it lip service, true support for free speech is rare on American public campuses, and it's dwindling. Official policies and informal practices reflect this. But there is good news. State legislatures have the power to enact legislation to ensure that public colleges and universities in their state maintain policies and practices consistent with the First Amendment. State legislatures have a duty to ensure that public universities that violate students' First Amendment rights are held accountable.

Along with American Legislative Exchange Council and other First Amendment advocates, ADF co-authored draft model state legislation known as the Forming Open and Robust University Minds Act (FORUM). Since 2017, twelve states have enacted some version of this act. All public universities in states that pass this type of legislation are required to modify their policies and keep them in compliance with state law. FORUM accomplishes three major objectives. First, it prohibits speech zones and policies requiring students to obtain prior permission before speaking in outdoor areas of campus. It also classifies the generally accessible outdoor areas of campus (that is, grassy areas, walkways, and other common areas) as public forums for members of the campus community (that is, students, administrators, faculty, and staff). This prevents schools from restricting access by reclassifying these areas as nonpublic forums.

Second, FORUM prohibits speech codes that unconstitutionally censor or suppress speech that may be considered controversial because other students or faculty disagree with or object to the speech. Under FORUM, universities are only allowed to punish or prohibit speech that the Supreme Court has defined as unlawful harassment: expression that is unwelcome, so severe, pervasive, and subjectively and objectively offensive that a student is effectively denied equal access to educational opportunities or benefits provided by the university (*Davis v. Monroe City Board of Education*, 526 U.S. 629, 1999). FORUM also protects the rights of students to peacefully protest while addressing the problem of shoutdowns and other disruptive activities.

Third, FORUM protects students' freedom of association. Universities are prohibited from denying a religious, political, or ideological student organization any benefit or privilege available to any other student organization based on the expression of the student organization. It expressly affirms that student groups may require its leaders or members to affirm and adhere to the organization's sincerely held beliefs, comply with the organization's standards of conduct, or further the organization's mission or purpose as defined by the student organization.

FORUM employs two important mechanisms to ensure compliance. First, it allows students to file a civil cause of action against university officials who violate the act. If a court finds a violation, it must award damages to the student of at least $5,000 and reimburse the students' costs and attorneys' fees. Second, FORUM creates public accountability by requiring universities to issue an annual report on the state of free speech on their campuses, including (1) any incidents of disruption of free expression on campus, and (2) whether the university has been sued for an alleged First Amendment violation.

CONCLUSION

The rise of our current culture of censorship and illiberality did not happen overnight. And we cannot change it overnight. It will take perseverance and dedication to the cause. However, we can achieve the goal if we stay true to our principles and dedicated to the task. Because freedom is worth fighting for.

In the words of the great Ronald Reagan:

Freedom is never more than one generation away from extinction. We didn't pass it to our children in the bloodstream. It must be fought for, protected, and handed on for them to do the same, or one day we will spend our sunset years telling our children and our children's children what it was once like in the United States where men were free.

Getting Right on Crime

by Marc Levin and Vikrant Reddy

Throughout the years, one of America's most challenging areas of public policy has been addressing crime and maintaining public safety. As conservatives, we know that law and order in the United States historically has meant locking up criminals for long periods of time in an effort to deter criminal activity. After many decades of dramatically increased rates of incarceration in the United States, we have come to realize today that crime rates can often be reduced with programs supporting less frequent incarceration. The criminal justice reform movement began in the states and has gained tremendous traction with the goal of maintaining public safety—most importantly—but also by providing smarter pathways to rehabilitation and the hope of redemption for nonviolent offenders. Marc Levin leads all criminal justice reform efforts at the Texas Public Policy Foundation (TPPF) and created the Right on Crime initiative, which has been instrumental in implementing conservative reforms nationwide. Vikrant Reddy is the senior research fellow at the Charles Koch Institute, where he focuses on criminal justice reform. Marc and Vikrant worked together for many years at TPPF, where they rolled out the Right on Crime initiative nationally. They are widely recognized as two of the leading experts in the field of criminal justice reform. It was my great privilege to work with Marc and Vikrant and invite them to regularly testify before the Texas House of Representatives Corrections Committee when I served as chairman. Many of our state's reforms have spread across the country, ultimately culminating nationally with President Trump signing into law the First Step Act in December 2018. Criminal justice reform is a critical subject that more Americans need to learn more about, and I'm most grateful to Marc and Vikrant for accepting my invitation to participate in *Making Government Work*.

—Tan Parker

INTRODUCTION

What conservative would say the value of any government program corresponds to its size, scope, and cost? Yet for too long, many on the right took this carte blanche approach to criminal justice, and particularly to prisons. In addition to exponentially more people in prison and on community supervision, we have also seen growth in the number and breadth of criminal laws, with more than 4,500 federal crimes now in statute and as many as 300,000 federal regulations (created by unelected agency officials) carrying criminal penalties.

As conservatives, we know public safety is a core function of government and that when someone breaks the law, there must be accountability. However, fulfilling this mandate does not require leaving core principles aside, including skepticism of state power, insistence on government accountability, and observance of due process and other constitutional rights. The imperatives to recognize the possibility of redemption and to treat people with dignity, even those who have made serious mistakes, also follow from the credo of many people of faith in public life, that all people are created in the image of God.

While the high cost of incarceration has brought many policy-makers to the table, the main course must be enhancing public safety, keeping families together, promoting redemption, and reintegrating people into the workforce. With the aging of our society and frequent shortages in many trades, such as welding and plumbing, the latter motivation for reform has taken on greater significance.

Fortunately, developments over the last fifteen years in Texas and across the nation have demonstrated that criminal justice reforms consistent with conservative principles can advance both public safety and second chances. The First Step Act, passed by a conservative House and Senate and signed by President Trump in December 2018, was both a culmination of successful state reforms that informed the positions of many members of Congress and the president, and a reflection of how the nation, and particularly conservatives, have embraced a new approach to this issue—an approach that balances justice with mercy.

EVOLUTION OF CONSERVATIVE THOUGHT
ON CRIMINAL JUSTICE

To be fair, the impulse on the right to expand government to keep us safe did not come from nowhere. Instead, it was a reaction to 1960s leftism typified by attitudes such as "if it feels good, do it" and the related movement to eschew personal responsibility and instead pin crime primarily on social causes.[1]

Unfortunately, the pendulum swung further than necessary, leading to a five-fold increase in incarceration from the early 1970s to the mid-2000s. This unprecedented rise in incarceration may have contributed to about a quarter of the decline in crime,[2] but other factors such as improved policing and demographic changes accounted for more of the decline. The increase in incarceration also, however, resulted in many nonviolent and low-risk people being unnecessarily swept into jails and prisons. Still others were kept behind bars long after their risk to public safety had dissipated.

Importantly, the historic growth in state and federal prisoners, from about 200,000 prisoners in 1975 to about 1.5 million in 2005, was a bipartisan undertaking. Among the liberal Democrat leaders who presided over massive prison-building campaigns were Governors Mario Cuomo, Michael Dukakis, and Ann Richards. At the federal level, the 1994 crime bill won overwhelming passage, led by then senator Joe Biden, with support coming even from socialist Bernie Sanders, then Vermont's sole congressman.

There are many reasons why the pendulum swung too far, including initially rising crime rates that created public pressure and the crack cocaine epidemic that contributed to harsh realities in many inner-city areas and public demands for action. However, crime peaked in 1991, and dramatic increases in incarceration nevertheless continued for more than a decade after that point.[3]

The extraordinarily high rate of imprisonment in the United States is a recent phenomenon. Before 1980, the highest imprisonment rate in U.S. history was recorded in 1939, when 137 out of every 100,000 Americans were behind bars.[4] The dramatic rise in the U.S. incarceration rate is particularly observable in the federal prison system. In the thirty-year period from 1950 to 1980, federal prisons gained about 6,600 inmates.[5] In the thirty-year period from 1980 to 2010, they gained over 185,500 inmates.[6] This difference cannot be explained by the fact that America's population grew more quickly from 1980 to 2010 than it did from 1950 to 1980, for the population did not grow 186 percent more quickly. The simple explanation is that in the 1980s and 1990s, America became far more punitive; more individuals were prosecuted, and sentence lengths grew longer.[7]

According to the International Centre for Prison Studies, the United States has the highest incarceration rate in the democratic world.[8] About 2.2 million Americans, or 716 out of every 100,000, are serving time behind bars.[9] This figure is striking when compared to figures from other nations of the Anglo-American common law tradition. In England and Wales, only 148 out of every 100,000 persons are incarcerated.[10] Australia was founded as a prison colony, yet it incarcerates only 130 out of every 100,000 persons.[11] Canada incarcerates 118 out of every 100,000.[12] This is to say nothing of democratic nations outside the Anglo-American common law tradition. France incarcerates 98 out of every 100,000 persons,[13] and Japan incarcerates 51 out of every 100,000 persons.[14]

In an important book on incarceration, *The Collapse of American Criminal Justice*, Professor William Stuntz noted that, with the important exception of homicide, American crime rates are fairly comparable to crime rates in Western democracies such as Great Britain and France.[15] Therefore, he wrote, "If Western nations' crime rates determine the size of their prison populations, the United States should imprison roughly the same share of its citizenry as do the British or the French . . . not four to seven times as many."[16]

Policies focused on incarceration emerged as a response to skyrocketing crime rates in the 1960s.[17] Urban crime had become an epidemic, and nowhere was this more true than in New York City.[18] In fact, in 1963, New York City was known as the "murder capital of the nation."[19] A *Time* magazine cover with the caption "The Rotting of the Big Apple" portrayed the muggings, robberies, and murders for which New York—and Times Square in particular—had become notorious.[20] Small business owner Bernie Goetz became a vigilante icon when he shot four teenage subway muggers in 1985.[21] Movies like *Serpico, Taxi Driver,* and *Dirty Harry* depicted crime-ridden urban environments in which chaos ruled.[22]

Just as it is unclear what caused the crime decline of recent years, it is unclear what caused the crime spike that began in the 1960s. Sociologist James Q. Wilson, however, suggested that abrupt changes in cultural norms may have been responsible for the spike:

> At the deepest level, many . . . shifts, taken together, suggest that crime in the United States is falling [in the early 2000s]—even through the greatest economic downturn since the Great Depression—because of a big improvement in the culture. The cultural argument may strike some as vague, but writers have relied on it in the past to explain both the Great Depression's fall in crime and the explosion of crime during the sixties. In the first period, on this view, people took self-control seriously;

in the second, self-expression—at society's cost—became more prevalent. It is a plausible case.[23]

Psychologist Steven Pinker made a similar argument in his book, *The Better Angels of Our Nature*:

> The leveling of hierarchies and the harsh scrutiny of the power structure [in the 1960s] were unstoppable and in many ways desirable. But one of the side effects was to undermine the prestige of aristocratic and bourgeois lifestyles that had, over the course of several centuries, become less violent than those of the working class and underclass. Instead of values trickling down from the court, they bubbled up from the street, a process that was later called "proletarianization" and "defining deviancy down."[24]

From the 1960s through the early 1990s, crime arguably became the most important domestic issue in American politics. Liberal politicians and thinkers, however, were widely viewed as disengaged from the issue.[25] Many liberals of the period argued that because crime resulted from social pathologies, such as poverty and racism, crime would continue until the social pathologies were eradicated. In other words, public policy directed at reducing crime would have no effect.[26] In some extreme cases, liberals appeared not only to ignore crime but to celebrate it. Novelist Norman Mailer, for example, suggested that graffiti was not vandalism; it was artistic commentary on architecture.[27]

In response, conservatives insisted on incapacitation through more incarceration.[28] Conservative policy prescriptions of this period emphasized the importance of building new prison facilities, increasing sentence lengths, and enacting truth-in-sentencing laws that limited parole.[29] Richard Nixon made the fight against crime a cornerstone of his 1968 and 1972 presidential election victories.[30] George H. W. Bush capitalized on the issue in his 1988 U.S. presidential campaign by launching his

"Willie Horton" campaign, with a commercial criticizing Governor Michael Dukakis's support for weekend passes for convicted felons.[31] The commercial featured Willie Horton, a Massachusetts felon sentenced to life in prison who committed armed robbery and rape while on a weekend furlough.[32] In the minds of many Americans, Governor Dukakis's hapless response to the salacious advertisement became emblematic of the liberal attitude toward crime in this chaotic era.[33]

As the conservative position became increasingly attractive to a population that felt terrorized by crime, liberal political candidates began to adopt it too.[34] Soon, increasing incarceration became a bipartisan cause.[35] In Texas, the liberal icon Ann Richards showed as much enthusiasm for prison-building as did the Republican governor who served before her, Bill Clements, and the Republican governor who served after her, George W. Bush.[36] It is also worth noting that the first person to attempt to use the Willie Horton story against Michael Dukakis was not George H. W. Bush in the 1988 presidential election but Al Gore in the 1988 Democratic primary.[37] James Q. Wilson sardonically joked that "there are no more liberals on the crime and law-and-order issue . . . because they've all been mugged."[38]

Next, as any public-choice theorist could have predicted, labor unions interested in maximizing the number of jobs for corrections officers joined in the cause.[39] The most notorious mandatory sentencing law in the country, California's "three strikes" law, was supported by California's powerful prison guard unions.[40] A federal "three strikes" law was also supported by President Bill Clinton.[41] Unsurprisingly, California's prisons were filled to almost double design capacity in 2011 when, in *Brown v. Plata*, the U.S. Supreme Court upheld a federal district court's order that California release prisoners to alleviate unconstitutional overcrowding.[42] Some analysts suggest that private prison companies, which benefited financially from increased incarceration, played a role in the dramatic expansion of U.S. prisons.[43] There is no evidence, however, that the popularity of private prison companies reflected their political influence rather than their affordability. On the other hand, it is clear that unionized labor forces in state facilities contributed to the popularity of the private companies.[44]

The modern American politician who best combined fiscal conservatism, libertarianism, and social conservatism in an effective political platform was Ronald Reagan. As a politician, Reagan took pride in the reductions in incarceration that occurred on his watch. In his second gubernatorial inaugural address in California, for example, he boasted that California's "rehabilitation policies and improved parole system are attracting nationwide attention. Fewer parolees are being returned to prison than at any time in our history and our prison population is lower than at any time since 1963."[45] In 1971, he even attempted, albeit unsuccessfully, to close the infamous San Quentin Prison located north of San Francisco.[46]

In the scholarly world, a 1974 study by sociologist Robert Martinson cast a long shadow over the corrections field for a few decades, as it suggested rehabilitation programs were largely ineffective and therefore incarceration was the best option. This led to such developments in the late 1980s as the removal of rehabilitation as a stated purpose of federal sentencing.[47] While there is still a need to carefully evaluate rehabilitative interventions, in recent years we have gained more knowledge about what works, as well as relatively new strategies such as drug courts and medication-assisted treatment. Notably, counseling programs have gravitated from those in the 1960s that often emphasized building self-esteem, which some suggested simply made for confident criminals, to evidence-based techniques such as cognitive behavioral therapy and motivational interviewing that balance encouragement with requiring the person to come to terms with the attitudes and behaviors, such as lack of impulse control and empathy, that led to their wrongdoing.

The most important thing to realize about the period from the mid-1970s to mid-2000s, when incarceration spiked five-fold, is that historical exigencies—not ideological principles—were the driving forces behind public policy decisions on criminal justice. There is nothing inherent in traditional conservative thinking that favors incarceration over other methods of handling offenders. In fact, because incarceration is expensive and restricts individual liberty, conservative ideology would favor focusing the use of prolonged periods of incarceration on violent and habitual offenders whose incapacitation is necessary for public safety. Moreover, personal responsibility is at the heart of conservative ideology, and prisoners receiving "three hots and a cot" while not paying restitution, child support, and other obligations hardly maximizes personal responsibility.

As we have seen, by the turn of the twenty-first century (if not before), we reached a point where the pendulum had swung too far on this issue. Traditional fiscal conservatives were concerned about escalating costs and long-term sustainability.[48] Libertarians were uncomfortable with the scope of punitive government and its intrusion into the lives of citizens.[49] Social conservatives saw a link between the mass incarceration of young men and the breakdown of American families, especially lower-income families.[50]

Perhaps most importantly, rather than emerging rehabilitated, plenty of offenders exit prison in a worsened social condition.[51] It is sometimes ruefully joked that prisons are finishing schools for criminality.[52] Even offenders who emerge from incarceration relatively stable find it difficult to reenter society because a criminal record is a significant barrier to employment.[53] There are a number of states in which recidivism rates hover above 50 percent.[54] Reflecting on this figure, former Speaker of the House Newt Gingrich and former Virginia attorney general Mark Earley have asked whether Americans would accept other government programs with such a high failure rate: "If two-thirds of public school students dropped out, or two-thirds of all bridges built collapsed within three years, would citizens tolerate it?"[55]

TURNING THE TIDE IN TEXAS

If conservatives needed a convincing case study to take a new approach to criminal justice, Texas was the logical choice. The state has long prided itself on a generally no-nonsense mentality, and furthermore, as the national leader in executions, its reputation as a "tough on crime" state was unassailable. In 2005, the Texas Public Policy Foundation (TPPF), the state's most prominent free-market think tank, launched its criminal justice program. TPPF immediately began researching the existing system to identify the reasons why the state's jails and prisons continued to expand, along with costs to taxpayers, and to develop alternative approaches that could deliver more public safety for every dollar spent. It quickly became apparent that this meant reversing course from the last few decades in which the growing prison system had crowded out investments in probation, treatment, and problem-solving courts, the very interventions needed to safely divert people from prison.

The transformation in Texas began in 2005 and took off in 2007 when the Legislative Budget Board estimated that it would cost taxpayers $2 billion to build 17,000 prison beds to accommodate the expected increase in Texas's prison population by 2012.[56] Although Texas had a budget surplus that year, its legislators refused to spend the money; instead, they allocated a much smaller amount, approximately $241 million, to expanding community-based supervision options such as probation, problem-solving courts, and evidence-based drug treatment.[57]

In the Texas Senate, Democrat John Whitmire, a Houston lawyer, rallied support for community-based supervision.[58] In the House of Representatives, Republican Jerry Madden, a West Point alumnus and Dallas businessman, led the charge.[59] Madden believed, and Whitmire agreed, that costly prison space ought to be reserved for the people "we're afraid of, not the ones we're mad at."[60] The Republican-majority legislature followed Madden and Whitmire's lead, as did Republican governor Rick Perry, who signed the reform legislation into law.[61] Indeed, at the beginning of the 2007 legislative session, Governor Perry had explicitly announced his support for corrections reform in his State of the State Address: "[T]here are thousands of non-violent offenders in the system whose future we cannot ignore. Let's focus more resources on rehabilitating those offenders so we can ultimately spend less money locking them up again."[62]

The Texas transformation was anchored in two key budgetary changes and administrative improvements in parole supervision. Improvements to parole and probation are critical to any serious criminal justice reform effort because nearly half of all prison intakes nationally are of people revoked from these forms of supervision.

The first change came in 2005, when Texas lawmakers appropriated $55 million for probation departments that agreed to target 10 percent fewer prison revocations and to implement graduated sanctions—issuing swift, sure, and commensurate sanctions for rules violations such as missing meetings. These sanctions included increased reporting requirements, extended terms, electronic monitoring, weekends in jail, and other measures that held offenders accountable for rules violations. The alternative strategy—the strategy that had been tried unsuccessfully for years—was to let the violations pile up seemingly endlessly before suddenly revoking the probationer to prison. Most of the funding went toward reducing caseloads from nearly 150 probationers per officer in major urban areas to 110 probationers per officer and to expanding specialized, much smaller caseloads for subgroups such as mentally ill probationers. This facilitated closer supervision and the consistent application of such sanctions, leading to a decline in revocations in the participating probation departments, thus saving taxpayers $119 million.[63] Notably, the drop in probation revocations has been almost entirely attributable to the probation departments,[64] which account for the majority of the state's population, that opted to participate in this incentive funding program that began in 2005, thereby agreeing to implement graduated sanctions.

The second strategy was the appropriation of $241 million in 2007 for a package of prison alternatives that included more intermediate sanctions and substance abuse treatment beds, drug courts, and substance abuse and mental illness treatment slots. This package was passed in lieu of spending billions to build and operate 17,332 new prison beds that the Legislative Budget Board had otherwise projected to be needed by 2012. The search for alternatives came in response to statements from judges, prosecutors, and corrections officials, bolstered by data, indicating that an increasing number of low-level, nonviolent offenders were being directly sentenced, or revoked from probation, to prison. The criminal justice officials presenting these statements noted that they did not feel public safety was being advanced by putting these individuals behind bars, but because of long waiting lists for the alternative sanctions, they had no other option.

Furthermore, inmates who were granted parole often remained in prison because of waiting lists for halfway houses and programs they had to complete before release, another backlog addressed by the 2007 package. All told, the 2008–2009 budget added 4,000 new probation and parole treatment beds, 500 in-prison treatment beds, 1,200 halfway house beds, 1,500 mental health pre-trial diversion beds, and 3,000 outpatient drug treatment slots.

These programs were sustained through subsequent budget cycles. Indeed, the number of problem-solving courts in Texas has gone from 35 in 2007 to 143 today. Moreover, in 2011 lawmakers passed legislation allowing state jail felons (the lowest-level felony offenders—those convicted of nonviolent offenses such as theft or possession of less than a gram of drugs) to earn up to 20 percent off of their time behind bars by completing programs and demonstrating exemplary conduct. In 2015, Texas adjusted its property offense thresholds to account for decades of inflation. So, for example, whereas the line between misdemeanor theft and felony theft had previously been $500, it was now set at $2,500. Skeptics worried that property crimes would increase as a result, but property crimes—and in fact total crimes—continued to decline.

Finally, Texas's gains in parole effectiveness have not only been attributed to the expansion of in-prison treatment programs that better prepare parolees to succeed, but also to administrative changes in parole supervision since 2005, which have included the adoption of instant drug testing and referrals to treatment as well as the enhanced use of graduated sanctions.[65] Another important change may have been the restoration of parole chaplains, who provide counseling and refer interested parolees to religious congregations eager to receive them.

Since 2005, Texas's FBI index crime rate has plummeted 42.6 percent,[66] a sharper drop than the national decline,[67] while its incarceration rate has dropped more than a quarter. Not only has Texas avoided building more than 17,000 new prison beds that in January 2007 were projected to be necessary, but the state has also shuttered eight prisons, with another two set to close in 2020.

Additionally, success rates of people on probation and parole have increased. In FY 2005, there were a total of 24,030 probation revocations, including 13,455 technical revocations and 10,575 for new offenses.[68] In FY 2018, there were 21,435 revocations, including 11,204 for technical violations and 10,231 for new offenses.[69] Parole data shows even sharper declines in failure rates. In FY 2005, there were 10,609 parole revocations, including 7,573 for a new conviction. In FY 2018, there were 6,179 revocations, including 4,783 for a new conviction.[70]

Furthermore, with more nonviolent offenders going into alternatives such as drug courts, Texas's remaining 105 prisons now focus more on incarcerating violent offenders. In FY 2005, only 16.8 percent of Texas prison admissions were for violent offenses,[71] whereas in FY 2018 that figure was 24.69 percent.[72]

TEXAS'S SUCCESS GOES NATIONAL

This record of success in Texas attracted national attention and laid the groundwork for the 2010 launch of our Right on Crime initiative at the Texas Public Policy Foundation. Partnering with Prison Fellowship and later the American Conservative Union, we began with a statement of principles signed by conservative luminaries such as former House Speaker Newt Gingrich, former U.S. attorney general Edwin Meese, former U.S. attorney and current Arkansas governor Asa Hutchinson, and former Virginia attorney general and current White House official Ken Cuccinelli.[73]

Not only has Texas continued its reforms, but between 2007 and 2018 some thirty-five states adopted "justice reinvestment" approaches that redirected money that otherwise would have gone to prison to alternatives, such as problem-solving courts, mental health treatment, and the use of evidence-based practices in community supervision.[74] For example, Georgia, under Republican governor Nathan Deal, passed a sweeping corrections reform bill in 2012.[75] Like Governor Perry, Governor Deal showed a particular interest in rehabilitating drug offenders and framed his arguments in terms of reducing government waste: "If we fail to treat the addict's drug addiction, we haven't taken the first step in breaking the cycle of crime . . . a cycle that destroys lives and wastes taxpayer resources."[76]

Every state is different, but common policies that have been effective in multiple states include earned time for those who complete programs, performance-incentive funding for corrections systems, swift and certain sanctions for criminal offenders, and the introduction of problem-solving courts that are distinct from traditional adversarial courts.

ALTERNATIVES TO PRISON FOR PROVIDING ACCOUNTABILITY:

A. PERFORMANCE-INCENTIVE FUNDING

Perhaps the most significant criminal justice reform idea to receive conservative backing is performance-incentive funding. This idea is based on the conservative insight that prison funding should be based partly on performance, not just population numbers. Performance can be measured in several ways, including whether treatment is obtained, whether education is received, and whether restitution is paid to victims. Above all, though, performance should be measured in terms of recidivism. A prison that can boast a low recidivism rate among its inmates is doing something right by helping to preserve public safety and is the kind of facility toward which we ought to direct public resources.

Arizona presents a good example of how performance-incentive funding works in practice. In 2008, Arizona instituted a policy that allows a portion of state savings from reduced incarceration to be redirected to counties that pursue policies that divert offenders from prison, reduce recidivism, and ensure victim restitution.[77] The policy helps recipient counties implement proven strategies for better supervising probationers.[78] Between 2008 and 2010, the number of Arizona probationers revoked to prison fell 28 percent, and the number of new felony convictions among Arizona probationers fell 31 percent.[79]

In Ohio, a similar program, Reasonable and Equitable Community and Local Alternatives to the Incarceration of Minors (RECLAIM), has also been tremendously successful.[80] The recidivism rate for moderate-risk youth in Ohio state lockups fell from 54 percent to 22 percent under RECLAIM.[81] For conservatives who have long emphasized that incentives affect the behavior of both individuals and systems, the success of these policies is unsurprising.

B. SWIFT AND CERTAIN SANCTIONS AND POSITIVE INCENTIVES

Another especially promising practice consistent with traditional conservative insight is HOPE, a probation program that is organized around the principles that swiftness and certainty are more important for effective punishment than is severity. HOPE, which stands for Hawaii's Opportunity Probation with Enforcement, began in Honolulu under the leadership of Justice Steven Alm, a former federal prosecutor, and it is beginning to spread across the mainland.[82]

HOPE is partly rooted in the thinking of the eighteenth-century Italian jurist Cesare Beccaria, who is widely regarded as the first criminologist in Western civilization.[83] Beccaria's 1764 treatise, *On Crimes and Punishments*, was read by many of the Founding Fathers of the United States.[84] Beccaria made several arguments in the treatise that many of the Founding Fathers made and that many modern conservatives continue to make, such as the importance of a right to bear arms.[85]

One of Beccaria's most important arguments was that offenders respond better to immediate and certain punishments than they do to random but severe punishments.[86] Using this insight, the HOPE court applies swift, sure, and commensurate sanctions to promote compliance with drug tests and probation terms. For example, a judge might inform a drug offender that, rather than be prosecuted, the offender will be assigned a color.[87] The offender will have to call the court daily to learn whether his color has been chosen.[88] If his color has been selected, the offender will have to report to the court and pass a drug test.[89] If he fails to pass the drug test, he will have to spend an immediate stint in jail.[90] At first, the stint will be short—often just a weekend. However, if the offender continues to test positive for drugs, his sanctions will become more onerous.[91] In this way, lengthy and protracted processes are reduced in favor of immediate sanctions.[92]

HOPE has decreased substance abuse and probation failures in Hawaii by more than two-thirds.[93] Moreover, HOPE has helped Hawaii identify which of its drug offenders most desperately require treatment. The 20 to 30 percent of HOPE probationers who cannot pass the random drug tests apparently suffer from serious chemical addictions.[94] Hawaii can prioritize its limited treatment resources to help these offenders.

HOPE works because swift and certain sanctions are more effective responses to criminal behavior than are severe sanctions applied only after multiple probation violations. This was Beccaria's key insight, but an eighteenth-century treatise is hardly necessary to explain why this works. A parent disciplining a child understands the concept even more intuitively than does a professor.

The replications of the HOPE program in other states have achieved varying degrees of success[95] that seem to be tied to the level of collaboration among courts, law enforcement, and probation, but the concept of swift, certain, and commensurate sanctions combined with positive incentives has been incorporated into the operations of many probation and parole agencies.[96] Indeed, a 2019 Pew report described how states such as North Carolina and Missouri have used graduated sanctions and positive incentives to reduce revocations from community supervision while improving public safety.[97]

Conversely, positive incentives for completing programs and exemplary conduct, whether on community supervision or within correctional institutions, have been found to be even more effective at shaping behavior than sanctions. Among the incentives in a grid used by the Harris County (Houston, Texas) adult probation department are double time toward the completion of the probation term, reduced reporting, bus tokens, and written commendations.[98] Expanding state laws that allow for record sealing in many cases upon successful competition of probation also provide a compelling incentive. Given research showing that only 5 percent of eligible individuals apply for record sealing and the requirement in many states that a separate civil action be brought, states should ensure sealing can occur automatically through a Clean Slate law, as in Utah and Pennsylvania, or, in cases where it is discretionary, through an order by the criminal court judge upon discharging the person from probation. As always, a combination of both "carrots and sticks"—not just one or the other—makes for ideal public policy.

C. PROBLEM-SOLVING COURTS

Accountability courts, sometimes called problem-solving courts, are specialized courts in which a judge oversees the supervision and treatment of the offender.[99]

A mental health court, for example, provides certain offenders with appropriate treatment rather than traditional sentences.[100] Importantly, mental health courts are relatively inexpensive to create in comparison to their potential benefits. "Merrill Rotter, the Medical Director and Co-Project Director of the Bronx Mental Health Court, notes that some of the programs 'cost as little as $150,000 while others cost multiples of that.'"[101]

A RAND Corporation study of mental health courts found that "the leveling off of mental health treatment costs and the dramatic drop in jail costs yielded a large cost savings."[102] In the Washoe County Mental Health Court in Reno, Nevada, for instance, the 2007 class of 106 graduates went from 5,011 jail days one year prior to mental health court to 230 jail days one year after, a 95 percent reduction.[103] The overall cost to the system was reduced from $566,243 prior to the institution of mental health courts to $25,290 one year after.[104]

In Santa Barbara County in California, an evaluation of mental health courts found that the participants averaged fewer "jail days after treatment than before, with a greater reduction in jail days noted for participants in the [mental health court] than for participants in [the traditional judicial system]."[105] The *American Journal of Psychiatry* reported that "participation in the mental health court program was associated with longer time without any new criminal charges or new charges for violent crimes."[106]

Drug courts are another proven alternative to incarceration. They combine intensive judicial oversight of low-level drug offenders with mandatory drug testing and escalating sanctions to achieve results.[107] According to the National Association of Drug Court Professionals, the average recidivism rate for offenders who complete a drug court program is between 4 percent and 29 percent.[108] In contrast, the average recidivism rate for offenders who do not participate in a drug court program is a whopping 48 percent.[109] Similarly, the Government Accountability Office reports that re-arrest rates among drug court participants are 10 to 30 percentage points below re-arrest rates in a comparison group.[110]

Drug courts can be exceptionally cost-effective. Some drug courts cost less than $3,000 per participant, and their estimated net savings, taking into account both reduced corrections spending and avoided victims costs, average $11,000 per participant.[111]

Mental health courts and drug courts—along with other problem-solving courts such as veterans' courts[112] and prostitution diversion courts[113]—exist because the standard adversarial litigation model is not always optimal. The model may be effective for civil justice matters and for determining whether a defendant is guilty of a crime, but it has limited efficacy in addressing criminality.

ENSURING DUE PROCESS

Arriving at the right response to criminal activity cannot solely be about maximizing results, as it is also important to ensure the process is fair and safeguards individual rights protected by the U.S. and state constitutions. This is also critical to avoiding wrongful convictions. Important policy advances in recent years include strengthening indigent defense and adopting measures to reduce the risk of wrongful convictions and ensure those that occurred in the past are rectified.

Once again, Texas has emerged as a national leader, enacting legislation over the last decade such as the Michael Morton Act, which requires that exculpatory evidence in the possession of the prosecutor be promptly shared with the defense;[114] improving standards for forensic science; and adopting legislation requiring that when information from jailhouse informants is used any benefit offered to the informant is disclosed to the defense and the court.

When it comes to indigent defense, Texas implemented a pilot program providing for client choice among qualified defense attorneys in Comal County, which, according to an independent evaluation, enhanced client satisfaction and the percentage of cases taken to trial.[115] Similarly, a managed assigned counsel program in Lubbock County has improved representation by shifting the assignment role from judges to an independent county office, creating greater fidelity in the lawyer-client relationship.[116] Another model of indigent defense reform, holistic defense, relies on nonprofit entities, such as the Bronx Defenders, that not only represent clients in court but also connect them with resources such as treatment. A 2019 RAND Corporation report found that holistic defense led to fewer defendants being convicted and imprisoned without endangering public safety.[117] Criminal cases often take months to resolve, but during that interim holistic defense programs can connect defendants with urgently needed resources that will reduce the risk of recidivism. Many jurisdictions use more than one model of indigent defense, including a public defender's office, appointed counsel, and nonprofit providers. This approach of letting many flowers bloom provides flexibility, such as in cases involving multiple defendants where a conflict is created, but it also allows for results to be compared. The Texas Public Policy Foundation and Right on Crime issued a paper providing numerous solutions for ensuring timely provision of counsel.

REINING IN THE SCOPE OF CRIMINAL LAW AND CIVIL ASSET FORFEITURE

Another public policy challenge is reining in the number and scope of criminal offenses, addressing what the Heritage Foundation and others have referred to as overcriminalization.[118] Criminal laws have become so voluminous and broad that it is impossible for an ordinary citizen to know whether their ordinary business and recreational activities are actually crimes. Even worse, it has been estimated that there are hundreds of thousands of federal regulations that carry criminal penalties, as well as countless such state regulations.[119] In these cases, unelected bureaucrats have created crimes that are even more inscrutable to the average person. Moreover, many of the thousands of federal, state, and local offenses do not require a mens rea. Also known as a guilty state of mind or criminal intent, this is one of the oldest canons of our legal system. Mens rea, the criminal state of mind, along with actus reus, the criminal action, combine to make up the two essential parts of a crime, as opposed to a mere accident. A properly drafted criminal statute will always ensure that a mens rea (either negligent, reckless, knowingly, or willfully) is specified. In recent years, however, this bedrock due process protection has been all too often ignored by legislators.

Fortunately, there are solutions.[120] First, states and the federal government can follow Texas in creating a commission to review existing crimes and identify those that should be repealed, narrowed, or modified to include a culpable mental state. Second, since many criminal laws are silent on mens rea, some twenty states, and the American Legislative Exchange Council (ALEC) through its model legislation, have adopted a default mens rea provision that applies in such cases.[121] State legislatures and Congress should also remove the authority of agencies to create new offenses, or specify that a regulation can only carry criminal penalties if expressly authorized by the legislation that provided the authority for the agency to adopt the regulation.

Perhaps no aspect of criminal justice reform has come more naturally to the conservative movement than paring back civil asset forfeiture. After all, the taking of a person's property without a conviction is an affront not just to due process but also to cherished private property rights. Moreover, in most jurisdictions, the proceeds of forfeitures are split between police and prosecutors. Though there have been examples of such funds being misused on extravagances like margarita machines and a prosecutor's trip to Hawaii (both examples that come, we are embarrassed to admit, from our home state of Texas),[122] most of these funds do go to important purposes. This is hardly a justification, however. Private property cannot be taken by government agents merely because "it's for a good cause." There are processes for going before the representatives of the people to seek funding for important things such as police vehicles, uniforms, weapons, and so on. No part of government—not even law enforcement—is exempt from this kind of accountability to taxpayers.

Fortunately, in the last decade some fifteen states have significantly curbed, if not abolished, civil asset forfeiture. Several points are important in this regard. First, seizure is different from forfeiture, as the latter refers to title passing to the government. Even abolishing civil forfeiture and thereby requiring a conviction, or criminal forfeiture, does not restrict initial seizure. Second, model legislation from ALEC that states may adopt (and adapt)[123] makes appropriate exceptions where a conviction would not be required, such as with unclaimed property or where the individual or entity, like a foreign gang, cannot be prosecuted for jurisdictional reasons. Short of requiring a conviction, other reforms can limit the worst aspects of civil asset forfeiture. For example, the burden of proof that the property was connected with criminal activity can at least be raised from the civil "preponderance of the evidence" standard to a higher "clear and convincing evidence" standard. Additionally, if the underlying criminal case is dropped, the burden should be on the government to initiate a civil proceeding within a specified time frame or else the property should be automatically returned to the owner.

CONCLUSION

Prisons are, of course, a necessary part of any society. In *The Scarlet Letter*, Nathaniel Hawthorne observed that "[t]he founders of a new colony, whatever Utopia of human virtue and happiness they might originally project, have invariably recognized it among their earliest practical necessities to allot a portion of the virgin soil . . . as the site of a prison."[124]

Conflict and crime will always exist. So too will prisons.

Prisons, however, are not a source of pride. Conservative philosophy recognizes that an unusually high number of prison cells indicates a society with too much crime, too much punishment, or both. This understanding was set aside in the 1960s to deal with perceived emergency conditions, but the bottom line is that prisons evince nothing about conservative political and legal principles. First principles in conservative thought counsel skepticism of all government programs—including prisons. Our devotion to limited government and individual liberty also require that we zealously safeguard due process and rein in the scope of criminal law so that it is not a tool to grow government and punish conduct that is unwitting and which the average person would not even know was against the law.

All conservatives—fiscal conservatives, libertarians, and social conservatives—are now returning to first principles in criminal justice. Conservatives know that there are methods other than incarceration for holding offenders accountable. These methods can improve public safety and increase the likelihood that victims receive restitution. Utilizing these methods does not mean making excuses for criminal behavior; it simply means "thinking outside the cell" when it comes to ensuring public safety and accountability, while doing the least collateral damage possible.

The Texas Model of Tort Reform

by Dick Trabulsi

"The most important thing that generated 38 percent of our jobs [in Texas] is tort reform. . . ."

—Richard Fisher, president and CEO, Federal Reserve Bank of Dallas

Tort reform is one of the most crucial policies that states can implement to foster economic vibrancy. Restricting frivolous litigation has been an instrumental component in the tremendous success Texas has enjoyed economically for over twenty years. Dick Trabulsi has been leading this effort in Texas from the beginning as the co-founder and chairman of Texans for Lawsuit Reform. No one in the country has a better understanding of the importance of tort reform or a deeper understanding of how it can be achieved in every state. His is a critical story that more Americans need to read and learn from. I'm most grateful that he accepted my invitation to participate in *Making Government Work*.
—Tan Parker

The Texas economy was struggling in the 1980s and early 1990s. The energy business was in recession, hundreds of banks had closed, and hundreds of thousands of Texans had lost their jobs—but the lawsuit business was booming.

It was crucial for the state to restart its market-based engine and once again make itself a fruitful place to do business. But since Texas was ground zero in the national litigation explosion, there was no way the Texas economy could prosper without first making its civil justice system fair and predictable so that disputes could be decided on their merits and in an impartial manner.

This is the story of how Texas moved from "the Wild West of Litigation" twenty-five years ago to the model of tort reform emulated by other states.

In 1994, when we formed Texans for Lawsuit Reform (TLR), such a reversal of fortunes in the Texas civil justice system seemed impossible. The personal injury lawyers who benefited from the status quo were fantastically wealthy and extraordinarily politically connected. They effectively controlled the legislature and many Texas courtrooms, and they were fanatically committed to fending off any serious legal reform.

At the outset, we in TLR were met with warnings, skepticism, and even derision. But we went to work to prove the skeptics wrong. We developed specific and comprehensive reform proposals, ranging from venue, to proportionate responsibility, to punitive damages, to overly broad consumer protection statutes and more.

As we traveled our vast state, we encountered real-life stories of lawsuit abuse. We built a network of citizen-leaders in our communities, industries, and professions. We retained highly skilled lawyers, who understood the legal issues as well as the problems and abuses, to craft commonsense solutions. Volunteer speakers spanned out to every part of Texas. We built a team of specialists for public and legislative advocacy. We established a political action committee to engage in state elections, because you can't produce good public policy if you don't elect good people to public office.

In many states today, plaintiff lawyers who are wealthy from personal injury and mass tort lawsuits continue to control the legislature and judiciary. The citizens of those states are paying a tort tax through increased costs for goods and services and decreased economic activity—just as Texas experienced twenty-five years ago. Those seeking to reform the civil justice systems in litigious states will benefit from knowing how Texas reformed its statutes and overturned discredited judicial precedents to establish laws and procedures to give all parties—plaintiffs and defendants alike—the opportunity for a fair resolution of disputes.

TEXAS TORT REFORM UNDER GOVERNOR GEORGE W. BUSH

Tort reform was jump-started when then gubernatorial candidate George W. Bush made TLR's tort reform package a central plank in his 1994 campaign platform, which led to numerous important civil justice reforms being enacted in the first legislative session following Bush's election. Recently, former U.S. president Bush reflected on the transformative 1995 legislative session in his first term as Texas governor:

> Lawsuit abuse was a crushing burden on our economy. Employers wouldn't move to or expand in Texas because of our unfair legal system, and doctors were fleeing the state because of our outrageous medical liability costs. As a result, families were suffering, whether as a result of limited job opportunities, the ever-present tort tax or simply not having access to health care.
>
> Lawsuit reform was a pillar of my campaign for governor in 1994. And in my first legislative session as governor, I was proud to sign eight major tort reform bills into law. Those reforms were the first steps in transforming Texas' economy into the powerhouse it is today—the running start into the next 25 years of work to make Texas a better place for families and businesses.

Prior to the 1995 reforms, judge-shopping was rampant in Texas. An injury that occurred in a traffic accident in Dallas might have been tried in a court in McAllen because the plaintiff's lawyer thought he could get a better outcome from a judge and jury in the Rio Grande Valley. Also, Texas was often the forum of choice for out-of-state and even out-of-country plaintiffs. To address those issues, the following reforms were enacted, which have effectively curbed court-shopping:

- Texas abolished highly permissive venue rules and established venue in the county in which the injury occurred, in which an individual defendant resides, or in which a corporate defendant has its principal place of business.
- When a trial court allows multiple plaintiffs to join a case (thereby impacting venue), a party may seek an immediate appeal to determine whether particular plaintiffs properly belong in the case to prevent a plaintiff's lawyer from naming a party solely to establish venue in a particular county.
- To discourage out-of-state and foreign forum shopping into Texas, state *forum non conveniens* rules were modified to give Texas trial judges broad discretion to dismiss cases that should be pursued in another state or country.

Historically, few guidelines were in place governing the awarding of punitive damages, which often resulted in wildly excessive awards. For example, in the famous *Pennzoil vs. Texaco* case, punitive damages of billions of dollars were awarded against Texaco, forcing it into bankruptcy proceedings. So in 1995 and subsequent years, Texas reformed punitive damages in these ways:

- Limited punitive damages to the greater of: (1) $200,000 or (2) two times economic damages plus the amount awarded for non-economic damages up to $750,000
- Enhanced the burden of proof, permitting an award of punitive damages only upon a showing of "clear and convincing evidence," rather than a mere "preponderance of the evidence"

- Subsequent legislation requires a unanimous 12–0 jury verdict for the award of punitive damages, rather than a 10–2 verdict allowed for an award of actual damages

TEXAS TORT REFORM UNDER GOVERNOR RICK PERRY

While the initial eight reforms passed in 1995 were critically important, several of them needed supplemental legislation, which was accomplished in the Omnibus Tort Reform Bill of 2003 when Rick Perry was governor. This bill also addressed other meaningful issues, especially in medical liability litigation. Texas doctors, nurses, and hospitals were being sued at such a rate that doctors were fleeing the state, emergency clinics were closing, and many parts of our state could not attract needed specialists, such as obstetricians and orthopedic surgeons. To address the health care crisis caused by abusive lawsuits, these reforms were enacted during Governor Perry's administration:

- Legislation enhanced an existing requirement that a plaintiff seeking to sue a health care provider file an affidavit by a qualified physician explaining how the target defendant violated the applicable standard of care, and an appellate remedy was added to the law to allow immediate review of the necessity for and quality of any such affidavit.
- Caps on non-economic damages (such as pain and suffering) were imposed on all health care liability cases: a $250,000 per-claimant cap applies to all doctors and nurses, and a separate $250,000 cap applies to each health care institution on a per-defendant basis, subject to a $500,000 aggregate non-economic damages cap in favor of all health care institutions in the case.

- An existing limitation on personal liability of government employees was extended to other health care professionals in government hospitals as well as to nonprofit operators of city hospitals or hospitals operated by special hospital districts.
- Additional liability limits were applied to nonprofit hospitals or systems that provide (1) charity care and community benefits in an amount equal to at least 8 percent of the net patient revenue of the hospital or system and (2) at least 40 percent of the charity care provided in the county in which the hospital or system is located.

As a result of these reforms, access to health care in Texas was greatly enhanced. The number of health care lawsuits fell, and insurance premiums for health care providers were reduced dramatically. Since then, physicians have flocked to the state, providing services to high-risk patients and in underserved areas.

Governor Perry also addressed a major abuse by a cadre of plaintiff lawyers in lawsuits alleging asbestos-caused diseases, which constitute the United States' longest-running mass tort litigation. Because Texas has a strong industrial sector and had permissive statutes governing venue, proportionate responsibility, and punitive damages, Texas was the preferred forum for asbestos lawsuits. Tens of thousands of plaintiffs filed asbestos lawsuits in Texas's courts in the 1980s and 1990s. In many of the cases, the plaintiff showed no sign of an asbestos-caused health problem. Then, in the early 2000s, the asbestos lawsuit model was applied to alleged silica-related injuries. Again, most of the plaintiffs showed no sign of a silica-caused disease.

To prevent the abusive lawyer tactics that bankrupted hundreds of American companies and extorted outrageous settlements from solvent companies, Texas enacted these reforms, among others:

- All asbestos and silica cases filed in a Texas state court, whether pending at the time the new law passed or filed afterward, are transferred to two multidistrict litigation courts (MDLs) for coordinated and efficient pretrial proceedings;
- Whether the case was pending at the time the new law passed or filed afterward, trial courts were compelled to apply strict, medically sound diagnostic criteria to determine if the plaintiff truly had a disease caused by exposure to asbestos or silica, to address the problem of lawyers filing lawsuits on behalf of unimpaired people;
- Cases filed by unimpaired plaintiffs that were pending when the new law was passed were moved to "inactive dockets" managed by the MDL courts, where they remain pending until each plaintiff establishes an actual impairment under the statutory medical criteria. New asbestos or silica cases that do not satisfy the statutory medical criteria are dismissed;
- Prohibited "bundling" of hundreds of plaintiffs' asbestos or silica cases into a single lawsuit, a tool regularly used before 2005 by personal injury trial lawyers to extort settlements on behalf of unimpaired plaintiffs; and
- Extended the statute of limitations to allow an asbestos or silica lawsuit to be filed within two years after diagnosis of actual impairment, no matter when the harmful exposure happened. Even a person whose case was previously dismissed because of a failure to fulfill the medical criteria can take advantage of the almost unlimited statute of limitations. As a result, access to the courts for anyone suffering from an asbestos- or silica-caused disease is virtually guaranteed, and cases in which the plaintiff met the medical criteria, thus showing a real disease, were accelerated to trial, giving true asbestos victims their day in court.

In addition, legislation enacted in 2015 (under Governor Greg Abbott) requires asbestos claimants to pursue their claims against special bankruptcy trusts that have funds available to compensate claimants for asbestos-related illnesses before a lawsuit against solvent defendants can move forward in a Texas court. The claimants must file all possible trust claims—and disclose the claims and money received from them—to the defendants in the lawsuit.

Claims filed with the asbestos trusts move quickly, meaning that filing these claims at the outset has no effect on the timing of the lawsuit. Yet, by requiring plaintiffs to proceed in an organized fashion and to make the required disclosures to defendants, asbestos lawyers are prevented from making inconsistent allegations in the bankruptcy trust process and the lawsuit. In other words, the lawyer cannot allege that companies X, Y, and Z are solely responsible for a claimant's injury in the bankruptcy process, and then say that companies A, B, and C are solely responsible for the same injury in the lawsuit.

Texas's asbestos and silica reform bills have been fair, reasonable, and effective. They are the model for the nation. The filing of thousands of lawsuits on behalf of unimpaired claimants was eliminated. "Gaming" the bankruptcy trust system was circumscribed. Yet any Texan actually suffering from an asbestos- or silica-caused disease is benefited by a generous statute of limitations and enjoys priority treatment in Texas courts.

Former U.S. energy secretary Rick Perry recently commented on the significant impact of tort reform in his long tenure as Texas governor:

> It's not often that a governor remains in office long enough to see ideas go from conception to reality to resounding long-term success. But as the longest serving governor in Texas history, I watched the fruits of our efforts to create the strongest economy in the nation not only bloom, but thrive, over my 14 years in the Governor's Office. Each principled, common-sense lawsuit reform and each election cycle built on the

progress of the last, eventually catapulting Texas to the top in terms of job creation, corporate relocation, quality of life and consistent rankings as the best place in our nation to do business.

But in addition to the big reforms were countless smaller, but meaningful, measures that improved the way Texas' courts work and shut down certain unscrupulous lawyers who exploited Texas statutes to manufacture unnecessary and baseless lawsuits.

TEXAS TORT REFORM UNDER GOVERNOR GREG ABBOTT

In 2019, the legislature passed numerous important bills that were signed into law by Governor Greg Abbott, including important legislation concerning attorney television advertising and the hiring of contingent fee lawyers by local governments.

Advertisements for legal services often are designed to frighten consumers into becoming new clients. Numerous cases have been documented of people who have quit taking prescription medication due to scare-tactic lawyer advertising, to the detriment of their health. The Texas legislature amended the statutes governing attorneys' television advertising in the following ways:

- Attorneys' television advertising is required to disclose that it is an *advertisement* and identify the sponsor of the ad.
- The advertisement is required to disclose the name of the attorney who will represent a person who responds to the advertisement. Selection of an attorney is the most important decision a person makes when considering a civil lawsuit. But because the advertisements are often sponsored by solicitors who do not actually provide legal services in Texas, the prospective client is farmed out to an unknown lawyer.

- If the purpose of the advertisement is to generate clients to sue for prescription drug–related injury, the ad must state that the viewer should *not* discontinue use of a prescription medicine without first consulting a physician.
- Either the attorney general or a local prosecutor can force the removal of a noncompliant advertisement from the airwaves, but if the advertising was pre-approved by the State Bar of Texas, the lawyer must be given notice and an opportunity to voluntarily withdraw the advertisement.

State and local governments in Texas, and throughout the country, are heavily recruited by attorneys to file lawsuits against private companies for all kinds of cases, from lawsuits against general contractors for alleged defects in construction to lawsuits against pharmaceutical companies for harm caused by opioids. The attorneys promise "no-cost" representation unless the case is successful. Often, these are arrangements involving taxpayer resources without public input or consideration of the payment terms. Because taxpayers populate the juries, these lawsuits are uniquely challenging to defendants.

- Since 1999 (under Governor Bush), Texas has prohibited the award of contingent legal fees for representing the state based on a percentage of the recovery. This law was a direct result of the state paying over $3 billion to four law firms in tobacco litigation for relatively little work. Only hourly-based contingent fee arrangements are permitted, though the attorney may be paid a premium fee of up to four times a reasonable hourly rate to account for the litigation risk.
- In 2007 (under Governor Perry), the legislature expanded the law to reach many local governments, providing that they too could not enter into a percentage-based

contingent fee contract with a private attorney without complying with the same restrictions applicable to the state. These local governments' contracts became subject to review and approval by the comptroller of public accounts. But the law was often ignored because the comptroller had no enforcement authority, and it did not reach all local governments.

- In 2019, the legislature shifted the contract-review process from the comptroller to the attorney general, gave the AG power to enforce the law, and made restrictions on contingent-fee contracting applicable to *all* local governments. In addition, local governments must use a public and transparent process to retain contingent-fee lawyers.

Governor Abbott, who has also served Texas as a state district judge, Texas supreme court justice, and state attorney general, recently observed:

The Texas of today is very different than the Texas of 25 years ago. . . . Back then, our civil justice system was an embarrassment—ridiculed around the world—and the subject of an infamous *60 Minutes* episode titled "Justice for Sale." Jackpot justice took a heavy toll on the rule of law and our economy.

Today we are known as a leader in creating and maintaining a fair, efficient and accessible legal system for all Texans. And today, our economy leads the nation largely because of it. When I speak to CEOs around the country, our strong state legal system and the common-sense lawsuit reforms we have enacted over the past 25 years are hailed as critical assets that set Texas apart from other states. We have come a long way from the days when Texas' legal system was a burden on economic growth and was forcing our doctors to flee the state because they could not afford the medical liability premiums caused by excessive litigation.

THE FUTURE OF TEXAS TORT REFORM

In addition to the reforms discussed above, Texas has enacted many other meaningful tort reforms, including those related to class actions, proportionate responsibility, appeal bonds, multi-district litigation, and product liability. But our civil justice system is not a static or closed universe, and entrepreneurial lawyers are constantly finding new ways to exploit statutes for self-gain.

For example, all Texas seaports are man-made, typically at the mouths of rivers emptying into the Gulf, and must be regularly dredged to function. The companies that dredge Texas's seaports experienced an unusual increase in personal injury lawsuits by former employees, filed in notoriously litigious southern Texas counties far from the location of the accidents. In many instances, the employee had never reported an injury before filing a lawsuit. Dredging companies were leaving Texas because of their exposure to abusive litigation, putting all of Texas's ports at risk of shutting down.

To address the lawyer-driven spike in litigation, Texas reformed its venue statute that allowed lawsuits to be pursued in the county in which the plaintiff resides. "Injuries on the seas" now must be pursued in the county in which the injury occurred or the county in which the defendant has its principal place of business in Texas. As a result of this reform, abusive dredging lawsuits evaporated.

The above example of lawyer abuse is just one of many that requires constant vigilance on the part of those who want a fair and balanced civil justice system. Recently, we have had to address lawyer-driven litigation abuses in weather-related damage claims against insurers. This lawsuit abuse disrupted certain insurance markets in Texas to the extent that property owners could not get insurance or had to pay significantly higher premiums.

We know that the future will not be different from the past—we will forever be responding to new challenges to the fair administration of justice in Texas, as will other states.

THE NEED FOR A STABLE, IMPARTIAL, AND HIGHLY QUALIFIED JUDICIARY

Good laws and sound legal precedent are instruments for the rule of law only in the hands of honest, fair, and competent judges. Judges who are ignorant of the law, dishonest, or biased in its application are unswayed by statute or precedent.

Today, the biggest challenge in the Texas justice system is the manner in which we select judges. Texas is one of only six states that chooses all of its judges by partisan elections, from the state supreme court to justices of the peace. There are almost two thousand elected judicial positions in Texas. In major urban counties, there may be more than seventy judicial positions on the ballot.

There is no way voters can make informed decisions in these judicial races. And in our urban counties, judicial races are subject to see-saw partisan sweeps, with only Republican judicial candidates winning in some years and only Democrat candidates winning in others, completely regardless of the qualifications of candidates of either party.

Nathan Hecht, chief justice of the Texas supreme court, observed:

No method of judicial selection is perfect. . . . Still, partisan election is among the very worst methods of judicial selection. Voters understandably want accountability, and they should have it, but knowing almost nothing about judicial candidates, they end up throwing out very good judges who happen to be on the wrong side of races higher on the ballot.

Partisan sweeps—they have gone both ways over the years, and whichever way they went, I protested—partisan sweeps are demoralizing to judges, disruptive to the legal system and degrading to the administration of justice. Even worse, when partisan politics is the driving force, and the political climate is as harsh as ours has become, judicial elections make judges more political, and judicial independence is the casualty. Make no mistake: a judicial selection system that continues to sow the political wind will reap the whirlwind.

And there is this: judges in Texas are forced to be politicians in seeking election to what decidedly should not be political offices. They are not representatives of the people in the same way as elected officials of the legislative and executive branches. A state legislator is to represent the interests and views of his or her constituents, consistent with the legislator's conscience. A judge is to apply the law objectively, knowledgeably, and fairly. Therefore, impartiality, integrity, and experience in the law should be the deciding factors in whether a person serves as a judge.

A judicial selection system should make qualifications, not personal political views or partisan affiliation, the paramount factor in choosing and retaining judges.

Over the past twenty-five years, Texas has led the way in reforming our civil justice laws to be fair and balanced. We must now lead the way in establishing a stable, fair, highly qualified, and professional judiciary, keeping it accountable to the people but removed from shifting political winds.

CONCLUSION

Texas tort reform has succeeded due to the many servant-leaders in our citizenry and in elected offices who have had the wisdom, courage, and determination to transform the Texas civil justice system from one that was feared and derided to one that is the nationwide model for reform. U.S. Supreme Court justice Louis Brandeis once admonished: "If we desire respect for the law, we must first make the law respectable." Since our law is a living instrument, making and keeping the law respectable is a forever project.

The U.S. Infrastructure Crisis: Enough Talk Already

by Bob Hellman

Without a healthy and robust infrastructure in this nation that supports our daily lives, where would we be as a society? Investing in our nation's infrastructure is one of the most important decisions that government, at both the state and federal level, can make. Today, much of our rapidly aging and deteriorating infrastructure across the United States is badly in need of very significant investment in order to keep America moving and our citizens safe. Most states in the country and the federal government itself have not done a good enough job of making infrastructure investments a priority. There are a few exceptions—including Texas, which has led the way by streamlining regulatory processes and putting in place creative solutions to address the infrastructure challenge. To fix the situation, unnecessary regulations at the federal and state levels must be removed in order to allow more flexibility in finding solutions. Additionally, tax policy needs to change, and we must find new ways to attract private capital. Bob Hellman is the managing director and CEO of American Infrastructure Funds, and for more than thirty years he has been one of the most highly regarded experts in the nation on both the infrastructure challenges facing America today and the solutions we must deploy. I am very thankful for his participation in *Making Government Work* and for his clear and specific guidance that provides an extremely insightful road map for policy-makers and all Americans.

—Tan Parker

By almost any measurable standard, the infrastructure of the United States is in a condition that would prompt the word "crisis" or, by those who would criticize most strongly, "third-world-country" level. The American Society of Civil Engineers (the folks who are responsible for building and maintaining infrastructure) recently rated the general nationwide condition of U.S. infrastructure as a D+. This is the type of grade that typically induces a crisis-type response, and yet debates about solving the problem at a federal or even state level often devolve into who is to blame as opposed to finding meaningful solutions.

In this chapter, we will examine the breadth and location of our nation's infrastructure crisis and some of the reasons behind the lack of action. We will also outline a strategy that could be applied today that will lead our nation out of these circumstances.

In many parts of the United States, the infrastructure—the assets and operations we all rely upon in our daily lives—is well past its useful life and in desperate need of replacement. Its present condition endangers lives, the environment, and economic progress and prosperity. Our water delivery systems are providing tainted water to our citizens; our wastewater treatment plants regularly discharge sewage into our public waterways; our roads and bridges are often plagued by disrepair and capacity constraints creating delays, lost hours, and increased air pollution; and our national electrical grid is experiencing a growing rate of capacity failure. These are just a few of the areas of infrastructure upon which we all rely that are in desperate need of upgrade or replacement.

It is often said that 80 percent of infrastructure is local—owned and/or controlled by local governments. Yet as bridges threaten collapse, capacity congestion and potholes create delays, grids overload, and schools and libraries fall apart, there seems to be little awareness on the part of some local leaders as to the breadth of financial options available for them to solve these problems. Therefore, after years of depending almost entirely upon federal and state funding coupled with heavy reliance on municipal bond financing, most local governments operate at or near a cash deficit and lack the financial resources to fix these assets.

The task of replacing or upgrading our nation's infrastructure will require trillions of dollars—the latest estimate is over $3 trillion per year for the foreseeable future—dollars that are either unavailable from government sources or do not exist.

At the federal level, our leaders universally applaud the need for infrastructure spending at the State of the Union address, but don't agree on the best way to accomplish the goal. Many want increased transportation funding to implement social engineering objectives that have little to do with infrastructure and more to do with climate change and increasing regulatory mandates. A $1 trillion program (which would barely scratch the surface of the problem nationwide) seems perpetually out of reach. State resources are equally tapped out. Many states are faced with federal mandates that require significant investments in health care, education, and other entitlements, leaving spending on these crucial assets very limited. Local communities have often gone well beyond their spending limits in accessing municipal bonds (capital markets have made it easy), leaving them also financially strapped and unable to fund their basic infrastructure needs. As a result, our infrastructure in the U.S. requires a recapitalization plan—one involving a "down round" (as the venture capital industry calls it), that is, new funds from third parties coming in to finance these needs.

FROM PROBLEM TO SOLUTION

Thankfully, we are not stuck with these circumstances. Solutions do exist! Private capital providers have developed viable means of financing the replacement and upgrade of infrastructure in partnership with local governments around the world that maximize the strengths of each stakeholder in these structures. And while private capital may not be a solution for all types of infrastructure needs, it can relieve major portions of funding shortfalls, leaving government funding to attack remaining needs less suited for private financing while protecting the taxpayer.

Because private capital will require a financial return, there must be a funding model (that is, generation of cash flow) to facilitate the access to this funding source. With this filter in mind, infrastructure falls into three categories when it comes to financing:

- Assets for which there is a clear funding model, such as charging a toll on a new bridge or a fee for wastewater disposal services
- Assets for which there is no clear funding model, such as river locks, where the fee required to fund replacement locks would be far too large to be feasible for river users such as barges and pleasure boats
- Assets where innovation can result in unique funding solutions and thus create access to private capital

Utilizing this framework, scarce government resources must be focused on the second of these asset types, as many of them are in the most desperate shape. It has been reported, for example, that the failure of a single lock on the Ohio River would raise the cost of a loaf of bread in the upper Midwest materially, given the volume of wheat transported on our nation's rivers and canals.

The world of infrastructure investing has developed quite well outside of the United States, and a number of models exist that guide investors as to the types of assets that could fit into the first and third of the aforementioned asset types. However, for private capital to be accessible for U.S. needs, we must also address several fundamental issues unique to the United States that have limited private capital deployment to date.

TAX BARRIERS TO CAPITAL FLOWS

FIRPTA (Foreign Investment in Real Property Tax) and ECI (Effectively Connected Income) are just two of several taxes that were created to address different issues but which remain on our books today as barriers to capital flowing into U.S. infrastructure. Millions are spent creating structures to avoid these taxes, when a simple exemption from these taxes for new capital invested in new U.S. infrastructure would work much more efficiently and ultimately better serve U.S. interests.

LEGACY REGULATORY BARRIERS THAT SLOW OR IMPEDE PROGRESS

A number of legacy regulations exist that slow the application of private capital to replacing aging infrastructure. As an example, if funds were supplied by the Federal Highway Administration (FHWA) for the construction of a road or bridge, private capital cannot acquire and replace the legacy asset, even if it is out of service, without negotiating a reimbursement with the FHWA. The FHWA does not have the funding to replace these broken assets, yet this regulation (which I am sure was well-intentioned at its writing), tends to limit the interest level of private financing entities from stepping forward.

LACK OF ABILITY FOR FEDERAL ASSETS TO ACCESS PRIVATE CAPITAL

In the same vein of the burden of legacy regulations, current laws provide that tolls collected on federal highways can only be used for the maintenance and repair of those assets. Yet the capital required to replace major portions of our national interstate network does not exist in current government coffers. Tolling would be a viable solution if tolls could provide a return on the private capital utilized to finance the asset replacement, but this solution is not available under current federal laws.

REGULATORY APPROVAL OF PERMITS FOR REPLACEMENT INFRASTRUCTURE

The Trump administration has appropriately cheered the halving of approval time for infrastructure projects from an average of four years to two. While recognizing that in many cases modest design, environmental, or technology changes may be involved, if a project is simply replacing broken assets on a substantially like-for-like basis, and if all funding is lined up from private sources, why does the approval process take longer than just sixty days? President Trump would probably agree, given his unique understanding of the building industry and the inherent benefits that would accrue from more rapid regulatory approval. This would eliminate a material backlog in environmental, U.S. Army Corps, and Coast Guard regulatory offices across the country, allowing personnel to then focus on projects that are more complex than the simple replacement of assets.

GOVERNMENT-MANDATED MULTI-BID REQUIREMENTS FOR ALL PHASES OF CONTRACTING

Currently, proposals for the replacement of critical infrastructure require extensive (and expensive!) bidding processes for all phases of work. The challenge is that these types of Request for Proposal (RFP) processes have devolved into multi-year, consultant-driven processes costing millions of dollars in professional fees. Often, but not in all cases, they have resulted in a "one decision" approach (that is, one decision is made for the entire replacement process), which has required participants to team together on capital, design and engineering, and contracting and has often impeded true competition on the critical expense items, such as steel and cement. An alternative, which is currently being tested in Australia, would be to allow unsolicited proposals to be proffered by developers while the city, if it is interested in such a proposal, organizes an expedited "alternative bidder" approach—all designed to seek a developer who has full capital funding and would team with the city to find the lowest-cost sources of the most expensive elements of a project.

INABILITY OF ASSET OWNERS TO RECYCLE CAPITAL

One of the more innovative developments in infrastructure outside of the United States has been clearance provided by local governments to sell existing "brownfield" infrastructure assets in competitive auctions, with the express plan of utilizing sale proceeds purely for the financing of new infrastructure. Such a "government as developer" approach has been successful in Europe and Australia in creating funding for projects that might otherwise be difficult to fund up front.

POOR LOCAL ENGAGEMENT BY CAPITAL SOURCES

Not all challenges with getting private funding to replace broken U.S. infrastructure are the result of government regulation or inaction. Local communities understandably have a high degree of suspicion about the trustworthiness of private capital. As one mayor asked me, "How do I know you aren't a twenty-first-century version of a carpetbagger?" Local communities will often require weeks—if not months—of "getting to know" a private capital provider, as well as solid references from other communities in which the capital source has made similar investments. Infrastructure investments into U.S. opportunities require investors who are willing to show their commitments to local leaders and businesses.

LACK OF EFFORT TO ADDRESS EQUITY ISSUES

Models are being developed for the subsidizing of low-income housing, employer-provided toll transponders, the addition of managed lanes, and other programs to help address the important issue of equity so that new infrastructure can enhance and revitalize a community rather than create an excessive financial burden.

CONFUSION AS TO THE URGENCY OF SOLUTIONS AT LOCAL LEVELS

Inevitably, when local infrastructure assets reach a crisis level, a search for free money ensues. This, coupled with the tendency of some local leaders to defer decision-making, has caused the crisis we are in today. Federal and state leaders could greatly accelerate solutions by clearly communicating two things: first, they cannot provide funding for certain types of assets (those that can be privately funded); and, second, they will force the closure of failing assets (for example, bridges and wastewater plants) to induce action on the part of local leaders as necessary.

CONFUSION ON "HOW?" (THAT IS, "WHERE DO I START?")

In the waning weeks of 2019, an unusual set of parallel meetings occurred. Two conferences outside of the United States were filled with institutional investors focused on their desire to invest in infrastructure assets, with a strong desire expressed for United States–based opportunities. During that same week, over three hundred community leaders from across the United States were gathered in Washington, D.C., all focused on learning how their communities might access infrastructure funding to meet their critical needs. While there are clearly some communities and regions (for example, North Texas) within the United States that have successfully developed private-capital-led infrastructure solutions, most have not—and more education of our leaders is needed on this topic.

The bottom line is that the infrastructure problem in this country is not a money problem—there is plenty of capital to fund the rebuilding of our nation's infrastructure. It is a problem of:

- Unnecessary tax barriers to entry for worldwide capital sources
- A set of approval and permitting processes that induce unnecessary or excess uncertainty for capital providers

- False hope by some local communities that someone will provide "free" capital
- Confusion over how to access private funding
- Some state governments' prohibiting private investment and alternate funding methods

I have tried to provide a number of brief recommendations to address each of these issues. Some are admittedly aggressive. Some require an investment in time to educate local communities and leaders. None of these recommendations results in free money, but reducing tax cost and uncertainty will lower the cost of private capital. "Cheap" is not "free"—but it is far preferable to "not available."

CONCLUSION

Our nation's infrastructure is at the point of crisis. So, at the risk of being excessively prescriptive, I will summarize a series of actions that, if taken, I believe would dramatically change the pace of the rebuilding and replacing of these critical assets upon which we rely daily:

1. Eliminate FIRPTA, ECI, and capital gains taxes for new capital invested in replacing designated infrastructure assets, provided that this capital remains in place for at least five years following the completion of construction.

2. Eliminate federal regulations that require reimbursement of federal investments in infrastructure which were made more than twenty-five years ago, and when the government has acknowledged it does not have the funding to replace the depleted asset. Alternatively, allow long-term (for example, ninety-nine-year) lease agreements on federally funded assets in need of such replacement.

3. Similarly, eliminate federal regulations and limitations regarding the tolling of interstate highway assets. Increase the number of project types that qualify for nationwide permits for private capital funding.

4. Allow for unsolicited proposals for the funding of replacement of failing infrastructure assets at all levels of government and create a specific process with a required short timetable (that is, three months or less) in which governments are required to respond "yes" or "no" to such proposals.

5. Allow governments to contract for the private funding of replacement of critical infrastructure provided that open bidding occurs on the high-cost items somewhere during the process.

6. Eliminate restrictions on the sale of government assets, provided that 100 percent of the proceeds of such sales are re-deployed into the construction of replacement assets for failing state and local infrastructure.

7. Fund training seminars in conjunction with the United States Conference of Mayors (and similar organizations) for local leaders to learn about how to access, structure, and negotiate private capital for their community's infrastructure needs. Invite other entities and organizations that have successfully implemented CDAs, private capital projects, and design builds to share their knowledge. Develop a small (that is, fewer than ten people) office of experts who can answer questions of government leaders as they attempt to navigate such arrangements.

8. Provide local governments with information and preparation templates on critical infrastructure needs in their communities, and then hold a series of capital-access sessions across the United States in which government leaders meet and pitch infrastructure investors on their

community's funding needs. These events are held in a number of other industries—why not infrastructure?

9. Pursue federal legislation that mandates that states must evaluate every major-capital roadway improvement of more than $150 million for its viability for private investment. If a state fails to comply, the federal government can withhold highway funding, in the same way it enforced the seatbelt and speed limit laws.

Fortunately, we as Americans are not stuck in the world of D+ infrastructure. As Americans, we do not accept anything that is subpar. The United States is a very attractive place for private capital to invest. With clear property rights and a clear demand and need, capital sources are clamoring to invest in U.S. infrastructure.

And in a world awash in capital (where dollars compete with euros and yen to bid up the prices of brownfield assets), providing funds to create new (or replacement) infrastructure assets can be quite attractive for investors. While private capital may not be a solution for all types of infrastructure needs, it can relieve major portions of funding shortfalls, leaving government funding to attack remaining needs.

Let us make it easy to invest in our country's critical infrastructure needs. Solutions are readily available and actionable if we wish to access them.

The Conservative Path to Immigration and Border Security Reform

by James Jay Carafano

Perhaps no public policy topic in America today is surrounded by more misinformation and distortion than the importance of border security and of addressing illegal immigration. America is a nation founded upon the rule of law, and our laws must be upheld. Protecting the sovereignty and security of our country is essential for the survival of our republic. We can advocate for this while still recognizing that we are a nation of immigrants. Our nation was built upon those who came to this country lawfully and created the most prosperous and generous country the world has ever known. Our diversity as a nation is one of our greatest strengths, and as long as we stay focused on what unites us as a people, our future holds unlimited potential. James Carafano is one of America's most recognized and knowledgeable experts on national security and foreign policy. As such, no one has a better grasp of the importance of border security and the necessity of addressing illegal immigration. James is the vice president of the Kathryn and Shelby Cullom Davis Institute for National Security and Foreign Policy and is the E. W. Richardson Fellow at the Heritage Foundation. More Americans need to read his thoughts on these matters, and I'm most grateful he accepted my invitation to participate.

—Tan Parker

Since 9/11, Americans have been whipsawed by seemingly endless bickering over immigration and border security. But let's be honest. The Left would like to frame this as a debate about being for or against immigration. It is not. No one knows that better than America's conservatives. Immigrants have added much to the American community. That is a proud tradition that American conservatives would like to see continue. And that aspiration is widely shared by a vast majority of all Americans. Fighting for immigration and border security reforms that are in the best interests of all Americans is a cause worth fighting for. American conservatives should muster the strength for this fight.[1]

A FUTURE WITH A PAST

It is worth reviewing how we got here. The American vision of immigration was always encapsulated in the idealization of the "American dream." Immigrants travel to America with the hope of joining the American community, each generation building on the hard work of their forefathers—mastering English, gaining an education, embracing an American civic identity, establishing themselves as productive contributors to American society.

For more than two centuries, the United States has welcomed millions of people from every corner of the globe. During the Constitutional Convention of 1787, James Madison expressed his wish "to invite foreigners of merit and republican principles among us. . . . America was indebted to emigration for her settlement and prosperity." That open, welcoming attitude exists today, as evidenced by the fact that the United States lawfully admits more than a million foreigners per year—more than any other country.

No one can deny that this model has had its ups and downs. American attitudes toward immigration have never been fixed, impacted as they are by a complex web of socio-economic and political issues. The immigration system of 1924, for instance, banned immigration from Asia and limited immigration from Eastern Europe.

Yet Americans by and large remain aspirational in their hopes for keeping America an immigration nation. This aspiration has never been considered the province of the Right or the Left. It is just who we are.

Over decades, however, politics has transformed the nature of the debate. Arguably, this began in the 1960s under legislation advocated by the administration of President Lyndon Johnson that promoted the policy of "chain migration," or giving preference to the extended families of individuals already residing in the United States. As immigration to the United States began to come increasingly from Mexico, significant imbalances developed.

As the United States experienced slowing population growth, along with generally increasing per capita wealth, the trends in Latin America were the opposite. There, population growth accelerated even as the economies in those countries lagged, unable to deliver real wealth creation. This disparity fed a pattern of migration from south to north, with young unemployed Latin Americans looking for jobs in the United States because they could not find them at home.

Over time, the number of individuals illegally remaining in the U.S. began to grow—and it didn't stop. The situation remained unaddressed until the presidency of Ronald Reagan. In 1986, Reagan fashioned what he believed would be a workable compromise. The U.S. would grant amnesty to what it believed was a population of about one million living here illegally. In exchange, Congress would support ramped-up border security and strict enforcement of immigration laws and temporary worker programs to fill jobs that had been held by illegal immigrants.

Nothing in this solution worked out as planned. The U.S. granted asylum to about 3.5 million individuals, and many of those claims were likely fraudulent. Furthermore, none of the enforcement measures were fully implemented or proved adequate. Indeed, many people—both inside and outside the U.S.—saw granting amnesties as little more than an incentive for future illegal immigration.

The problem festered, exacerbated by the dramatic rise of criminal cartels in Latin America. The cartels emerged as multi-billion-dollar criminal enterprises that trafficked in guns, money, drugs, and people. Human smuggling became a profitable enterprise for the cartels, as well as a means to disrupt border security to make their other criminal ventures more lucrative. Crime increased not just in border communities, but throughout the U.S. It included a vast expansion in transnational gang activity. As a result, immigration and border security became an even more acute public safety problem, as well as an economic and immigration enforcement challenge.

By the turn of the century, the illegal population in the U.S. had swelled to over eleven million. The problem was only getting worse.

After 9/11, when concerns over border security became a front-page issue, President George W. Bush was determined to use concern over the issue to propose a sweeping solution to address border security and illegal immigration. As a native Texan, Bush was sympathetic to challenges faced on the border and the plight of illegal immigrants, who lived in the shadows without access to the American dream. He proposed a legislative fix comparable to Reagan's 1986 proposal, but it failed in Congress.

Reagan's attorney general Edwin Meese recalled that even Reagan later acknowledged his proposal had been a mistake. Amnesty was not the answer for solving the border security and illegal immigration problem.

Nevertheless, when Barack Obama became president, the same package was presented to Congress—and failed to win passage during his two terms in office. Obama had heavily courted the support of illegal immigrants "rights" activists during both of his presidential campaigns. To continue to ensure their support, he began a series of unilateral executive measures that pleased his base. But those measures undermined the effectiveness of immigration enforcement, including blocking the deportation of individuals who had illegally migrated to the U.S. as minors. If they registered under a program he established called Deferred Action for Childhood Arrivals (DACA), they could be granted permission to remain in the United States.

In the end, Obama embraced policies that would open and deepen the partisan divide between those on the left and right, both of whom struggled with how to solve what increasingly appeared to be an intractable problem.

When Donald Trump ran for president, he made securing the border and enforcing immigration laws his signature campaign issue. This was not merely a passion for the president; he knew this issue resonated with supporters. In addition, among the myriad challenges surrounding illegal immigration, two issues dominated—one economic and one cultural.

The recession of 2007 and the slow economic recovery during the Obama years exacerbated concerns over unemployment and slow wage growth. Immigration in general and illegal immigration in particular were seen by some as having a demonstrably negative impact on job creation and wage growth.

Those concerns were not without merit. In the economics literature, it is widely accepted that the overall economic impact of immigration is positive. Businesses tend to respond to increased immigration by investing in new capital (for example, by building additional factories), which suggests that immigration does not crowd out existing work. However, other research suggests that immigration may have a downward impact on per capita GDP.

In truth, it can be difficult to tease out the impact of immigration from all the other factors affecting the economy. Nevertheless, it is true that expanding the size of the economy does not necessarily mean that per capita incomes will increase. This is particularly true if immigration supplies a majority of low-skilled workers rather than high-skilled technical workers. Addressing such concerns requires sound immigration policies and pro-growth economic policies that will allow American workers and the American economy to prosper.

The second factor worrying the president's supporters was the apparent breakdown of the traditional instruments of assimilation—work, family, language, and education. Fifteen years ago, Ed Meese, who then was my colleague at the Heritage Foundation, observed that "more than any other nation in history, our country and its system of equal justice and economic freedom beckons not only the downtrodden and the persecuted—indeed all those 'yearning to breathe free'—but also those who seek opportunity and a better future for themselves and their posterity."[2] Those sentiments are as true today as they were then.

This attitude did not come into being all by itself; at all levels, governments and institutions played an active role in the Americanization process. The Founders knew that the new country would attract even more immigrants, so they believed in assimilating and educating them to instill the nation's philosophy into a new population, giving American democracy its "demos."

Over the past few decades, however, America has drifted away from assimilating immigrants. Elites in government, the culture, and academia have led a push toward multiculturalism, which emphasizes group differences. This transformation has taken place with little input from rank-and-file Americans, who overwhelmingly support assimilation.[3] This issue has become one that is increasingly worrisome to Americans. It was a concern that Trump tapped into during the 2016 election.

Once he became president, Trump pressed forward with an aggressive agenda to secure the border, including building a stronger wall along a portion of the border, aggressively enforcing immigration laws, and seeking to reform the laws governing legal migration.

The liberal response was to embrace an agenda diametrically opposed to Trump's. If Trump was for it, they were against it.

Even elements of the border and immigration debate that enjoyed bipartisan consensus fell away. For example, a bill was passed in 2006 to secure the border with a fence. The bill enjoyed bipartisan support. Now, the president's opposition uniformly and summarily rejects funding for a border wall.

Until recently, most on the left generally recognized the importance of detaining and deporting illegal immigrants, particularly those who have committed violent felonies. Now it is commonplace for progressive politicians to call for abolishing Immigration and Customs Enforcement (ICE), the agency responsible for enforcing immigration laws. Leading progressive candidates for president have called for a moratorium on deportations. Furthermore, they called for a vast expansion of rights and privileges for illegal immigrants—including publicly funded health care.

In addition, liberal politicians have led the effort to establish sanctuary cities, counties, and states that refuse to cooperate with federal officials enforcing immigration laws. Instead of cooperating with officials to ensure the removal and deportation of dangerous felons directly from detention, sanctuary localities ignore ICE's requests for detainers and release these criminals back into communities, where they have often committed additional felonies, including murder and rape.

Rather than look for compromise solutions or common ground, the Left has embraced the belief that enforcing immigration laws and border security is racist, immoral, ineffective, and unjust.

The U.S. has consistently admitted more than 1 million immigrants as lawful permanent residents each year for fifteen of the last eighteen years. Of that million, more than one-third have been admitted from Asian countries annually for at least the last three years. In addition, more than 100,000 were admitted annually from Africa and Central and South America for the last three years. Beyond the 1 million-plus permanent immigrants admitted each year, the U.S., on average, naturalized 720,000 new citizens annually for the past ten years, granted asylum or refugee status to more than 88,000 annually for the past ten years, and admitted 182 million temporary visitors for the past three years.

Yet the Left ignores this generosity (and diversity) and focuses solely on illegal immigration. This has involved well-known tactics of the Left—pick the target, freeze it, personalize it, and polarize it, as well as ridicule opponents. The Left demands that illegal immigrants be admitted into, and remain in, the U.S. It amplifies emotional stories of illegal immigrants, individual by individual. In addition, the Left uses ridicule by labeling anyone who argues against admitting illegal immigrants into the U.S. a racist.

The Left's tactics, however, cannot overcome Americans' fundamentally understood principle that there is a difference between legal and illegal immigration. Also, Americans don't like to be erroneously labeled racist, and they have grown tired of how this tactic is used to shut down debate. Without productive debate, immigration issues continue unresolved.

WHERE WE ARE

The partisan political voices have split into two irreconcilable camps—one focusing solely on enforcing the law, the other seemingly promoting policies that would lead to open borders.

Conservatives are not alone in their frustration with the current state of affairs. The vast majority of Americans certainly don't want our laws abolished. On the other hand, they have concerns they feel are not being adequately addressed. There are three main concerns.

First, Americans don't like a system that is unfair. They don't like the idea that some people get to jump the line to come here while those who patiently wait and obey the law are put at a disadvantage. They don't like the fact that legitimate refugees have to wait behind a sea of meritless asylum claims.

Second, Americans don't like bearing the fiscal burdens of illegal immigration. These burdens take myriad forms, from public charges, to local communities bearing the burdens of those unlawfully present on their education systems, to hospitals that have to provide services in their emergency rooms.

Third, Americans have real concerns about public safety. They fret about the violence caused by transnational criminal cartels. They don't want transnational gangs in their communities. They detest all the horrific activity associated with human trafficking, including sexual exploitation, kidnapping, extortion, rape, pedophilia, and murder. They also worry about what else could come across America's porous borders—including, perhaps, another wave of terrorist threats.

In addressing these concerns, conservatives contend they are not just championing an agenda for the Right. They are tackling issues that the vast majority of Americans want solved. They want America to be a successful immigration nation.

CONSERVATIVE SOLUTIONS

What do conservatives have to offer? A lot. Following conservative principles, our nation can deliver solutions that the vast majority of Americans would find not only reasonable, but desirable. What's more, most Americans would recognize that these ideas are rational, practical, and doable.

To remain true to the foundations established by the Constitution and to repair border security, enforcement, and immigration law, we must observe four principles that reflect conservative ideas and values. They are:

RESPECT THE CONSENT OF THE GOVERNED

There is no right to become a citizen or remain unlawfully present in the United States; there is no place in America for a policy of "open borders."

The United States is a sovereign nation. The very idea of sovereignty implies that each nation has the responsibility and obligation to determine its own conditions for immigration, naturalization, and citizenship.

Individuals who are not citizens do not have a right to American citizenship without the consent of the American people, as expressed through the laws of the United States. Through those laws, the people of the United States invite individuals from other countries, under certain conditions, to join them as residents and fellow citizens. Congress has the constitutional responsibility "[t]o establish an uniform Rule of Naturalization" that sets the conditions of immigration and citizenship and ensures the fairness and integrity of the legal process by which immigrants may enter the country legally and, in many cases, become American citizens.

PRESERVE PATRIOTIC ASSIMILATION

This is a nation in which immigrants of all nations become Americans, and it must remain so.

The United States has always welcomed immigrants who come to this country honestly, with their work ethic and appreciation of freedom, seeking the promises and opportunities of the American dream. The founding principles of this nation imply that an individual of any ethnic heritage or racial background can become an American.

However, those same principles also call for a successful immigration policy that is only possible by means of a deliberate and self-confident policy to assimilate immigrants and educate them about this country's political principles, history, institutions, and civic culture. This may be a nation of immigrants, but it is more accurate to say that this is a nation where immigrants are Americanized, sharing the benefits, responsibilities, and attachments of American citizenship. While this happens mostly through social interactions, private institutions of civil society, and public and private education, the federal government has a significant, albeit limited, role to play in ensuring the success of this crucial process.

Patriotic assimilation is the bond that allows America to be a nation of immigrants. Without it, America either ceases to be a nation with a distinct character, becoming instead a hodgepodge of groups, or it becomes a nation that can no longer welcome immigrants. It cannot be both a unified nation and a place that welcomes immigrants without patriotic assimilation.

DO NOT COMPROMISE NATIONAL SECURITY AND PUBLIC SAFETY

We must know who is entering the country and have resilient and effective means to screen against malicious threats and to remove people who break the law or are a danger to American citizens.

Every nation has the right, recognized by both international and domestic law, to secure its borders and ports of entry and thereby control the goods and persons coming into its territory. Americans have always been and remain a generous people, but that does not mitigate the duty imposed on the United States government to know who is entering, to set the terms and conditions of entry and exit, and to control that entry and exit through fair and just means.

This task is all the more important after the events of September 11, 2001. A disorganized and chaotic immigration system encourages the circumvention of immigration laws and is a clear invitation to those who wish to take advantage of our openness to harm this nation. Secure borders, especially in a time of terrorist threat, are crucial to American national security.

RESPECT THE RULE OF LAW

Those who enter illegally are violating the rule of law; the Law of Nations clause of the U.S. Constitution guarantees the power to control immigration.

Those who enter and remain in the country illegally are violating the law, and condoning or encouraging such violations causes a general disrespect for the law and encourages further illegal conduct. Forgiving the intentional violation of the law in one context because it serves policy objectives in another also undermines the rule of law. Amnesty is appropriate only when the law unintentionally causes great injustice or when particular cases serve the larger purposes of the law. Those who break immigration laws should not be rewarded with legal status or other benefits, but should instead be penalized on any road to citizenship.

No sovereign nation can exist without clearly delineating its borders and having the power to defend them. The Constitution clearly presumes this by granting Congress the authority, for example, to demarcate the nation's borders by adding new states to the Union. So too is the power granted to "repel Invasions." In addition, Article 4, Section 4, guarantees that the United States shall protect each state "against Invasion." If these powers are granted to Congress in order to protect the nation's sovereignty from foreign threats, it is inconceivable that Congress would not also possess the power to regulate foreign migration into the nation.

Without control of the nation's borders, American sovereignty would be effectively defined by foreigners and foreign nations.

These are the foundational conservative ideas that can serve as the bedrock of good policy.

THE WAY FORWARD

If there were easy answers to these problems, if we could depend on politicians in Washington to adopt principled practical solutions, and if politics were not trumping service to the people, then all these principles could easily be satisfied with good public policies. Those are not the conditions we face now. Nor are we likely to get good policies unless good conservatives take tough stands.

Fixing the problem requires some tough medicine. Amnesty is not the answer. We must stand strong against those who advocate open borders. Our borders must be secured—and yes, that means building more barriers (a wall, if you will) along our southern border. Individuals who are here illegally do not have a right to stay. Our laws have to be enforced. It is only fair to millions of Americans that we expect those who join our great nation to respect its laws and add to its wealth and welfare. We need to turn this clarion call into action.

A CONSERVATIVE REFORM AGENDA:
WE MUST IMPLEMENT EFFECTIVE BORDER SECURITY

We must insist Congress support border security measures paired with robust enforcement. These initiatives include such controversial but essential steps as building additional sections of the border "wall," expanding detention space, and (as required) the temporary and effective use of support from the Department of Defense.

The reality is that despite liberal opposition, the Trump administration has made great progress. To date, the signature act of resistance has been opposing funding border security. On December 21, 2018,

Congress started the longest government shutdown in U.S. history, in part over the refusal of the president's political opponents to fund the wall. Rather than throw up his hands, President Trump initiated a controversial program to divert other appropriations to repair and expand the wall along the U.S.–Mexico border. Efforts to block him failed in the courts. As a result, the administration now has the plan, money, resources, contracts, and land to put in place 450 miles of state-of-the-art border wall by the end of 2020.

The wall is going to happen whether the president's opponents like it or not. And the wall is going to have impact. When completed, it will cover the most heavily trafficked migrant routes across the border, making illegal border crossing significantly more difficult.

Indeed, obstacles are already having an impact. In addition to building more wall, the administration has adopted a number of measures to deter and discourage illegal immigration. For example, the Department of Homeland Security has tried to discourage abuse of asylum claims by requiring applications to be adjudicated in Mexico before migrants enter the U.S. Recently, the government sent five thousand individuals who had illegally crossed the border and applied for refugee status back to Mexico to await the processing of their claims. Of the five thousand, two—that's right, two—cases were determined to have merit. The vast majority were not real refugees. They accepted bus rides back to their home countries or simply left on their own and didn't bother to wait for their applications to be processed.

By cracking down on meritless claims, loopholes, and abuses, even without the cooperation of Congress, the administration is sending a strong message that the U.S. means business.

The president has also been winning in the courts, where high-profile cases are increasingly turning the administration's way. Recently, for example, a Supreme Court ruling allowed the Trump administration to enforce nationwide restrictions that would prevent most Central American immigrants from seeking asylum.

In short, the president has won round one in the fight against liberal opposition to border security. That victory, however, will soon prove to be hollow if our national leaders do not commit to sustained solutions.

DEAL WITH ILLEGAL IMMIGRATION AND UNLAWFUL PRESENCE

Amnesty must not be granted. Amnesty undermines the rule of law and encourages more unlawful migration.

If America suddenly awards legal status to immigrants unlawfully in the United States, it will be treating them better than it treats immigrants abroad who have followed America's immigration procedures and patiently awaited their opportunity to get a visa authorizing them to come to the United States. Such action—as past amnesties have proved—will also spur more immigrants to enter or remain unlawfully in the United States, in the confident expectation that Congress will repeat the process. The government should pursue a wide range of approaches to a wide variety of immigration issues, but in all events it should exclude amnesty for immigrants unlawfully in the United States.

IMPROVE IMMIGRATION ENFORCEMENT

Instead of throwing out the rule of law, we must make the existing system work. We should increase funding for immigration court judges, prosecutors, and associated staff. The U.S. immigration adjudication and court system is falling further and further behind. More immigration judges, prosecutors, and staff to assist in immigration proceedings, as well as more U.S. Citizenship and Immigration Services asylum officers, are essential to enforcing U.S. immigration laws in a timely and effective manner.

With the right assets in place, the administration can fairly, effectively, and humanely deal with those here unlawfully, reducing that population without a sweeping amnesty in a manner that serves the best interests of all Americans.

There are four appropriate tools for dealing with illegal immigration that are already on the books. They are humane, adaptable, and practical. They are deportation and removal, voluntary departure, temporary relief from deportation, and cancellation of removal. By segmenting illegal immigrants and using the right tools for the right groups, the administration can proactively address the challenge of illegal immigrants without a comprehensive bill or a general amnesty.

ESTABLISH A MERIT-BASED IMMIGRATION SYSTEM

Congress should modify the family preference system and move to a new merit-based system of visas. This shift from family-based to merit-based immigration would prioritize economically and fiscally beneficial immigration and better serve the national interest.

Such a system should be designed in a way that recognizes that the market is the best and most objective way to identify those who will benefit the economy. This starts with requiring immigrants to have an offer of employment or financial means of self-support before entering the country. The government would not be picking winners and losers among industries, job categories, or immigrants. The offer of employment is an objective market signal. If there are more requests for green cards than are available, Congress could consider a limited points system that would place emphasis on the market. Another approach would be to implement an auction system, in which employers would pay for the permits of the immigrant labor they need.

Congress should allow immediate family to remain uncapped while restricting the definition of immediate family to one's spouse and minor children. Congress should cut all or almost all of the current family preferences for extended family, thus ending chain migration. U.S. citizens could continue to sponsor their parents, but only for a renewable temporary visa that would not make them eligible for any welfare benefits and would require the citizens to provide proof of health insurance and financial support of their parents. It is worth noting that these extended family members may have other legal avenues for immigrating to the U.S.

ENCOURAGE PATRIOTIC ASSIMILATION

Those who wish to see immigration continue must see to it that the whole edifice of victimhood, oppressor–oppressed, compensatory justice, racial preferences, coercive diversity, and so on is dismantled. This is a large undertaking, but if America is to continue to take in immigrants—and we will—policy-makers must be ready to overhaul policies that do not blend well with immigration.

Congress must put an end to measures that coerce immigrants and their American children and grandchildren into pan-ethnic identity traps. We must stop categorizing them as victims with protected status and start expecting them to participate in all aspects of society. Immigrants came to be Americans, not to join synthetic nations within the nation.

The executive branch should stop dividing society into groups by rescinding the 1977 OMB directive and its 1997 revision that divide the population into "Hispanics," "Asians," and so on, and the courts should finally declare racial preferences in admissions and government contracts to be unconstitutional.

Candidates for citizenship should demonstrate a strong understanding of America's language (English), history, and civic life. The patriotic rituals surrounding the naturalization ceremony should be augmented to reinforce the transformational character of the event. Once immigrants go through naturalization, they are expected to have no other national loyalty—neither to the lands of their birth nor to a "nation within a nation"—while at the same time being a part of the great American Melting Pot.

THE ROLE OF STATE AND LOCAL GOVERNMENT

While immigration and border security are federal responsibilities, there are many steps that individuals can demand that their state and local governments take to play a positive role in restoring the integrity of America's border and immigration policies. They can, for example, push back against politicians who wish to establish sanctuary cities, counties, and states. Establishing these "sanctuaries" isn't an act of compassion; instead, it creates magnets for crime and public safety risks to citizens and illegal immigrants alike.

State and local governments can be encouraged to participate with federal authorities in 287(g) programs. Designed to enable state and local governments to help enforce federal immigration laws, 287(g) programs were under assault during the Obama administration, which sought to cut funding, access to, and use of the programs. Citizens can advocate for their government to participate in and promote widening 287(g) usage by calling for increasing funding for the program and requiring the Department of Homeland Security to enter into a 287(g) agreement with any state or local government that requests entry into the program—with significant consequences should the department not meet this requirement in a timely fashion.

Finally, citizens can call on their government to be more transparent and provide data about the illegal immigrant population in their communities so that voters can make decisions based on real data. For instance, governments ought to be required to provide information on illegal immigrants in state and local jails and prisons and estimates of the fiscal costs of populations unlawfully present in their communities.

A TIME FOR CHOOSING

Conservatives can shrink from the fight for responsible immigration and border policies. They can avoid all the terrible labels liberals will slap on them for rejecting the view that open borders is the only humane approach to the issue.

Or conservatives can stand up.

They can stand for policies that are in the best interest of all Americans. They can stand for policies that will make America better and stronger. They can stand for policies that respect the Constitution and the rule of law. They can fight to keep America a successful nation of immigrants.

Make no mistake, this is a choice conservatives can't avoid. If they do nothing and say nothing, that's a choice. The Left wins. If they stand up, then getting it right is not assured—but there is a better chance than if they stood back and did nothing.

From Serving the Nation to Coming Home: How State and Local Governments Can Assist in Veteran Transition

by Captain Scott O'Grady

No individuals in our society have done more throughout our history as a nation to preserve and protect our rights and freedoms than our brave men and women in the United States Armed Forces. They represent the best of America with their unwavering patriotism, bravery, dedication, and selflessness. These men and women have carried an even greater burden since the despicable acts of terror inflicted on our nation on September 11, 2001, led to the war in Iraq and the longest war in American history, the conflict in Afghanistan. As such, both our states and our federal government must be prepared to play an even greater role in supporting our heroes as they transition from the battlefield to Main Street. Captain Scott O'Grady is one of the greatest American heroes of the century. On June 2, 1995, while serving as a United States Air Force fighter pilot and enforcing the NATO no-fly zone policy over Bosnia, he was shot down in his F-16 and had to survive in enemy territory for six days before his rescue. Since departing from the Air Force, Scott O'Grady has become one of the biggest advocates in the country supporting the successful and positive transition of our veterans by championing specific public policies that can be pursued by the states.

I'm greatly honored that my good friend agreed to participate in *Making Government Work*. More Americans need to hear his views and beliefs.
    —Tan Parker

For all the good that the Veterans Administration (VA) does to help our nation's eighteen million plus veterans, approximately 7 percent of the adult population, there is still much need for local entities and individuals who have the heart to help meet veterans' individual challenges.[1] Veterans served, sacrificed, and suffered to protect and preserve the quality of life, prosperity, and freedoms that all Americans enjoy. It is the obligation of every citizen in our country to repay our veterans, not with handouts but with a hand up to help them heal physically, mentally, emotionally, and spiritually. Above all others, our veterans and their families deserve to enjoy the prosperity and happiness that their fellow Americans enjoy but never suffered to preserve.

The population of veterans has been on the decline for years. In 1990, veterans were 14 percent of the adult population.[2] Now, in 2020, veterans make up just above 7 percent of the civilian population eighteen years and older. Currently, less than 1 percent of the population is serving in the active duty military.[3] Since 1990, with the Base Realignment and Closure (BRAC), the U.S. active duty military has been reduced by nearly 40 percent.[4] Yet for the past thirty years, Americans have sent our military to fight without respite to protect us from terrorists and nation-states that intend to destroy our way of life.

Never in the history of America have so few for so long sacrificed and suffered for the rest of the nation.

Not since World War II has our country collectively served and mobilized for war. In the conflicts since, we have sent a small minority of Americans, our military, to fight, sacrifice, and suffer on behalf of the nation so we may remain a free people. Our veterans did not go to war grudgingly. Instead they proudly served and would do so again. For they love America, our U.S. constitutional freedoms, their families, and their fellow veterans who share in the burden of their sacrifices.

As a nation, we owe our veterans a debt of gratitude. It has been said that a nation is judged by how well it treats its veterans. Our country's future will be contingent upon the treatment of veterans. It has also been stated that the willingness with which our young people are likely to serve in any war, no matter how justified, shall be directly proportional to how they perceive the way veterans of earlier wars were treated and appreciated by their nation. With today's all-volunteer military, the treatment of our veterans directly impacts recruitment. How veterans are treated is a matter of national security. In the past thirty years, a higher percentage of veterans are disabled from physical and mental wounds because of constant wars and conflicts to which our country has sent a small minority of patriots to fight on our behalf. So how can we best serve our veterans when they return home?

VETERANS' MENTAL HEALTH AND SUICIDE

It is my opinion that the number one priority is to assist veterans with mental health issues, such as post-traumatic stress disorder (PTSD). Approximately sixteen veterans a day commit suicide.[5] That's more than six thousand veterans every year. Recently, I attended the funeral of a Marine who served in Iraq. He had been a part of the Marine unit that saved my life years earlier during the Bosnian War.

Even one veteran suicide is one too many. Our nation is obligated to care for each veteran, but is the VA at large equipped to handle its case-load and provide proper effective treatments? One size does not fit all, and individual care is necessary. Therefore, the recent report from the VA on veteran suicide was accompanied by a statement from VA secretary Robert Wilkie emphasizing that the crisis of veteran suicide went beyond the VA's capacity to address it and that there needs to be a coordinated approach with state, local, and private partners.

The VA Veterans Crisis Line is available day or night, 24/7:

- Phone 1-800-273-8255 and press 1

- Text 838225
- Live chat at VA.Gov
- TTY hearing loss 800-799-4889

If you are a veteran or a family member or friend of a veteran in need of help do not hesitate to contact the VA Veterans Crisis Line. Help is available day or night every day of the year. You are not alone! Please go online to Make the Connection (VA) at www.maketheconnection.net for information, resources, and videos of testimonials from dozens of veterans who have recovered from mental health issues.

State and local governments and private partners (veterans' service organizations and centers) along with individuals should take the following steps:

1. Lobby to ensure that no veteran need fear losing his or her job for seeking mental health treatment inside or outside the VA, regardless of discharge type or disability rating.
2. Lobby to ensure that veterans who have been diagnosed with PTSD or other mental health issues are not required to take VA prescription drugs to maintain VA disability compensation, especially if they show that alternative treatments are helping.
3. Promote a campaign of awareness to remove the unfair stigma of veterans' mental health issues and post-traumatic stress disorder.
4. Veterans should be referred to local charitable organizations, private veterans' service centers, veterans' service organizations, and any health provider or clinic that provides mental health treatments. All alternative care beyond pharmaceuticals should be explored, such as brain therapies and supplements, oxygen therapies, faith-based counseling, group therapy safe spaces, therapeutic

retreats, meditation and yoga, essential oils, and other non-traditional therapies that anecdotally have shown positive healing results. An example is Mt. Carmel Veterans Service Center in Colorado Springs, which works with dozens of local partners to provide a safe space as well as wellness and career services that veterans need to stabilize their lives.

5. State and local funding and grants should be considered to support local veterans' centers and clinics that are showing positive results with helping veterans.

VETERANS' BENEFITS

It is very important that every veteran connect with either a state, county, or local Veterans Service Officer (VSO), an accredited representative, who can file claims with the VA on behalf of the veteran. VSOs are not employees of the VA but have been certified to be advocates for a veteran's VA benefits. VSOs are available in every state and most counties. Plus, many are connected with local veterans' service organizations.

Veterans Service Officers are the best advocates for veterans and their families to ensure they receive their maximum benefits, such as disability compensation, health care, GI benefits, job training and placement, mortgage loans, military records, and so on. Veterans Service Officers, in conjunction with veterans' service organizations and private groups like Dallas-based Allies in Service, which has an extensive partnership with dozens of industry leaders, help to prepare, equip, and place veterans in civilian careers. All VSO services should be free to the veteran, so ask in advance and, if need be, find a different VSO. State and county VSOs are typically located at government offices. So that every veteran is connected to a local VSO, I recommend that state, county, and local officials receive performance and outreach reports from their VSOs on a regular basis.

VETERANS' EDUCATION, TRAINING, AND EMPLOYMENT

The G.I. Bills (MGIB, Post 9/11, Forever) and other VA education benefits can be applied for with the help of VSOs and online at VA.gov. These are good educational and training benefits for veterans. The best state education benefit for veterans comes from Texas. The Hazlewood Act allows Texas residents who enter the military to earn 150 credit hours from public state universities. See the Texas Veterans Commission website for details.[6] Every state should look to provide the same benefits for its residents who join the military.

State, county, and local governments should encourage preferential hiring of veterans seeking to be civil servants. They should also encourage trade and union groups to offer training at no charge to veterans who want careers as welders, electricians, plumbers, mechanics, carpenters, truck drivers, and so on. Veterans make excellent employees. They are disciplined, listen to instructions, have leadership skills, and know how to work as team players.

Local groups, such as veterans' service organizations and veterans' service centers, and private groups, such as Allies in Service, that provide assistance in career job placement should be supported by local government if they are providing concrete results.

VETERANS' HOMESTEAD PROPERTY TAX RELIEF

One of the most helpful benefits that a state and local government should provide to disabled veterans is homestead property tax relief. Each state provides different property tax relief to disabled veterans, and many have not updated benefits in decades to meet the current markets. Many states provide little to no relief, and in my opinion all states should do better. There are fewer than five million disabled veterans (25 percent of the veteran population), which is less than 2 percent of the adult population in the United States.[7] If anyone has earned the right to homestead property tax relief, it is disabled veterans, especially the most severely disabled.

The VA disability rating system is the best benchmark for states to use as criteria for benefits. Veterans are thoroughly examined by the VA disability claims and rating system, which makes it exponentially more difficult for a veteran to be awarded a higher overall disability rating. Approximately one-third of disabled veterans are rated with a 70 percent or greater overall disability rating by the VA.[8] Yet the most severely disabled veterans have a higher unemployment rate. Plus, more than 50 percent of homeless veterans have disabilities, and homeless veterans have a higher suicide rate.[9] By providing homestead property tax relief to disabled veterans, especially the most severely disabled (70 percent or greater), states and local governments are greatly helping to curb veteran homelessness and suicide.

Homestead property tax relief should be equal to the percentage of the disabled veteran's overall VA disability rating (examples: 100 percent disabled veteran receives 100 percent homestead property tax relief; 70 percent disabled veteran receives 70 percent homestead property tax relief; and so on). State legislatures should immediately pass state constitutional amendments for disabled veteran homestead property tax relief based on this recommended percentage of relief and allow taxpayers to vote on it for approval and ratification.

I highly recommend that a state constitutional amendment initially focus on helping the most severely disabled veterans (70 percent or greater) who need help first and foremost. Once this is accomplished, states and local governments can look to extend property tax relief to the remaining disabled veterans. Just as in battle, we should first look to help our soldiers and veterans who require the greatest care and attention.

Property tax relief for disabled veterans should not be based on home values, which need to be consistently revised to keep up with current markets. Nor should property tax relief be evaluated on the income level of the disabled veteran. This is not a social welfare handout. If it were not for the service and permanent disabilities of the veterans, no American would enjoy their prosperity today. Disabled veterans paid for homestead property tax relief with their sacrifices, blood, sweat, and tears. Homestead property tax relief is a debt of gratitude owed to our disabled veterans.

SUMMARY

The VA is a federal government agency that provides much-needed care and benefits to our veterans. State and local governments and private partners also have an important role in helping veterans transition home, because they work best in solving local problems and providing assistance to those individuals in need within the local community. State and local governments, along with local private entities, should (1) focus on helping veterans with mental health issues, (2) connect all veterans with a local VSO for benefits, (3) support entities that provide job training and employment placement, and (4) states should quickly pass meaningful, long-standing homestead property tax relief for our disabled patriots. It will be the states, local governments, private entities, and individuals that will make the difference in the lives of our veterans.

Legislative Aftershock

by House Majority Leader Dick Armey

Controlling the growth of government at all levels is a fundamental hallmark of conservative belief. As conservatives, we know that as government grows, our freedoms and liberties contract. As such, finding mechanisms that allow for oversight of necessary new legislation is imperative to striking the proper regulatory balance. Oftentimes, legislation passed at the state or federal level takes on a life of its own, well beyond the original intentions of the legislator who authored the bill. This is a function of government agencies' abuse of the rule-making process. Another critical topic facing America now more than ever is finding the proper balance between advancement in information technology and the importance of privacy. As Americans, we cherish our privacy and freedoms and do not look favorably on those precious rights being trampled upon. However, in this modern world, every action on our electronic devices is tracked in great detail. We must find the optimal regulatory framework to protect the rights of the individual from the inherent desires of government and private industry, both of which seek to utilize such information. Dick Armey, the former majority leader of the United States House of Representatives, has a truly unique perspective and wisdom on these matters. During his time in public service, he was focused on addressing these most serious issues. While most people remember Leader Armey for his tenacious commitment to fiscal discipline, his greatest personal interest while serving in the U.S. House of Representatives was defining the proper role of regulation and grappling with the importance of protecting the privacy of our citizens. I'm most grateful that he chose to participate in *Making Government Work*, because his insights and teaching are timeless and something every American should know more about.

—Tan Parker

During my teaching years, while dabbling in public choice theory, I created the notion of "bureaucratic zealots." It was my observation that people tended to seek employment in various government bureaus or agencies because they had a predetermined set of convictions in agreement with what they perceived to be the agency's missions. These people frequently see themselves as the hero-soldiers of a movement and are often unrestrained in their commitment to extending the agency's reach and control. For example, eco-evangelicals tend to join the EPA, antiterrorists join the CIA, and law-and-order enthusiasts join the Justice Department. They tend to "burrow in" and retain lifetime employment in their respective agencies. Since their inherent desire is to expand the government's dominion in the area of their chosen passion, they tend also to affiliate with the Democratic Party in American politics because it is the party of big government.

While they may find their way into the agency through many avenues, the most insidious portal is through the "revolving door" between the agency and the legislative body that created it and therefore has the duty to oversee its activities. We seem to have a widely held understanding of the revolving door between government and the private sector, and the consequent tendency for that bureaucratic symbiosis to result in the regulatory agencies' becoming subservient to the private firms they are charged with regulating. We have yet to understand the revolving door between the agencies and the legislative bodies that create and oversee them. It is only through completing that circle of understanding that we are able to see the larger threat to personal liberty and economic efficiency.

While serving in Congress, I became intensely aware of an extra-legislative expansion of the law, done all too often in concert with Democratic congressmen and executed by bureaucratic zealots. I called it the "legislative aftershock." This is the way it happens. While the legislative body is creating an administrative or regulatory agency or an expansion of authority for an existing agency, they leave aspects of the law unspecified or ill-defined. They leave it vague and open, to be resolved when the agency writes the regulations by which they will implement the law. Often the legislators work with the agency employees, who are, in turn, former staff members of the legislators themselves, to write the regulations in order to expand the jurisdiction and increase the agency's authorities beyond those which were stipulated in the law.

Hence, there is a legislative aftershock, an extension of state power and diminution of private liberty beyond that which is stipulated in the law.

It was an awareness of how powerful this process is that prompted one iconic legislator in Congress to announce, "If I could have it my way, I'd let you write the law and I'd write the regulations for its implementation." It is not unusual for representatives of the private sector (stakeholders) who will be affected to participate in the entire process. That is how we got a Medicare law that required all private insurance to discontinue hospital benefits for even lifetime policyholders once they reached the age of eligibility for Medicare. The circle is unbroken when it includes a working group of individuals from the legislative body, the agencies, and the private sector—all of whom are friends and colleagues passing through revolving doors in order to always be in a position to grow big government.

A second way for legislators to create legislative aftershocks resulting in growing government is to leave the legislative language ambiguous in order that it might be resolved in the courts. The principal reason for doing things this way is that some legislators are betting they can get through the courts what they cannot pass through their legislative bodies. If they are correct, there is another type of legislative aftershock, in the form of a court ruling, through which our personal liberty is diminished and the power of government enhanced.

Let me clarify a little. It may seem harsh and partisan for me to emphasize that this mischief is done by the Democrats. Be assured that this is not a partisan diatribe. It is an observation of fact. It is my observation that the Democrats are the principal perpetrators of this mischief—for good reasons. Democrats are the primary proponents of expanding government in this country. For them, these are strategies that serve well their "labor of love"—the love of big government and the power and control they derive by its growth. Also, the principal beneficiary of the first legislative aftershock is the agency employee who is able to see his enterprise grow and his powers grow within it. Federal agencies and employees are an important voting constituency of the Democrats, and it serves them well to increase the numbers and influence of their allied constituents.

By the same token, the principal beneficiaries of the second legislative aftershock are the trial lawyers who are also an active and well-funded constituency of the Democratic Party. It must be understood that all of this is a big part of the Democrats' way of doing business at every legislative level. When I first observed this phenomenon, I checked with many others and found the practice to be prevalent throughout the entire set of congressional committees, at the state level as well as the federal level. I further found a great similarity in the language used to explain what was being done at the time of its commission. It is not random. It is integral to the way Democrats plan out legislative initiatives.

By the time we established the federal House Republican majority in 1994, there had been forty years of unconstrained and congressionally abetted mischief along these lines. My position was that since every agency of the government was created by the legislative branch, the legislative branch had both the right and the duty, through oversight, to require that its activities conformed to the letter of the law. I saw our majority as being in an excellent position to halt and even reverse that legislative aftershock mischief with legislative oversight. Speaker Newt Gingrich understood and agreed with me when I said I could do more to limit excessive government with oversight, which could discover the illegitimate excesses and roll them back, than with new legislation. Together we agreed to reward each committee that established an oversight subcommittee. Most of them did. Newt also agreed that my office should have a specialized division to coordinate and reward responsible legislative oversight.

My office established an extraordinarily good working relationship with the Government Accountability Office (GAO), which was staffed by some of the finest professionals with whom I have been privileged to work during my time in office. Additionally, my office created a special award to incentivize and recognize House members who did exceptional oversight.

Legislative oversight is difficult and unglamorous. It requires detailed examination of agency activities to contain them within the law as written by Congress and to compel them to work in a cost-effective manner. The professionals at GAO were frustrated over the legacy of (at best) congressional indifference or (at worst) congressional complicity in agency excesses. They were pleased and optimistic to see our commitment. Unfortunately, we achieved very little success. Time after time, our efforts were met with agency staff having a history of working as staff to high-ranking and well-placed congressmen, whose trust they enjoyed, simply encouraging them to accept that everything was fine.

For example, long before the housing bubble burst in 2006, Congressman Richard Baker from Louisiana came to me with his concerns about Fannie Mae and Freddie Mac. Richard was one of the brightest and hardest-working members of the House Banking Committee. He had good information that was extremely foreboding about the tenuous position of these two government-sponsored enterprises and, indeed, the whole housing and mortgage industry. He argued that it was urgent that we should look into it. It turned out that virtually every agency and enterprise involved in the debacle had well-placed people, from their boards to their government operations departments, who had been highly placed as trusted staff on both sides of the aisle in both legislative bodies. They were aggressively assuring everyone that there were no problems nor reasons for alarm. Richard and I could not get to first base with our concerns. When the bubble burst and Congress had to vote on the proposed bailouts, those same trusted former Capitol Hill staffers were all over the Capitol, spinning the matter as a crisis and an emergency and gathering the votes.

I left Congress at the age of sixty-two, and my wife and I are able to continue our participation in the congressional group health insurance plan for the duration of both our lives. I therefore had no need for Medicare and thought it to be a good thing that Susan and I would not be a burden on an already overburdened system. However, when I tried to enroll for my Social Security benefits at the age of sixty-five, I was told that I either had to enroll for Medicare or forfeit my retirement benefits. This was disconcerting, because I had been compelled by the law to pay into Social Security with after-tax dollars since I was sixteen years old. I went through a difficult period of anxiety and research and, as I had thought, that requirement was not in the law. It was not even in the regulations. It was in a policy memo written in 1993. I got busy and tried to get my old friends in Congress to address the matter. My first response was from the chairman of Ways and Means, who said his guy checked and it was not in the regulations, so it couldn't be real. I then asked how he explained the agency's refusing to remit me my retirement benefits unless I enrolled in Medicare. His response was that it must have been my misunderstanding.

I did manage to get two different House members to drop bills to correct the matter, but they went nowhere. I joined a class action lawsuit to try to correct the matter. It was eventually dismissed. By 2003, the agency had discovered that some people were getting around the requirement by enrolling in Social Security before they were eligible for Medicare. They wrote a new memo. If you did not enroll in Medicare when you were first eligible, you lost your Social Security and had to refund all funds you had previously received. The point is that agencies are now able to rewrite the law with memos, and legislative bodies offer very little to discipline the system. What to do?

In the Medicare case just cited, the problem can be resolved by a simple executive order that prohibits the agencies from continuing to enforce the memo. And that is the answer. The executive branch of government has the ability and must have the discipline to end such excesses. If it does not, then I fear we can never correct the situation. That is why a president like Donald Trump is important. He can discipline the excessive government establishment because he is not part of it, has no history with it, and even has a healthy contempt for it. President Reagan did the same during his presidency.

There is an even more insidious circumstance found in the legislative process at all levels of government. It is the fear that legislators have of being seen as unresponsive to a perceived crisis. Many legislators are only passively involved in their own jobs and are more involved both by way of emotion and activity with their reelection. Oftentimes, a legislator perceives a catastrophe that might affect or inflame the concern of his or her constituents, and he or she sees a "crisis." It doesn't matter if it is real or merely perceived; it could affect his or her reelection if constituents think it is real. Because of this common insecurity, every catastrophe, no matter how insignificant or unreal, becomes a "crisis" to even the most complacent legislators. And every crisis precipitates a legislative panic, expressed in such pleadings as, "We have got to get out ahead of this thing. We can't be seen as not doing something." This whining is generally directed at the leadership of the legislative body, who, it is felt, must provide us with something that we can support and vote for as a demonstration of our concern and involvement.

Furthermore, it is amply demonstrated that during a legislative panic nearly anything can be passed. It has been my observation that with almost everyone in government, every crisis is the newest, most urgent reason that we should do exactly what they have been advocating all along. For example: When the economy overheats, the Republicans say it is time to lower taxes, and the Democrats argue that it is necessary to raise taxes. The same thing takes place when the economy cools down. The Democrats say it is time to raise taxes and the Republicans argue that it is necessary to lower taxes. The importance of this phenomenon is well understood by the advocates of government growth. One of the most integrated, recurring, well-placed, and well-connected political operatives of the Left, Chicago's own Rahm Emanuel, made that clear when he said, "Never let a good crisis go to waste. What I mean by that is, in the aftermath of a crisis you can often do what you could not do before." The idea did not originate with Emanuel. It goes back to Saul Alinsky's *Rules for Radicals*. The reader can rest assured that it is an integral part of the big government control strategy of the Left in American politics today.

The September 11, 2001, attack on the World Trade Center precipitated the largest American federal legislative panic in modern times, and it hit to the heart of our most precious national values, individual liberty and personal privacy. Indeed, in the aftermath of the attack, there was national debate about how much we must forsake our liberties and our privacy in the interests of our security. There were many luminaries of conservatism who aggressively argued for security over liberty. I had been working on protecting individual liberty and personal privacy from bureaucratic encroachment for some time, so I was quite familiar with the players and the issues that would erupt on the scene in the aftermath of the attack. I was deeply involved with efforts to eliminate red light cameras and other electronic surveillance devices and, on the internet, an initiative called "Carnivore" by the Justice Department to indiscriminately spy on personal email. I mention red light cameras because it is important to be aware that government can be reckless against personal liberty at all levels—from local to national.

During the period of time when I was so blessed to serve in the House of Representatives, the question of whether to give up our liberties for the hope of possible additional physical security was just one aspect of the debate around privacy. The other, which has dramatically accelerated since I left office, is the loss of privacy for consumers through the rise of big technology companies that collect enormous amounts of data daily on each of us. In the years ahead we must continue to safeguard individual liberties and privacy through the application of regulation where necessary and appropriate to keep up with the dramatic advances in technology that are occurring.

Of course, the "big enchilada" of legislative responses in the aftermath of the World Trade Center attack was the anti-terrorist legislation titled "Uniting and Strengthening of America to Provide Appropriate Tools Required to Intercept and Obstruct Terrorism Act of 2001," or the USA PATRIOT Act. The acronym is powerful in that it is "buzzword blackmail." Who is prepared to vote against patriotism in the aftermath of such an attack? No one, even if it is a monster piece of legislation amounting to 342 pages, covering 350 subject areas, encompassing 40 federal agencies, and carrying 21 legal amendments.

The House Judiciary Committee chairman introduced the legislation on October 2, 2001. It became law on October 26 of that year. This was record-breaking, made possible only by forcing the pace to the point that serious debate and discussion were made impossible by the restricted timescale and the "urgent" demand for political action. It would be impossible to detail here all the trespasses against personal liberty contained in the bill, but we can have a summary.

The act created, among other things, sweeping powers of detention and surveillance for the executive and law enforcement agencies. It also deprived the courts of meaningful judicial oversight of the exercise of those powers. The secretary of state was empowered to designate any group, foreign or domestic, as "terrorist." This power was not subject to review. A new crime, "domestic terrorism," was created. It included activities that involved acts dangerous to human life that were a violation of the criminal law, if it appeared to be intended (1) to intimidate or coerce a civilian population; (2) to influence the policy of government by intimidation or coercion; or (3) to affect the conduct of a government by mass destruction, assassination, or kidnapping. It permitted investigations based on unlawful First Amendment activity if that activity could be tied to intelligence purposes. It undermined the privacy protection of the Fourth Amendment by eroding the line between intelligence gathering and gathering evidence for criminal proceedings. It expanded the ability of the government to spy by wiretaps and computer surveillance. It provided access to medical, financial, business, and educational records and allowed secret searches of homes and offices. It undermined due process procedures by permitting the government to detain noncitizens indefinitely even if they have never been convicted of a crime.

The possible uses and outcomes of this legislation horrified many of us who felt heavily invested in personal liberty and privacy. But only a few of us fought it. I had a personal confrontation with some arrogant young lawyers in the Justice Department over Carnivore. I recall one of them defiantly saying, "We've been asking for this for a long time." I responded, "And we've been saying 'No!' for a long time." I did manage to get some judicial oversight into its implementation, and I did manage to get a fairly comprehensive set of sunset provisions into the bill. My idea was that after some time passed, more sober reflection might distill the excesses.

For a modern nation created largely by immigrants, the new laws covering noncitizens are ironically harsh. Section 412 of the act permits indefinite detention of immigrants and other noncitizens. I argued that the shame of our World War II experience under President Roosevelt, which resulted in the incarceration of more than 110,000 people of Japanese origin, 11,000 of German origin, and 3,000 of Italian origin, was now being replicated, despite the best of intentions. It had been argued that these detention powers were merely precautionary and unlikely to be utilized.

The final illustration of the new wave of legislation was the Military Order of November 13, 2001, which allowed for noncitizens suspected of involvement in "international terrorism" to be tried by special military commissions. These commissions were not subject to the regular rules and safeguards that cover military court-martials. These commissions were empowered to act in secret and to pass the death penalty by a two-thirds majority, and their decisions could not be appealed to other courts.

In addition to the PATRIOT Act, Congress expanded the size and scope of the Department of Transportation by creating the Transportation Security Administration (TSA), which subjects us all to a rigorous and annoying search every time we try to board an airplane or train. Finally, it created a whole new cabinet office, the Department of Homeland Security, and moved TSA there. There had been several people advocating such a cabinet-level organization for years, but they had been unable to get anyone interested. Once the "legislative panic" took hold, it was impossible to slow that stampede down. Despite all of my concerns with the legislation, I ultimately voted for the bill myself. The ironic thing was that the people who had been doing the studying and planning about how such an agency could best be created were left out of the process.

The other glaring example of legislative panic and excessive regulation in recent memory was the passage of the Dodd-Frank Wall Street Reform and Consumer Protection Act in 2010 in response to the financial crisis the nation experienced in 2008. This legislation was a huge expansion of federal power over our financial system and passed almost exclusively with Democratic support. It was signed into law by President Obama. This legislation did nothing but hurt America's small banks and their ability to survive, due to the absurd new levels of regulation. The ridiculous regulatory burdens imposed by the legislation also slowed business lending, particularly to small businesses and middle-market companies. The net impact was that Dodd-Frank slowed our nation's growth in dramatic ways. Many of the elements within the bill were Democratic wish-list items for many years, but it took the financial crisis and the ensuing legislative panic for the legislation to pass. The good news is that many aspects of this legislative disaster and excess were repealed under Republican leadership and signed into law by President Trump in May 2018.

We must be vigilant in stopping the excessive spread of big government. The world changes, but the tactics remain the same. Each new generation of conservatives must pick up the mantle to keep our government accountable and working for its citizens, not just its representatives.

Defending the Second Amendment

by Chuck Norris

Few subjects in America today ignite as passionate a response as the constitutionally protected right to keep and bear arms. As conservatives, we believe deeply that the United States Constitution's Second Amendment is a sacred freedom passed down from our nation's Founding Fathers. It allows every American the right to protect his or her home and to provide for his or her self-defense against those that would seek to do harm. It was James Madison himself, in *Federalist* No. 46, who spoke about the Second Amendment as a great advantage that America had over European nations. America's citizens were armed and therefore could not be controlled through military force or invasion. Madison recognized that the Second Amendment provided a hedge of protection, a privilege not afforded to other nations. This brings me to our author. Chuck Norris is unparalleled in both his knowledge of and passionate beliefs regarding the Second Amendment and for his generosity and kindness toward his fellow Americans. Chuck is not only a legendary figure in the martial arts, but he's also one of the most successful action film stars in history, a producer, a bestselling author, an Air Force veteran, a successful businessman, a husband and father and, throughout his life, a fierce defender of the Second Amendment. I am deeply grateful for his participation and for the opportunity for all Americans to understand and read for themselves his beliefs in this most important area of public policy.

—Tan Parker

Those Chuck Norris "facts" we see on the internet are full of levity. It is said, for example, that "Chuck Norris doesn't wear a watch; he simply decides what time it is." It is said that "when Chuck Norris does a push-up, he's not lifting himself up—he's pushing the Earth down." It is even said that "Chuck Norris has a grizzly bear carpet in his room; the bear isn't dead, it's just afraid to move."

These quips have been a real compliment to me and have provided a way for me to reconnect with young people throughout the world. I am an actor and an activist, a martial artist and a philanthropist. I am a husband, a father, and a man of faith. I was a military policeman in the U.S. Air Force. Little-known fact: because of the efforts of this book's editor, Tan Parker, and of former Texas governor Rick Perry, I am also an honorary Texas Ranger.

I play an action hero. In my movies and in my television series, I defend the defenseless, and in those appearances, my character uses deadly force when necessary—and only when necessary.

But in real life, thousands of Americans defend themselves—and the defenseless—every year, and they are able to do so because of the Second Amendment to the U.S. Constitution.

"A well-regulated militia being necessary to the security of a free state, the right of the people to keep and bear arms, shall not be infringed," the amendment says.

Our right to defend ourselves and our families is God-given.[1] It is not something granted to us by the government—nor can it legitimately be taken away from us by the government.

So, when ordinary citizens avail themselves of this right, they are not exceeding their authority. They are not doing the police officer's job.

They are taking upon themselves the responsibility to care for that which God has given them—their families, their lives, and the precious gift of liberty.

I want to tell you some of their stories now. And each story will illustrate an important, broader point about our Second Amendment rights. I am indebted to the Heritage Foundation, which keeps a very useful database of defensive gun-use incidents.[2]

CINCINNATI, OHIO

Early one June morning, a Cincinnati mother of five heard something from her living room—it was her ex-boyfriend, attempting to enter her home. She had a protective order against the man, Dante Ruff. But she also had a concealed carry permit—and a handgun.[3] When he apparently could not force open the door, he went to the window.

The noise she heard was Ruff attempting to kick out the air conditioner so he could enter. She fired her gun through the window, hitting Ruff multiple times in the abdomen.

She was safe—and so were her children. And the local prosecutor affirmed that she did the right thing.

"Thank goodness she had a Concealed Carry Permit and was able to defend herself and her 5 children," Hamilton County prosecutor Attorney Joseph Deters told the local news station. "It is hard to imagine what might have happened to her or her children if she had not been able to protect herself and her family."[4]

The broader lesson for us here is that protective orders only go so far. We cannot simply leave it to the courts and the judicial system to defend our lives and our families. Yet those who wish to take away your Second Amendment rights often say that you can depend on the legal system to protect you.

Here's how that argument was made recently in *The Atlantic*: "Gun regulation offers another such path to self-defense, one vastly more efficacious and preferred by the American public. It represents a mode of preemptive self-defense, whereby the state is tasked by its citizens with limiting access to deadly force."[5]

Of course, the state is incapable of "limiting access to deadly force" by those who would do us harm. If they do not have access to guns, they have access to knives, clubs, fists, and improvised weapons. And women are often at a disadvantage to even an unarmed man. Even if the state could uphold its side of the bargain (keeping bad people disarmed), it still has no legitimacy in trying to prevent us from defending ourselves.

ROCHESTER, NEW HAMPSHIRE

A man with his two small children in the car drove into his own driveway to see a man attempting to break into his home. The father confronted the man, and held him at gunpoint until the police arrived.

Later, the man's son asked his father if he shot the intruder.

"I said, 'No, buddy, I had no reason to kill him,'" the father explained. "I don't carry a gun to kill people. I carry a gun to neutralize threatening situations."

And that is the broader lesson here. Defensive handgun use is not about killing people. Nor is the Second Amendment. They are about protecting lives. Often, the presence of a gun is enough to achieve this purpose. Statistics show that guns save lives.

Writing for the Foundation for Economic Education (FEE), Lawrence Reed explains, "Liberty isn't the only thing likely to be lost when gun laws are passed to appease emotions over reason, evidence, logic, and rights. Lives will most assuredly be lost, too. Lots of them."[6]

The numbers are astounding.

"Guns prevent an estimated 2.5 million crimes a year, or 6,849 every day," Reed notes. "Most often, the gun is never fired, and no blood (including the criminal's) is shed. Every year, 400,000 life-threatening violent crimes are prevented using firearms."[7]

This is the very opposite of the vigilante justice gun-control advocates say will fill our streets unless guns are taken away.

WINSTON, MISSOURI

A female police officer transporting a male prisoner was overpowered by the man, who managed to wrestle her handgun out of the holster as she drove. He shot her in the abdomen, though he was shot in the hand.[8]

The car they were in came to a rolling stop on the side of the highway, near a convenience store. The inmate, thirty-eight-year-old Jamey Griffin, tried to force the officer to drive away, but some nearby citizens saw the struggle and intervened, chasing the slowly moving vehicle for another quarter mile. One of them, who was legally carrying his own firearm, used that weapon to stop Griffin, then forced him out of the vehicle. He held the suspect at gunpoint until other law enforcement vehicles arrived, while other bystanders rendered aid to the severely wounded police officer.

The police officer, a single mother to a five-year-old daughter, underwent multiple surgeries and survived. She later met the Good Samaritans who saved her. The community held fundraisers to help with her expenses.

The larger principle here is that it is not "us and them." It is not police officers (who should be allowed to carry firearms) and citizens (who others argue should not). We are in this together.

Of course, gun control advocates truly believe that only cops should carry guns. As former New York City mayor (and anti–Second Amendment activist) Michael Bloomberg said following a tragic shooting in a Texas church, "It's the job of law enforcement to have guns and to decide when to shoot. You just do not want the average citizen carrying a gun in a crowded place."[9]

Yet it was a gun owner, lawfully carrying his firearm, who ended that shooting before it could get much, much worse. As the Associated Press reported, that man's "single shot quickly ended the attack. . . . He said the entire confrontation was over in no more than six seconds. More than 240 congregants were in the church at the time."[10]

Video of the incident shows that other church members, also lawfully carrying their own firearms, also responded (if not as quickly). As many as six other parishioners drew their own weapons to assist the former sheriff's reserve officer.[11]

Citizens come to the aid of police officers more often than you might expect. Cops are human, too. They can be overpowered, overcome, even outgunned. Citizens often step in.

In one case in Arizona, a cop was shot by an assailant.[12] The bullet hit his unprotected shoulder, making him unable to draw his pistol. A passerby saw the struggle and intervened. The police officer is alive; his assailant is not.

American citizens are beneficiaries of what our Founders thought of as "ordered liberty." But we are not merely supposed to enjoy the liberty; our duties include helping to maintain that order as well.

TAMPA, FLORIDA

Two masked and armed men broke into a family's home late one October night.[13] They severely beat the father, demanding money. They aimed their guns at the eleven-year-old daughter, threatening to shoot. The mom, who was eight months pregnant, was in a back room. She peeked out and was fired on. With her family in mortal danger, she grabbed her husband's AR-15 rifle and returned fire, killing one home invader and chasing the other off.

Many gun control advocates say that no civilian needs a "high-powered" weapon or an "assault rifle."[14] Do not be deceived; that argument is saying that your right to defend yourself and your family should be limited to what they think is acceptable.

The husband in that family feels that the AR-15, the most popular sporting rifle in America, was absolutely critical to keeping that family safe.[15]

"Them guys came in with two normal pistols and my AR stopped it," he said. "(My wife) evened the playing field and kept them from killing me."[16]

The truth is that there is no such thing as an "assault rifle." It is a subjective term, mostly used by the media—not firearms manufacturers or gun owners. [17] So, efforts to ban them are based on opinion—and the clear opinion of gun control advocates is that they know better than you what you need to protect yourself.

DEFENSE AGAINST TYRANNY

We have the right to defend ourselves against criminals and those who would do us harm. That is why Thomas Jefferson, in a letter to his nephew Peter Carr, advised him: "Let your gun therefore be the constant companion of your walks."

But our Founding Fathers did not merely have self-defense against criminals in mind when they authored the Second Amendment. They also had in mind the defense of liberty against tyranny. If the government decides to become a tyrannical government, our guns are to protect us against that.

Author Robert Tracinski explained it well recently in the Federalist:

> The Founding Fathers didn't ask why it was necessary to provide the people the means to resist a tyrannical central government. It was a problem they had very recently encountered in real life, in the form of thousands of Redcoats sent across the Atlantic by a distant central government to suspend civil rights and enforce oppressive laws. So when they drafted their own system of central government and provided it sufficient military force to repel or deter foreign threats, they were profoundly concerned that this new national government would not be able to turn its power back against its own citizens.[18]

It is not all bad news. Recently, there has been a movement to establish Second Amendment sanctuary counties, particularly in my home state of Texas.[19] Sheriffs and other county officials, who are sworn to uphold the U.S. Constitution, are taking a stand against unconstitutional legislation that might come down from Washington, D.C.

I could not agree more.

It is encouraging to see counties, and even many states, stepping in to support the Second Amendment. Even as many national politicians—including Bloomberg and many others—signal their intention to curtail our rights, states, counties, and cities can and should be ready to stand up to them.

The title of this book is *Making Government Work: A Conservative Agenda for the States.* The agenda for the states is clear—ensure your citizens can fully enjoy their God-given right to keep and bear arms.

We are not asking our elected leaders for anything. We are simply requiring them to abide by the oaths they took. The Second Amendment is not a gift to us from the government. It is the enumeration of a right we have inherent in our being. And it is a strict limitation on government.

And it is worth defending.

America's Greatest Asset: The Family

by Chad Hennings

I have always passionately believed that the family unit is the bedrock of not only our nation but of civilization itself. We can judge the health of our nation in large part by looking at the health of our families. Ideally, we learn our most important attributes within the family: character, integrity, unconditional love, the values of hard work, faith, patriotism, and service to others. After he was drafted by the Dallas Cowboys, Chad Hennings delayed his NFL career to serve his country as an Air Force fighter pilot. Upon his return home, he joined his team and became a three-time Super Bowl champion. Chad has also been one of America's leading advocates for protecting the family and inspiring men to be leaders within their families and communities. Through his personal testimony, books, and ministry involvement, he is changing our culture for the better. I am blessed to call him my friend and very grateful that he accepted my invitation to participate in this 2020 version of *Making Government Work*.

—Tan Parker

INTRODUCTION

I have come into contact with some powerful forces in my life. Whether when firing the GAU-8 Avenger Gatling gun on board the A-10 Warthog fighter jets I flew serving as a pilot in the Air Force or feeling the bone-jarring impact of slamming into the elite offensive linemen I lined up against during my time with the Dallas Cowboys, I'll never forget the moments when I came into contact with raw power.

Yet, one of the most powerful forces on the planet is not found on the battlefield or gridiron—it's found in homes and neighborhoods all across our great nation. The force I am talking about is the family.

It is easy to look back on the past two and a half decades since the original edition of *Making Government Work* was first published in 1994 and mourn the apparent weakening of the institution of the family. Many of the threats that Gary Bauer, the author of this chapter for the original edition, warned of have come to fruition. Pornography is so accessible through the internet that more than a dozen states have acted to declare it a public health crisis.[1] Marriage and birthrates continue to decline.[2] More American children live in single-parent homes than anywhere else in the world.[3]

These trends have led many leading conservative thinkers, notably Rod Dreher of the magazine *The American Conservative*, to declare that the culture war is effectively over and that conservatives have been roundly defeated by the rising tide of secularization.[4] Turn on the nightly news for just ten minutes and you'll find considerable evidence to support such pessimism.

But dig a little deeper and you will find much cause for hope. Divorce rates are declining, recently hitting a forty-year low for those under age fifty-five.[5] Abortion, likewise, is on the decline, recently hitting its lowest rate since *Roe v. Wade*, driven by the one-two punch of fewer unintended pregnancies overall and more mothers choosing to carry their babies to term.[6] Economic prosperity among households with married parents is rising.[7]

I write this not to discount the very clear threats faced by the American family, but to warn against despair. Conservatism at its core is a philosophy rooted in hope. Now, more than ever, it is critical for conservatives to hold tightly to the truth of who we are and what we believe as we chart a new path forward.

"Conservative family policy" has become so synonymous with culture war issues like same-sex marriage and abortion that mainstream Americans have all but tuned out. Even as I write this, I can almost see the reader's eyes glazing over. Yet conservative family policy encompasses so much more than the social issues that have dominated political discourse over the past two decades. These issues are not the root but rather symptoms of larger societal issues with which conservatives must engage.

This chapter seeks to reorient conservative understanding of what it means to have a pro-family agenda. By proposing practical solutions and inspiring hope through the stories of everyday Americans who are on the front lines of reinvigorating the awesome power of the family, we hope to help chart a new direction for both conservatives and the nation. We also hope that this chapter will be thought-provoking for those readers who do not consider themselves conservative, and inspire a productive dialogue around issues where all Americans can and should find common ground. As you will soon see, this new direction is less about effecting change through the levers of government and more about what each of us can do in our homes and neighborhoods to promote liberty, dignity, and opportunity for all Americans.

THE IMPORTANCE OF MARRIAGE AND FATHERHOOD

The best day of my life was not the day I was drafted to play professional football. It was the day I got married, followed closely by the day I became a father. Although I will forever be known as a three-time Super Bowl champion, my true legacy will be the people my son and daughter become and the lives they touch. Throughout their lives, I have worked hard to teach my children to take ownership of who they are. Establish an identity. Work hard and be financially responsible. Serve others. These lessons have the power to create revolutionary societal change.

All of these lessons were intended to help my kids develop high moral and functional characters. Kids do not learn how to develop character through a government program or by attending even the best schools in the nation. They learn it, primarily, through family.

Unfortunately, the married-parent family is on the decline in the United States. Today, roughly half of all American adults are married—a historically low rate that shows little sign of reversing.[8] Family formation is also on the decline, with the nation's fertility rate recently hitting an all-time low of 1.73 births per woman.[9] At the same time, an increasing number of children are growing up with only one parent active in their lives. These trends, if left unaddressed, threaten not only the character of our nation but its future prosperity.

Today, nearly 40 percent of all births in the United States are to unwed mothers, and the United States leads the world in the rate of children—close to one in four—growing up in single-parent households.[10] This has profound ramifications for these children, as well as the health of society as a whole.

Now, I want to be very clear that this is not to disparage the millions of single parents, mostly mothers, who are doing absolutely heroic work daily providing for their families and raising their children to become people of strong character. But we must be clear-eyed about the reality of what current economic, psychological, and sociological research shows regarding the challenges faced by children who grow up in single-parent households.

Sadly, children born to single parents fare much worse across a number of well-being indicators as compared with their peers who are born to married parents.[11] Seven in ten children living with a single parent are either low-income or in poverty.[12] Less than one-third of children with married parents fall into this category.[13] Married-parent families earn, on average, three times as much in annual income as single-parent households.[14] There are a number of unique factors contributing to this disparity, but statistically speaking, children of married parents are significantly more likely to experience positive economic outcomes.

Interestingly, similar disparities in outcomes are also seen among children who live in households headed by unmarried, cohabitating parents.[15] More than 20 percent of cohabitating stepparent families and almost one-third of cohabitating biological families live at or below the poverty line.[16] Only about 10 to 11 percent of married families, whether biological or stepparent, live at or below the poverty line.[17]

But it is not just about economics. Children born to single mothers are also more likely to struggle academically and experience other behavioral and developmental issues.[18] This is not to suggest that all children who grow up in a single-parent home are damaged or lacking in some way, merely that they are statistically at higher risk of experiencing these challenges.

Quite simply, marriage matters. Marriage and family formation are societal goods that are critical prerequisites for a healthy, prosperous society. But marriage and family formation alone are not sufficient for building strong communities. Parents must be proactive in molding their children's characters, and fathers have an especially important role to play.

Dr. David Popenoe, a leading sociologist whose research focuses on the impact of fathers in child development, has famously noted that "involved fathers bring positive benefits to their children that no other person is as likely to bring."[19] Research has shown that children who grow up with involved fathers achieve better educational outcomes, tend to be more emotionally secure, and demonstrate better behavioral outcomes than those who do not.[20] They are also safer. Kids who live with two married biological parents are eight times less likely to be victims of abuse or neglect.[21]

I firmly believe that our nation is facing a crisis of character, driven in large part by the erosion of the nuclear family. Character is not innate. It is a kinetic force that develops and evolves over time. If you recall your high school science lessons, kinetic energy is the energy of an object due to its motion. But objects will not move forward on their own; some outside force—known as "work" in scientific terms—must be applied to get things started. But any number of outside influences can slow, or even stop, forward progress. The A-10 jets I piloted for the Air Force did not fly on their own. The combustion of fuel in the engine produced the thrust needed to get the plane up to a high enough speed to generate the lift required to propel it skyward. Once airborne, that energy needed to be maintained. If I ran out of fuel, there was nothing I could do to keep the plane from falling out of the sky. My skills as a pilot might help me avoid disaster by making an emergency landing, but no amount of fancy flying could keep that plane airborne.

It is the same with character. A person's character is shaped by a number of forces, including the people who have influence in his or her life and the choices—both big and small—he or she makes on a daily basis. Perhaps the most important influence on the development of a child's character is the example set by its parents.

Ever increasing rates of children growing up in single-parent households mean that fewer and fewer children have the advantage of learning the finer details of character development by watching how their parents interact, support each other, and handle conflict. Those without involved fathers miss out on the priceless opportunity to spend quality time playing and working with their dads, which, research shows, aids in healthy psychological and emotional development.[22] This is not to discount the critically important role mothers play in their child's development, but as a father, I am passionate about helping other fathers understand and embrace their equally important role.

I have experienced the benefits of having an involved father in my own life. My family's farm in Iowa has been in our family for more than 150 years. From an early age, my identity and character were shaped by working alongside my father and my grandfather. These men taught me about the value and dignity of hard work and what it means to be a man of strong moral character simply by demonstrating these qualities in their own daily lives. True, there were times when direct lessons were taught, but the majority of my education in character came through following their silent example.

Given the important role marriage, family formation, and engaged fathers play in the lives of children and a strong society, we are right to be concerned by their decline. Addressing this concern requires us to first consider why fewer Americans are choosing to get married and have families.

Numerous explanations for declines in marriage and fertility rates have been proposed in recent years. These include younger Americans stating that they chose to delay marriage until much later in life than previous generations because of socioeconomic factors like education and the cost of living.[23] While there are certainly a number of outside factors contributing to the decline in marriage and family formation, a close look at the data reveals that for most people the decision of whether or not to get married and have children is more rooted in lifestyle choices and personal desires than any factor external to the individual.

In 2018, the *New York Times* commissioned one of the most comprehensive surveys of the reasons American adults were choosing to have fewer children.[24] The survey asked nearly two thousand men and women between the ages of twenty and forty-five why they either were choosing not to have children or having fewer children than they would like. Among those surveyed who said they didn't want children or were not sure, the top reason given—36 percent of all respondents—was a desire for more leisure time.[25] Even though it was not the top reason given, 42 percent of respondents who already had children said a desire for more leisure time was a major factor in their decision not to have more.[26]

The *New York Times* survey is a snapshot of a trend that has been developing over the past three decades. In 2010, Andrew Cherlin, a sociologist at Johns Hopkins University, published his landmark book, *The Marriage-Go-Round*, which tracked Americans' evolving ideas about marriage and family formation. Foremost among his findings was that marriage is no longer viewed as foundational to American life, but as a "capstone" event entered into only after already having achieved success and stability. This view of marriage has been particularly embraced by Americans of the millennial generation, whose decision to delay marriage has driven the median age of marriage up to twenty-nine years for men and twenty-seven years for women.[27] A 2018 study commissioned by the online dating website eHarmony found that Americans between the ages of twenty-five and thirty-four are spending more time—roughly six and a half years—getting to know their eventual spouse before tying the knot.[28]

Dr. Helen Fisher, an anthropologist and senior research fellow at the Kinsey Institute, cites this delay in marriage among millennials as an embrace of what she calls the "age of slow love."[29] According to Dr. Fisher's research, two-thirds of single men and half of single women reported that they had engaged in a one-night stand.[30] Similar numbers reported having a so-called "friends with benefits" relationship, which involves regular sexual encounters with the same person without the commitment of an actual relationship.[31]

Dr. Fisher celebrates this culture of "fast sex, slow love" as a healthy development that will lead to more happy, long-term relationships.[32] But there's more to marriage than personal happiness and, as we have seen, the choice to delay or even forgo marriage carries significant risk of negative outcomes for children, economic prosperity, and society at large.

Incredible prosperity in the decades following the end of World War II has enabled access to a standard of living that was once only attainable by the wealthiest Americans. This prosperity, combined with increasing equality and more options for Americans of all walks of life, has created an enormous amount of good. But it has also created an increasingly self-focused population, something exemplified by the millennial generation's embrace of the "fast sex, slow love" philosophy.

CULTURE AND COMMUNITY ARE KEY

Thus, the root problem we must solve if we want to increase the number of Americans choosing to get married and have children isn't economic, educational, or environmental—it's cultural. While there are certain steps that government can take to reduce barriers that prevent individuals from making these important decisions, promoting this type of cultural shift is ultimately not the role of government.

I recognize that this is, in some ways, a shocking statement to make in a book about policy solutions. It is, however, the proper conservative position. Our philosophy is rooted in a belief that individuals, families, and communities do best when left alone to exercise their God-given freedoms and to provide for themselves and for one other. Government exists merely to protect and preserve these freedoms. It is rather for individuals, religious communities, and other institutions of civil society to take the lead in reorienting American society toward a culture that prioritizes marriage and family formation.

I am honored to be on the board of one organization that is seeking to do just that. Promise Keepers is an evangelical Christian men's ministry focused on helping men live with integrity and become the husbands and fathers God has called them to be. Founded in 1990 by legendary University of Colorado football coach Bill McCartney, Promise Keepers convened hundreds of thousands of men at gatherings across the nation during its peak in the mid-'90s.

But the America of the 2020s is very different from the America of the 1990s. Considerable ink has been spilled in recent years over the question of what it means to be a man. For some, masculinity is toxic, the root cause of horrific acts of sexual exploitation and violence. For others, masculinity is under attack from progressive forces seeking to eradicate the influence of men in society. Both sides are operating from different, yet equally false, definitions of masculinity. That is why I'm so excited to be part of the team that is relaunching Promise Keepers at a time when it is critically important that we rediscover the true definition of manhood.

While it is true that masculinity is in crisis, it is not the type of masculinity being debated endlessly in the mass media. The true masculinity I am talking about is exemplified by men of integrity who walk in humility, honor women, serve those in need in their communities, and put their children and families above themselves. If we are serious about revitalizing the family, it is of the utmost importance that we revitalize true, biblical manhood.

I firmly believe that many of the challenges facing the American family today are the result of a generation of men who failed to show their sons what it means to work hard and sacrificially love their wives and children. This failure of leadership has resulted in more men struggling with isolation, loneliness, addiction, narcissism, and depression than ever before. It has resulted in a crisis of character.

As I mentioned earlier, character is kinetic—it must be continually developed over time. The work that goes into establishing and growing one's character is incredibly difficult and virtually impossible to do in isolation. One of our main goals at Promise Keepers is to go after the poison of isolation that is undermining the ability of men to realize their true purpose. Very few men have close friends or mentors modeling true manhood and helping them hone their characters. By creating a space where men can be mentored and are pushed to develop deep, healthy relationships with other men of character, we hope to positively transform a generation of men and, in the process, the nation.

FAITH AS A KEY INGREDIENT

The Promise Keepers model creates transformational change through the power of relationships between individuals and within communities, not a government program. While it may seem overly idealistic to an increasingly cynical society, individual relationships and community-driven efforts are infinitely more effective at creating lasting, positive change than government. Consider the incredible story of how a few churches and nonprofit organizations in Jacksonville, Florida, utterly transformed the culture of marriage in their city.

Between 2015 and 2017 something significant happened in Jacksonville, Florida—the divorce rate plummeted by 28 percent.[33] To put this number in context, the national divorce rate fell by 6 percent during this same period of time.[34] Researchers looking into what caused the dramatic decrease in divorces concluded that the change could not "be classified as a chance occurrence," but "resulted from an interaction that was timely, effective, and resulted from program providers in Jacksonville who focused on keeping marriages together rather than allowing them to separate."[35]

At the center of this change was a coordinated effort among nonprofits and local church congregations focused on strengthening marriage in Jacksonville. Led by the Culture of Freedom Initiative (COFI), a project of The Philanthropy Roundtable[36] since spun off as an independent nonprofit called Communio, and Live the Life, a Florida nonprofit focused on marriage enrichment, this movement brought together more than fifty Jacksonville area churches to reach over fifty thousand people with relationship and faith development programs.[37]

The entire initiative was privately funded and driven by the local community, which is especially impressive when you compare the results achieved in Jacksonville with similar federally funded programs. In 2001, the U.S. Department of Health and Human Services Administration for Children and Families (ACF) launched the Healthy Marriage Initiative (HMI) with the goal of promoting and strengthening marriage in the United States. Between 2001 and 2014, the federal government spent over $600 million on marriage education, skills training, mentoring, and public awareness campaigns designed to help Americans form and sustain healthy marriages.[38]

By any measure, the program was an absolute failure. Despite a massive investment of taxpayer dollars, the nation's divorce rate remained relatively stable while the marriage rate decreased by 26 percent from 2001 to 2010.[39]

So why did the Culture of Freedom Initiative succeed with a budget of only $1.75 million per year while a $600 million government-driven program failed? One key variable was the role of community organizations, specifically the role of local churches, in leading program implementation.

In contrast with HMI's top-down approach that awarded grants to organizations to develop and implement marriage-strengthening programs, COFI's program was based on coordinating and enhancing the existing marriage-strengthening capabilities of local community organizations, focusing primarily on churches.[40] Leveraging local congregations allowed COFI to saturate the Jacksonville market with its programs while employing a sophisticated online micro-targeting strategy to drive interest among Jacksonville residents.[41] Rather than using local churches merely as a program delivery mechanism, however, COFI specifically structured its program to incorporate the spiritual beliefs of the participating congregations. Thus, COFI was able to leverage a powerful force for change that HMI, as a government-funded initiative, cut from its programs—faith.

Unsurprisingly, faith is a key driver of community service. More than half of all Americans who donate to charitable causes cite their religious beliefs as an important motivator for their giving.[42] Healthy, active community institutions, like churches, are the catalysts of fundamental social change. By artificially uncoupling the act of service from the values that inspire the desire to serve, we risk sabotaging the work. For family-strengthening efforts to be truly effective, we must not only engage these institutions but also free them to deploy their unique strengths in the service of others.

SPORTS AS A TOOL FOR CULTURE CHANGE

The old cliché "actions speak louder than words" has never been truer. Americans, and especially youth, are constantly bombarded with information and conflicting messages through social media. This onslaught has forced us to develop mental filters to help decipher the real from the fake. Preaching to kids about the importance of character is not enough. If you are not authentic, if your life does not match your message, they will smell you out from a mile away.

One of the best opportunities outside of the home for demonstrating and instilling character in children is sports. My heroes growing up, aside from my father and grandfather, were my coaches. I was fortunate to have coaches who taught me much about how to excel both on and off the field. The most important lessons I learned were not about the skills required to be an elite athlete, but about work ethic, overcoming adversity, supporting others, and living a life of integrity. Few of these lessons were conveyed with words.

Unfortunately, youth participation in sports is declining. A recent study by the Aspen Institute found that just 38 percent of children between the ages of six and twelve played individual or team sports on a regular basis in 2018.[43] This is down from 45 percent in 2008. The decline is especially pronounced among youth from low-income households. Only 22 percent of children whose families make $25,000 or less regularly participate in sports. As I travel around the country, it breaks my heart to see empty fields that were once filled with kids playing and learning critical life skills.

Gone are the days of *The Sandlot*, the nostalgic coming-of-age film about a group of childhood friends whose greatest joy in life was playing baseball together. In that movie, the main characters would gather every afternoon at a run-down dirt field in their small town to spend countless hours playing the game they loved. The kids of *The Sandlot* were not particularly talented athletes. Only one, Benny, would go on to achieve the dream they shared of playing in the major leagues. But through the unstructured, self-organized games they played together, they developed deep bonds and learned lessons that they carried with them into adulthood.

Today, the loosely structured pickup games idealized by *The Sandlot*, as well as town- or church-sponsored little leagues, have largely given way to a lucrative professionalized model that seeks to identify and develop "elite" talent in kids as young as ten years old.[44] It is becoming increasingly common for top college programs like Alabama and Michigan to offer scholarships to promising middle schoolers.[45] This has resulted in a sort of "arms race" among parents willing to pay top dollar for their kids to join highly selective developmental leagues in hopes of getting a leg up in the quest to achieve professional success.

While this model is certainly valuable for the rare kids who are blessed with elite-level talent, it is costing the vast majority of kids who will never make the jump to "the League" but who need the character development that organized sports provide. If we are serious about revitalizing community and helping our children develop strong characters that will serve them well when they inevitably (in the words of a memorable NCAA public service announcement) "go pro in something other than sports," then we need to put the time and effort into resurrecting community recreational leagues.[46]

This presents a prime opportunity for fathers to invest in their own children as well as children in their communities who lack an involved father. Instead of spending thousands upon thousands of dollars each year on travel teams and private coaching, consider volunteering to organize a league or coach a recreational team in your local community. I can guarantee the return on investment from developing the characters of your kids and the kids in your community will be infinitely more valuable than any signing bonus or shoe endorsement.

STRENGTHENING FAMILIES BY LIMITING GOVERNMENT

The family is not only the most powerful force for shaping character and setting children up for future success, it is also the foundation of a free and prosperous society. It is, in the words of priest and legal scholar Robert J. Araujo, "more than a mere juridical, social, and economic unit. It is a community based on love and solidarity, which is uniquely suited to teach and transmit cultural, ethical, social, spiritual, and religious values essential to the well-being of its members and of the larger society beyond it."[47] The health of society, Father Araujo argues, is inextricably linked with the health of the family. "When the family prospers, so does the society surrounding and beyond it. When it does not, society becomes all the poorer."[48] While, as we observed earlier, there is little that government can do to create the cultural shifts necessary for promoting and strengthening the family, government actions can—and often do—significantly weaken this most critical institution.

Given the fundamental importance of the family to a healthy, functioning society, Western civilization has long made a clear distinction between the role of parents and the role of the state and protected the family against interference from the state except in the most extreme circumstances. The English philosopher John Locke, whose ideas profoundly influenced America's Founding Fathers, explored this distinction in his classic work, *Two Treatises of Government*. Unlike the political power vested in government, which Locke writes is conveyed by man giving up a portion of the power he naturally possesses to society as a whole, parental power exists independently of any conveyance and is a natural form of government derived from "the affection and tenderness God hath planted in the breasts of parents towards their children."[49] Locke likens the role of parents in the life of their child to the role of a sovereign over his people. Every parent, Locke writes, "has as much parental power over his children as the prince has over his."[50] Under Locke's formulation, even the sovereign himself is limited by the natural order of the family, owing to his parents "as much filial duty and obedience as the meanest of his subjects do theirs."[51]

The Lockean idea of the family as a natural form of government that exists independently of, and, indeed, outlives the state is an integral part of American constitutional jurisprudence. Nearly a century of U.S. Supreme Court precedent has recognized the parent-child relationship as a fundamental right under the Constitution. The Court in *Meyer v. Nebraska* held that the Fourteenth Amendment protects "the right of the individual to contract, to engage in any of the common occupations of life, to acquire useful knowledge, to marry, establish a home and bring up children . . . as essential to the orderly pursuit of happiness by free men."[52] More recently, Justice Sandra Day O'Connor, writing for a plurality of the Court in the case of *Troxel v. Granville*, noted that "the interest of parents in the care, custody, and control of their children is perhaps the oldest of the fundamental liberty interests recognized by this court."[53]

To put it in simpler terms, the family relationship is so important that our society has constructed a system of governance that protects it from any kind of government interference absent the strongest justification. Even in instances where a so-called "compelling interest" exists, the intervention by government into the life of a family must be the most limited and precise way to achieve that interest.

There is good reason for this, and it is rooted in our earlier discussion of the critical role parents play in shaping the character of their children. While the fundamental right of family members in their relationships with one another is colloquially referred to as "parental rights," these rights do not belong solely to parents. Children, as the ultimate beneficiaries of the exercise of these rights, have a constitutionally protected interest in maintaining the "emotional attachments that derive from the intimacy of daily association" with parents and siblings.[54] This interest derives from the duty of parents to "take care of their offspring during the imperfect state of childhood," to "preserve, nourish and educate" them, and to "prepare [them] for additional obligations."[55]

The concept of the family in American jurisprudence rests on two primary presumptions. First, "that parents possess what a child lacks in maturity, experience, and capacity for judgment required for making life's difficult decisions."[56] Second, and most importantly, "that natural bonds of affection lead parents to act in the best interests of children."[57] These two presumptions find their source in the universal truth that it is the proper role of the family to shape a child's character so that he or she can grow to become a contributing member of society. For this reason, "the statist notion that governmental power should supersede parental authority . . . is repugnant to American tradition."[58]

Yet, despite these clear lines of separation between the family and the state, government is inserting itself more and more into the private realm of the family. Contemporary American society is increasingly fragmented as the ideals and institutions once held sacrosanct are increasingly being questioned and, in some cases, completely rejected. As we saw with the declining marriage rate, the family is not immune.

A troubling consequence of the public's increased questioning of fundamental social institutions is a growing acceptance of government intervention and micromanagement of the family. Some, like James G. Dwyer, a law professor at the William & Mary Law School, are shockingly honest in advocating for increased government regulation of families. Dwyer, a self-identified liberal, has been outspoken in his calls for draconian levels of state intervention, including the mandatory removal of children born to parents who live in neighborhoods the state deems "unfit" if the parents do not voluntarily relocate.[59] He has also advocated for a categorical presumption of unfitness for certain parents, ostensibly determined through some type of predictive risk modeling, and requiring those deemed "unfit" to present evidence proving their ability to raise their children before the state recognizes them as their child's legal parent.[60] While one could easily dismiss Dwyer's ideas as an extreme example of progressive utopian ideology, some self-professed conservatives are beginning to make similar, albeit less expansive arguments in favor of increased state intervention in the family.[61] These policy proposals include lowering the legal standards the state is required to meet before placing children into foster care and utilizing big data to allow the state to preemptively identify "at-risk" families and intervene.[62]

To be clear, the fundamental rights of parents do not include the right to abuse their children. Such actions are contrary to the duty of parents to nurture and care for their children, and the state, through its police powers, is justified in intervening in the parent-child relationship to protect children who have been abused or are in imminent danger of harm. Contrary to the insistence by Dwyer and others that government should have broad authority to intervene even in cases where the risk of harm is entirely speculative, the Constitution requires that the type of harm justifying government intervention be narrowly defined and the intervention itself be limited solely to those actions necessary to protect the child. The Supreme Court has consistently given broad deference and protection to the liberty interest of parents and children in their relationship with one another, going so far as to note that this interest "does not evaporate simply because they have not been model parents."[63]

Yet, too often, children are removed from their parents and placed in the foster care system for reasons unrelated to actual or imminent maltreatment. During fiscal year 2018, 62 percent of all children who entered the foster care system did so solely due to neglect, a broadly defined category that is frequently confused with poverty.[64] Jerry Milner, whom President Trump appointed to serve as associate commissioner of the U.S. Children's Bureau at the Department of Health and Human Services in 2017, has been outspoken about the need for reforms that make it "resoundingly clear that a child should never be removed from his or her family due to poverty alone."[65]

The tendency to confuse poverty with neglect is one symptom of a growing government bureaucracy that increasingly inserts itself into the private realm of the family—sometimes without any justification whatsoever. Take, for example, a recent case out of Texas involving four-year-old Drake Pardo.

Drake has a complicated medical history. During his short life, he has undergone brain surgery, was diagnosed with cerebral palsy, and struggled with serious eating issues. After his physician refused to see him during a multi-day hospitalization, Drake's parents, Ashley and Daniel Pardo, filed a complaint with the hospital. Shortly thereafter, a physician specializing in child abuse filed a report with Child Protective Services expressing concerns for medical child abuse. The doctor would later admit in court that her concerns were entirely speculative as she had not seen Drake in person prior to filing her report. Nevertheless, Child Protective Services obtained a court order based on the doctor's report and removed Drake into foster care.[66]

The removal sparked a four-month court battle that went all the way to the Texas Supreme Court. Ultimately, the court ruled in favor of the Pardo family, finding that the Department of Family and Protective Services failed to show that Drake was in substantial danger of harm and ordering his immediate return home.[67] In an interview following the conclusion of the case, Texas Supreme Court justice Jimmy Blacklock indicated that ordering the return of Drake was an easy decision because "the government had not satisfied the statutory standards for taking the child away and for keeping the child away."[68] Although the Pardo family's ordeal had a happy ending, the case highlights the incredible power of the state to forever destroy families and the need for strict limits on this power. While these limits are of the utmost importance for protecting the fundamental constitutional rights of families and preventing unnecessary trauma to children, they are also critical for providing CPS caseworkers with appropriate guidance as they engage in the difficult but necessary work of protecting children who are in actual danger of harm.

INCREASING THE ROLE OF LOCAL COMMUNITIES

Government's leading role in child protection, which gives rise to its power to separate families, is a relatively new phenomenon. Prior to President Franklin D. Roosevelt's New Deal, child protection was primarily handled by local communities—specifically faith-based organizations.

The first institution dedicated to caring for orphaned children in North America was affiliated with the church. In 1729, Ursuline nuns in New Orleans founded an orphanage to care for the children of French settlers who were killed in an attack by members of the Natchez tribe.[69] Just over a century later, in 1874, the first formal organization for protecting children from abuse would be established by a group of philanthropists in New York City.[70] By 1922, there were more than three hundred private, charitable organizations across the country dedicated to protecting children from abuse.[71]

The Great Depression changed the entire course of child welfare. The Social Security Act of 1935 created the Aid to Families with Dependent Children program, which provided economic aid to poor families with children. More importantly, it also created the Children's Bureau to facilitate cooperation between the federal government and "state public-welfare agencies in establishing, extending, and strengthening . . . public-welfare services . . . for the protection and care of homeless, dependent, and neglected children, and children in danger of becoming delinquent."[72]

From that point forward, community-led solutions were crowded out or absorbed into government-run programs. By the 1960s, nearly every state had laws placing primary responsibility for child welfare in the hands of government. The enactment of the Child Abuse Prevention and Treatment Act in 1974 and the Adoption and Safe Families Act in 1997 solidified government control over child protection, foster care, and adoption.

Tragically, this centralized control has, in many ways, proven harmful for the children it was intended to protect. In 1974, the year the Child Abuse Prevention and Treatment Act was signed, there were approximately 60,000 reports of abuse and neglect each year.[73] In 2018, there were 4.3 million reports alleging maltreatment involving nearly 8 million children.[74] Of these 8 million children, 3.5 million received some type of intervention from CPS.[75] Ultimately, 678,000 children were confirmed as victims of abuse or neglect.[76] While this is an absolutely heartbreaking number, it means that roughly 2.8 million children who had meaningful contact with CPS were later ruled to be non-victims.[77] The government's casting a wider net that brings more children and families into contact with CPS does not necessarily translate to better protections. In fact, as we will see, it carries the potential of causing more harm.

Increases in reports have led to an increase in children entering the foster care system. Since 2012, the number of children entering state custody has increased almost every year despite an overall downward trend in the number of children who are confirmed as victims of abuse or neglect.[78] The most recent data show that there are 437,000 children living in the foster care system with 237,000 new entries each year.[79] Although this was a slight decrease from the year prior, the overall trend has been one of increased government intervention.

This intervention, while often necessary, is far from benign. Less than half of those who enter foster care will ever be reunited with their families.[80] Approximately 8 percent of children who leave foster care, more than 17,000 in 2018, will "age out" when they turn eighteen without ever finding a permanent home.[81] These children, many of whom have spent most of their childhoods in the care of the state, exit to a challenging future in which it is more likely that they will experience poverty, homelessness, and incarceration than graduate from college.[82]

Government-run foster care has consistently failed the very children it is charged with protecting. Things in Texas got so bad, in fact, that in 2015 a federal judge ruled that the foster care system operated by the Department of Family and Protective Services actually violated the constitutional rights of the children in its care. Judge Janis Jack found that Texas foster children faced an unreasonably high risk of physical abuse, sexual abuse, and suicide before concluding that these children "uniformly leave State custody more damaged than when they entered."[83] Paradoxically, the harm caused to children by the government-run foster care system in Texas would result in the termination of the rights of a parent.

Due to these failures, many states, Texas among them, are questioning the centralized model of child welfare that has dominated the better part of the last century and are enacting sweeping reforms. Many have found the answer by going back to the place where child welfare originated—local communities and faith-based organizations.

The state of Florida was one of the first to undertake such a comprehensive transformation of its child welfare system. Beginning in 1996, Florida shifted a majority of the responsibility for providing foster care and adoption services away from government and to local private and nonprofit charities.[84] Full implementation of the model, known as community-based care, was completed in 2005, and since then the state has seen significant improvement in several key outcomes for children, including reducing the amount of time it takes to move a child from foster care to a permanent home and increasing the number of older youth in care who are either reunified with their families or adopted.[85] The community-based model has produced an additional benefit for Florida. Not only is the state achieving better results when compared with government-run models, it is also spending less per child than the national average.[86]

Partially inspired by Florida's success, Texas is pursuing similar community-based reforms to its foster care system. In the wake of the 2015 court ruling, Governor Greg Abbott declared foster care reform the top "emergency item" to be tackled by the 85th Legislature.[87] By the time the session concluded, Texas lawmakers had successfully enacted revolutionary changes that moved the state to a localized, community-driven foster care system.[88] Although still in the early phases of implementation, regions currently operating under the new community-based care model are already outperforming the old state-run system.[89]

Why are community-based models succeeding where government-run models have failed? A key to the success lies in the combination of localization and decentralization. Localizing child welfare services gives communities skin in the game, and decentralizing authority gives them the power to actually make life better for the most vulnerable children in their neighborhoods. No longer are these children merely "foster kids"; they're "our kids." This sense of ownership is key to increasing the number of people who sign up to foster or adopt and for generating innovative new ways of making the system more responsive to the unique needs of the children who enter it. If we are truly serious about strengthening the family, then decentralization is key. The lion's share of the work to meet the needs of children and families should be done at the neighborhood and municipal levels rather than outsourced to the state and federal governments.

STRENGTHEN FAMILIES BY STRENGTHENING COMMUNITIES

At the root of the factors contributing to the weakening of the American family is a breakdown of the American community. Problems that were once solved by neighbors helping neighbors are increasingly being ceded to or taken over by government. Civic institutions that were once a dominant feature of American society are all but disappearing.

In his famous book *Bowling Alone*, political scientist Robert Putnam highlights the critical role of interpersonal relationships to the overall health of society. Putnam argues that individuals and communities are happier, healthier, and more prosperous the more they connect and interact with one another on a personal level.[90] Conversely, communities that are more isolated, often as a result of a loss of clubs, churches, and other centers of communal life, tend to be plagued by lower levels of educational performance, higher rates of violent crime, poorer overall health, and higher rates of premature death.[91] In short, humans are social creatures and need meaningful relationships with one another in order to lead happy, prosperous lives.

Unfortunately for our modern society, technology has given us the illusion of relationship while actually taking it away. The rise of social media has, in one sense, allowed human beings to connect in a way never before seen in all of human history. Thanks to platforms like Facebook, Instagram, and Twitter, we can instantly connect with people all over the world. In theory, we should be more connected with our fellow man. The reality, however, is just the opposite. Numerous studies have found that increased use of social media is directly correlated with an individual's sense of social isolation.[92] Social isolation—a person's lack of a sense of belonging or of having true, supportive relationships with others—is associated with a number of negative health outcomes.[93] Researchers have found that the more heavily a person uses social media, the more likely they are to feel socially isolated. For example, study participants who reported using social media for two hours or more per day were two times as likely to report feelings of loneliness as those who used social media for only thirty minutes per day.[94]

THE ROLE OF CHURCHES

The rise of personal technology has roughly coincided with a decline in church membership. Over the last two decades, church attendance in the United States has dropped by 20 percent.[95] Only about half of all

Americans report that they are members of a church, synagogue, or mosque.[96] Between the late 1930s and mid-1970s, this number was over 70 percent.[97] Today, roughly one quarter of all Americans claim no religious affiliation whatsoever.[98]

In *Alienated America*, Tim Carney makes a compelling case that many of the ills plaguing struggling communities can be traced to the secularization of America. Citing numerous sociological studies, Carney writes that "the Americans who are turning away from religion, particularly among the working class, are doing worse than those maintaining their connection to religion."[99] Those who attend church regularly, by contrast, tend to experience greater economic success, have more stable families, and lower incidence of spousal or child abuse, drug use, criminality, and suicide.[100]

Carney's findings are consistent with other studies that have found that those who are active in their faith are more likely to invest in the health of their communities through volunteering and charitable giving.[101] Practicing Christians, for instance, are more than twice as likely to adopt and 50 percent more likely to foster when compared with the general population.[102] Yet, despite the proven importance of religious communities to the overall health of society, government often makes it harder for the religious to serve the public good.

During the winter of 2019, for example, zoning restrictions in Dallas, Texas, made it illegal for religious organizations to shelter the homeless on freezing nights.[103] Many churches and faith-based charities in Dallas chose to defy the ban. Wayne Walker, the executive director of a discipleship ministry for the homeless called OurCalling, proudly displays a code violation he received from the city for sheltering the homeless on a cold night in February 2018 on the wall of his office.[104]

While Dallas's zoning restrictions can be chalked up to unintended consequences of poor city planning, other government regulations are directly targeted at preventing religious organizations from engaging in certain activities due to their sincerely held beliefs. Numerous cities across the country have lost adoption and foster care capacity by placing restrictions on the ability of faith-based organizations to operate in accordance with their belief systems. In 2018, the city of Philadelphia terminated its contract with Catholic Charities to provide foster and adoption services over its organizational policies that adhered to traditional Catholic teachings about marriage.[105] At the same time that it terminated its contract with Catholic Charities, Philadelphia was in the midst of an emergency shortage of foster families and put out an urgent call for 300 more approved foster families to meet the city's need for placements.[106] The year prior, Catholic Charities had served 2,200 foster children.[107]

Similar stories of governments shooting themselves in the foot by making it harder for faith-based agencies to provide foster and adoptive services have played out in Boston, Illinois, San Francisco, and Washington, D.C. Yet, there is reason for hope. In late 2019, the Trump administration moved to reverse an Obama-era rule that prohibited faith-based agencies that receive federal grants from having religious qualifications for their foster and adoptive families.[108] The proposed rule change would require states that distribute federal grant money for foster and adoptive services to comply with nondiscrimination provisions that expressly protect the religious liberty of service providers.[109]

In his classic work *Democracy in America*, Alexis de Tocqueville observes that "religion, which among Americans never directly takes part in the government of society, must be considered as the first of their political institutions; for if it does not give them the taste for liberty, it singularly facilitates their use of it."[110] A unique aspect of the role of religion in American society that Tocqueville highlights is how, despite a diversity in beliefs among the "innumerable multitude of sects in the United States," all are united in their beliefs concerning the "duties of men toward one another."[111] Foremost among man's duties to his fellow man is his duty to his family. The strengthening of the American family, then, is inextricably linked with increasing religious participation.

CONCLUSION

There are many things that make America exceptional among the nations of the earth. Foremost among them is our republican system of government that puts the power to chart the course of the nation in the hands of the people. For the average American, it is not the politician in Washington, D.C., or even at the state capital who has the most influence on his daily life. It is the people in his home, neighborhood, and place of worship. As I noted at the beginning of this chapter, the most powerful force for change that I have experienced is the American family. To strengthen the family, conservatives must continue to prioritize limiting and decentralizing government. But more than that, we need to embrace the truth of the old adage that "politics is downstream from culture," and actively engage in and reinvigorate community life in the neighborhoods we call home. If we do that, and do it well, then we will make life better for generations to come.

Every Life Matters

by Kathy Ireland

In our society today, no issue is more passionately debated than the right to life. It truly is an issue unlike any other, and our nation is deeply divided on this most crucial of matters. As pro-life advocates, we believe that every human life is precious, a gift from God. Each child is created in God's image and likeness. We believe that every human life should be protected from conception to natural death. We also believe that the Fifth Amendment to the United States Constitution protects the unborn, as it reads "nor be deprived of life, liberty or property, without due process." Over the years, many individual states have advanced pro-life legislation successfully. These efforts are alive and well across the nation today. The fight to protect every human life from abortion is the human rights issue of our time. Without life, which is the most essential right, no other rights have applicability or meaning. Not only is Kathy Ireland one of the world's most famous supermodels and actresses, but she is also one of the world's most successful entrepreneurs as the founder and CEO of kathy ireland Worldwide (kiWW). She is renowned for her charitable and philanthropic efforts protecting children, eradicating disease and hunger, and serving our veterans. She is incredibly humble and kind and would share that her greatest achievement in this world is her family. Kathy is one of the most articulate and passionate defenders of life in America today. With grace and tremendous clarity, she puts forth arguments based on science and reason, as well as her strong Christian faith, that expose the lies of the abortion industry. I am honored that Kathy chose to participate in *Making Government Work*. Her passionate defense of all human life needs to be read and understood by all Americans.

—Tan Parker

You are valuable. You are unique. There never has been and never will be another person just like you. No matter our differences, I will fight for your right to live.

The definition of "child" in the *Merriam-Webster Dictionary* is "an unborn or recently born person."

Science changed the trajectory of my life. I went from being someone who identified as pro-choice to being a fierce advocate for life and human rights at every age, including for the most vulnerable humans residing in the womb.

Statistics tell us that one in four women in America have had an abortion.[1] Please know, this is absolutely not an indictment of any woman. When an abortion takes place, there are always several victims—some known, some not. Women, unborn children, and often men suffer silently. As women, we are usually not given the needed information and facts regarding life and abortion. We are told abortion is our God-given right and a freedom we must fight for and protect.

As a little girl growing up in the 1970s, I found it encouraging to watch women find their voices and take bold stands. There was hope for more opportunities than those that were available to my mom and grandma.

In my high school drivers' education class, we were surprised one day by a guest speaker, a schoolmate who volunteered for Planned Parenthood (PP). This student explained that we had the right to have an abortion, and our parents did not need to know. The teacher nodded in approval and led the class in applause for this presentation. While I never thought I would have an abortion, who was I to tell another girl what she could and couldn't do with her body? At an age when many impressionable teens believe parents are clueless, it felt liberating to have a peer—as well as adults—advocate for us adolescents. My heart breaks as I remember that day, for the vulnerable girls in that class who believed that when life was growing within them it could quietly be erased with no lasting repercussions.

In our state of California, this law continues today. In addition to being CEO of his businesses, my husband Greg is a heroic emergency room physician. If Greg were to give a minor an aspirin in the hospital without a parent's permission, he could face costly litigation and potentially have his medical license revoked. Yet our daughters could have a surgery that would kill a human life and forever change theirs, and this could be unknown to us forever.

Four decades ago, PP targeted me as a teenager. Today, through the California Healthy Youth Act, PP still introduces itself to children as a group of advocates. Its members even speak in kindergarten classes. Please educate yourself on these dangerous laws and take appropriate actions to protect our youth. Please don't believe that the rest of our country, and world, is immune to these attacks on our children.

Though I became a Christian at age eighteen, I regret that, due to biblical illiteracy, I identified as a pro-choice Christian. But it was science, not the Bible, that first taught me the truth about life. The topic of abortion became relevant, and upon deep reflection, I had more questions than answers. I recognized I wasn't truly pro-choice; rather, I was on the fence. I detest being on the fence on any matter, especially matters of life and death. Determined not to be distracted by emotions, opinions, politics, or man-made religion, I went directly to medical science, seeking facts.

I learned that at the moment of conception, a new life comes into existence. The complete genetic blueprint and DNA, entirely separate from both parents, is determined. The blood type, the sex, and the unique set of fingerprints are all in place at conception. We know this is a continually growing life. We must know what kind of life this is before we decide if it is acceptable to kill it. According to the Law of Biogenesis, all life comes from pre-existing life, and each species reproduces after its own kind. Human beings can only reproduce human beings. We don't begin as one species and become human sometime during gestation.

Though I was searching for truth, becoming pro-life was not what I wanted. Perhaps subconsciously, I feared that in the worlds of entertainment, media, and politics, I might be described (along with other pro-life people) as unstable, ignorant, or crazy.

I picked up the phone and called the organization that first put me on this journey, PP.

"Help!" I said. "What's your best argument for being pro-choice?"

I was told, "It's just a clump of cells. If you get it early enough, it doesn't even look like a baby."

Even in my earliest stages of seeking facts, it was shocking to hear that this was their best defense. We are all clumps of cells. The unborn human doesn't look like a baby in the same way that a baby doesn't resemble an adolescent or an octogenarian. That unborn human looks exactly the way human beings are supposed to look at that stage of life. Viewing the miraculous details of children in the womb had been an impossibility. However, technology has made incredible strides since *Roe v. Wade*.

I called my pro-choice friends to see if they could offer better help. They shared the same information I believed before taking an unbiased look at science.

"It's a woman's body," they said. "It needs to be her choice. It's a private matter between a woman and her doctor."

We can all agree that choice and privacy are good as long as another human being is not being hurt. None of us has complete autonomy over our bodies if our actions could harm another. Drinking and driving is illegal, and we cannot deceptively yell, "Fire!" in a theater.

We know the unborn person's DNA and fingerprints are unique from the parents' DNA and fingerprints. There is also a 50 percent chance that the baby the woman is carrying is a male child with a penis. Clearly, the mother doesn't have a penis; therefore, the unborn child is not part of her body. Rather, the unborn child resides within her body.

Other arguments for abortion include financial hardship, health challenges of the baby, bad timing, inconvenience, parents not equipped to bring a child into the world, and emotional distress. These real challenges surrounding an unintended pregnancy must be addressed and are arguments for birth control—not for the killing of a human being. We don't kill innocent people when they become expensive, develop health issues, or become inconvenient.

I believe all who claim to be pro-life must do everything that they can to support the tangible needs of women and children in unplanned pregnancies, offering love and support without judgment. I always have and always will fight for the rights of women. Abortion is not a women's rights issue; it is a human rights crisis of disastrous proportions.

The research of NIH's Eunice Kennedy Shriver National Institute of Child Health and Human Development informs us that 9 percent of men and about 11 percent of women of reproductive age in the United States have experienced fertility problems.[2] The CDC shares that one in eight couples, or 12 percent of married women, or 6.1 million women, have trouble getting pregnant or sustaining a pregnancy. Many sources estimate there are currently 2 million couples waiting to adopt in the U.S., which means that for every birth and abortion there are thirty-six couples waiting to adopt.[3] Today's adoption process empowers the birth mother with every choice: open or closed adoption, involvement or no involvement in the child's life, selection of adoptive parents, and the covering of prenatal and labor costs.

I've asked leading scientists throughout our country and world to please provide evidence that the unborn is not a human being. A scientist once dismissively told me, "Kathy, it's a little bit more complicated than that." I replied that it was actually quite simple. The surrounding issues of an unplanned pregnancy can be complicated and must be addressed.

That is a separate issue, and facts, rather than emotion, are needed to make the most compassionate decision.

Who—or what—is the unborn child? If the unborn child is not a human being, have as many abortions as you like. No justification is needed. If the unborn is a human being, no justification is adequate, unless another human life is in jeopardy—the life of the mother. In this rare occurrence, you are acting to save a life. As a result of the mother's life being saved, the unborn child tragically dies. However, your intent is to save a life. With abortion, the sole intent is to kill. As you ask these questions of others, please don't allow anyone to dismiss you. Refute? Yes. Dismiss? Never. An excellent book I recommend that scientifically explains the facts surrounding abortion is *Precious Unborn Human Persons* by Gregory Koukl.

Article III of the UN's Universal Declaration of Human Rights states, "Everyone has the right to life, liberty and the security of person." Yet, since *Roe v. Wade*, there have been more than 60 million abortions in the United States, and the World Health Organization reports that 125,000 children are aborted every single day globally. Horrific.

Please don't rely on my research; love children enough to do your own independent research and find out why the United States is one of seven countries that allows elective abortions after twenty weeks of pregnancy. Two of the nations that share our country's position on late-term abortion are North Korea and China, both notorious for committing human rights atrocities.

Recently, I met a neighbor who serves on the board of our local PP. We quickly learned that we have very differing viewpoints on life. It was refreshing when this neighbor agreed to meet for coffee in an effort for each of us to better understand the other's perspective. As our respectful dialogue was coming to a close, it didn't appear that either of our positions would be changed, so I asked, "Please help me understand, if it is a woman's choice, why would we not do everything to give her all the information so she could make an informed, educated choice? We know

PP has ultrasound machines in its clinics; why are women not encouraged, in fact allowed, to look at their sonogram?"

My neighbor said this was incorrect, and she later confirmed this for me. She said that while PP doesn't force an ultrasound, one is available to any woman who asks for it.

I did what any skeptical person who has been in this battle for years would do—I called PP, asking to schedule an ultrasound appointment, saying that if I were pregnant then I needed to know how developed the baby was so I could make a decision.

PP answered, "We don't do ultrasounds. We do abortions."

The woman on the phone said I would have to go somewhere else for an ultrasound, and the only way I would get an ultrasound from them is if I scheduled an abortion. She explained that the abortion would cost $1,086 and take fifteen minutes, but that I should plan on two hours for filling out paperwork and recovery.

When I asked what would happen to me after the abortion, she said, "Nothing. You can go back to your normal life." I asked if I would be given counseling afterward, and she said they don't do that. I asked if they could help me with adoption if I wanted to keep my baby, and was told they don't do that either. I explained that I didn't understand. If they have an ultrasound in the clinic, why couldn't I benefit from that information before scheduling an abortion? She had no answer.

When our call ended, my heart was broken for the girls who honestly make those desperate calls, and for the woman I talked with and her colleagues all over the country who give out that deadly information day after day.

After sharing this conversation with my neighbor via email, she wrote back, saying she had learned that this woman who gave the information was a new hire and mistaken. Yet when I called other PP clinics in different parts of the state, I got the same answer each time.

I contacted my friend Lila Rose, founder of Live Action. Lila shared a video that covers her journey to PP clinics around the country asking this very question. Everywhere she went, she was given the same response

I received. I explained to my neighbor that because PP benefits financially from abortion and far less from women giving birth to babies, many believe PP is in the abortion business. I believe that if PP changed its policy by intentionally offering an ultrasound to every woman who is pregnant, the group could demonstrate true concern for women.

PP could do everything in its power to equip women with an informed choice. I asked my neighbor: Even though our differences on abortion were antithetical, couldn't we come together to improve the adoption process since we shared the common ground of loving and deeply caring about women? I'm still waiting; I haven't heard back.

As long as babies are being killed through abortion, I'll fight for their lives.

For models in the last century, the job description was essentially "Shut up and pose." I reject that today—I won't shut up—and I am grateful for every opportunity to speak the truth about life. Rejection was the greatest gift from that long ago modeling career. It prepared me to be a CEO in the worlds of business and philanthropy, where "No" can mean, "We're talking; I'll come back tomorrow. Maybe you'll have facts. Maybe your position will change and someone else will be the decision-maker."

When you believe in something, please don't surrender. Please never give up on these vulnerable, precious children.

THE AFTERMATH OF ABORTION

This is something most people don't talk about. A friend who had an abortion speaks about this often. As I mentioned earlier, since *Roe v. Wade*, it's estimated that one in four women in America has had an abortion. For everyone who was born after 1973, this means one-fourth of your peers were killed before you ever got to meet them. When an abortion takes place, there is always more than one victim. The mother's life and oftentimes the father's life are forever impacted.

Several years ago, at a women's retreat held in a football stadium in Bakersfield, California, a speaker shared that while she hadn't been intending to discuss this, it was on her heart to pray for those attending who had undergone an abortion. She said, "If you've never told your boyfriend or husband or others, don't feel pressure to come forward." She invited anyone who wished to come forward onto the field to do so, and she would pray for them, as well as pray for those sitting in their seats.

It began with a trickle of women making their way down the aisles to the field, but it became a flood of women. The stadium became mostly empty as the field filled with women weeping and praying. As their cries filled the air, my heart broke for these women—these victims of abortion. No one told them the pain they would experience in the deepest part of their soul. The women knew that God's love is unconditional. They knew He would forgive them of anything they brought before Him. I'm so grateful that when we confess and repent of our sins, not only does God forgive, His Word tells us He remembers them no more. Still, what these women were carrying was among the heaviest of burdens.

Some people champion abortions in cases of rape. But I have a dear friend who was conceived in rape, and she boldly declares that her life matters. Many people believe abortion is the answer to the evil and violent crime of rape. In *Real Choices*, Frederica Mathewes-Green chronicles the aftermath of abortions in women's lives, including those who were raped who share that the abortion felt like being raped all over again. Abortion doesn't change reality. It doesn't take away hurt and pain. Abortion kills, and women suffer, most often silently. Love and support is needed.

It is a privilege I take seriously to be named by UCLA as one of the top ten advocates for women's health in the United States. It's an honor to participate in the work of neonatal intensive care units (NICUs) all over the country and be introduced to successful surgeries in the womb. It is a joy and serious responsibility to serve as International Youth Chair for the National Pediatric Cancer Foundation (NPCF). Our portfolio at NPCF includes over 150 researchers as well as 25 leading hospitals.

Each child is wanted. Each child has immeasurable value, regardless of the challenges faced by the child and the family. Being an advocate for human life at every stage is not restricted by race, religion, gender, or any other factor. As a major donor and ambassador for the Elizabeth Taylor AIDS Foundation, it's powerful for our company to experience the passion for life, including for children in the womb, from people whose views are different in many ways from the stereotypical pro-life images that the media portrays.

My teenage years were spent in fashion, surrounded by gifted people, photographers, executives, art directors, designers, hair and makeup artists, and wonderful people who are very different from me. Through this, I learned that countless people are quiet supporters of life and that they remain silent because of fear. I am watching that silence begin to evaporate.

There is harsh division in our country. For decades, abortion has been a political football. This must cease. Unborn children need our protection, regardless of who is in power. I'm saddened to realize that because of this division, the mere mention of a politician's name can cause some not only to become angry or tune others out, but instantly to reject any discussion of this life-and-death crisis of abortion.

To Republicans, Democrats, Independents, and people of other political parties, I say let's not dehumanize people who have different perspectives. The title of Texas State Representative Tan Parker's book, *Making Government Work*, is powerful. To truly make government work, it needs to work for all people. We can and must always strive to make needed change, do better, learn from past mistakes, and treat those with whom we disagree with respect and love. If we only associate with people who are just like us, how will we ever initiate positive change? We must commit to investigating the issues deeply and honestly and to acting on information received rather than simply relying on sound bites.

When someone with whom we disagree on one issue takes positive action on another, an action that impacts and saves many lives, we should acknowledge this. I am deeply grateful to every person in government, from legislators and lobbyists to our president, vice president, and secretary of state, for taking bold, unwavering positions helping to protect unborn babies. We thank those who are bringing truth to life, like the Susan B. Anthony List, which advocates for political leaders of every political background who stand for life.

Deep appreciation and respect goes to people in every sector of business and life who stand for unborn children, often at great personal cost. It is critical that life advocates come together and begin a peaceful sea change with appreciation and respect for life at every stage, from conception to adolescence, our young adults to our seniors. It's crucial to remember that abortion and euthanasia are opposite ends of the same coin that threatens the precious gift of life. Just as every child is wanted, we need every warrior of peace in this battle. As we stand firm on our convictions, let us come together in love and include all in the battle to save the lives of children in the womb. People of many faiths, Muslims, Jewish, and Christians, those who identify as atheist, people of every color, every race, every age, every sexual orientation, people of every political identity, every person, no matter their economic strata or current circumstance, must come together to stand in love for life. We cannot and we must not surrender to the largest genocide in recorded history.

Jesus is my Lord and Savior. He is my foundation and the anchor to my soul. He is firm and secure, regardless of circumstance. I intentionally didn't begin this chapter with my faith. My biggest regret is having the arrogance to ignore the very thing that led me to the Lord in the first place—the Bible—which I didn't read in its entirety until I was forty-four years old. I didn't know what His perfect, unchanging Word says about life.

I'm a slow learner and deeply flawed. I continually thank Him for His forgiveness, patience, grace, and unconditional love. The science that began my life journey simply affirms God's truth, which was there all along. He never changes. While I'll joyfully share my faith with anyone, I will not impose it. Belief is truly a personal choice that must be made by each individual, including our children, because God doesn't have grandchildren.

I can, however, impose myself when I see any human being suffering abuse. If I see someone beating a toddler, I will intervene. It becomes my duty. To do nothing is to participate in the crime. Until someone can provide scientific evidence that the unborn are not human beings, I will continue to do all I can to intervene. You don't have to share my faith to accept that it's a universal wrong to kill a human being except in self-defense. People of many different faiths and people with no faith at all share this understanding.

To all the pastors, priests, rabbis, and religious leaders who teach the inerrancy of God's Word and the truth about life and abortion, you are faithful heroes. Tragically, the majority of pastors in our country do not encourage their congregations to read the Bible. Most do not teach the inerrancy of scripture or talk about life and abortion in their church with their congregants.

Care Net found in a survey of 1,038 women who have had abortions in the United States that 70 percent claim a Christian religious preference, and 43 percent reported attending church monthly or more often at the time of an abortion.[4]

There are women in our churches suffering silently and alone. Because abortion is not discussed, many fear it is too terrible for God to forgive or believe that God is OK with abortion. This lie must end. Apathy in the church is what made it possible for me to identify as a "pro-choice Christian." The Word of God must be taught in its entirety and never taken out of context to suit any agenda. God's grace, forgiveness, and passionate heart for children of every age, including those who reside in the womb, is evident throughout both the Old Testament and New Testament. I deeply regret believing the lie that I could pick and choose the verses of scripture I deemed relevant and disregard the rest.

Ignorance is not bliss, it's deadly. The enemy seeks to kill, steal, and destroy. God seeks to give life and give it more abundantly.

As we study history in the Old Testament and learn of the atrocities of rampant child sacrifice among many nations, we see that God's response to this evil shows us that His heart is grieved because of His perfect love for life at every stage and age. God speaks volumes on life. Here are a few of my favorite verses from scripture:

"Let the children alone, and do not hinder them from coming to Me" Matthew 19:14 (NASB).

"And whoever receives one such child in My name receives Me; but whoever causes one of these little ones who believe in Me to stumble, it would be better for him to have a heavy millstone hung around his neck, and to be drowned in the depth of the sea" Matthew 18:5–6 (NASB).

"For You created my inmost being; You knit me together in my mother's womb. I praise You because I am fearfully and wonderfully made; Your works are wonderful, I know that full well. My frame was not hidden from You when I was made in the secret place, when I was woven together in the depths of the earth. Your eyes saw my unformed body; all the days ordained for me were written in Your Book before one of them came to be" Psalm 139:13–16 (NIV).

"This day I call the heavens and the earth as witnesses against you that I have set before you life and death, blessings and curses. Now choose life, so that you and your children may live and that you may love the Lord your God, listen to His voice, and hold fast to Him. For the Lord is your life, and He will give you many years in the land He swore to give your fathers, Abraham, Isaac and Jacob" Deuteronomy 30:19–20 (NIV).

"Open your mouth for the speechless, in the cause of all who are appointed to die" Proverbs 31:8 (NKJV).

In Genesis, the first four words out of Satan's mouth are, "Did God really say. . . ?" The enemy seeks to distort and keep us from God's Word. When we read the entirety of scripture and don't allow it to be taken out of context, we experience not only how God views life, but we learn of His absolute love for people of every tongue, tribe, and nation. The Author of Life created each of us uniquely in His image. He loves all people. Racism, anti-Semitism, and bullying of every kind are at variance with scripture.

According to the Kaiser Family Foundation, 40 percent of all abortions in the United States in 2015 were performed on black children, though black Americans make up only 13 percent of our population.[5] The eugenic philosophy of Planned Parenthood's founder, Margaret Sanger, tragically propagates the evil lie that some lives are more valuable than others.[6]

Many people believe that the agenda to overturn *Roe v. Wade* is the main goal of all people who are pro-life. But that simply isn't true. *Roe v. Wade* is settled law. This is about changing hearts and minds, not merely the law. *Roe v. Wade* is a very bad law based in ignorance, not science and truth, and it must be challenged. Still, many life advocates realize that reversing *Roe v. Wade* will not stop the horrific, worldwide industry of abortion.

It bears repeating: Abortion is not a women's rights issue. It's a human rights crisis of disastrous proportions.

To end abortion, we must educate minds and open hearts. When we as a people come together and demand that this genocide cease throughout our country and the rest of the world, politicians who currently repeat the rhetorical lies of pro-choice marketing will fall in line. PP tells us every child should be wanted. We know that every child is in fact, wanted by someone.

There is much to learn from a powerful nun who lived a life of serving others in impoverished Calcutta, India. Mother Teresa shared, "Any country that accepts abortion is not teaching its people to love, but to use any violence to get what they want. This is why the greatest destroyer of love is abortion."

Let us all commit to never give up fighting for the lives of each precious unborn child and every human being at every stage of life. Let us be a voice for those who cannot speak for themselves.

Addressing the Social Fabric of Our Society

by Representative Tan Parker

Being a conservative means far more than just caring about economic growth and tax policy. Contrary to stereotypes, conservatives care deeply for people and their well-being. As conservatives, we of course believe in limited government and the ability of generous citizens and corporations alike to address philanthropic need, as opposed to government growth and creating a myriad of bureaucracies. We also believe that government has inherent limitations on its power and that being conservative means government must not only be limited, but effective and responsive to its citizens. As President Ronald Reagan said himself in his 1964 "A Time for Choosing" speech:

> It's not my intention to do away with government. It is rather to make it work—work with us, not over us; to stand by our side, not ride on our back. Government can and must provide opportunity, not smother it; foster productivity, not stifle it.[1]

With those words powerfully engrained in the minds and hearts of conservatives, the states today are serving as real laboratories for innovation across a wide range of public policy initiatives. Often, individual states pioneer new approaches that are then replicated across multiple other states. Once the impact or footprint becomes significant enough in scale, it will catch the attention of federal lawmakers, who then implement such initiatives nationally. This chapter seeks to highlight some of these innovative policies being rolled out in the states by conservatives that address, in particular, the social fabric of our nation. It's essential that as conservatives, we are driving innovation and creativity in all aspects of our society while honoring our constitutional rights as Americans.

But as conservatives who cherish individual freedoms, liberty, and economic prosperity, we are also strongly grounded in the right to life—and that includes protecting life at all stages, from the moment of conception to natural death. Through the years, Republicans have been most widely known for successes in protecting the unborn and providing for end-of-life safeguards. Yet being pro-life also includes our belief that we, as a society, have an obligation to protect every child from abuse and neglect while also making certain that children have, at minimum, the necessities of life. Every life is precious, and we must safeguard every child once they arrive in this world.

PREVENTING CHILD SEXUAL ABUSE

In this day and age, it's hard to comprehend that the abuse of children is so prevalent, with approximately five children senselessly dying each day in our country and well over 3.5 million cases of child abuse being reported each year.[2] The vast majority of child abuse victims also know the perpetrator,[3] who is all too frequently a member of the family.

Child sexual abuse knows no boundaries; it affects children from every state, every ethnicity, and from rich and poor communities alike. It's a pervasive problem of the heart. I was blessed early in my legislative career to work with a courageous young survivor by the name of Jenna Quinn. My wife, Beth, and I met Jenna just after my election to the Texas House of Representatives in 2007. After meeting Jenna at our local

Children's Advocacy Center and learning about her suffering, it was crystal clear to Beth and me that something needed to be done to stop this horrific scourge on innocent children.

After much deliberation, analysis, and prayer, I decided in 2009 to file a bill to prevent child sexual abuse by making certain that training for all K–12 students and school staff would occur in Texas public schools. Through the bravery and strength of Jenna and her testimony in the legislature, I was able to pass this legislation that became the first law in the nation to address this horrible crime in such a manner. Appropriately, I named this hallmark legislation Jenna's Law. Over the years, I have worked to further strengthen and enhance the legislation to have the greatest possible impact on our society. The law has spread across many states since its passage and, in 2019, was introduced by U.S. Senator John Cornyn (R-TX) into the United States Senate, in an effort to make it the law across the nation.

Most importantly, the legislation is working. The data in Texas shows that since the law was passed in 2009, educators reported child sexual abuse at a rate of almost four times more often after training than during their pre-training careers.[4] It's been a powerful tool in the fight to protect our nation's most precious asset, our children. It's also an example of the type of legislation that the states are passing as they serve as laboratories of democracy and bring real innovation to solving some of the most pressing issues facing the country today.

STOPPING HUMAN TRAFFICKING

Over the years, there has not been a more complex atrocity committed against children and adults than human trafficking. It is a global problem of enormous scale, but the United States is tragically one of the countries where this societal darkness is most prevalent. This coercion of human beings primarily for forced sexual exploitation and labor is estimated worldwide to be a $150 billion industry each year.[5] It has impacted tens of millions of people around the world, destroying countless lives. Here in the United States, it is estimated that there are several hundred thousand victims currently trapped in this modern form of slavery. It impacts men and women, girls and boys. On average, a victim is tragically first trafficked as a mere child at age eleven to fourteen, and in many cases, victims can be under the age of ten.[6] The average age of a survivor who is finally identified in the United States is twenty-six.

Human trafficking victims are not faceless strangers; they are our own children, our sons and daughters, from every state in this nation. Children are kidnapped and forcibly trafficked often through the threat of violence against them or a loved one. Reflect for a moment on what that awful, unimaginable circumstance is like for a child or young adult. It's clear why lawmakers are taking aggressive policy measures to address this atrocity occurring in our own nation.

Such victims find themselves enslaved, often for many, many years before being liberated—if they are ever fortunate enough to escape. Human trafficking cases are believed to be chronically underreported due to the nature of the crime itself. The complexity of a crime that occurs over many years, and in some cases decades, further complicates reporting, arrests, and prosecutions.

California, Florida, Texas, and New York are believed to be the states with the highest concentration of cases.[7] Additional high concentrations of victims exist in cities like Las Vegas, Atlanta, and Washington, D.C. For twenty years, U.S. presidents of both parties have understood the importance of addressing this crime against humanity. Most recently, President Donald Trump signed nine pieces of legislation to fight this horrific crime and made the elimination of human trafficking a top priority of his administration. While the federal government is working to combat this crime, the states themselves have had to address this enormous challenge with creativity and innovation. Oftentimes, policies created in the states on this subject have shaped federal law itself.

I'm proud of the work that Texas and many other states have done to achieve great successes in passing new legislation on this most important issue. New laws that create enhanced penalties for the crime of human trafficking have passed in numerous states. Laws that provide increased training and awareness have also been put into effect. In addition, laws are in place to deliver better support for survivors through having their criminal records protected from public view if they can demonstrate innocence.

The states have also in many cases increased funding for law enforcement itself, enhanced coordination among agencies, and restructured law enforcement departments to more effectively combat these crimes. Furthermore, states have recognized and taken legislative action to address the links between teenage runaways, the high percentage of children in foster care who become victims of human trafficking, and the homeless teenager crisis—all of which contribute to fuel the growth of human trafficking victims.[8]

Understanding the interconnected aspects of this despicable crime is essential to being able to effectively combat it. And despite the successful work being done, one of the most important and necessary actions that must continue is to provide the survivors of human trafficking of any age with the ability to fight and restore their lives. We must continue enacting strong measures that provide a pathway for upward mobility in order for these brave survivors to get a job or go back to school without fear of a proverbial "Scarlet Letter" being placed on their chests.

ADVANCING MEDICAL FREEDOM

The moral fabric of our nation is shaped not only by how we take care of the unborn, our children, and elderly populations, but is also directly tied to allowing citizens one of the most precious of all freedoms—the right to fight for one's own life when faced with a terminal medical condition. Providing terminal patients access to investigative and non–FDA approved drugs, biologics, and devices is a moral imperative. These medical therapies often offer the hope of continued life, healing, and restoration. What right do we have that could be more fundamental to our core values and beliefs as Americans?

The "Right to Try" was first established in Colorado in 2014. From that point forward, the movement grew across the country and was adopted by forty-one states before it was championed by Republican U.S. Senator Ron Johnson of Wisconsin, with the strong support of President Donald Trump, who ultimately signed into law the federal "Right to Try" Bill on May 30, 2018.[9]

For several decades in this country, prior to the establishment of "Right to Try" laws in the states and the federal law in 2018, terminal patients who wanted to pursue experimental therapies were effectively prevented from being able to do so despite the FDA's expanded access law being in effect since the late 1970s.[10] Enormous amounts of red tape had to be navigated, and this took extensive amounts of time, all while those pursuing treatment literally raced against the clock to save a loved one.

With expanded access, better known as "compassionate use," a physician has to first request approval from a particular biotechnology company to determine if the company would grant access to its therapy on behalf of the physician's patient. This has often proven over the years to be a near-impossible task and created false hope for many terminal patients. For the lucky few who have been able to overcome that enormous hurdle and find a willing company open to providing its therapy, the physician and patient then had to jointly apply to the FDA to receive approval to proceed. While the FDA historically grants a large majority of the applications, the paperwork process is very extensive and burdensome, and worst of all, enormously time-consuming when literally every hour counts in fighting to save the life of a terminal patient.

Due to this extremely inefficient and difficult process, the "Right to Try" gained traction across the states. "Right to Try" laws allow patients to bypass the FDA and contact a company directly to request access to their therapy—as long as the patient is terminal, has exhausted all other medical options, and the therapeutic has passed an FDA Phase 1 trial. This newly streamlined approach to supporting the needs of terminal patients, coupled with greater responsiveness from biotechnology companies due to heightened public awareness, will save countless American lives in the years to come. It's a great story about the states listening to their constituencies and being both responsive and innovative on their behalf.

The states are continually innovating in the realm of medical freedom. I was privileged in recent years to work to expand the "Right to Try" in Texas. Initially, it only applied to patients with terminal conditions; we included patients who are living with severe, chronic conditions. My fundamental belief is that these chronically ill patients should have the same rights and privileges extended to them in order to improve the quality of their lives. Why would we as a society not support medically documented, chronically ill patients with the ability to have real hope for a brighter tomorrow? Therefore, I filed legislation in January 2017 that extends the benefits of "Right to Try" to the chronically ill, and to specifically allow access to adult stem cell therapies. With the support of my colleagues in the Texas legislature, I named this bill Charlie's Law in honor of a dear friend and legislator who tragically lost his battle with cancer.[11]

Adult stem cell therapies offer tremendous hope for patients facing virtually any type of medical condition, from autoimmune diseases and multiple sclerosis to cancer and heart failure.[12] Incidentally, former Texas governor, U.S. energy secretary, and *Making Government Work* contributor Rick Perry is a huge advocate for adult stem cell therapies because of the incredible benefits he has personally derived from treatments over the years. Adult stem cells are the repair cells of your own body and offer the promise of true regenerative medicine. I encourage all Americans to learn more about their enormous potential and capabilities. I also wish to clarify that my support of stem cell therapy and the passage of Charlie's Law is focused exclusively on adult stem cell therapy and *not* the unethical utilization of embryonic stem cells.

Prior to this legislation's passing, adult stem cell therapies that allowed for the expansion of adult stem cells, even those from your own body, were prohibited from being used in the United States by the FDA. As a result, hundreds of thousands of American citizens each year have traveled outside of the United States to seek these treatments around the world. With the passage of Charlie's Law, Texas became the first state in the nation to approve such treatments for patients with no other option and to put in place an appropriate regulatory structure managed by the Texas Department of State Health Services to protect citizens while allowing for the promise of medical innovation and life-saving treatments. It's simple really— medical freedom and liberty should be a protected right for every American citizen who wants to fight to improve his or her quality of life or fight for his or her own survival.

Furthermore, the Tenth Amendment to the United States Constitution affords each individual state, and in this specific example Texas, the right to govern itself and to make decisions on what is best for its citizens. Expanding medical freedom is another example of how this cherished constitutional right established over two centuries ago is being utilized to provide the meaningful innovation that's taking place today.

PROTECTING THE MEDICALLY FRAGILE

Another critically important area of public policy where conservatives in the states are more actively engaging is protecting medically fragile children in our nation.

All too often, public policy has not adequately recognized the unique needs of the approximately three million children in this country who are medically fragile. Whether a child was born with great physical or developmental challenges or was tragically injured during childhood, the medically fragile deserve health care that is responsive to their needs.

Many families face unimaginable financial and emotional challenges when raising these very special kids. Addressing these realities as a matter of public policy is philosophically aligned with the conservative values of protecting life, recognizing families as the strength of our nation, and ultimately reducing taxpayer costs that result from an overreliance on state-managed institutionalized care. Furthermore, these challenging circumstances increase risks associated with parental employment loss and ultimately result in families facing a higher probability of financial vulnerability.

Due to the nature of their complex medical conditions, the medically fragile population often requires around-the-clock care, specialists, equipment, and support services to simply survive.[13] As lawmakers, we need a more honest dialogue on preserving the most cost-effective aspects of delivery models. We cannot fight for the ability to have life but then essentially remove the ability to live.

It was President Ronald Reagan who emerged as an early pioneer on the specific topic of protecting these very special children when he embraced what became the Katie Beckett waiver in 1981. At just four months of age, Katie Beckett contracted viral encephalitis, an inflammation of the brain, which left her partially paralyzed and dependent on a ventilator. Medicaid rules during this time forced her family to keep Katie hospitalized instead of allowing her family to care for her at home. This battle ensued for three years until then vice president George H. W. Bush shared their story with President Ronald Reagan, who recognized the injustice:

Now, by what sense do we have a regulation in government that says we'll pay $6,000 a month to keep someone in a hospital that we believe would be better off at home, but the family cannot afford one-sixth that amount to keep them at home?[14]

President Reagan was exactly right and asked the precisely correct question. This resulted in the official adoption of the Katie Beckett waiver that specifically allowed medically fragile children the option to receive their critical medical care at home while still retaining their Medicaid coverage.

President Reagan's innovative vision for recognizing the importance of assisting these children has inspired conservative policy-makers in many states and at the federal level to work to create support structures that understand the uniqueness of this population and the necessity of tailoring the delivery of medical solutions to best meet their needs.

Optimal delivery of medical services to this population requires a strong focus on keeping these children at home when feasible, with regular medical support, as opposed to constantly in the emergency room, hospitalized or institutionalized, away from their families and any chance of a normal childhood.[15] Achieving this goal is what's best for these children and enabling them to live as normal of a life as humanly possible. Every life is a precious and priceless gift from our Creator. As a matter of practicality in policy, it's also in the best interest of taxpayers to enable families to take care of these children in their homes, as more and more families desire to do.[16] As policy-makers, we must be willing to recognize that this is what pro-life looks like in action.

Republican legislators across the nation are more actively addressing the unique needs of the medically fragile, and their actions speak to the heart of conservatism.[17] We have a moral obligation to fight for every life, from conception to natural death. Helping to lessen the suffering of these children and their loving families needs to be a top priority for conservatives—and all legislators across the country.

We have started the journey. However, we still have much work to do to aggressively provide innovative solutions and support, making certain that we uphold President Reagan's standard of care and that our rhetoric matches our actions when it comes to delivering meaningful results for this most special group of children.

As Republicans, we can engage in grassroots activism and pass laws at all levels of government that protect the unborn, which is crucial, but unless we are willing to address the realities of the medically fragile population as part of our conservative platform, we are not fulfilling our true calling.

INNOVATION IN FIGHTING CANCER

Additionally, in recent years many states have taken the lead in pursuing the expansion of access to cancer clinical trials—for underserved populations in particular. World-class organizations like the Lazarex Cancer Foundation and other nonprofits are partnering with individual states to bring private sector resources and coordination to support such programming.[18] Expanding participation in cancer clinical trials is critically important to finding new treatments for the disease. One of the greatest challenges to having successful clinical trials is overcoming the complexities of recruitment. Frequently, misinformation and a lack of knowledge about available trials prevent cancer patients from participating. Expanding enrollment of racially and ethnically diverse populations is often further complicated by a lack of available transportation, as well as the costs associated with travel to what can be a distant trial site location. Addressing these obstacles is essential to the further development of new life-saving therapies and assisting these underrepresented populations, who are often disproportionately impacted by cancer. As such, more and more states are making increased trial engagement a key priority.

Of course, the focus on cancer clinical trials is an extension of the innovative work done over the last decade by many states to provide programming and resources in the fight against cancer. The battle to raise awareness and the need for additional federal funding to fight pediatric cancer in particular has also been a significant focus for several states. Over the years, some states have passed legislation to recognize September as Childhood Cancer Awareness Month. Many other states, such as Kentucky and Wisconsin, have created Childhood Cancer license plate programs that raise revenue to fund more pediatric cancer research. In other states, like Florida and Virginia, innovative waivers have been passed that enable enhanced pediatric hospice care in a child's home.

Over the years, these state initiatives have led to a greater awareness in Washington, D.C.—which in turn has paved the way to a nationally coordinated effort recognizing the critical importance of increasing funding for pediatric cancer research. Many of the innovative policies utilized in the states through the years are component pieces of new federal legislation. No better example exists than the Childhood Cancer Survivorship, Treatment, Access and Research (STAR) Act signed into law by President Donald Trump on June 5, 2018. This legislation was the most substantial federal legislation in the history of our nation to address pediatric cancer. It was championed by my fellow Texans, Republican Congressman Michael McCaul, a great advocate for enhanced pediatric cancer funding for many years, and a heroic and incredibly courageous young pediatric cancer survivor named Sadie Keller from Lantana, Texas.[19]

Conservatives are shaping public policy across the states and care deeply about the social fabric of our society. The states are, in fact, functioning well as incubators of discovery, breakthrough, and policy innovation. As conservatives, we also have an unwavering moral commitment to the protection of life in all its stages. We have the passion to seek out new ideas while preserving precious freedoms that make government work most effectively—for all our citizens.

The Media: "Goodbye, Iphigene"

by Merrie Spaeth

The media landscape has changed dramatically in the twenty-six years since the original publishing of *Making Government Work*. With the advent of the twenty-four-hour news cycle, the growth of the internet, and new and emerging social media platforms, public policy and politics itself has been permanently altered. No one in the country better understands this phenomenon and the implications for our society than Merrie Spaeth. Merrie has been at the peak of her profession for over forty years, working as a reporter, a *20/20* producer, special assistant to FBI director William Webster, White House director of media relations for President Reagan, and an advisor and counselor to clients worldwide in her private practice. Her insights into optimal media messaging and trends are even more relevant now than they were in the 1980s when she was serving President Reagan. Imagine being the media director for the Great Communicator, President Ronald Reagan! Merrie has been a dear friend and mentor to me for almost thirty years. Americans will greatly benefit from reading her unique wisdom and insight.

—Tan Parker

In 1984, I was the director of media relations for Ronald Reagan's White House. It was a dream job. Everyone is familiar with the White House press corps, the reporters accredited full-time to cover the president and the White House—the group of well-dressed, well-groomed reporters who scream questions at the president and whose main goal in life is to get a minute or two on their newscasts.

By contrast, the media relations office was set up by President Carter in recognition of the fact that most Americans get their news from other sources—local newspapers and TV, industry or trade press, specialty press like women's magazines, or other sources. President Carter also foresaw that the press office would guard its power jealously; he had media relations report to the chief of staff, so the press office couldn't quash it. During my time with the Reagan White House, the chief of staff was James Baker, and the deputy chief of staff was Michael Deaver.

This chapter looks at what's changed in twenty-five years, how media affects policy and politics, what we can expect in the future, and what proponents of limited government or conservative principles should do to advance these ideas.

Back to 1984 again: when I talk about media relations in the Reagan White House, my children roll their eyes and say, "Mom, that was the last century." (Then they realized it was the last millennium, which they thought was even funnier.)

The initial director of media relations, Karna Small, had been one of the deputy press secretaries under Jim Brady. When Brady was shot, Larry Speakes became press secretary and Karna was asked to run media relations. Because she was a known and respected figure in Washington, national publications like the *Washington Post* sought her insights.

Small's talents were quickly recognized and snapped up by the National Security Council, and Baker and Deaver turned to FTC chairman and former OMB deputy director Jim Miller, who was getting high marks for advancing Reagan's de-regulatory initiative, including getting balanced press coverage outside of Washington, D.C. Miller gave credit to my office, public affairs, and to me as the director and confirmed I would be an excellent choice for the office.

The day after White House communications director David Gergen left, Baker and Deaver called me in, told me to take over the media relations, and requested that I tell them what I'd do differently. The media relations office was sending out multiple press releases each week to about six thousand publications and media outlets. As far as I could tell, these got zero pickup because they were being mailed. Even in the last century, it was clear that "daily" news meant it had to arrive daily. We had fax machines (imagine that), but there was no way to send mass quantities of faxes of releases.

What the White House did have was location, location, location. We could invite members of the press to the White House, and they would come. Media relations was doing a briefing or so a week. The goal would be one or two a day. Women's magazines, agricultural publications, banking publications, weekly newspapers, education columnists—there were endless ways to tailor briefings to different media.

The White House could also utilize technology. At the FTC, I wanted to see what other departments were doing to get the word out about their accomplishments. The Agriculture Department had set up an arrangement with ITT Dialcom. It was the first commercial electronic mail service. If you had an account, a (primitive) computer, and a contraption with two rubber cups, you put your phone in the cups, dialed a telephone number, it made strange shrieks and up on your black and white monitor came "AGRICULTURE NEWS." The minute I saw it, I was in love. Thus, the White House news service came into being.

This was the first body blow to the White House press corps' monopoly on information. Now, any media outlet with a phone, a monitor, and an ITT Dialcom account could have everything the press corp had and more. If I could get my hands on it, I would load it into the White House news service.

Technology also advanced at exactly the right moment to allow us to ramp up remote television interviews. We could approach the groups of stations with corporate owners or Washington offices, or we could create our own groups. The U.S. Chamber of Commerce had just set up its own TV studio and bought a huge block of satellite time. We cut a deal that allowed us to use their studio (and satellite time). I could pick five local stations to do sequential, five-minute, "live-on-tape" interviews remotely with an administration official, and the Chamber's anchor would get the sixth interview in studio. This meant that if steel policy was a priority, I could call stations in cities where it was news.

I started calling local stations. I'm not ashamed to tell you that I loved calling and asking for the news director because when the person answering the phone said, "He's busy," I'd say, "I'm calling from the White House." It always elicited, "I'll get him."

The rules? Stations had to conduct at least two interviews with cabinet officials, then they could have an interview with Vice President George H. W. Bush and then they would be in line to interview the president.

Local media, both in the White House briefings and for the "live-on-tape" remote TV interviews, could be counted on to ask penetrating but not "gotcha" questions.

I used to say Larry Speakes, who had to deal with the national reporters, had the world's worst job, and I had the world's best job.

Before I move on from the last century with an eye to what government and conservatives should do in the future, one of the things I didn't do at the White House but did successfully at the FTC was set up an aggressive outreach program to deploy knowledge experts as speakers. Of the 1,100 career lawyers and economists at the commission, about fifty volunteered to participate in the program. This meant putting them through training to become motivating speakers in addition to being knowledgeable about their specific corner of the FTC and learning how to become good interviews for local newspapers, TV, and radio.

The lawyers and economists saw it as an opportunity for professional development. In fact, I now make my living building on the techniques developed to make the commission's speaker outreach program good enough to generate word-of-mouth invitations and balanced publicity.

The key to enlisting employees, particularly government employees, is to enable them to talk about the agency's mission, to explain bureaucratic jargon to average citizens, to equip them to answer all kinds of questions, and to practice. I'll return to the importance of outreach at the end of the chapter.

Fast-forward to 2020. What's different? What's better? What's the future?

We now live in a 24/7 news cycle, and the speed—or velocity—with which information travels has accelerated in a manner we couldn't have foreseen in the Reagan days.

Change One: Everyone is a reporter. Social media and traditional media have merged.

My current illustrative teaching example is from India. In 2018, a plane took off from Mumbai and the pilots neglected to pressurize the cabin, so when the plane reached twenty thousand feet in altitude, passengers experienced nosebleeds. Oxygen masks dropped from the ceiling, but no oxygen flowed. What did all the passengers do? They pulled out their cell phones and started posting pictures and videos. The incident made worldwide news, driven by the passengers' postings. We have heard that the airline management learned of the situation from the passengers' postings. The media learned of the incident from the passengers before the airline management publicly acknowledged it.

This phenomenon started when CNN began encouraging viewers to send in their home videos, particularly those of disasters. Now, nobody needs to be asked.

Change Two: The internet has let like-minded people find each other to create a critical mass.

While this opportunity was initially viewed as one of the most positive developments of the internet, it has a decidedly dark side. We could pick any number of topics, such as child trafficking, but one of the most documented examples is the anti-vaccination movement, which demonstrates the media's empowerment of this trend and the resulting impact on policy and politics.

Most readers will need only a quick refresher: an English doctor and researcher, Andrew Wakefield, published a paper in 1998 claiming a link between autism and vaccinations for MMR (measles, mumps, and rubella).[1] The "study" only included twelve patients and was seriously flawed in several respects. Ninety percent of children in the UK are vaccinated for MMR, and the vaccine is administered at about the time autism is detected, so there was no proof of causation. In addition, the Wakefield paper had other serious flaws.

Wakefield repeated studies in 2002, but they were subsequently scientifically debunked, and he was finally found to have accepted funds from trial lawyers seeking to sue manufacturers of vaccines.[2]

The supposed link between the measles vaccine and autism has been thoroughly examined and found to be false, but the media coverage has had a worldwide impact. Celebrities like Jenny McCarthy and Robert F. Kennedy Jr. took active roles promoting the link between autism and the measles vaccine, with clearly identifiable results.

Following the release of the Wakefield study, the vaccination rate in the UK fell below 80 percent. In the U.S., parents' groups lobbied state legislatures to pass or expand exemptions beyond medical circumstances and religious prohibitions to allow for philosophical objections.

The World Health Organization (WHO) reported a 300 percent increase in the numbers of measles cases in 2019 compared with 2018. Americans think of measles as a non-threatening rash of spots, but measles is one of the most contagious diseases on the planet. It can cause severe complications, including death, and aggravate other conditions. The WHO estimates that 110,000 people, mostly children, die of measles each year.

In the U.S., action is mostly at the state level. Health officials in Maine were worried that the non-vaccination rate was 6.2 percent of the population. Scientific guidelines say that 95 percent of a population needs to be vaccinated to achieve what's called "herd immunity," the protection created when almost everyone has been vaccinated so that few people become infected. This protects the most vulnerable segments of the population.

The media has played a significant role in the American and global situation by giving a platform to the anti-vax movement. While some publications have carried a few facts about the side effects or complications of measles or noted that whooping cough, which had been wiped out, has made a comeback, television in particular has failed to visually explain the horrors of diseases like diphtheria.

News stories during the summer of 2019 reported that migrant children in custody wouldn't be receiving the flu vaccine.[3] Buried in the stories was the fact that Customs and Border Protection had never administered vaccinations, but the headline read "Three Migrant Children Have Died from Flu in Custody but U.S. Won't Provide Vaccines." Again, remembering that the internet enables like-minded people to find one other and the media enables and amplifies it, one can see that this kind of headline is likely to be shared by many people and foster an unfavorable impression.

This helps demonstrate the phenomenon of people finding one other and learning from one other, which is globally enabled and amplified by media.

The protests in Hong Kong have been well documented in the media. What started as a spontaneous reaction to the proposal that China be allowed to extradite people accused of crimes to the mainland, where they would be prosecuted by the notoriously political courts, has morphed into a genuine revolt against the mainland Communist regime, which has steadily eroded the protections guaranteed under Hong Kong's "special arrangement."

The world watched as local media coverage went national and then international, including protesters in the Catalonia region of Spain, which has long had its own active separatist movement. The Catalans adopted the Hong Kong students' slogan, "Be water," the fighting philosophy of martial arts luminary Bruce Lee. The slogan means participants should move quickly and fluidly, gathering a presence in visible spaces, disappearing and then appearing elsewhere. The Catalan protestors took to brandishing umbrellas as the Hong Kong students had in their demonstrations starting in 2014. They are wearing masks—like the Hong Kong students—and they have sought to gain international attention to pressure domestic leaders.

Change Three: The national media became an arm of the Democratic Party.

Conservatives suspect that reporters and members of the media are overwhelmingly Democrats hostile to Republicans, conservatives, and the idea of limited government. They are right.

The authors of the book *The American Journalist in the Digital Age* conducted a study in 2014 built on surveys conducted in 1971, 1982, 1992, and 2002. In 1971, 35.5 percent of reporters identified themselves as Democrats versus 25.7 percent as Republicans and 32.5 percent as Independents. In subsequent surveys, the number of reporters who identified as Democrats grew to 38.5 percent and 44.1 percent, and then the majority migrated to Independents, who in 2014 made up just over 50 percent of reporters. However, 28.1 percent identified as Democrats and only 7.1 percent as Republicans.[4]

It is clear that more reporters now claim to be Independent, but the most sizeable cohort are Democrats and only 7 percent are Republicans. Furthermore, as Chris Cillizza of the *Washington Post* observed, these are the figures for all reporters in all fields. The studies do not separately analyze reporters who cover politics, but we suspect the reporters who call themselves Independents are actually Democrats or left-leaning.

This is more than an academic debate. The philosophy of the reporter and his or her media outlet directly influences what he or she reports and how he or she reports it—sometimes with hilarious obviousness.

When Islamic State leader Abu Bakr al-Baghdadi was killed in a military raid, the *Washington Post* headlined the news and his obituary as "Abu Bakr al-Baghdadi, Austere Religious Scholar at Helm of Islamic State, Dies at 48."

An avalanche of satirical tweets ridiculed the headline:

"Genghis Khan, beloved father of thousands, expert horse breeder at helm of Mongolia, dies" (David Bernstein).

Hitler was an obvious theme:

"Adolf Hitler, simple Austrian painter at helm of Nazi Party, dies at 56" (Eylon Levy).

"Adolph Hitler, noted diversity critic, dies in Berlin" (Kurt Schlichter).

My favorites: "Jeffrey Dahmer, connoisseur of exotic and locally sourced meats, dies at 34" (Josh Jordan).

"Charles Manson, folk singer, noted Lothario and counter-culture celeb, passed" (Gary Berg).

While this example is easy to poke fun at, there are many examples of media bias in the press. Others are more insidious and indicate a mindset or ideological framework that creeps into what appear to be evenhanded stories. For example, the *New York Times* wrote about a growing movement demanding old-fashioned dishwashers be made available again. Why? Because they actually worked and performed their desired function, washing dishes.[5]

Those pining for older washers identify the culprit correctly as over-regulation. In the middle of a generally fair story, the writer noted that the Trump administration is pursuing "weakening energy standards for lightbulbs," unaware that another point of view—the same point of view reflected by those demanding dishwashers that actually wash—would describe these as "streamlining," or perhaps "rationalizing," standards, or "weighing the costs versus benefits."

The media bias is directly related to the alarming unanimity of opinion in our universities, a development that has been widely reported and addressed by people like Ben Shapiro, Dinesh D'Souza, Brent Bozell, and, of course, one of my fellow *Making Government Work* contributors, Tyson Langhofer. A 2017 survey by the *Yale Daily News* found that 75 percent of faculty members describe themselves as "liberal" or "very liberal" and only 7 percent lean conservative, numbers very close to the last survey reported above.

I include this because in December, famed computer science professor David Gelernter wrote to his colleagues that political diversity at Yale was "0%."[6] His widely circulated and equally widely ignored email was picked up by the *Wall Street Journal*, which talked to other Yale professors who identified themselves as liberal and agreed with Gelernter but did not want to be identified by name. The *Daily News* interviewed a history professor, Carlos Eire, who escaped from Cuba as a child. The *Journal* reported that Eire said he "mostly keeps quiet on political matters."[7]

Coverage and commentary about the appalling lack of diversity of thought is increasing. The *Wall Street Journal* wrote about the faculty of the University of Chicago, noting that university employees had made $193,985 in political donations with only $1,475 going to conservative candidates and causes and only one $250 donation to President Trump, which came from an officer in the campus police department.[8]

And this is where the problem of media bias is compounded: people are intimidated and afraid to discuss their ideas because they will be attacked as racists or other epithets.

"THERE'S NO EVIDENCE IT WAS FICTION."

The media outlet that most exemplifies how the national media has become a captive of the Left and for what used to be considered extreme policies is the *New York Times*. The above quote also illustrates how journalistic standards have been turned upside down.

In 1979, when I was the co-host of Warner Communications' nightly TV show, *Columbus Alive!*, an intern was assigned to stop at the airport each morning on the way to work to snag a copy of the *New York Times*. You couldn't be an informed citizen without reading the *New York Times*.

Readers will recognize the name Sulzberger, the family that built the *New York Times*, but they probably don't know that Iphigene Ochs Sulzberger, the daughter of the founder, wife of his successor as editor, and mother to his successor, played an incredibly important role in personifying what she considered the values of the *Times*.[9]

Her obituary noted that she was an advocate of using the *Times* as a classroom teaching tool. The subsidized program was a key factor in making the paper the most widely circulated publication in schools and universities. As students grew up and moved outside New York City, they took with them the habit of reading the *Times*, just as I did in Columbus, Ohio.

At Columbia Business School, I wrote a paper comparing the *Times'* decision to subsidize classroom use with the New York *Daily News'* decisions over time not to. The *Times* always justified the decision by saying they were "breaking even," a statistic they engineered by not counting any sunk costs. The *Daily News* vetoed the idea numerous times, claiming it was "too expensive," a cost they arrived at by including all kinds of operating expenses. But the real difference was Iphigene. She was the internal champion. She believed that the *Times* set the standard for journalism and that people needed the paper. It's a lesson that has influenced my thirty years of consulting. Internal, passionate champions who believe they are on a mission are vital.

I titled this chapter of *Making Government Work* "Goodbye Iphigene" because the paper and values she championed are almost completely gone.

How else can one defend the decision by the *New York Times* to hire as an editorial board writer Sarah Jeong, a former writer for the Verge, a media outlet owned by Vox Media. Jeong's Twitter account included dozens of tweets and retweets that ooze hate and racism. Some examples:

"Dumbass [expletive redacted] white people marking up the internet with their opinions like dogs pissing on the hydrants."

"Are white people genetically predisposed to burn faster in the sun, thus logically being only fit to live underground like groveling goblins."

"I dare you to get on Wikipedia and play 'things white people can definitely take credit for' it's really hard."

"Oh man, it's kind of sick how much joy I get out of being cruel to old white men."

It is sick. Just as sick, when the tweets were widely circulated, the *Times* defended her and their decision to hire her, claiming that as an Asian woman she had been harassed online and was simply returning the rhetoric, and that they had "candid conversations with Sarah" and that "she understands what is acceptable at the *Times*." What's obviously acceptable at the *Times* is hiring those with a history of publicly expressing vile sentiments.

What's also acceptable is publicly admitting that the paper was switching its coverage of the Trump administration from Russian collusion to describing Trump as a racist. Well, actually, it wasn't supposed to be public. Editor Dean Baquet made the announcement at an employee town hall meeting in August 2019, a meeting that was supposed to be private and confidential. It's ironic that the meeting was secretly recorded and leaked.[10]

The meeting was spurred by reaction to a *Times* front-page story following the shootings in El Paso. The *Times* reported the president's denunciation of white supremacy under the headline, "Trump Urges Unity vs. Racism." Readers and employees went ballistic that the headline wasn't critical of the president, so within hours, the headline was changed to "Assailing Hate but Not Guns."

This brings us to the line "No evidence it was fiction" and the implications for standards of journalism.

The *New York Times* reporters Robin Pogrebin and Kate Kelly wrote a book purporting to have uncovered new, sensational, and convincing evidence of Supreme Court justice Brett Kavanaugh's despicable behavior as a college teenager. The *Times* published an excerpt in advance of publication to promote the book, *The Education of Brett Kavanaugh: An Investigation*, claiming it "sheds new light on a matter of significant national interest."

The trumpeted allegation involved a new, unreported young woman into whose hand Kavanaugh pushed his penis at a party.

Seems pretty bad, doesn't it? Left out of the excerpt in the *Times* were salient facts that were included in the book (although significantly downplayed). The female student in question declined to talk to Pogrebin and Kelly. Her friend, who did talk to them, said she doesn't recall the incident, and one of the supposed witnesses who did report to the Senate and FBI what he may have seen said that people were so drunk they didn't remember.

Molly Hemingway of the Federalist got an advance copy of the book, noted the excerpt did not include the exculpatory material, and called the paper on it. The *Times* was humiliated into adding a correction, saying weakly, "An earlier version of this article, which was adapted from a forthcoming book, did not include one element of the book's account regarding an assertion by a Yale classmate that friends of Brett Kavanaugh pushed his penis into the hand of a female student at a drunken dorm party. The book reports that the female student declined to be interviewed and friends say she does not recall the incident. That information has been added to the article."[11]

Former *Times* executive editor Jill Abramson stepped forward to defend the paper, acknowledging to Fox News' Harris Faulkner, "It's true that a material fact was left out," but claiming that "[n]o one has challenged the basic accuracy of the story." Faulkner jumped on Abramson, asking how she could claim that if "the alleged victim doesn't remember any assault," to which Abramson responded with the line that I think sums up journalism today, "There's no evidence it was fiction."

Think what applying this new standard of journalism means for public policy and politics.

A glimmer of Iphigene's work ethic can sometimes still shine through in the pages of the *New York Times*. See the extraordinary reporting by Austin Ramzy and Chris Buckley about what's going on in China, "'Absolutely No Mercy': Inside China's Mass Detentions."[12] The lengthy, in-depth article in November 2019 should be mandatory reading for all elected officials and—as Iphigene believed—for anyone who wants to be an informed citizen.

MOVING FORWARD

What do some of the recognized great journalists think of the current state of the media?

Emmett Tyrrell, writer, magazine creator, and political commentator, is sought after for his insights. I asked him for his comments on the state of the media and the implications for the nation.

MS: In your long experience, has media coverage gotten worse, or is this just our perception with current biases?

Tyrrell: It's definitely gotten worse. I began in Iowa with Spiro Agnew denouncing bias in the media. . . . Here we are decades later with the same debate going on but a few more atrocities.

MS: Do you see any way to return to real journalism?

Tyrrell: I don't see a way back to real journalism because the people in mainstream journalism are the same class, supposedly educated, and their sense of reality is not penetrated by facts.

MS: What do you predict for the future?

Tyrrell: Five years from now, there will be changes—but for the worse. You can't expect the mainstream media to become more diverse or bring on conservatives, so it will get more and more radical. Conservative media isn't even 10 percent of the media, but will continue because that's where the money is. The *New York Times* and *Washington Post* are riding an anti-Trump wave and when he's no longer president, there will be real cutbacks.

SO WHAT DOES THE FUTURE HOLD?

Reason, a Libertarian powerhouse organization, which today includes a foundation, the well-known magazine, a podcast, a speaker series, and other offshoots, has a weekly round table, which they begin by asking the participants, "What media have you consumed this week?" Note, participants aren't watching or reading, they're "consuming." That's probably the correct way to think about media in the future—just as we decide whether we want Italian or Thai for dinner and, if Italian, do we want pizza or pesto linguini?

William Faulkner penned the oft-quoted, "The past is never dead. It's not even past." Today, he'd write, "The future isn't in the future. It's already here." The future is individual media universes that we each construct and customize for ourselves. There are an estimated 700,000 podcasts, and many of them represent what can only be described as complete alternative universes. They offer the opportunity for different ideas, particularly conservative ones, to flourish, because as Emmett Tyrrell observed, "That's where the money is."

Here are just two examples:

DR. R. ALBERT MOHLER JR.

Dr. Mohler is an American historical theologian and president of the Southern Baptist Theological Seminary. He is one of America's most influential evangelicals, but he's much more than that. Mohler does twenty-five to twenty-eight minutes of conversation or lecture five days a week on news and world events called "The Briefing." The topics are indeed infused with biblical references, but he tackles wide-ranging topics, from "A Study Reveals Another Difference between Men and Women: When Disaster Strikes, Men Run to the Window to Watch," to "Maybe Moderates Aren't as Moderate as We Might Think; People Tend to be Moderately Partisan, Not Truly Undecided."

Mohler's material is carried on his website as well as on iTunes, Spotify, and other outlets, with approximately 375,000 downloads weekly, making his audience bigger than a number of American cities, and his listeners are in all fifty states.

GLENN BECK

Rather than enumerating what Glenn Beck does, it might be simpler to list what he doesn't do. Beck describes himself—depending on the time of day—as an entertainer, a commentator, an author, an entrepreneur, and a philanthropist, and he is certainly all of those things. Most of all, he's an example of someone who has created a broad range of activities and vehicles knit together with "media."

Glenn started as a radio talk show host, bouncing around the country but clearly capable of attracting and building an audience. He rose to be the third most popular radio host in the country behind Rush Limbaugh and Sean Hannity. After a stint at CNN, he moved to Fox News with a nightly show at 5:00 p.m., a time slot typically regarded as the dead hour but which he built into a powerhouse. At one point, it had more viewers than three other cable networks combined for its time slot. Part of his appeal is his transparency in sharing his personal story of struggles.

To call Glenn a "personality" is to understate the meaning of the word. Today, by means of his holding company Mercury Radio Arts, Glenn has radio shows five days a week, carried by Premiere Media as well as on the internet via his creation, the Blaze; rallies; tours; books; and video. Beck has written fiction, nonfiction, children's books, and self-help publications, and has seen most go to number one on the *New York Times* and other bestseller lists.

But the next component of his operation is the most important: he has always been involved with charities, and his efforts today include rescuing over thirty thousand stranded Christians from the Islamic State in the Middle East, working globally with organizations to rescue women trapped as sex slaves and bring their captors to justice, and developing a combination museum, research institution, family destination, and educational mission for what he considers a complete view of American history.

Estimates are that his footprint reaches fifty million people a month, and *Forbes* estimates his combined activities bring in $90 million annually and that his net worth is $250 million.

Most important for this chapter, Beck was among the first—if not the very first—to recognize the potential of streaming video. Starting his operation when Netflix and HBO were just beginning, he has been recognized as a major disruptor of the media industry, being awarded

Disruptor of the Year by the Tribeca Film Festival. He said, "It must have killed them to give it to me." But because he has the ability to anticipate the future, the model he has built is worth studying for its success and for what it portends for the future.

THE FUTURE OF CONSERVATIVE IDEAS AND POLICIES

The message from Dr. Mohler and Glenn Beck is "get out and compete."

Conservatives need to continue to mount a proactive outreach to media by highlighting policies, particularly policies based on good intentions or ideologies that had far-ranging and damaging results. There is now deep research on many policies. For example, rent control sounds like a really great deal, but New York City has proven the result is greatly reduced affordable housing. A fifteen-dollar minimum "living" wage sounds compassionate until Seattle becomes a case study that can track the number of restaurants that have closed and jobs that have been lost.

We should draw a bright line on policy differences between conservative and liberal/progressive thought. For example, Democrats have largely abandoned support for charter schools that enjoy huge support in the Latino and African American communities. There are countless stories with quotes from minority parents desperate to get their kids into rigorous schools with discipline.

We need to find and tell anecdotes—stories. The liberal, pro-government advocates have an endless list of anecdotes of something going wrong for someone, and we try to counter with facts. They'll dredge up a sad story of someone who needs surgery, medication, and everything else, but who has no health insurance and is left to die a cold and lonely death. We reply, "But 90 percent of Americans are covered by health insurance already!" That's a losing competition.

We need to reframe the discussion by finding and quoting "Sam Smith," who has health insurance that provided a kidney transplant for his wife of forty years, thus freeing her from three-times-a-week dialysis.

Ask Sam if he wants to keep his health insurance and quote him saying, "Heck yes!"

You don't counter individual anecdotes by saying, "The market will solve the problem," or with facts and statistics. You have to use competitive quotes and stories from real people and situations.

Social media can help spread those stories to like-minded people, just the way the Catalan activists followed the protestors in Hong Kong.

Most of all, it's time to channel Ronald Reagan, first with his comment that if you agree with me 80 percent, you're an 80-percent friend, not a 20-percent enemy.

Next, we need to promote the most important and American commodity. In 2011, on the anniversary of what would have been Ronald Reagan's one-hundredth birthday, Ken Rudin wrote for NPR, "Bill Clinton may have been the man from Hope, and Barack Obama certainly campaigned on hope. But Ronald Reagan was the embodiment of hope. And of optimism."[13]

Hope and optimism may not be bacterial, but they are contagious. All the chapters in this update of *Making Government Work* have one thing in common: hope and optimism in the American ability.

Glenn Beck's predictive abilities are worth the closing thought: "Technology is going to continue to change everything. Things will be very different in five, ten years. If we don't stop believing all the lies about how bad we are and start believing the truth of how good we are, we won't make it and the world will plunge into darkness. But it's up to us. Democrat, Republican, Independent doesn't matter. What matters is to do the right thing. We want our kids to have a better life and not just financially, but in all ways. The future is bright if we choose right, but the time to choose is right now."

Revitalizing Low-Income Communities—from the Bottom Up and the Inside Out

by Robert L. Woodson Sr.

One of the most pressing public policy challenges of this century has been how to best support our inner cities and address systemic poverty. As conservatives, we believe in the power of the individual, but as the legendary Robert Woodson has demonstrated throughout this chapter, we must also embrace the power of community. The challenges facing America's poor today can best be addressed with solutions developed and implemented by men and women in the neighborhoods suffering the problems, supported by the philanthropy and generosity of organizations, corporations, and everyday Americans. It's critical that we also understand the origins of youth crime and the links between crime and isolation from one's community. We must turn to what Robert Woodson calls "neighborhood healers" in order to holistically address this most pressing challenge for America. No one in the country has more depth of experience than Robert Woodson in these matters. He has dedicated a lifetime of service to inner cities and the poorest communities, where he has worked tirelessly to bring about societal and economic revitalization and the restoration of hope. His remarkable career spans from his beginnings as a civil rights activist in the 1960s, to working side by side with Congressman Jack Kemp, to advising former president George W. Bush. For his service, he was awarded the prestigious Presidential Citizens Award. No one in the country has their finger on the pulse of America's inner cities more than Robert Woodson. He understands how best to address and overcome the issues of welfare dependence, poverty, substance abuse, and youth crime. I'm so grateful for the honor and privilege of having Mr. Woodson accept my invitation to participate in *Making Government Work*. Millions of Americans will benefit from reading his firsthand accounts of his unique ministry of hope and healing.

—Tan Parker

As campaign rhetoric heats up for electoral battles, both sides use the conditions of disinvested low-income neighborhoods as a way to fire at their rivals. The Right characterizes the Left as perpetrators of a socialized nanny state that promotes the massive growth of government intrusion and out-of-control spending. Meanwhile, the Left portrays the Right as hard-hearted and tight-fisted, oblivious to the conditions of those who are in need.

As a protracted political tug-of-war continues between those who would expand government programs and those who demand budget cuts, the poor are spoken about and spoken around but never spoken to. As the old African saying goes, "When bull elephants fight, the grass always loses."

But what if an effective response to poverty with sustainable impact could be forged? What if it were possible to decrease the rolls of welfare, add to the ranks of self-sufficient productive citizens, strengthen families and communities, and effectively address debilitating societal problems while spending fewer taxpayer dollars? Exploring this possibility means calling a moratorium on political grandstanding and gladiatorial ideological combat in which each side vies to exhibit the best argument.

What candidates ought to be debating is not which political party has crafted a superior *argument*, but which has the superior *agenda*—which, when implemented, could measurably improve the conditions of those who are most in need. That should be the new standard for today—not who can posture with the most convincing rhetoric but who can offer the clearest example of real remedies to our nation's most pressing problems. As I will explain, the true experts in this project are unexpected and grassroots. The living evidence of their victories trumps any rhetorical flourish.

A FAILED PARADIGM

After more than fifty years and the investment of $25 trillion of taxpayer money, poverty statistics have virtually remained the same, while conditions in low-income neighborhoods have spiraled downward. The ranks of the poor, as well as devastating family dissolution and rates of crime and violence, have continued to increase. The reality is that poverty will never be reduced by channeling even more money into the same failed bureaucratic programs that have yet to make a dent in poverty.

As the funding flow for poverty programs has steadily increased, 70 percent of the money has gone to those who service the poor rather than those who are impoverished. Since the War on Poverty was launched in the 1960s, a virtual poverty industrial complex has emerged—an entire industry revolving around pathology. A huge provider base of psychologists, social workers, and counselors emerged in response to the funding that was allocated. For every problem, there was a different master's degree or professional certificate.

Unfortunately, providers tended to ask not which problems were solvable but which ones were fundable. Priorities were driven by government grant possibilities, which meant that providers were rewarded not for solving problems but, in effect, for the proliferation of problems and dependency, since the larger a problem was, the larger the grant and salaries would be, and the more extensive the staff.

This is not to argue that everything that was done to address poverty was harmful or motivated by self-interest. Those who go into the field of social work certainly don't go into it for the money. But even in the absence of an intent to harm, misguided good intentions have injured with the helping hand. As Dietrich Bonhoeffer wrote in his *Letters from Prison*, "Folly is a more dangerous enemy to the good than malice. You can protest against malice, you can unmask it, or prevent it by force. . . . There is no defense against folly."

The massive welfare system that we know today had its roots with the launch of the War on Poverty and was based on a failed paradigm that entailed numerous perverse incentives. The system sapped its dependents of the dignity of an expectation of reciprocity and discouraged effort and initiative.

Welfare policies undermined healthy communities and disincentivized work and marriage—key ingredients of progress toward self-sufficiency. For example, if an unmarried woman receiving public assistance married a man who was gainfully employed, her benefits would be terminated. Rent was fixed at 30 percent of income for people receiving public assistance, so, in effect, an increase in earnings was penalized. Programs rewarded illegitimacy by giving a mother more money for each additional child she had.

ELITISM INHERENT IN THE ANTIPOVERTY AGENDA

The most debilitating obstacle limiting the ability of those on the bottom rung of society's ladder to begin to rise is a fundamental and pervasive elitism. The conventional, elitist approach to solving problems of poverty is to have credentialed professionals design social theories for which they develop programs, access funding, and then "parachute" projects into the afflicted communities. When the community doesn't respond in a way that is consistent with the expectations, the fundamental nature of the intervention is never questioned, and instead it's decided that more funding and more programs are needed.

RACE-GRIEVANCE AGENDA MIMICS THE POVERTY PARADIGM

The same elitist mentality permeates a race-based response to the problems of afflicted communities. Portraying the poor as helpless victims of racism denies the capacities and potential of those who suffer the greatest economic and societal problems and places their deliverance in the hands of others to dole out restitution.

Racism may exist, but it doesn't have to be the determining force. As syndicated columnist Bill Raspberry once put it, viewing all problems through the race prism presents the barrier of myopia. What you see may not be inaccurate, but it is inadequate.

To say that the conditions of the poor are the inevitable result of racism is to ignore the rich history of the black community in America. Why is it that the black family was strong and black enterprise thrived in earlier eras, in the midst of legalized segregation and racial discrimination? Why is there such social and economic decline today in the presence of the greatest opportunity? In 1954, there were 96,000 blacks in prison—a number corresponding to the percentage of blacks in the general population. That number has soared to nearly 900,000 today.

In order to challenge the faulty assumptions of the race-grievance spokespersons, we need to look at black America in past eras. The core of the black community in the hundred years between the end of the Civil War and the War on Poverty was the family, a belief in God, and business formation. Until 1965, the marriage rate for blacks was over 80 percent. In fact, during the Depression, the black marriage rate was higher than that of whites.

In the first fifty years after the Emancipation Proclamation, black Americans had accumulated a personal wealth of $700 million. They owned over 40,000 businesses, and 937,000 farms. The literacy rate had climbed from 5 to 75 percent. Black commercial enclaves in Durham, North Carolina, and the Greenwood Avenue section of Tulsa, Oklahoma, were together known as the Black Wall Street.

Another element of strength was the belief in solid moral and spiritual tenets that guided the black community in the late 1800s and early 1900s. Mutual aid societies were established as part of the National Negro Movement. In every one of these self-help associations, moral competency was a requirement. Mother Bethel Church in Philadelphia, for example, had one of the first recorded welfare systems—entailing principles of reciprocity and personal responsibility. Its members were taxed a shilling a week and individuals could not qualify for aid if their poverty was due to their own "slothfulness or immorality."

A continued focus on race and support for those who profit from maintaining a grievance industry are keeping this nation from addressing the nation's most pressing problems. If complete racial reconciliation were immediately possible, it still would not answer the high rates of black-on-black homicide and out-of-wedlock pregnancy.

IDENTIFYING SOLUTIONS TO POVERTY

If the public and private sectors are to refocus their efforts so that their contributions will have a positive impact for those who are in need, several crucial questions must be answered: Who are the true experts of social and moral revitalization? What principles should guide funding decisions? What qualities are common to all effective programs?

Unfortunately, as a nation, we are prone to place our trust in irrelevant authority. Just as commercials lead consumers to believe that sports stars are experts on nutrition or footwear, there are those who would have us believe that the MBAs and sociologists in distant universities can provide expert advice in salvaging our inner-city neighborhoods and impoverished communities. But the solutions to the problems of our nation's Harlems will never be found in the Harvards of this nation.

The good news is that solutions do exist. Today, in the most devastated, poverty-ridden communities, there are oases of health and restoration. I use the biblical figures of Joseph and the pharaoh as a metaphor to describe these grassroots leaders and the relationships and support that can empower them to continue and expand their transformative outreach.

When the Egyptian pharaoh was troubled by ominous dreams that none of his counselors or astrologers could interpret, he was willing to seek guidance from a young Hebrew boy who was being held in his own prison. He followed the young man's guidance for his kingdom and even appointed him to oversee the strategy he advised to make preparations for times of hardship. When a famine came, the pharaoh's was the only land that was prepared. The Bible recounts that Egypt not only survived the famine but also prospered for four hundred years until "there arose a pharaoh who knew not Joseph."

The pharaoh trusted Joseph in spite of his humble status because he recognized that he had the capacity that others with authority lacked. Today, in communities throughout the nation, hundreds of modern-day "Josephs" are at work restoring spiritual health in their neighborhoods, guiding others to lives of value and fulfillment, and helping people who were once considered to be hopelessly lost to reclaim and redirect their lives.

Many of these community healers have emerged from the worst conditions. Some have been called to responsibility from jails, from drugs, from crime, from prostitution. They have passion for and faith in the people they serve—in impoverished neighborhoods infested with drugs and crime—because they have personally experienced a transformation in their own lives. Their authority is attested to not by their position and prestige in society, but by the thousands of lives they have been able to reach and change.

They work with individuals that conventional service providers have given up on. They take on the worst cases and they work with meager resources, yet their effectiveness eclipses that of conventional professional remedies.

Among the hundreds of neighborhood healers I have met throughout the last forty years were Freddie and Ninfa Garcia, the founders of Victory Fellowship, a powerful San Antonio–based rehabilitation initiative for hard-core drug addicts and alcoholics.

Victory Fellowship had, to put it mildly, humble beginnings. Freddie and Ninfa were themselves former addicts. Freddie first met Ninfa when she was driving the getaway car in a convenience-store robbery. In 1966, their lives were reclaimed through the outreach of ex-addicts in the faith-based Teen Challenge program founded by David Wilkerson, author of *The Cross and the Switchblade.*

After their lives were transformed, Freddie and Ninfa could have simply gone on to live happily and peacefully with their children, pursuing their personal goals. But they could not bear to witness the lives of the people in their community being wasted and lost to addiction. In 1972, they launched Victory Fellowship from their one-bedroom home, moving their furniture into the yard to make room for the addicts and alcoholics they invited to live with them. Their ministry continued to expand, and, through their personal 24/7 outreach and long-term commitment, thousands of even the most hardened addicts were empowered to turn their lives around.

Today, Victory Fellowship's programs have spread to more than seventy satellite centers with international outreach and have transformed more than thirteen thousand lives. Although Pastor Freddie has passed away, his son Jubal continues the efforts of his parents.

Another unforgettable "Joseph" I met is Bob Cote. Bob was a former boxer with some business acumen whose alcoholism had driven him to desperation and homelessness. After he broke the chains of addiction and achieved sobriety, he felt called to reach out to other men who had lost control of their lives because of drugs and alcohol.

Because Bob personally knew life on the streets and the ploys addicts use to feed their addictions, the recovery center he set up for the homeless in a skid-row section of Denver—dubbed Step 13—employed a no-nonsense approach that entailed personal responsibility and reciprocity. Bob criticized the conventional homeless shelters and soup kitchens in the city that garnered funding by inflating the number of people served. He described them as "heads in beds" warehouses that gave drunks a donut in the morning before they put them back on the streets. In contrast, Step 13's motto was "Real Change, Not Spare Change."

Step 13 established an amazing track record of success in helping people that everyone had given up on and empowering them to redirect and reclaim their lives. He worked with the hardest cases. One recovered alcoholic tells of how Bob took him in one winter night after finding him frozen to the sidewalk in his own vomit. Men who came to Bob with no life and no hope progressed through different living arrangements in the program—from a bunk room, to their own room, and, eventually, to their own homes after they achieved self-sufficiency and emerged as responsible spouses, fathers, and employees.

There are as many different types of Josephs as there are different needs, but there are a number of defining characteristics they all hold in common:

1. Their programs are open to all comers. The grassroots leaders do not target their services exclusively to individuals of any particular race or background. Help is offered, instead, on the basis of the need a person has and his or her desire to change.

2. Neighborhood healers live in the same "geographic and cultural zip code" as the people they serve. They have firsthand knowledge of the challenges they face and they have a personal stake in the success of their solutions.

3. Their approach is flexible. They know that every person cannot be reached in exactly the same way. Even in programs that are guided by a certain theology or philosophy, every participant is not expected to embrace it or be affected by it in the same way.

4. Effective grassroots programs contain an essential element of reciprocity. They do not practice blind charity but require something in return from the individuals they serve. They recognize that treating them only as "recipients" denies their capacity and potential.

5. Clear behavioral guidelines and discipline are an important part of their programs.

6. Grassroots healers fulfill the role of a surrogate parent or mentor, providing not only authority and structure, but

also the love that is necessary for an individual to undergo healing, growth, and development. Like a parent, their love is unconditional and resilient. They never withdraw their support, in spite of backsliding and even in the face of betrayal.

7. Grassroots leaders are committed for the long haul. Most of them began their outreach with their own meager resources. They are committed for a lifetime, not for the duration of a grant that funds a program.

8. They are on call virtually twenty-four hours a day, in contrast to a therapist who comes once a week for a forty-five-minute session or professional service provider who comes from 9:00 a.m. to 5:00 p.m. and then returns to his distant home. The homes of grassroots leaders are always open to the people they serve.

9. The healing they offer involves an immersion in an environment of care and mutual support with a community of individuals who are trying to accomplish the same changes in their lives.

10. These Josephs are united in a brotherhood of service. They are eager to share ideas and strategies. They offer earnest support to each other in times of struggle and sincerely celebrate one another's victories.

NOT AN ANOMALY

Our nation's grassroots Josephs go unrecognized, unappreciated, and underutilized. They work with the hardest cases, yet their effectiveness eclipses that of conventional professional remedies.

Why haven't we heard more about these leaders? Why isn't their success common knowledge? Elitism has caused us to dismiss the possibility that remedies could emerge from low-income neighborhoods.

With silent prejudice, faith-based strategies are dismissed out of hand in spite of their consistent track records of effectiveness.

Even in instances where recognition is given to the transformations accomplished through the outreach of grassroots leaders, praise often comes with a caveat that those cases are "anomalies" and can't be brought to scale to address the enormous societal problems facing the nation.

Two examples provide evidence that this is not true, and that with well-earned support from both the public and private sector, neighborhood programs can be both duplicated and scaled up.

RESIDENT MANAGEMENT OF PUBLIC HOUSING

As early as 1973, a handful of trailblazing women living in public housing projects were frustrated by the neglect and opportunism that typically characterized the public housing authorities funded to manage their properties. These courageous residents determined that they would reclaim their crime-ridden, drug-infested, neglected housing projects and organized their counterparts to take action. In their struggle to determine their own destiny, they understood that, just as the management of the properties had to become accountable for its performance, the residents of their neighborhoods, likewise, needed to change and improve their conduct so as to earn the trust, respect, and support of those who invested funds in the properties.

One of the earliest groups of residents to take action lived in the Bromley Heath housing project in Boston, led by a woman named Mildred Hailey. One of the first resident initiatives she led was the formation of a security patrol in the neighborhood, which had been virtually abandoned by the police. The group next sought to supply social services to the residents, given that the city took no responsibility for making those services available in federally owned housing developments. The resident group received a grant to open a maternity and infant-care clinic, which was later expanded as a comprehensive family health facility. In addition, the residents revitalized a community recreation facility, established a babysitting service, day care centers, and even a radio station.

Public housing residents in St. Louis, likewise, rose to action when lax management by the bureaucratic housing authorities allowed conditions to deteriorate to the point that the project looked like a virtual war zone. Hundreds of windows were missing (many had flown from their frames during high winds due to poor structural design), and the top four floors of a twelve-story high-rise were uninhabitable for more than twelve years because the maintenance crew had gutted those 250 units to make repairs on other floors. In the midst of this squalor, crime, vandalism, and drug-related killings soared. Under the leadership of a determined woman named Bertha Gilkey, residents organized to create a volunteer maintenance crew that began to repair the site. Once they had shown the effectiveness of collaborative community action, the resident group went on to secure a grant from the city to create a comprehensive plan for revitalizing the development and also received both public and private revitalization funds. In 1976, the group negotiated a contract with the city's housing authority and officially became the Cochran Tenant Management Corporation.

A leader among those grassroots leaders, Kimi Gray of the Kenilworth-Parkside public housing development in Washington, D.C., became the face of the resident movement. Because of the neglect of the public housing authority, the housing project had deteriorated to squalid conditions, and some residents went without heat and water for a three-year period. Roofs were literally collapsing, while drugs and crime infested the community. Kimi—a no-nonsense, fast-thinking and fast-talking mover—was determined to reclaim her community and rose to action. In 1974, she launched a College Here We Come program for youth in the development, which provided tutoring, guidance with college applications, and even organized college site visits for students who exhibited effort and commitment. Kimi's vision was that if the young people could be exposed to different environments, they would see higher vistas for their lives and their communities and would work to improve conditions when they returned.

Kimi was right. Many graduates of the program returned to the development to take part in ongoing programs that enriched the lives of the residents. An architectural student supervised a major building rehabilitation program and the revitalization of a townhouse development that was funded through a HUD grant.

The neighborhood would go on to establish its own co-op market, laundromats, barber and beauty shops, and catering company, as well as a health clinic and day care facility. In addition, an innovative "reverse commute" project was launched to provide transportation that enabled inner-city residents to take jobs in the suburbs. Within four years, teenaged pregnancy and welfare dependency were reduced by 50 percent and crime fell by 75 percent, while rental receipts rose by 77 percent. A cost-benefit analysis conducted by one of the nation's largest and most respected accountancy firms projected that resident management would bring the District's government savings of $4.5 million over ten years.

In the mid-1980s, my organization, the National Center for Neighborhood Enterprise (NCNE), (now the Woodson Center), brought resident leaders together in a series of forums, conferences, and meetings to exchange ideas and information, strengthen their capacities, and clarify their goals. The idea of resident management and entrepreneurism attracted the attention of Republican congressman Jack Kemp, who resonated with an anti-poverty agenda that was based on empowerment and market principles. When he learned of a meeting that I had scheduled with the resident leaders at my D.C. offices, he called asking if he could attend. Kemp was to become an ardent advocate of the movement and would play a key role in its progress in the policy arena.

The Amoco Foundation was impressed with the initiative and accomplishments of the public housing leaders and came to the table, providing $1.9 million for a three-year Public Housing Resident Management Demonstration that would be conducted in twelve public housing sites in eight cities. The project included training in four arenas: community organization and board development, fundamentals of management and supervision, business and real estate development, and home-ownership. In addition, NCNE supported enterprise development in the public housing neighborhoods.

To connect resident leaders with those who could influence public policy, NCNE arranged for busloads of residents to travel to Washington to brief their representatives on their accomplishments and the barriers they confronted. In 1985, the first legislative hearings on resident management were held. Two years later, landmark resident management and homeownership amendments were introduced with the Housing and Community Development Act of 1987, with bipartisan sponsorship in the House and Senate. The residents sat in the galley as Congress debated the bill—a presence that could not be ignored even by the legislators who were lobbied by special interest groups that were opposed to empowering the residents. The legislation passed 419 to 1 in the House and was unopposed in the Senate. In 1988, President Reagan signed the bill into law, flanked by public housing resident leaders, establishing the right of public housing residents to manage their properties. The right of resident management had been established.

By 1991, a national Association of Resident Management Corporations was established to raise up fledgling resident groups, and more than 1,300 residents from thirty cities throughout the nation attended its annual conference in Boston.

VIOLENCE-FREE ZONES

In 1997, shockwaves reverberated in Washington, D.C. (a city that had become calloused to youth violence and gang warfare), with a horrendous murder in the Benning Terrace public housing project. A rash of gang-related homicides climaxed with the discovery of the body of a twelve-year-old frozen in a ravine—the victim of a retaliatory execution.

A group of adult males who had grown up in the neighborhood stepped forward to intervene. This "Alliance of Concerned Men" knew the street culture and were able to identify the leaders of the two warring gangs and approached each individually. After a period of continuous and consistent investment, the youths began to trust them and respond to them and, as they began to change direction, their gang members followed. A peace council was held at my office for the gang leaders and their deputies. The youths filed in to our conference room after checking their guns in the reception area. Eventually, their leaders agreed to declare a truce.

NCNE connected with the acting head of the District's housing authority, David Gilmore. A street-smart and impassioned individual, Gilmore arranged to provide training and employment opportunities for the youths who had pledged to turn their lives around. Once the scourge of their neighborhood, these youths began to work to revitalize the community—doing landscape work, cleanup, and graffiti removal. The violence subsided, and for twelve years there was not a single homicide in the neighborhood that had been the site of fifty-three murders in a two-year period.

Key components of this remarkable intervention were the outreach of indigenous community leaders and the role that former gang leaders and members played as peer mentors. Since that time, the model of the Violence-Free Zone initiative that was launched in D.C. has been replicated in violence-plagued schools throughout the nation. At each site, a local community group worked with a team comprised of representatives of the police, school staff, administrators, and, most importantly, youth advisors—young adults who have redirected their lives and reach out to their counterparts to do the same.

Today, Violence-Free Zones have been established in more than thirty-five schools in five cities. Although the initiative targets schools with the highest levels of violence, three evaluations by university experts have found a measurable impact in reduced violence and crime, improved safety, reduction in suspensions and truancy, increased academic performance, and even a decline in crime in the surrounding neighborhoods. School administrators and law enforcement officers have testified about the initiatives' remarkable impact in changing the school culture.

SEARCHING FOR THE GOOD PHARAOH

Although today's Josephs deserve to be heeded by modern-day pharaohs (political leaders and leaders of the business and philanthropic community), their effectiveness is not dependent on such recognition. Long before support or acknowledgement came from the others, our nation's neighborhood healers committed themselves to lives of service, and they engendered miraculous changes in the lives they touched. Though these grassroots leaders accomplished extraordinary feats with little support, an alliance between today's Josephs and pharaohs could provide the support that is needed to allow their transforming efforts to expand and further develop to benefit the entire society.

This type of partnership requires a major overhaul in how we view the poor. Many policy-makers on both the left and the right see the poor as hopelessly lost in a sea of pathology, with few personal redeeming qualities. They assume that their only hope is rescue coming from the professionals and the intellectual elite. They cannot recognize the capacities that exist within America's low-income communities. Policy-makers and philanthropists must recognize, support, and strengthen the assets that exist within our nation's most impoverished communities.

A SOLUTION FOR BOTH SPIRITUAL AND MATERIAL POVERTY

The hundreds of grassroots leaders throughout the country are the embodiment of "social entrepreneurs" who have the vision, creativity, and commitment to forge innovative, workable solutions to the devastating societal crises that permeate not only our nation's inner cities but our rural and suburban communities as well.

The trailblazing innovation and committed outreach of our nation's Josephs are in need of one thing: support from policy-makers and venture capitalists of the corporate arena who recognize their potential and are willing to invest in their transforming efforts and to strengthen the organizational structure and management skills that will be needed to expand and export their remarkably effective outreach.

Like those who have led us through our nation's giant steps in the areas of science and industry, there exist even now hundreds of dedicated and inspired geniuses throughout the nation who can guide us in solving even our most entrenched and devastating social crises. An effective strategy does not begin with credentialed professionals' analysis of the problems but with a comprehensive and sustained effort to maximize the impact of the solutions that exist.

Moreover, "impoverishment" is not measured exclusively by economic status. Financial wealth does not equate with a life of value. The tragic scenarios of self-destruction and suicide that occur among the successful and the famous comprise a compelling testimony that our nation is desperately in search of meaning and purpose. All poverty is not material, and spiritual poverty has taken its toll in the lives of young people in affluent suburbs just as it has in our urban streets.

In an era of spiritual hunger and moral disarray, today's Josephs are a source of both spiritual and economic renewal that will have an impact beyond the boundaries of inner-city neighborhoods. Grassroots leaders who have proven that they can engender substantial and lasting transformations—sometimes at only a tenth of the cost of less effective but "credentialed" programs—have much to bring to the table.

If America's grassroots leaders can heal the heart of a hard-core drug addict who has been to prison and who once refused to yield to any and all figures of authority, if they can heal a person who has been so severely damaged and hardened, imagine what they can do for those who have gone astray but have the buffers of income, power, and influence.

One of the best opportunities for the states to address the challenges we all face is to embrace and reteach the timeless principles and lessons of Martin Luther King Jr. regarding the importance of peaceful protest to achieving societal change. During his lifetime, Martin Luther King Jr. took a peaceful approach to protesting against the abuses of segregation and racism. All American children should be educated on these events from our nation's history.

Currently, states like Tennessee, under the leadership of Governor Bill Lee, have now implemented just such an outstanding curriculum for all fifth- and ninth-grade students. I encourage all states to do the same.

Among the most devastated economic and social conditions today, oases of spiritual renewal have been created through the work of thousands of committed grassroots leaders. If these embers of hope and life can be nourished by those who have wealth and influence in society—today's pharaohs—the flames of revitalization can become a brushfire that may sweep across the nation, bringing revitalization and vision where there is now only cynicism, confusion, and despair.

Contributor Biographies

HOUSE MAJORITY LEADER DICK ARMEY

Elected to Congress in 1984, Dr. Richard "Dick" Armey went to Washington as a novice. As he has said many times, "When I came to Washington, the only congressman I'd known or spent much time with was the man I beat." Armey was a strong believer in the policies of Ronald Reagan. He quickly became known for his dedication to good public policy based on conservative principles, serving as House Majority Leader from 1995 to 2003.

Armey was the primary author of the Contract with America, which was a collection of ten bills that would be brought up for a vote during the first one hundred days of a Republican-controlled Congress. The Republicans took control of the House for the first time in forty years, and 60 percent of the Contract with America was signed into law.

Armey ran unopposed for Majority Leader in the 104th Congress, and that Congress passed the first balanced budged in a generation. He was influential in key legislation related to e-commerce and the economy, development of a flat tax, and homeland defense. He is also an author and former economics professor.

GOVERNOR JEB BUSH

Jeb Bush is the forty-third governor of the state of Florida, serving from 1999 through 2007. He was the third Republican elected to the state's highest office and the first Republican in the state's history to be reelected. He was most recently a candidate for the Republican presidential nomination in 2016.

Governor Bush remained true to his conservative principles throughout his two terms in office—cutting nearly $20 billion in taxes, vetoing more than $2.3 billion in earmarks, and reducing the state government workforce by more than thirteen thousand. His limited government approach helped unleash one of the most robust and dynamic economies in the nation, creating 1.3 million net new jobs and improving the state's credit ratings, including achieving the first ever triple-A bond rating for Florida.

During his two terms, Governor Bush championed major reform of government in areas ranging from health care and environmental protection to civil service and tax reform. His top priority was the overhaul of the state's failing education system. Under Governor Bush's leadership, Florida established a bold accountability system in public schools and created the most ambitious school choice programs in the nation. Today, Florida remains a national leader in education and is one of the only states in the nation to significantly narrow the achievement gap.

Governor Bush is also known for his leadership during two unprecedented back-to-back hurricane seasons, which brought eight hurricanes and four tropical storms to the state of Florida in less than two years. To protect the state from loss of life and damage caused by catastrophic events, such as hurricanes, Bush worked tirelessly to improve the state's ability to respond quickly and compassionately during emergencies, while also instilling a "culture of preparedness" in the state's citizenry.

Governor Bush joined the University of Pennsylvania as a non-resident Presidential Professor of Practice for the 2018–19 academic year. He has previously served as a visiting professor and fellow at Harvard University, an executive professor at Texas A&M University, and has been awarded several honorary doctorates from collegiate institutions across the country. Governor Bush has been recognized for his contributions to public policy by national organizations including the Manhattan Institute, the Lynde and Harry Bradley Foundation, and the Jack Kemp Foundation. Governor Bush earned his bachelor's degree in Latin American Studies from the University of Texas at Austin.

Governor Bush currently serves as chairman of Finback Investments Partners LLC and Dock Square Capital LLC, both merchant banks headquartered in Coral Gables.

Governor Bush maintains his passion for improving the quality of education for students across the country by serving as the chairman of the Foundation for Excellence in Education, a national nonprofit education reform organization he founded to transform education in America.

He has written three books: *Profiles in Character*, *Immigration Wars: Forging an American Solution*, and *Reply All: A Governor's Story 1999–2007*.

Governor Bush lives in Miami with his wife Columba. They have three children and four grandchildren.

JAMES JAY CARAFANO

James Jay Carafano is a leading expert in national security and foreign policy challenges, an accomplished historian and teacher, as well as a prolific writer and researcher. He currently serves as the Heritage Foundation's vice president, foreign and defense policy studies, assuming responsibility for Heritage's entire defense and foreign policy team; the E. W. Richardson Fellow; and the director of the Kathryn and Shelby Cullom Davis Institute for International Studies.

Carafano is a graduate of the U.S. Military Academy at West Point and served twenty-five years in the U.S. Army, retiring as a lieutenant colonel. He served in Europe, Korea, and the United States. His assignments included head speechwriter for the Army Chief of Staff, the service's highest-ranking officer. Before retiring, Carafano was executive editor of *Joint Force Quarterly*, the Defense Department's premiere professional military journal.

From 2012 to 2014, he served on the Homeland Security Advisory Council convened by the secretary of the U.S. Department of Homeland Security. He formerly was a senior fellow at George Washington University's Homeland Security Policy Institute. He also previously served on the congressionally mandated Advisory Panel on Department of Defense Capabilities for Support of Civil Authorities, the National Academy's Board on Army Science and Technology, and the Department of the Army Historical Advisory Committee.

Carafano holds a master's degree and a doctorate from Georgetown University as well as a master's degree in strategy from the U.S. Army War College. His recent research has focused on developing the national security required to secure the long-term interests of the United States—protecting the public, providing for economic growth, and preserving civil liberties.

JACKI DEASON

Jacki Deason is host of *The Jacki Daily Show* and a senior fellow at the Texas Public Policy Foundation, the nation's largest state-based policy shop. Prior to her current work, she has served as a litigator, as counsel to the chairman of the Subcommittee on the Constitution (of the U.S. House Judiciary Committee), and as an executive in a policy-directed nonprofit.

Jacki's show and podcast can be heard each week on Blaze Media. *The Jacki Daily Show* is also the dial in Texas and podcast twenty-four hours a day, seven days a week on iHeartRadio, iTunes, Google Play, and SoundCloud. You can follow her on social media through *The Jacki Daily Show* Facebook page, or via Twitter @JackiDailyShow.

PROFESSOR RICHARD J. DOUGHERTY

Dr. Richard J. Dougherty is professor of politics at the University of Dallas in Irving, Texas, director of the graduate program in politics, and the director of the university's Center for Christianity and the Common Good.

He received his B.A. from Belmont Abbey College in North Carolina and his M.A. and Ph.D. from the University of Dallas's Institute of Philosophic Studies. He edited and contributed to the 2019 work *Augustine's Political Thought* (University of Rochester Press), and is a contributor to the *Encyclopedia of the American Presidency* and to the three-volume work *The Oxford Guide to the Historical Reception of Augustine*. He has recently republished, with a new introductory essay, Charles McCoy's *The Structure of Political Thought* (Transaction Publications).

He is currently completing a book on executive prerogative power and American constitutionalism, and a second book on St. Thomas Aquinas' *Treatise on Law*. Dr. Dougherty has served as a visiting professor in the department of Comparative Political Science at the Catholic University of Eichstätt-Ingolstadt in Bavaria. He and his wife Julie have been blessed with nine children and seven grandchildren.

NICHOLAS C. DRINKWATER

Nicholas C. Drinkwater is chief operating officer at Laffer Associates. Nick joined Laffer Associates in 2010 as an intern. After graduating from Vanderbilt University in 2011 with a B.A. in economics, he joined Laffer Investments and Laffer Associates in a financial and economic research role. He is responsible for managing the firm's research program and consulting business.

Nick's research efforts have focused on the effects of fiscal policy on the economy, especially at the state and local level, through his involvement in projects such as serving as the primary data researcher for *NYT* bestseller *An Inquiry into the Nature and Causes of the Wealth of States*, and since 2012, overseeing all data collection and analysis related to producing the annual ALEC-Laffer State Economic Competitiveness Index known as Rich States, Poor States.

BECKY NORTON DUNLOP

Becky Norton Dunlop, a prominent leader, strategist, and counselor in the conservative movement, is the Heritage Foundation's Ronald Reagan Distinguished Fellow. Dunlop, who joined the leading think tank in 1998, holds the only policy chair in the country to be officially named for the fortieth president. She succeeds Ed Meese, the U.S. attorney general under Reagan, who assumed emeritus status.

Dunlop oversees special projects, travels as an ambassador for Heritage, and works tirelessly to ensure that the legacy of principles, policies, and practices represented by the life and service of Ronald Reagan remains in the hearts and minds of Americans.

Previously, Dunlop was Heritage's vice president for external relations from 1998 until May 2016. She served on the Trump transition team. Dunlop was a senior official in the Reagan administration from 1981–89 inside the White House, at the Justice Department, and at the Interior Department. She served from 1994–98 as secretary of natural resources for the Commonwealth of Virginia in the cabinet of then Virginia governor George Allen.

As political director for the American Conservative Union from 1973–77, she was instrumental in organizing grassroots activists for Reagan's unsuccessful 1976 race for the Republican nomination and advised his successful 1980 nomination and general election campaigns.

From Reagan's first inauguration in 1981 to 1985, her White House posts included deputy assistant to the president for presidential personnel and special assistant to the president and director of his cabinet office. During Reagan's second term, Dunlop served as senior special assistant to Meese, who was then the attorney general, in charge of managing cabinet-level domestic policy issues. She oversaw major policy reports on the environment, the family, federalism, tort reform, privatization, and welfare reform.

She completed her service in the Reagan administration as deputy undersecretary of the Interior Department and as assistant Interior secretary for fish, wildlife, and parks. Dunlop is one of the few of the insiders from the beginnings of the Reagan era who remain active in public policy leadership.

As Virginia's natural resources chief, Dunlop worked to streamline, decentralize, and downsize agencies while protecting and improving the environment. She is one of the few "free-market environmentalists" to have headed a state agency and put ideas into action. Her book *Clearing the Air* (Alexis de Tocqueville Institute, 2000) chronicles some of her experiences in advancing those principles.

In 2002, President George W. Bush appointed her to a part-time post as chairwoman of the Federal Service Impasses Panel. The seven-member panel resolves disputes between federal agencies' management and labor unions. Under her leadership, it took on several hundred cases and eliminated backlogs.

Other current leadership roles include the boards of the Virginia Institute for Public Policy, the Reagan Ranch Board of Governors, the Reagan Alumni Association, the Association for American Educators and the AAE Foundation, the Council for National Policy, and the American Conservative Union.

In addition to topics addressing conservative principles and their roots in the nation's founding, Dunlop is a sought-after public speaker on the idea that personnel is policy; on energy, natural resources, and the environment (including free market environmentalism); on federalism as a former member of a governor's cabinet; Capitalism and the Rule of Law; and on the Reagan administration (including the fortieth president's effective leadership style).

A graduate of Miami University in Ohio, she currently resides in Arlington, Virginia, with her husband, George S. Dunlop. The Dunlops are members of Oakland Baptist Church in Alexandria, Virginia.

PROFESSOR ROBERT P. GEORGE

Robert P. George is the McCormick Professor of Jurisprudence and director of the James Madison Program in American Ideals and Institutions at Princeton University. He has several times been a visiting professor at Harvard Law School. He has served as chairman of the U.S. Commission on International Religious Freedom and on the U.S. Commission on Civil Rights and the President's Council on Bioethics.

He has also served as the U.S. member of UNESCO's World Commission on the Ethics of Scientific Knowledge and Technology. He was a judicial fellow at the Supreme Court of the United States, where he received the Justice Tom C. Clark Award. A Phi Beta Kappa graduate of Swarthmore, he holds the degrees of J.D. and M.T.S. from Harvard University and the degrees of D.Phil., B.C.L., D.C.L., and D.Litt. from Oxford University, in addition to twenty-one honorary doctorates.

He is a recipient of the U.S. Presidential Citizens Medal, the Honorific Medal for the Defense of Human Rights of the Republic of Poland, the Canterbury Medal of the Becket Fund for Religious Liberty, the Bradley Prize, the Irving Kristol Award of the American Enterprise Institute, and Princeton University's President's Award for Distinguished Teaching. His books include *Making Men Moral: Civil Liberties and Public Morality* and *In Defense of Natural Law* (both published by Oxford University Press).

BOB HELLMAN

Bob Hellman is the founder and CEO of American Infrastructure Partners, the successor entity to American Infrastructure Funds, which he founded in 2006. Bob has been a real asset and infrastructure investor for over thirty years, building companies in such industries as building materials, energy distribution, school buildings, deathcare, and most recently transportation and last mile logistics.

He holds several patents on innovative financial securities, and his most recent creations include the New American Bridges Fund, dedicated to building replacement bridge infrastructure across the U.S., and the American Postal Infrastructure Fund, focused on acquiring post offices across the U.S. in partnership with the U.S. government.

Bob began his investment career at McCown De Leeuw in 1987, having previously worked as a consultant with Bain & Company, where he was one of the founding members of Bain's Tokyo office. Bob has served on the board of a number of public and private companies. He is also a member of the Board of the Stanford Institute for Economic Policy Research (SIEPR) and Past President of Stanford's DAPER Investment Fund.

He received an M.B.A. from the Harvard Business School with Baker Scholar honors, an M.S. in economics from the London School of Economics, and a B.A. in economics from Stanford University. Bob lives in Atherton, California, with his wife, Holly, and is father to two sets of twins (ages eight and twenty-five).

CHAD HENNINGS

Three-time Super Bowl champion and Air Force veteran Chad Hennings's successes began long before his professional football career. An accomplished lineman in high school, Hennings was offered full scholarships from universities across the nation. Instead, he chose to attend the

U.S. Air Force Academy, where he racked up numerous honors academically and on the gridiron.

Hennings's exemplary achievements put him at the top of many draft lists and earned him a spot on the Dallas Cowboys' roster, but Hennings postponed his entry into the National Football League to fulfill his commitment to the U.S. Air Force. He entered the Euro-NATO program, a training program for top pilots, and soon found himself at the controls of the A-10 Thunderbolt.

During his four-year stint with the Air Force, Hennings flew forty-five missions in support of Operation Provide Comfort in northern Iraq, an effort that helped provide relief and humanitarian aid to Kurdish refugees. He received two aerial achievement medals, a humanitarian award, and an outstanding unit award for his actions in the service.

After his discharge, Hennings joined the Dallas Cowboys, quickly earning a starting position as a defensive lineman. He spent his entire nine-year professional football career with the Cowboys, retiring in 2001 with three Super Bowl rings.

Since his retirement from the NFL, Hennings has found success as commercial real estate professional, author, and motivational speaker. He established Wingmen Ministries, a Christian men's ministry that concentrates on discipleship.

Hennings is a partner and principal with Rubicon Representation LLC. He is the author of three books: *It Takes Commitment*, *Rules of Engagement*, and *Forces of Character*.

He lives in Texas with his wife Tammy. They have two children, Chase and Brenna.

KATHY IRELAND

Kathy Ireland, chair of kathy ireland® Worldwide (kiWW®), is a fashion and home industry icon whose unprecedented American entrepreneurial success inspired the term "model-preneur." kiWW® is owned solely by Kathy's family trusts.

Kathy's first novel, *Fashion Jungle*, is co-authored with number one *New York Times* bestselling author Rachel Van Dyken. Kathy entered the "jungle" as a teenager, sheltered by loving parents, John and Barbara, of Santa Barbara, California. Covers of *Vogue, Teen,* and *Cosmopolitan* led to a record thirteen issues and all-time bestselling cover of *Sports Illustrated Swimsuit.* Kathy is the supermodel turned supermogul, hailed by *Harper's Bazaar* as the most successful "model in the world." kiWW® launched a single pair of socks during Kathy's first pregnancy. While selling over one hundred million pairs, retail expanded. kiWW® develops for home, office, fashion, luxury jewels, vacation destinations, weddings, lighting, flooring, furniture, personal care, media, and more. After billions of dollars in sales, kiWW®, a private company, was reported on by *Forbes.*

Kathy's story continues in global media, including three *Forbes* covers (two USA, one Asia), *Inc., Wall Street Journal,* Cheddar, *Success Magazine,* television, and online. Kathy speaks in America, the Middle East, Asia, and beyond. Residing in Santa Barbara, California, Kathy Ireland and Greg Olsen are parents to Lily, Chloe, Erik, and Erik's wife Bethany, their daughter-in-love.

Kathy holds numerous honorary doctorates of Humane Letters, including one from CSU Channel Islands. Kathy's philanthropy includes: women and children's health, HIV/AIDS, education, human freedom, life, and wars against religious persecution and violence. Kathy is a board member of the NFLPA, WNBPA Board of Advocates, an ambassador and donor for the Elizabeth Taylor AIDS Foundation, and international youth chair for the National Pediatric Cancer Society.

LIEUTENANT GOVERNOR
REBECCA KLEEFISCH

Rebecca Kleefisch is the jobs ambassador for Associated Builders and Contractors of Wisconsin, traveling the state to encourage more Wisconsin workers to choose well-paying jobs in construction trades.

The former executive director of the Women's Suffrage Centennial Commission, Kleefisch launched the country's efforts to commemorate and educate America about the one-hundredth anniversary of women earning the right to vote.

Previously, Rebecca served as lieutenant governor of Wisconsin, where she championed workforce and economic development for eight years. She is well known for her efforts in fighting poverty, focusing on prison reentry reform, where she pushed for the placement of job centers at corrections facilities. She helped create and chaired the Interagency Council on Homelessness, which produced Wisconsin's first action plan to end homelessness as we know it.

Rebecca also co-chaired the Governor's Task Force on Opioids Abuse and the Task Force on Minority Unemployment.

Rebecca started the Governor's Small Business Summit, a symposium for small business owners to gain exclusive all-day access to state leaders, and Small Business Academy, a free half-day seminar designed for minority and female potential entrepreneurs.

She is the former chairman of the Aerospace States Association, which articulates and advocates for aerospace and aviation policy across the country. She is the former chairman of the Republican Lieutenant Governors' Association.

Rebecca is a member of the Town Bank and the Joseph Project Boards of Directors, former owner of a small media and marketing firm, and a "recovering journalist." She lives in Concord, WI, with her husband Joel and daughters Ella and Violet.

DR. ARTHUR B. LAFFER

Arthur B. Laffer is the founder and chairman of Laffer Associates, an economic research and consulting firm, and Laffer Investments, an investment management firm.

Dr. Laffer's economic acumen and influence in triggering a worldwide tax-cutting movement in the 1980s have earned him the distinction in many publications as "The Father of Supply-Side Economics." One of his earliest successes in shaping public policy was his involvement in Proposition 13, the groundbreaking California initiative that drastically cut property taxes in the state in 1978.

Dr. Laffer was a member of President Reagan's Economic Policy Advisory Board for both of his two terms (1981–1989) and was a founding member of the Reagan Executive Advisory Committee for the presidential race of 1980. He also advised Prime Minister Margaret Thatcher on fiscal policy in the UK during the 1980s.

In June 2019, Dr. Laffer was awarded the Presidential Medal of Freedom by President Donald Trump.

Dr. Laffer has authored a number of books, including *An Inquiry into the Nature and Causes of the Wealth of States* (Wiley 2014) and, most recently, *Trumponomics: Inside the America First Plan to Revive Our Economy* (All Points Books 2018).

TYSON LANGHOFER

Tyson C. Langhofer serves as senior counsel and director of the Center for Academic Freedom with Alliance Defending Freedom. Langhofer has represented college students and student organizations throughout the country in defending their freedom of speech, freedom of association, and free exercise of religion.

In *Young America's Foundation v. Covino*, he successfully represented YAF, Ben Shapiro, and California State University–Los Angeles students in a lawsuit against university administrators for First Amendment violations when they allowed a mob of professors and students to physically block students from attending Shapiro's scheduled speech on the campus. In *Grace Christian Life v. Woodson*, he successfully represented a religious student group at North Carolina State University in a lawsuit against administrators for violating their First Amendment freedoms when they prevented students from discussing religious topics because they did not acquire the university's pre-approval.

Before joining ADF, Langhofer was a partner with Stinson LLP, where he worked as a commercial litigation attorney for fifteen years and earned Martindale-Hubbell's AV Preeminent® rating. Numerous media outlets have interviewed or featured Langhofer, including the *Washington Post, Washington Times,* Townhall, the Federalist, and the Daily Wire.

Langhofer earned his juris doctor from Regent University School of Law, where he graduated cum laude in 1999. He obtained a B.A. in international business with a minor in economics from Wichita State University in 1996. A member of the bar in Virginia, Kansas, and Arizona, Langhofer is also admitted to practice in numerous federal district courts.

MARC LEVIN

An attorney and accomplished author on legal and public policy issues, Levin began the Texas Public Policy Foundation's criminal justice program in 2005 and currently serves as chief of policy and innovation for its Right on Crime initiative.

This work has contributed to nationally praised policy changes that have been followed by dramatic declines in crime and incarceration in Texas. Building on this success, in 2010 Levin developed the concept for the Right on Crime initiative, which has become the national clearinghouse for conservative criminal justice reforms.

In 2014, Levin was named one of the "Politico 50" in the magazine's annual "list of thinkers, doers, and dreamers who really matter in this age of gridlock and dysfunction." Levin, who also serves on the National Association of Drug Court Professionals Board of Directors, has testified on criminal justice policy on four occasions before Congress and before numerous state legislatures. He also has met personally with leaders such as U.S. presidents, Speakers of the House, and the Justice Committee of the United Kingdom Parliament to share his ideas on criminal justice reform.

In 2007, he was honored in a resolution unanimously passed by the Texas House of Representatives that stated, "Mr. Levin's intellect is unparalleled and his research is impeccable." Since 2005, Levin has published dozens of policy papers on topics such as sentencing, probation, parole, reentry, and overcriminalization which are available on the TPPF website. Levin's articles on law and public policy have been featured in publications such as the *Wall Street Journal* and *USA Today*.

In 1999, Levin graduated with honors from the University of Texas with a B.A. in Plan II Honors and Government and in 2002 received his J.D. with honors from the University of Texas School of Law. Levin served as a law clerk to Judge Will Garwood on the U.S. Court of Appeals for the Fifth Circuit and staff attorney at the Texas Supreme Court.

CHUCK NORRIS

Chuck Norris is an international television and film star who has starred in twenty-four motion pictures such as *Delta Force, Code of Silence,* and *Missing in Action,* with his latest film role in *Expendables 2.* His television series *Walker, Texas Ranger,* ran for eight and a half years. With 203 episodes, it was the most successful Saturday night series on CBS since *Gunsmoke.* Internationally, it is seen in more than eighty countries worldwide with an average of one billion viewers daily.

Norris first made his mark as a renowned teacher of martial arts, and was a six-time undefeated World Professional Middle Weight Karate Champion. He is the first man from the Western Hemisphere in the over-4,500 year tradition of Tae Kwon Do to be awarded an eight degree Black Belt Grand Master ranking. By the 1970s, he had revolutionized martial arts in the U.S. and created his own system called "the Chuck

Norris System." He is also the founder and chairman of the United Fighting Arts Federation.

Chuck Norris is also a *New York Times* bestselling author of several books. They include *Black Belt Patriotism: How to Reawaken America*, and the 2004 autobiography *Against All Odds*. Norris has also penned two works of fiction, *The Justice Riders* and *A Threat to Justice*. In 2006, he added "columnist" to his list of credits with the launch of his popular internet column on the independent news site WorldNetDaily.com.

Modeling a life of health and fitness for more than five decades, Norris has promoted the importance of exercise by his endorsement of the Total Gym, a popular exercise machine that is sold internationally in more than eighty countries. In 2010, Chuck launched a syndicated weekly health and fitness column called C-Force to help inspire and improve the health and fitness of his readers by taking a holistic view of health—that wellness is obtained and maintained by treating ourselves as an integrated whole, in mind, body, and spirit.

A genuine internet phenomenon, Norris has become the subject of countless Paul Bunyan-type fictional "facts" of his exploits, submitted by fans. There are currently more than a million such "facts" floating around the internet. In November 2009, he came out with *The Official Chuck Norris Fact Book*, focusing on 101 of his favorite facts and stories.

A very popular public speaker, Norris is a strong supporter of our Second Amendment rights. He has also served as spokesperson for agencies such as the United Way and the Veterans Administration. An Air Force veteran, Norris was named an honorary member of the Marine Corps in 2007, which was an incredible honor demonstrating the appreciation the Corps felt for his two "handshake" tours of Iraq within a one-year period.

A man of deep religious convictions and a giving spirit, Chuck will say that next to his family, his most rewarding accomplishment is the creation in 1992 of his KICKSTART KIDS Foundation. With the purpose of building strong moral character in our youth through martial arts training, the foundation has become the most important mission of Chuck and his wife Gena's lives, following the development and well-being of their family. KICKSTART KIDS now serves nearly ten thousand at-risk youth on a daily basis as part of the daily school curriculum in middle schools. Since its inception, the program has graduated more than 100,000 kids. The goal is to expand the program all over Texas and eventually nationwide. See www.kickstartkids.org

Chuck has been married to his wife Gena for twenty-three years. They have seven children and thirteen grandchildren.

The Norrises live on their ranch near Houston, where they are raising their seventeen-year-old twins, Dakota and Danilee.

CAPTAIN SCOTT O'GRADY

Scott O'Grady is a former United States Air Force captain and Air Force fighter pilot who gained prominence after the June 2, 1995, Mrkonjic Grad incident, in which he ejected over Bosnia when his F-16C was shot down by a Bosnian Serb SA-6 while he was patrolling the no-fly zone. He survived for almost six days by eating leaves, grass, and ants and avoiding Serb patrols while trying to contact Magic, NATO's airborne command center. He evaded capture and was rescued on June 8 by U.S. Marines.

Scott served twelve years in the Air Force both active and reserve duty and continued to fly the F-16 three years after his rescue. He has over one thousand hours in the F-16.

O'Grady tells his incredible story of survival in his book, *Return with Honor*. In May 2007, he completed a master's degree in biblical studies at Dallas Theological Seminary in Dallas. He resides in Texas.

REPRESENTATIVE TAN PARKER

Tan Parker is a Republican member of the Texas House of Representatives who has the privilege of representing one of the fastest-growing areas in the nation. Since taking office in 2007, Tan has been recognized as a proven champion for economic development, job creation, strengthening border security, promoting fiscally responsible government spending, reducing tax burdens, promoting a culture of life, and enacting greater public safety measures. He is also known for his advocacy for the protection of children and vulnerable populations, as well as being an early leader in the fight against human trafficking.

Tan's legislative tenure has encompassed numerous leadership roles including two terms as the chairman of the Texas House Republican Caucus, in which he led the Republican majority. He is the former chairman of the Investments and Financial Services Committee, which had oversight of banks, savings and loans, credit unions, lending, securities, and cybersecurity initiatives. Prior to that role, Tan was chairman of the Corrections Committee, focusing on prison reform and the management of one of the largest prison systems in the United States.

In addition to serving as a lawmaker, Tan is a successful businessman who has, over the past two decades, worked in software, financial services, biotechnology, and private equity. A passionate advocate for community, Tan serves on the Board of Trustees for the University of Dallas and has had voluntary leadership roles for regional nonprofits such as Communities in Schools of North Texas, the Children's Advocacy Center for Denton County, Kyle's Place (a shelter for homeless teens), and Special Olympics Texas.

Prior to his election to the Texas House of Representatives, Tan was appointed by Texas governor Rick Perry to chair the Texas Industrial Development Corporation and was also an appointee of the Texas Comptroller, serving the state's e-Texas initiative. Tan began his involvement in the Republican Party as a youth and was influenced by the great leaders with whom he interacted, such as President Ronald Reagan, President George H. W. Bush, Majority Leader Dick Armey, and Tex Lezar, who orchestrated the original version of *Making Government Work*.

Tan is a graduate of the University of Dallas and the London School of Economics. He and his wife of twenty-five years, Beth, reside in Flower Mound, Texas, with their daughters, Lauren and Ashley.

SECRETARY RICK PERRY

Rick Perry served as the fourteenth United States secretary of energy from March 2017 to December 2019. As secretary, he was responsible for successfully executing President Donald J. Trump's energy agenda and the expansive mission of the Department of Energy (DOE), including maintaining the safety and security of the nation's nuclear arsenal, protecting the electric grid from cyber threats, ensuring access to reliable and affordable energy, overseeing scientific research and development, and promoting the development and export of American technology and energy all over the world. Under his leadership, the nation ushered in a historic energy era, becoming the number one producer of oil and gas in the world, a world leader in the production and generation of renewable energy, and the dominant global force in supercomputing, quantum computing, and artificial intelligence.

Prior to joining the Trump administration, Perry served as the forty-seventh governor of Texas from 2000–2015. As the longest-serving governor of the Lone Star State, he championed conservative pro-growth principles that made Texas the world's twelfth-largest economy and the economic envy of America. During his time in Austin, Governor Perry also implemented transformative reforms in the areas of security, criminal justice reform, energy, education, health care, and the economy.

As chief executive both as governor of Texas and secretary of energy, Perry understood that the success of government is only as strong as its partnerships with the private sector. He advocated for smart regulatory reforms and strong public-private partnerships, empowering industry rather that creating more bureaucratic barriers. He started the Texas Enterprise Fund, which lured hundreds of millions of dollars in private sector business and jobs to Texas. At DOE, he appointed the first ever chief commercialization officer, who was tasked with bridging the gap between the world-class R&D at the department's seventeen national laboratories and commercialization in the private sector.

Rick Perry is a veteran of the United States Air Force, where he flew a C-130 tactical airlift aircraft in Europe and the Middle East. Throughout his career, he has been deeply involved in supporting both the active duty and veteran community, most recently as an advocate for using the power of artificial intelligence (AI) to deliver precision health care to warriors suffering from post-traumatic stress disorder (PTSD), traumatic brain injury (TBI), and other conditions.

Perry earned distinction early in his life as an Eagle Scout. He was one of the first in his family to go to college, earning a degree in animal science from Texas A&M University, where he was a member of the Corps of Cadets and a yell leader. He is a lifetime member of both the NRA and American Legion Post #75.

Perry married his childhood sweetheart, Anita, in 1982. They have two children, two beautiful granddaughters, and a grandson who was born on the 4th of July in 2019.

VIKRANT REDDY

Vikrant Reddy is the senior research fellow at the Charles Koch Institute in Arlington, Virginia, where he focuses on criminal justice and policing reform. Reddy previously served as a senior policy analyst at the Texas Public Policy Foundation, where he managed the launch of their national Right on Crime initiative in 2010. He has also worked as a research assistant at the Cato Institute, as a law clerk to the Honorable Gina M. Benavides of the Thirteenth Court of Appeals of Texas, and as an attorney in private practice.

He is a member of the State Bar of Texas and an appointee to the executive committee of the Criminal Law Practice Group of the Federalist Society. He is also an appointee to the U.S. Commission on Civil Rights Texas State Advisory Committee.

Reddy graduated from the University of Texas at Austin with a bachelor's in Plan II honors, economics, and history and earned his law degree at the Southern Methodist University Dedman School of Law in Dallas.

SENATOR RICK SANTORUM

Rick Santorum was a candidate for the Republican nomination for president in 2012 and 2016—winning the 2012 Iowa caucuses, ten additional states, and nearly four million votes. Prior to his campaigns for president, Rick served two terms in both the House of Representatives and Senate, where he gained a reputation as one of the nation's leading government reformers, pro-life advocates, and national security experts.

Rick Santorum is the author of the 2005 *New York Times* bestseller *It Takes a Family*, *American Patriots: Answering the Call to Freedom*, and *Blue Collar Conservatives: Recommitting to an America that Works*. Rick and his wife Karen are also the co-authors of *Bella's Gift*, which chronicles the inspiring story of life with the Santorums' special-needs youngest child. Bella was born with a condition called Trisomy 18, and she wasn't expected to survive her first birthday. Beating all the odds, Bella turned twelve in May 2020.

Rick is currently a CNN senior political contributor.

PROFESSOR BRADLEY A. SMITH

Bradley A. Smith is the Josiah H. Blackmore/ Shirley M. Nault Professor of Law at Capital University in Columbus, Ohio. In 2000 he was nominated by President William Jefferson Clinton to fill a Republican-designated seat on the Federal Election Commission, where he served for five years, including as chairman of the commission in 2004. He has also held the Judge John T. Copenhaver Chair at West Virginia University College of Law.

His writings have appeared in numerous leading law journals, including the *Yale Law Journal*, *Georgetown Law Journal*, the *Harvard Journal of Legislation*, the *Pennsylvania Law Review*, and the *George Washington University Law Review*, and in popular publications such as the *Wall Street Journal*, *The Atlantic*, the *New York Times*, and the

Washington Post. He is the author of *Unfree Speech: The Folly of Campaign Finance Reform* (2001), and co-author of two leading textbooks on election law.

Professor Smith serves as chairman of the Institute for Free Speech in Washington, D.C., and the 1851 Center for Constitutional Law and the Buckeye Institute for Public Policy Solutions, both in Columbus. He is a cum laude graduate of Harvard Law School and Kalamazoo College.

MERRIE SPAETH

Merrie has a unique background in media, government, politics, business, and entertainment. She is a thought-leader in communication theory, a master of executive coaching, and acknowledged as one of the most influential communication counselors in the world.

Before founding Spaeth in 1987, Merrie was a producer for ABC's *20/20*, a speechwriter for the legendary founder and chairman of CBS, William S. Paley, and was assigned to FBI director Judge William Webster while serving as a White House fellow. All of this culminated into her role as director of public affairs for the Federal Trade Commission, and ultimately her appointment as director of media relations at the White House in the Reagan administration.

Merrie is a sought-after public speaker who provides strategic communication counseling for companies and executives across the globe.

DICK TRABULSI

Richard J. Trabulsi Jr. is a co-founder and chairman of Texans for Lawsuit Reform, chairman of TLRPAC, and director of the Texans for Lawsuit Reform Foundation.

Mr. Trabulsi is a native of Houston, Texas. He is married and has two adult children and four grandchildren.

Mr. Trabulsi attended the University of Texas at Austin in the pre-law program and received a J.D. from the University of Texas Law School, graduating with honors. Mr. Trabulsi was a chancellor, a member of the Order of the Coif, and articles editor of the *Texas Law Review*. He clerked for Judge Homer Thornberry of the United States Court of Appeals for the Fifth Circuit and was briefly an attorney at Vinson Elkins in Houston.

Mr. Trabulsi has been active in a variety of businesses, including retail, real estate, banking, ranching, and financial asset investments.

Mr. Trabulsi has served on several community boards, including the George Foundation, Covenant House, the Houston Museum of Natural Science, and the University of Texas Health Science Center at Houston.

GRACE-MARIE TURNER

Grace-Marie Turner is president of the Galen Institute, a public policy research organization she founded in 1995 to promote an informed debate over ideas to transfer power over health care decisions to doctors and patients. She has served on the Long Term Care Commission, the National Advisory Board for the Agency for Healthcare Research and Quality, and the Medicaid Commission.

She testifies regularly before Congress and has been published in hundreds of newspapers, including the *Wall Street Journal, New York Times,* and *USA Today.* She edited *Empowering Health Care Consumers through Tax Reform* and has contributed to numerous other books. She speaks extensively in the U.S. and abroad, including Harvard University, the London School of Economics, Oxford University, and the Gregorian University at the Vatican.

She received the 2007 Outstanding Achievement Award for Promotion of Consumer Driven Health Care from Consumer Health World.

KATHLEEN HARTNETT WHITE

The Honorable Kathleen Hartnett White joined the Texas Public Policy Foundation in January 2008. She is the director of the Armstrong Center for Energy & the Environment, a senior fellow for the Life: Powered project, and a distinguished senior fellow-in-residence.

Prior to joining the foundation, White served a six-year term as chairman and commissioner of the Texas Commission on Environmental Quality (TCEQ). With regulatory jurisdiction over air quality, water quality, water rights and utilities, and storage and disposal of waste, TCEQ's staff of three thousand, annual budget of over $600 million, and sixteen regional offices make it the second-largest environmental regulatory agency in the world after the U.S. Environmental Protection Agency.

Prior to Governor Rick Perry's appointment of White to the TCEQ in 2001, she served as then governor George Bush's appointee to the Texas Water Development Board, where she sat until appointed to TCEQ. She also served on the Texas Economic Development Commission and the Environmental Flows Study Commission. She recently completed her term as an officer and director of the Lower Colorado River Authority. White now sits on the editorial board of the Texas Water Foundation. Her writing has appeared in numerous publications including *National Review, Investors' Business Daily, Washington Examiner, Forbes*, the Daily Caller, *The Hill*, and major Texas newspapers. She most recently testified before the U.S. Senate Environment and Public Works Committee.

A writer and consultant on environmental laws, free market natural resource policy, private property rights, and ranching history, White received her bachelor's cum laude and master's degrees from Stanford

University, where for three years she held the Elizabeth Wheeler Lyman Scholarship for an Outstanding Woman in the Humanities. She was also awarded a Danforth National Fellowship for doctoral work at Princeton University in Comparative Religion and there won the Jonathan Edwards Award for Academic Excellence. She was also twice nominated by President Trump to chair the White House Council of Environmental Quality, and she studied law under a Lineberry Foundation Fellowship at Texas Tech University.

White was director of private lands and the environment for the National Cattlemen's Association in Washington, D.C. She has served as director of the Ranching Heritage Association and was a special assistant in the White House office of First Lady Nancy Reagan.

She is a member of the Texas and Southwestern Cattleraisers Association, the Texas Hereford Association, and the American Hereford Association. She is a former commissioner of the Texas Strategic Economic Development Planning Commission, a former board member of the Texas Wildlife Association, and the National Cattlemen's Legal Defense Fund.

A long-time breeder of national champion Jack Russell Terriers, Kathleen Hartnett White lives with her husband Beau Brite White in Bastrop County, Texas, outside of Austin, and in Presidio County, on the far southwestern border of Texas.

ROBERT L. WOODSON SR.

Robert L. Woodson Sr. is founder and president of the Woodson Center and 1776 Unites. He is an influential leader on issues of poverty alleviation and empowering disadvantaged communities to become agents of their own uplift. Woodson is a frequent advisor to local, state, and federal government officials as well as business and philanthropic organizations.

His social activism dates back to the 1960s, when as a young civil rights activist he developed and coordinated national and local community revitalization programs. During the 1970s, he directed the National Urban League's Administration of Justice division. Later he served as a resident fellow at the American Enterprise Institute.

Woodson is frequently featured as a social commentator in print and on-air media, including C-SPAN, CNN, *Tucker Carlson Tonight*, *Meet the Press*, *The O'Reilly Factor*, and other national and local broadcasts. He is a contributing editor to *The Hill*, the *Washington Examiner*, and the *Wall Street Journal*, and has published in influential newspapers and journals such as *Forbes*, *National Review*, the *Washington Post*, *Milwaukee Journal Sentinel*, *Harvard Journal of Law & Public Policy*, *Vanderbilt Law Review*, and other national and local media outlets.

He is the recipient of the prestigious John D. and Catherine T. MacArthur "Genius" Fellowship award, the Bradley Prizes presented by the Lynde and Harry Bradley Foundation, the Presidential Citizens Medal, the 2018 William Wilberforce Award, and many other awards and honors.

Woodson is the author of several books, including *On the Road to Economic Freedom* and *The Triumphs of Joseph: How Today's Community Healers are Reviving Our Streets and Neighborhood*.

Notes

FEDERALISM AND THE AMERICAN EXPERIMENT: THE INTENTION OF THE CONSTITUTION

1. The Fourteenth Amendment prohibits the state from depriving "persons" of the right to "life, liberty and property" without due process of law, thus a ruling recognizing the unborn as persons would likely trigger striking down abortion protections. On the public status of the question, see, for example, https://personhood.org/.

2. *The Federalist*, ed. Jacob E. Cooke (Middletown, Connecticut: Wesleyan University Press, 1961), No. 15, 93. In *Federalist* No. 23 Publius asserts that "there is an absolute necessity for an entire change in the first principles of the system; that if we are in earnest about giving the Union energy and duration, we must abandon the vain project of legislating upon the States in their collective capacities; we must extend the laws of the federal government to the individual citizens of America" (148).

3. On the way in which states failed to protect the rights of their citizens at the time of the founding, see, for example, the discussion in Charles C. Thach, *The Creation of the Presidency, 1775–1789: A Study in Constitutional History* (Indianapolis: Liberty Fund, Inc., 2007), especially Chapters II–III on state and federal executive power prior to the Constitutional Convention.

4. *Federalist* No. 9, 55.

5. Ibid., 257. Publius develops this point at some length in an earlier passage: "The difference between a federal and national government, as it relates to the operation of the Government, is supposed to consist in this, that in the former

the powers operate on the political bodies composing the Confederacy, in their political capacities; in the latter, on the individual citizens composing the nation, in their individual capacities. On trying the Constitution by this criterion, it falls under the National, not the Federal character; though perhaps not so completely as has been understood. In several cases, and particularly in the trial of controversies to which States may be parties, they must be viewed and proceeded against in their collective and political capacities only. So far the national countenance of the government on this side seems to be disfigured by a few federal features. But this blemish is perhaps unavoidable in any plan; and the operation of the government on the people, in their individual capacities, in its ordinary and most essential proceedings, may, on the whole, designate it, in this relation, a National government." (Ibid., 255–56).

6. *Federalist* No. 9, 256.
7. *Federalist* No. 56, 379.
8. It is important to recognize that the knowledge of "commerce" spoken of here does not include the far-reaching regulation of commerce the government comes to assume for itself; this issue will be addressed below.
9. *Federalist* No. 17, 107.
10. Ibid.
11. Of course we would also be remiss in not mentioning the expansion of the powers of the states themselves, but it is also the case that the burgeoning of many state and local intrusions into the lives of their citizens is a result of federal mandates.
12. Chief Justice Rehnquist provides a helpful summary account of the Court's interpretation of the commerce clause in his majority opinion in *United States v. Lopez*, 514 U.S. 549 (1995). His concluding remarks note the continued authority of state governments under this line of jurisprudence: "Under this line of precedent, the Court held that certain categories of activity such as 'production,' 'manufacturing,' and 'mining' were within the province of state governments, and thus were beyond the power of Congress under the Commerce Clause" (554).
13. *Hammer v. Dagenhart*, 247 U.S. 251 (1918).
14. Ibid., 275.
15. This is not a new argument, though, as it is most clearly articulated in the Court's decision in *United States v. E. C. Knight*: "Doubtless the power to control the manufacture of a given thing involves, in a certain sense, the control of its disposition, but this is a secondary, and not the primary, sense; and, although the exercise of that power may result in bringing the operation of commerce into play, it does not control it, and affects it only incidentally and indirectly. Commerce succeeds to manufacture, and is not a part of it."
16. *Gibbons v. Ogden*, 22 U.S. 1 (1824), 196.
17. *Hammer v. Dagenhart*, 275.
18. The Court struck down the Agricultural Adjustment Act in *United States v. Butler*, 297 U.S. 1 (1936), the National Industrial Recovery Act in *Panama*

Refining Company v. Ryan, 293 U.S. 388 (1935), *Schechter Poultry Corp. v. United States*, 295 U.S. 495 (1935), and the Bituminous Coal Conservation Act of 1935 in *Carter v. Carter Coal Company*, 298 U.S. 398 (1936).

19. *United States v. Darby Lumber Company*, 312 U.S. 100 (1941).

20. Ibid., 118.

21. Thomas Jefferson, among others, noted the manner in which specific grants of power can be expanded into broad grants of power (the context of the passage being a consideration of a bill granting a federal charter to a mining company): "Congress are authorized to defend the nation. Ships are necessary for defence; copper is necessary for ships; mines, necessary for copper; a company necessary to work the mines; and who can doubt this reasoning who has ever played at "This is the House that Jack Built?" Under such a process of filiation of necessities the sweeping clause makes clean work" (*The Writings of Thomas Jefferson* 8:262 (ed. Ford), quoted in Gerald Gunther, *Constitutional Law* [Mineola, New York: Foundation Press, Inc., 1985], eleventh edition, 87).

22. *United States v. Darby Lumber Company*, 124.

23. *Granholm v. Heald*, 544 U.S. 460 (2005); New York had passed a similar law, and its law was also struck down in the same case.

24. Ibid., 493.

25. For example, the state of Michigan had claimed that allowing out-of-state shipments would make it easier for minors to get access to alcohol, but the Court was not convinced by the claim.

26. I thank Dominic Dougherty for alerting me to this fascinating example.

27. *Paul v. Virginia*, 75 U.S. 168 (1869; Justice Field for the majority), 183.

28. *New York Life Insurance Company v. Deer Lodge County*, 231 U.S. 495 (1912).

29. *United States v. South-Eastern Underwriters Association*, 322 U.S. 533 (1944).

30. Ibid., 545.

31. The act as reflected in the United States Code can be found at: https://www.law. cornell.edu/uscode/text/15/6701.

32. See the brief discussion, for example, at the website of the National Association of Insurance Commissioners, noting the continued relevance of the Act in light of recent developments: https://content.naic.org/cipr_topics/topic_mccarran_ ferguson_act.htm.

33. Alexis de Tocqueville, *Democracy in America*, trans. Harvey C. Mansfield and Delba Winthrop (Chicago: University of Chicago Press, 2000), 156.

34. Tocqueville, *Democracy in America*, 381; see also his earlier discussion of the exercise of local authority and popular sovereignty: "The people reign over the American political world as does God over the universe" (55).

35. *Federal Trade Commission v. Ruberoid Co.*, 343 U.S. 470 (1952), 487–88, dissenting opinion.

GUIDELINES FOR PRO-GROWTH TAX REFORM FOR THE STATES

1. The distinction between "earned" and "unearned" income taxes is that earned income taxes typically apply to wage income, while unearned income taxes typically apply to income from dividends and interest. In 2020, Tennessee and New Hampshire are the only states with no earned income taxes but with separate unearned income taxes. Tennessee's unearned income tax, called the Hall Income Tax, has been falling according to a phase-out schedule in recent years and will be completely eliminated starting in tax year 2021.

2. Greg Bordonaro and Matt Pilon, "Hartford's Stifling Property Taxes Make It Difficult for Businesses to Prosper—and Remain in the City," *Hartford Courant*, July 7, 2019, https://www.courant.com/community/hartford/hc-news-hartford-high-commercial-tax-rate-20190707-rvwiub3c2jhznfl7c26hjzrs7i-story.html.

3. "What You Should Know about Home Rule," Real Property Alliance, 2019, https://realpropertyalliance.org/home-rule/.

4. Adam H. Edelen, "Ghost Government: A Report on Special Districts in Kentucky," Commonwealth of Kentucky, Auditor of Public Accounts, 2012, http://apps.auditor.ky.gov/public/theregistry/2012GhostGovernmentSpecialDistrictsReport.pdf.

5. "FactSheet: Kentucky Business Taxes," Cabinet for Economic Development, December 2015, https://www.thinkkentucky.com/kyedc/pdfs/KYBusinessTaxes.pdf.

6. Ibid.

7. Ibid.

8. "2015 Property Tax Handbook," Kentucky Department of Revenue, 2015.

9. For more on the history of California's Proposition 13, see: https://ballotpedia.org/California_Proposition_13,_Tax_Limitations_Initiative_(1978).

10. They are "stackable" in that these are a collection of tax rates that a consumer or business owner must sum, or "stack," on top of each other in order to calculate the total sales tax rate.

11. "2018 Sales and Use Tax Rate Tables," Missouri Department of Revenue, http://dor.mo.gov/business/sales/rates/2018/.

12. Ibid.

13. Joel Walters, "Tax Policy Reform: Issue to Be Addressed to the Benefit of All Missourians," 2017.

14. U.S. Census Bureau State and Local Finances, Bureau of Economic Analysis, Tax Foundation State and Local Sales Tax Rates, Laffer Associates Calculations.

15. Joel Walters, "Tax Policy Reform: Issue to Addressed to the Benefit of All Missourians," 2017.

16. Arthur B. Laffer and Wayne H. Winegarden, "The Economic Consequences of Tennessee's Gift and Estate Tax," Laffer Center and Beacon Center of Tennessee, March 2012.

17. The nineteen states with a separate estate tax do not include Ohio, which has passed legislation to repeal its estate tax effective January 1, 2013. Connecticut and Tennessee are the only states with gift taxes.
18. U.S. Census Bureau, State Government Tax Collections.

A COMMONSENSE GUIDE FOR THE STATES: THE TEXAS MODEL

1. "Texas Governor Swearing-In," C-SPAN, December 21, 2000, https://www.c-span.org/video/?161458-1/texas-governor-swearing.
2. Rick Perry, "Rick Perry: Follow the Texas Model of Success," *USA Today*, October 28, 2013, https://www.usatoday.com/story/opinion/2013/10/28/governor-rick-perry-texas-tour-jobs-editorials-debates/3290927/.
3. *Southwest Economy* no. 2, Federal Reserve Bank of Dallas (March/April 2001), https://www.dallasfed.org/~/media/documents/research/swe/2001/swe0102a.pdf.
4. Ibid.
5. Ibid.
6. Ibid.
7. "How Much Did the September 11 Terrorist Attack Cost America?" Institute for the Analysis of Global Security, http://www.iags.org/costof911.html.
8. Ezra Klein, "Bin Laden's War against the U.S. Economy," *Washington Post*, May 3, 2011, https://www.washingtonpost.com/blogs/ezra-klein/post/bin-ladens-war-against-the-us-economy/2011/04/27/AFDOPjfF_blog.html.
9. Eric Aasen, "On This Day in 1958, a TI Engineer Invented a Chip That Changed the World," KERA News, September 12, 2014, https://www.keranews.org/post/day-1958-ti-engineer-invented-chip-changed-world.
10. Stephanie Landsman, "Tech Rally Shows Troubling Parallels to Dot-Com Bubble, Warns Long-Time Bull," CNBC, March 14, 2019, https://www.cnbc.com/2019/03/14/tech-rally-shows-troubling-parallel-to-dot-com-bubble-rich-bernstein.html.
11. Michael J. Martinez, "Dot-Com Bubble's Legacy: Unrealistic Expectations," *Houston Chronicle*, January 13, 2005, https://www.chron.com/business/technology/article/Dot-com-bubble-s-legacy-unrealistic-expectations-1930927.php.
12. Scott, "Revisiting the Effect of the Dot-Com Bust on Austin," BP3, November 16, 2015, https://www.bp-3.com/blog/revisiting-the-effect-of-the-dot-com-bust-on-austin/.
13. *Southwest Economy* no. 2, Federal Reserve Bank of Dallas (March/April 2004), https://www.dallasfed.org/~/media/documents/research/swe/2004/swe0402a.pdf.
14. "Comptroller's Biennial Revenue Estimate Outlines Budgetary Challenges," Texas Senate website, January 13, 2003, https://senate.texas.gov/news.php?id=20030113a&lang=en.

15. "Governor Rick Perry's Remarks at Post-Session News Conference," Legislative Reference Library of Texas, June 4, 2003, https://lrl.texas.gov/scanned/govdocs/Rick%20Perry/2003/speech060403.pdf.

16. *Southwest Economy* no. 2, Federal Reserve Bank of Dallas (March/April 2004).

17. Ibid.

18. Joey Berlin, "Coming of Age: Celebrating 15 Years of Texas Tort Reform," Texas Medical Association, https://www.texmed.org/Template.aspx?id=48427.

19. "Governor Perry Speaks at Med Mal Bill Signing," Legislative Reference Library of Texas, July 11, 2003, https://lrl.texas.gov/scanned/govdocs/Rick%20Perry/2003/speech071103.pdf.

20. Berlin, "Coming of Age."

21. "Petroleum & Other Liquids," U.S. Energy Information Administration, https://www.eia.gov/dnav/pet/hist/LeafHandler.ashx?n=PET&s=MTTIMUS1&f=M.

22. Ibid.

23. Matt Mandel, "Experts: Shale Revolution Has Improved U.S. Energy Security and Is 'Shifting the Geopolitical Balance,'" Energy in Depth, May 25, 2018, https://www.energyindepth.org/experts-shale-revolution-improved-u-s-energy-security-shifting-geopolitical-balance/.

24. Jordan Blum, "Rebounding Haynesville Shale Breaks 2011 Production Record," *Houston Chronicle*, April 19, 2019, https://www.houstonchronicle.com/business/energy/article/Rebounding-Haynesville-shale-breaks-2011-13778387.php.

25. Kathleen Hartnett White, "The Shale Revolution Is a Uniquely American Story," Texas Public Policy Foundation, June 18, 2018, https://www.texaspolicy.com/the-shale-revolution-is-a-uniquely-american-story/.

26. Barry Smitherman, "3 Reasons Rick Perry Is Good for American Energy," *Dallas Morning News*, December 16, 2016, https://www.dallasnews.com/opinion/commentary/2016/12/16/3-reasons-rick-perry-is-good-for-american-energy/.

27. Ibid.

28. "Text of Gov. Rick Perry's Remarks at Post-Session News Conference," Legislative Reference Library of Texas, June 3, 2004, https://lrl.texas.gov/scanned/govdocs/Rick%20Perry/2004/remarks060304.pdf.

29. Robert Rich, "The Great Recession," Federal Reserve History, November 22, 2013, https://www.federalreservehistory.org/essays/great_recession_of_200709.

30. Laura Kusisto, "Many Who Lost Homes to Foreclosure in Last Decade Won't Return—NAR," *Wall Street Journal*, April 20, 2015, https://www.wsj.com/articles/many-who-lost-homes-to-foreclosure-in-last-decade-wont-return-nar-1429548640.

31. Estimated Impact of the American Recovery and Reinvestment Act on Employment and Economic Output from October 2011 through December 2011, Congressional Budget Office, Washington, D.C., February 2012, http://www.cbo.gov/sites/default/files/cbofiles/attachments/02-22-ARRA.pdf.

32. Bill Peacock, "The Texas Economic Miracle: Can We Weather the Current Economic Storm?" Texas Public Policy Foundation, https://files.texaspolicy.com/uploads/2018/08/16093115/2009-TTIAPresentation-bp.pdf.
33. Bill Peacock, "The Texas Model Works," Texas Model, Center for Economic Freedom, August 2011, https://files.texaspolicy.com/uploads/2018/08/16094403/2011-08-PB35-TexasModel-CEF-bpeacock.pdf.
34. Derek Thompson, "Rick Perry and the Economics of the Texas Miracle," *The Atlantic*, August 15, 2011, https://www.theatlantic.com/business/archive/2011/08/rick-perry-and-the-economics-of-the-texas-miracle/243619/.
35. James Taylor, "Rick Perry Is the Perfect Choice for Energy Secretary," *Forbes*, December 14, 2016, https://www.forbes.com/sites/jamestaylor/2016/12/14/rick-perry-is-the-perfect-choice-for-energy-secretary/#75721a6b5c26.
36. "Governor Perry Remarks to the Dallas Regional Chamber," Legislative Reference Library of Texas, October 21, 2008, https://lrl.texas.gov/scanned/govdocs/Rick%20Perry/2008/speech102108.pdf.
37. "Address by the Governor," Legislative Reference Library of Texas, January 11, 2011, https://lrl.texas.gov/scanned/govdocs/Rick%20Perry/2011/speech011111House.pdf.
38. "Governor Perry Gives Remarks at Texas Public Policy Foundation's Policy Orientation," Legislative Reference Library of Texas, January 10, 2013, https://lrl.texas.gov/scanned/govdocs/Rick%20Perry/2013/speech011013.pdf.
39. Thomas Lindsay, "Texas Takes the Next Step to Make College More Affordable," Texas Public Policy Foundation, December 26, 2018, https://www.texaspolicy.com/texas-takes-the-next-step-to-make-college-more-affordable/.
40. Vance Ginn, "The Texas Miracle Isn't All about Oil," Texas Public Policy Foundation, June 9, 2016, https://www.texaspolicy.com/the-texas-miracle-isnt-all-about-oil/.
41. Ibid.

MAKING AMERICAN HEALTH CARE GREAT: A CONSERVATIVE AGENDA FOR STATES TO CREATE INNOVATIVE HEALTH CARE MARKETS

1. John H. Cushman Jr., "Senator Heinz and 6 Others Killed in Midair Crash Near Philadelphia," *New York Times*, April 5, 1991, https://www.nytimes.com/1991/04/05/us/senator-heinz-and-6-others-killed-in-midair-crash-near-philadelphia.html.
2. Wofford served out the three remaining years of the late Senator Heinz's term. His successor was then Pennsylvania representative Rick Santorum.
3. Paul Starr, *The Social Transformation of American Medicine: The Rise of a Sovereign Profession and the Making of a Vast Industry* (New York: Basic Books, 1982), 235.
4. G. M. Turner et al., *Why Obamacare Is Wrong for America* (New York: Harper-Collins, 2011).

5. "Paul Ryan on Health Care and the Steep Climb to Reclaim the American Idea," U.S. House of Representatives, Floor debate on H.R. 3590 and H.R. 4872, March 21, 2010, http://www.house.gov/budget_republicans/press/2007/pr20100323speech.pdf.

6. Angie Drobnic Holan, "Lie of the Year: 'If You Like Your Health Care Plan, You Can Keep It,'" PolitiFact, December 12, 2013, https://www.politifact.com/truth-o-meter/article/2013/dec/12/lie-year-if-you-like-your-health-care-plan-keep-it/.

7. Mark Pauly, "Will Health Care's Immediate Future Look a Lot like the Recent Past?" American Enterprise Institute, June 7, 2019, https://www.aei.org/publication/health-cares-future-public-sector-funding-delivery-administration/.

8. "National Health Expenditure Data," Centers for Medicare and Medicaid Services, https://www.cms.gov/Research-Statistics-Data-and-Systems/Statistics-Trends-and-Reports/NationalHealthExpendData/index?utm_source.

9. Grace-Marie Turner, "Health Care Choices Proposal: A New Generation of Health Reform," Forbes, June 22, 2018, https://www.forbes.com/sites/gracemarieturner/2018/06/22/health-care-choices-proposal-a-new-generation-of-health-reform/#1106ce6664f1.

10. "Data on 2019 Individual Health Insurance Market Conditions," Centers for Medicare and Medicaid Services, October 11, 2018, https://www.cms.gov/newsroom/fact-sheets/data-2019-individual-health-insurance-market-conditions.

11. Brian Blase, "Health Reform Progress," Galen Institute, September 2019, https://galen.org/assets/Health-Reform-Progress-Brian_Blase.pdf.

12. Kev Coleman, "First Phase of New Association Health Plans Reveal Promising Trends," Association Health Plan News, January 2019, https://www.associationhealthplans.com/reports/new-ahp-study/.

13. Paige Winfield Cunningham, "The Health 202: Association Health Plans Expanded under Trump Look Promising So Far," Washington Post, January 30, 2019, https://www.washingtonpost.com/news/powerpost/paloma/the-health-202/2019/01/30/the-health-202-association-health-plans-expanded-under-trump-look-promising-so-far/5c50ba751b326b29c3778d05/?noredirect=on&utm_term=.6435676a70d4.

14. "Short-Term, Limited-Duration Insurance," Federal Register, August 3, 2018, https://www.federalregister.gov/documents/2018/08/03/2018-16568/short-term-limited-duration-insurance.

15. Linda J. Blumberg, Matthew Buettgens, Robin Wang, "Updated: The Potential Impact of Short-Term Limited-Duration Policies on Insurance Coverage, Premiums, and Federal Spending," Urban Institute, March 2018, https://www.urban.org/sites/default/files/publication/96781/2001727_updated_finalized.pdf.

16. Doug Badger and Whitney Jones, "Five Steps Policymakers Can Take to Permit the Sale and Renewal of Affordable Alternatives to Obamacare Policies," Heritage Foundation, April 26, 2018, https://www.heritage.org/

health-care-reform/report/
five-steps-policymakers-can-take-permit-the-sale-and-renewal-affordable.

17. Council of Economic Advisers, "Deregulating Health Insurance Markets: Value to Market Participants," White House, February 2019, https://www.whitehouse. gov/wp-content/uploads/2019/02/Deregulating-Health-Insurance-Markets-FINAL.pdf.

18. Presidential Executive Order Promoting Healthcare Choice and Competition across the United States, White House, October 12, 2017, https://www. whitehouse.gov/presidential-actions/ presidential-executive-order-promoting-healthcare-choice-competition-across-united-states/.

19. Doug Badger, Ed Haislmaier, "State Innovation: The Key to Affordable Health Care Choices," Heritage Foundation, September 27, 2018, https://www.heritage. org/health-care-reform/report/ state-innovation-the-key-affordable-health-care-coverage-choices.

20. Grace-Marie Turner, Doug Badger, "Several States Have Found Ways to Mitigate Obamacare's Damage to Their Health Insurance Markets," *Forbes*, October 3, 2018, https://www.forbes.com/sites/gracemarieturner/2018/10/03/ several-states-have-found-ways-to-mitigate-obamacares-damage-to-their-health-insurance-markets/#56d1b71730da.

21. Doug Badger, "How Health Care Premiums Are Declining in States That Seek Relief from Obamacare's Mandates," Heritage Foundation, August 13, 2019, https://www.heritage.org/health-care-reform/report/ how-health-care-premiums-are-declining-states-seek-relief-obamacares.

22. Emily M. Mitchell, "Concentration of Health Expenditures in the U.S. Civilian Noninstitutionalized Population, 2014," Agency for Healthcare Research and Quality, November 2016, https://meps.ahrq.gov/data_files/publications/st497/ stat497.pdf.

23. "Health Care Wait Times," Fraser Institute, last updated December 10, 2019, https://www.fraserinstitute.org/categories/health-care-wait-times.

24. Dennis Campbell, "16,900 People in a Week Kept in NHS Ambulances Waiting for Hospital Care," *The Guardian*, January 4, 2018, https://www.theguardian. com/society/2018/jan/04/16900-people-in-a-week-kept-in-nhs-ambulances-waiting-for-hospital-care.

25. Nick Triggle, "Patients 'Dying in Hospital Corridors,'" BBC, January 11, 2018, https://www.bbc.com/news/health-42572116.

26. Sally Pipes, "Britain's Version of 'Medicare for All' Is Struggling with Long Waits for Care," *Forbes*, April 1, 2019, https://www.forbes.com/sites/ sallypipes/2019/04/01/ britains-version-of-medicare-for-all-is-collapsing/#2c4418a536b8.

27. "About CCGs," NHS Clinical Commissioners website, https://www.nhscc.org/ ccgs/.

28. Sean Rai-Roche, "CCGs in England Restrict Access to Cataract Surgery," March 20, 2019, https://www.opticianonline.net/news/ccgs-restrict-cataract-surgery-in-nhs-england-1.

29. "NHS Hospitals Need Plan to Tackle Backlog of Patients, Warns RCS," Royal College of Surgeons of England, March 14, 2019, https://www.rcseng.ac.uk/news-and-events/media-centre/press-releases/nhs-stats-march-2019/.

30. Ibid.

31. Doug Badger, "Replacing Employer-Sponsored Health Insurance with Government-Financed Coverage: Considerations for Policymakers," Galen Institute, December 2018, https://galen.org/assets/Replacing-Empl-Spons-Insur-112618.pdf.

32. Stuart Heiser, "New Findings Confirm Predictions on Physician Shortage," Association of American Medical Colleges, April 23, 2019, https://news.aamc.org/press-releases/article/workforce_report_shortage_04112018/.

33. "The Complexities of Physician Supply and Demand: Projections from 2017–2032," Association of American Medical Colleges, April 2019, https://aamc-black.global.ssl.fastly.net/production/media/filer_public/31/13/3113ee5c-a038-4c16-89af-294a69826650/2019_update_-_the_complexities_of_physician_supply_and_demand_-_projections_from_2017-2032.pdf.

34. Peter St. Onge, "What Bernie Sanders Isn't Telling You about Canadian Health Care," Daily Signal, February 27, 2020, https://www.dailysignal.com/2020/02/27/what-bernie-sanders-isnt-telling-you-about-canadian-health-care/.

35. Sally Pipes, False Premise. False Promise. The Disastrous Reality of Medicare for All (New York: Encounter Books, 2020).

36. Grace-Marie Turner and Thomas Miller, "ObamaCare Co-ops: Cause Célèbre or Costly Conundrum?" Galen Institute, June 29, 2015, https://galen.org/2015/obamacare-co-ops-cause-celebre-or-costly-conundrum-2/.

37. "Health Co-op," Center for Insurance Policy and Research, February 12, 2020, https://www.naic.org/cipr_topics/topic_health_co-op.htm.

38. Medicare premiums are community rated, and they do not vary by age. A disabled forty-year-old beneficiary pays the same premium as a ninety-year-old. The monthly premium for Part A is $437. Part B is $135.50, but 75 percent is subsidized. The full, unsubsidized premium would thus be $542. The average Part D premium is $33. Eliminating the subsidy would raise that to $132. Thus, without government subsidies, the monthly premium for Medicare would be $1,111. Source for A and B premiums: https://www.cms.gov/newsroom/fact-sheets/2019-medicare-parts-b-premiums-and-deductibles. Source for D premiums: https://www.mymedicarematters.org/costs/part-d/.

39. Brian Blase, "Transparent Prices Will Help Consumers and Employers Reduce Health Spending," Galen Institute, September 27, 2019, https://galen.org/assets/Blase_Transparency_Paper_092719.pdf.

40. Brian Blase and Aaron Yelowitz, "The ACA's Medicaid Expansion: A Review of Ineligible Enrollees and Improper Payments," Mercatus Center, November 2019, https://www.mercatus.org/system/files/blase-medicaid-expansion-mercatus-research-v2_2.pdf; Brian Blase, "Why Obama Stopped Auditing Medicaid," *Wall Street Journal*, November 18, 2019, https://www.wsj.com/articles/why-obama-stopped-auditing-medicaid-11574121931.
41. Daniel R. Levinson, "California Made Medicaid Payments on Behalf of Non-Newly Eligible Beneficiaries Who Did Not Meet Federal and State Requirements," Department of Health and Human Services, Office of Inspector General, December 2018, https://oig.hhs.gov/oas/reports/region9/91702002.pdf?mod=article_inline.
42. Hayley Dixon, "Terminally Ill Boy Denied 'Potentially Life-Saving' Treatment by NHS 'Would Be Given It in Any US Hospital," *Telegraph*, April 3, 2017, https://www.telegraph.co.uk/news/2017/04/03/terminally-boy-denied-potentially-life-saving-treatment-nhs/.
43. Julie Zauzmer, "Alfie Evans Update: Parents to Meet with Doctors to Ask If They Can Take Their Ailing Son Home," *Washington Post*, April 26, 2018, https://www.washingtonpost.com/news/acts-of-faith/wp/2018/04/24/judge-rules-against-letting-alfie-evans-a-terminally-ill-british-child-go-to-the-popes-hospital/?utm_term=.5f284047564b.
44. Grace-Marie Turner, "Health Care Choices Proposal: A New Generation of Health Reform," *Forbes*, June 22, 2018, https://www.forbes.com/sites/gracemarieturner/2018/06/22/health-care-choices-proposal-a-new-generation-of-health-reform/#740e5ce864f1.
45. "The Health Care Choices Proposal," Center for Health and Economy, http://healthandeconomy.org/the-health-care-choices-proposal/.
46. More details of the plan are available at www.HealthCareChoices2020.org.
47. "Janet's Story: High Medical Costs, Worse Coverage," Health Care Choices 2020 Testimonies, May 22, 2018, https://www.healthcarechoices2020.org/testimonial/janets-story-high-medical-costs-worse-coverage/.

RELIGIOUS LIBERTY AND THE HUMAN GOOD

1. Martin Luther King, *Letter from Birmingham Jail* (New York: Harper Collins, 1994). The letter was written and originally published in 1963.
2. John Rawls, "On the Priority of Right and Ideas of the Good," *Philosophy and Public Affairs* 17, no. 4 (1988), 251–76.
3. There are, of course, many people today who contest my view that the life of a human being is intrinsically and not merely instrumentally valuable. So it needs to be defended. For a defense see Patrick Lee and Robert P. George, *Body-Self Dualism in Contemporary Ethics and Politics* (New York: Cambridge University Press, 2008), 160–62. See also Germain Grisez, John Finnis, and

Joseph M. Boyle Jr., *Nuclear Deterrence, Morality and Realism* (Oxford: Clarendon Press, 1987), 304–9.

4. On religion as a basic human good, see John Finnis, *Natural Law and Natural Rights* (Oxford: Oxford University Press, 1980), 89–90.

5. For a deeply informed and sensitive treatment of similarities and differences in the world historical religions, see Augustine DiNoia, *The Diversity of Religions: A Christian Perspective* (Washington, D.C.: Catholic University Press, 1992).

6. See Kevin J. Hasson, *The Right to Be Wrong: Ending the Culture War over Religion in America* (New York: Encounter Books, 2005).

7. *Dignitatis Humanae*, 2–3.

8. On natural law and religious freedom in the Jewish tradition, see David Novak, *In Defense of Religious Liberty* (Wilmington, Delaware: ISI Books, 2009). (Rabbi Novak kindly dedicated this fine work to me. Inasmuch as this is the first time I have had occasion to cite it in a public forum, I am happy to have the opportunity to express gratitude for what I consider to be a high honor.)

9. John Rawls, *Political Liberalism* (New York: Columbia University Press, 1993), 137.

THREE CHEERS FOR THE ELECTORAL COLLEGE

1. Donald Lutz, Philip Abbott, Barbara Allen, and Russell Hanson, "The Electoral College in Philosophical Perspective," in Paul D. Schumaker and Burdett A. Loomis, eds., *Choosing a President: The Electoral College and Beyond* (New York: Seven Bridges Press, 2002), 31.

2. Erwin Chemerinsky, "Reforming the Electoral College," *Orange County Register*, September, 15, 2016, https://www.law.uci.edu/news/in-the-news/2016/ocregister-chemerinsky-reforming-electoral-college-091516.pdf.

3. Tara Ross and Robert M. Hardaway, "The Compact Clause and National Popular Vote: Implications for the Federal Structure," *New Mexico Law Review* 44, no. 383 (Summer 2014), 402.

4. This insight comes from UCLA Law professor Daniel Lowenstein. Professor Lowenstein is generally recognized as the founder of election law as an independent field of legal study.

LABOR UNIONS AND THE PUBLIC SECTOR

1. Joan Gucciardi, "The Imbalance Between Public and Private Pensions in Wisconsin," Badger Institute, February 2010, https://www.badgerinstitute.org/Reports/2010/The-Imbalance-Between-Public-and-Private-Pensions-in-Wisconsin.htm.

2. Dean Mosiman, "Madison Metro Driver Highest Paid City Employee," *Wisconsin State Journal*, February 7, 2010, https://madison.com/wsj/news/local/govt_and_politics/madison-metro-driver-highest-paid-city-employee/article_24af32d4-13f4-11df-86b2-001cc4c002e0.html.

3. Warren Todd Huston, "Union Abuses in Wisconsin," Publius Forum, March 9, 2011, http://www.chicagonow.com/publius-forum/2011/03/union-abuses-in-wisconsin/.

4. Journal Times Editorial Board, "Union's Grievance Feeds Walker's Plan," *Journal Times*, March 3, 2011, https://journaltimes.com/news/opinion/editorial/article_4163c08e-4607-11e0-8d0c-001cc4c03286.html.

5. Email from Senator Scott Fitzgerald to Legislative Senate Republicans, "GOP Senate Weekly Update – April 29, 2011," April 29, 2011, https://www.scribd.com/document/95335394/20120523143512439.

6. Mark Browne and Linda Leetch, "Health Insurance for Public School Teachers in Wisconsin: A Good Value for Taxpayers or a Case of Market Abuse?" Wisconsin Policy Research Institute Report, December 2000, https://www.badgerinstitute.org/BI-Files/Special-Reports/Reports-Documents/Vol13no8.pdf.

OUR ENERGY FUTURE

1. "Interview with Former CIA Director, Ambassador James Woolsey on Iran & Middle East," *Jacki Daily Show*, The Blaze Radio Network, October 12, 2015. "Oil and gas are . . . instruments of power . . . Saddam [Hussein] was 100 miles from controlling half of the world's oil, and that's why we went to war in '91" at minute 27:00. "Low oil prices make trouble for Maduro, Putin, and Khomeini" at minute 22–23.

2. Testimony of General James L. Jones, USMC (Ret.) before the U.S. Senate Committee on Foreign Relations, "Keystone XL and the National Interest Determination," March 13, 2014; "Interview with Gen. James Jones," *Jacki Daily Show*, KLIF FM 96.3, AM 570, September 30, 2014.

3. "21st Century U.S. Energy Sources: A Primer," Congressional Research Service, November 5, 2018, https://www.everycrsreport.com/files/20181105_R44854_5 65cc0d6cf6eab708f415bdb7c9d0bf1a37f612a.pdf; Annual Energy Outlook 2019 with Projections to 2050, U.S. Energy Information Administration, January 24, 2019, https://www.eia.gov/outlooks/aeo/pdf/aeo2019.pdf; North American Energy Inventory, Institute for Energy Research, December 2011, http://instituteforenergyresearch.org/wp-content/uploads/2013/01/Energy-Inventory.pdf; "The U.S. Leads Global Petroleum and Natural Gas Production with Record Growth in 2018," U.S. Energy Information Administration, August 20, 2019, https://www.eia.gov/todayinenergy/detail.php?id=40973. "Shale Revolution" is the twenty-first-century surge in U.S. oil and natural gas production from the advancement of hydraulic fracturing techniques, combined with horizontal drilling.

4. "Nuclear Explained," U.S. Energy Information Administration, April 16, 2020, https://www.eia.gov/energyexplained/nuclear/nuclear-power-plants.php.

5. "Fossil Energy Study Guide: Coal," U.S. Department of Energy, https://www.energy.gov/sites/prod/files/2013/04/f0/MS_Coal_Studyguide_draft1.pdf.

6. "Monthly U.S. Crude Oil Imports from OPEC Fall to a 30-Year Low," Today in Energy, U.S. Energy Information Administration, https://www.eia.gov/todayinenergy/detail.php?id=39852&src=email.

7. This figure does not include unfunded mandates such as entitlement spending. "The Debt to the Penny and Who Holds It," Treasury Direct, https://treasurydirect.gov/NP/debt/current; see "The 2019 Long-Term Budget Outlook in 23 Slides," Congressional Budget Office, August 2019, https://www.cbo.gov/system/files/2019-08/55544-CBO-LTBO-in-23-slides.pdf. For a real-time running debt total, see https://www.usdebtclock.org/

8. Kathleen Hartnett White and Stephen Moore, *Fueling Freedom: Exposing the Mad War on Energy* (Washington, D.C.: Regnery Publishing, 2016), 229–47.

9. This figure does not include unfunded mandates such as entitlement spending. See "The Debt to the Penny and Who Holds It" and "The 2019 Long-Term Budget Outlook in 23 Slides." For a real-time running debt total, see https://www.usdebtclock.org/.

10. "Oil and Gas Industry Employment Growing Much Faster Than Total Private Sector Employment," U.S. Energy Information Administration, August 8, 2013, https://www.eia.gov/todayinenergy/detail.

11. Tom DiChristopher, "Harold Hamm Fires Back at Russia: They Said We'd Never Be a Natural Gas Exporter. Look at Us Now," CNBC, January 25, 2017, https://www.cnbc.com/2017/01/25/harold-hamm-fires-back-at-russian-exec-over-us-energy-independence.html; Matthew J. Belvedere, "Trump Would Get Us to Energy Independence in about Six Years," CNBC, October 21, 2016, https://www.cnbc.com/2016/10/21/trump-would-get-us-to-energy-independence-in-about-6-years-advisor-harold-hamm.html.

12. Belvedere, "Trump Would Get Us to Energy Independence in about Six Years."

13. Ibid.

14. "Economic Growth with Cleaner Air," United States Environmental Protection Agency. See graph entitled "Comparison of Growth Areas and Declining Emissions 1970–2018," https://gispub.epa.gov/air/trendsreport/2019/#growth

15. Texas Public Policy Foundation, "America Is the World Leader in Clean Air," YouTube, May 2, 2019, https://www.youtube.com/watch?v=xcqpwgoQqfY&list=PLLF4kBvOHH68ebdbauXox9huo65ocaXzE&index=3&t=0s.

16. Ibid.

17. Kathleen Hartnett White and Brent Bennett, "The U.S. Leads the World in Clean Air: The Case for Environmental Optimism," Texas Public Policy Foundation, November 2018, https://files.texaspolicy.com/uploads/2018/11/27165514/2018-11-RR-US-Leads-the-World-in-Clean-Air-ACEE-White.pdf.

18. "Fact Check: Is the U.S. Really a World Leader in Clean Air?" Life:Powered, July 8, 2019, https://lifepowered.org/fact-check-is-the-us-really-a-world-leader-in-clean-air/.

19. Robert Rapier, "Yes, the U.S. Leads All Countries in Reducing Carbon Emissions," *Forbes*, October 24, 2017, https://www.forbes.com/sites/

rrapier/2017/10/24/
yes-the-u-s-leads-all-countries-in-reducing-carbon-emissions/#5a92beb83535.

20. Between the years 1970 and 2018, the population grew from approximately 203 million to approximately 327 million. "Population," United States Census Bureau, https://www.census.gov/topics/population.html; "Census of Population and Housing," United States Census Bureau, https://www.census.gov/prod/www/decennial.html.

21. "Travel Monitoring," Office of Highway Policy Information, U.S. Department of Transportation, http://www.fhwa.dot.gov/policyinformation/travel_monitoring/tvt.cfm; "Economic Growth with Cleaner Air," U.S. Environmental Protection Agency, https://gispub.epa.gov/air/trendsreport/2019/#growth_w_cleaner_air.

22. "Economic Growth with Cleaner Air," U.S. Environmental Protection Agency.

23. "Cleaner Air in America," Life:Powered, Texas Public Policy Foundation, 2019.

24. Texas Public Policy Foundation, "America is the World Leader in Clean Air."

25. The U.S. is a signatory to the Kyoto agreement, but did not ratify it: "7. A Kyoto Protocol to the United Nations Framework Convention on Climate Change," United Nations Treaty Collection, https://treaties.un.org/Pages/ViewDetails.aspx?src=TREATY&mtdsg_no=XXVII-7-a&chapter=27&clang=_en.

26. See endnote four at "7. D Paris Agreement," United Nations Treaty Collection, https://treaties.un.org/pages/ViewDetails.aspx?src=IND&mtdsg_no=XXVII-7-d&chapter=27&clang=_en#4.

27. Drew Johnson, "Unlike in Europe, the US Approach to Climate Change Is Actually Working," Washington Examiner, February 10, 2020, https://www.washingtonexaminer.com/opinion/op-eds/unlike-in-europe-the-us-approach-to-climate-change-is-actually-working.

28. Between 1980 and 2016, the U.S. population grew 43.3 percent, GDP grew 165 percent, and Americans drove 111.2 percent more miles. Texas Public Policy Foundation, "America is the World Leader in Clean Air." See also Jason Isaac, "Washington Examiner: This Earth Day, Thank America, the World Leader in Clean Air," Life:Powered, April 22, 2019, https://lifepowered.org/this-earth-day-thank-america-the-world-leader-in-clean-air/.

29. Meiyun Lin et al., "U.S. Surface Ozone Trends and Extremes from 1980 to 2014: Quantifying the Roles of Rising Asian Emissions, Domestic Controls, Wildfires, and Climate," Atmospheric Chemistry and Physics 17 (2017): 2943–70, https://www.atmos-chem-phys.net/17/2943/2017/.

30. "Past EPA Administrator Sets the Record Straight: An Interview with Scott Pruitt," Jacki Daily Show, The Blaze Radio Network, April 7, 2019, minute 42. See also, "Ryan Zinke and Scott Pruitt on Energy and Environment Policy," C-SPAN, March 21, 2019, https://www.c-span.org/video/?458968-1/ryan-zinke-scott-pruitt-environment-energy-policy.

31. Jacki Pick, "Fracking Is Our Clean Power Plan," Forbes, August 25, 2015, https://www.forbes.com/sites/realspin/2015/08/25/fracking-is-our-clean-power-plan/#52b0617e1cf5.

32. "The Value of U.S. Energy Innovation and Policies Supporting the Shale Revolution," Council of Economic Advisors, Executive Office of the President of the United States, October 2019, https://www.whitehouse.gov/wp-content/uploads/2019/10/The-Value-of-U.S.-Energy-Innovation-and-Policies-Supporting-the-Shale-Revolution.pdf.

33. Mike Nasi, "EPA's ACE Rule: A Step towards Returning the EPA to the American Model for Proper Environmental Regulation," Life:Powered, August 29, 2018, https://lifepowered.org/ace-rule-commentary-full/.

34. Kathleen Hartnett White, "The Facts about the Clean Power Plan," Texas Public Policy Foundation, January 2016, https://files.texaspolicy.com/uploads/2018/08/16101356/Key-Points-The-Facts-About-the-Clean-Power-Plan.pdf.

35. Jonathan H. Adler, "Supreme Court Puts the Brakes on the EPA's Clean Power Plan," Washington Post, February 9, 2016, https://www.washingtonpost.com/news/volokh-conspiracy/wp/2016/02/09/supreme-court-puts-the-brakes-on-the-epas-clean-power-plan/.

36. Chris Mooney, "Amid Record Global Temperatures, Senate Votes to Block Obama's Clean Power Plan," Washington Post, November 17, 2015, https://www.washingtonpost.com/news/energy-environment/wp/2015/11/17/amid-record-global-temperatures-congress-to-vote-to-stop-obamas-clean-power-plan/.

37. Nasi, "EPA's ACE Rule."

38. Ibid.

39. Michelle Jamrisko and Wei Lu, "Germany Breaks Korea's Six-Year Streak as Most Innovative Nation," Bloomberg, January 18, 2020, https://www.bloomberg.com/news/articles/2020-01-18/germany-breaks-korea-s-six-year-streak-as-most-innovative-nation.

40. Rebecca Elliott and Luis Santiago, "A Decade in Which Fracking Rocked the Oil World," Wall Street Journal, December 17, 2019, https://www.wsj.com/articles/a-decade-in-which-fracking-rocked-the-oil-world-11576630807.

41. Christi Parsons, "Obama Calls for Expanded Use of Natural Gas," Los Angeles Times, January 26, 2012, https://www.latimes.com/world/la-xpm-2012-jan-26-la-na-obama-energy-20120127-story.html.

42. "The Value of U.S. Energy Innovation and Policies Supporting the Shale Revolution," Council of Economic Advisors, Executive Office of the President of the United States, October 2019, https://www.whitehouse.gov/wp-content/uploads/2019/10/The-Value-of-U.S.-Energy-Innovation-and-Policies-Supporting-the-Shale-Revolution.pdf.

43. Akshat Rathi and Jeremy Hodges, "Even under Trump, U.S. Renewable Investment Hit a Record in 2019," Bloomberg, January 16, 2020, https://www.bloomberg.com/news/articles/2020-01-16/even-under-trump-u-s-renewable-investment-hits-a-record.

44. "U.S. Energy Facts Explained," U.S. Energy Information Administration, last updated May 7, 2020, https://www.eia.gov/energyexplained/us-energy-facts/.

45. Ibid.
46. Julia Pyper, "Tom Steyer Calls on Activists to Push for Clean Energy Solutions Post-Keystone," Green Tech Media, November 11, 2015, https://www.greentechmedia.com/articles/read/tom-steyer-calls-on-activists-to-push-for-clean-energy-solutions.
47. Ibid.
48. "2. Public Opinion on Renewables and Other Energy Sources," Pew Research Center, October 4, 2016, https://www.pewresearch.org/science/2016/10/04/public-opinion-on-renewables-and-other-energy-sources/.
49. Angela C. Erickson, "The Production Tax Credit: Corporate Subsidies & Renewable Energy," Texas Public Policy Foundation, November 1, 2018, https://www.texaspolicy.com/the-production-tax-credit-corporate-subsidies-renewable-energy/.
50. Mark Clayton, "America's Wind Corridor," Christian Science Monitor, February 5, 2009, https://www.csmonitor.com/Business/2009/0205/america-s-wind-corridor.
51. Jim Malewitz, "$7 Billion Wind Power Project Nears Finish," Texas Tribune, October 14, 2013, https://www.texastribune.org/2013/10/14/7-billion-crez-project-nears-finish-aiding-wind-po/.
52. Erickson, "The Production Tax Credit."
53. Cutter Gonzalez, "Chapters 312 and 313 Are Supposed to Bring Jobs—Renewables Don't," Texas Public Policy Foundation, November 27, 2018, https://www.texaspolicy.com/chapters-312-and-313-are-supposed-to-bring-jobs-renewables-dont/.
54. Brandon T. Hooker, "California's Green Economy Trends: Relationships between Firms and Their Employment Outcomes," Working Paper 1, California Employment Development Department, August 2013, https://www.labormarketinfo.edd.ca.gov/specialreports/CA_LMI_Trends_GreenFirmsStudy.pdf https://www.politico.com/story/2019/09/04/california-green-jobs-1479996.
55. "Renewable Energy and Energy Mandates," Texas Public Policy Foundation, 2015–2016, https://files.texaspolicy.com/uploads/2018/08/16100014/Renewable-Energy-and-Energy-Mandates.pdf.
56. Chuck DeVore, "'Green New Deal' Preview? Texas Town's Lofty Environmentalism Leaves Residents with a Nightmare," Texas Public Policy Foundation, August 28, 2019, https://www.texaspolicy.com/green-new-deal-preview-texas-towns-lofty-environmentalism-leaves-residents-with-a-nightmare/.
57. Ali Linan, "Bloomberg Terminates $1 Million Grant Award to City of Georgetown," Community Impact, August 14, 2019, https://communityimpact.com/austin/georgetown/city-county/2019/08/13/bloomberg-terminates-1-million-grant-award-to-city-of-georgetown/.
58. DeVore, "'Green New Deal' Preview?"

59. Mark P. Mills, "The 'New Energy Economy': An Exercise in Magical Thinking," Manhattan Institute, March 26, 2019, https://www.manhattan-institute.org/green-energy-revolution-near-impossible.

60. Bill Peacock, "Markets, Not 'Renewable Energy' Magic, Ensure the Affordable Supply of Electricity," Texas Public Policy Foundation, August 25, 2018, https://www.texaspolicy.com/markets-not-renewable-energy-magic-ensure-the-affordable-supply-of-electricity/.

61. "2019–20 Legislator's Guide to the Issues" (Austin, Texas: Texas Public Policy Foundation, 2018), https://files.texaspolicy.com/uploads/2018/10/03133012/2019-20-LegeGuide-WEB.pdf.

62. Brent Bennett, "What's the True Cost of Renewables?" Texas Public Policy Foundation, July 7, 2019, https://www.texaspolicy.com/whats-the-true-cost-of-renewables/.

63. Xiaojing Sun, "Solar Technology Got Cheaper and Better in the 2010s. Now What?" Green Tech Media, December 17, 2019, https://www.greentechmedia.com/articles/read/solar-pv-has-become-cheaper-and-better-in-the-2010s-now-what.

64. Cutter J. Gonzalez, "The '100 by 32' Green Energy Fad Means Higher Costs, Less Reliability for DC Residents," Texas Public Policy Foundation, January 16, 2019, https://www.texaspolicy.com/the-100-by-32-green-energy-fad-means-higher-costs-less-reliability-for-dc-residents/.

65. Lisa Linowes, *The Texas Wind Power Story: Part 1: How Subsidies Drive Texas Wind Power Development*, Texas Public Policy Foundation, May 2018, https://files.texaspolicy.com/uploads/2018/06/07165735/2018-04-RR-TexasWindPowerStoryPart1-ACEE-LisaLinowes.pdf.

66. "Texas Oil and Natural Gas Industry Paid $13.8 Billion in Taxes and Royalties in 2015, Second Most in Texas History," Texas Oil and Gas Association, February 2, 2016, https://www.txoga.org/texas-oil-and-natural-gas-industry-paid-13-8-billion-in-taxes-and-royalties-in-2015-second-most-in-texas-history/.

67. *Annual Energy Outlook 2019 with Projections to 2050*, U.S. Energy Information Administration.

68. "Frequently Asked Questions," U.S. Energy Information Administration, https://www.eia.gov/tools/faqs/faq.php?id=58&t=8; "Oil," BP, https://www.bp.com/en/global/corporate/energy-economics/statistical-review-of-world-energy/oil.html.html#oil-reserves.

69. Brigham McCown, former acting administrator of the Pipelines and Hazardous Materials Safety Administration, Alliance for Innovation and Infrastructure.

70. Pipeline 101, https://pipeline101.org/Where-Are-Pipelines-Located.

71. Bev Betkowski, "Pipelines Easier on the Environment Than Rail," University of Alberta Faculty of Engineering, December 13, 2016, https://www.ualberta.ca/

engineering/news/2016/december/pipelineseasierontheenvironmentthanrail. html.

72. Shant Shahrigian, "Homes, Businesses in Limbo as National Grid Denies Natural Gas Services," *Daily News*, August 27, 2019, https://www.nydailynews. com/news/politics/ny-national-grid-natural-gas-brooklyn-queens-long-island-20190828-g5evy3scjrdwleejqws55snqli-story.html.

73. See for example, *Denbury Green Pipeline-Texas, LLC, v Texas Rice Land Partners Ltd., et al*, No. 15-0225 (2016). "[A common carrier] serve[s] the public by transporting a product for one or more customers who will either retain ownership or sell it to parties other than the carrier."

74. University of Texas System Office of the Controller, Available University Fund Report, Report to the Legislature and Governor, December 2018, https://www. utsystem.edu/sites/default/files/documents/Availablepercent20University percent20Fundpercent20Reportpercent3Apercent20FYpercent202016/ auf-report-fy-2016-final.pdf.

75. Alex Samuels, "Hey, Texplainer: How Does Texas' Budget Use Taxes from Oil and Natural Gas Production?" *Texas Tribune*, January 5, 2018, https://www. texastribune.org/2018/01/05/ hey-texplainer-how-does-texas-budget-use-taxes-oil-and-natural-gas-pro/.

76. Definition of common carrier under the Texas code: https://codes.findlaw.com/ tx/natural-resources-code/nat-res-sect-111-002.html.

77. *Stewart v. City of Dallas*, 361 SW 3d 562 Texas Supreme Court (2012); *Laws v. Texas*, NO. 4:15-CV-0652 (S.D. Tex. Apr. 9, 2015); *Denbury Green Pipeline-Texas, LLC, v Texas Rice Land Partners Ltd., et al.*, No. 15-0225 (2016).

78. The State of Texas Landowner's Bill of Rights, Tex. Gov. Code §402.031; Tex. Prop. Code Ch. 21, https://www.texasattorneygeneral.gov/sites/default/files/files/ divisions/general-oag/LandownersBillofRights.pdf.

CHOOSING THE BEST FOR OUR CHILDREN

1. Michael Chui, James Manyika, and Mehdi Miremadi, "Where Machines Could Replace Humans—and Where They Can't (Yet)," McKinsey, July 8, 2016, https://www.mckinsey.com/business-functions/mckinsey-digital/our-insights/ where-machines-could-replace-humans-and-where-they-cant-yet#.

2. Zeger van der Wal and Yifei Yan, "Could Robots Do Better Than Our Current Leaders?" World Economic Forum, October 17, 2018, https://www.weforum. org/agenda/2018/10/could-robot-government-lead-better-current-politicians-ai/.

3. Sigal Samuel, "A Quarter of Europeans Want AI to Replace Politicians. That's a Terrible Idea," Vox, March 27, 2019, https://www.vox.com/future-perfect/2019/3/27/18283992/ai-replace-politicians-europe-survey.

4. Lauren Camera, "High School Seniors Aren't College-Ready," U.S. News and World Report, April 27, 2016, https://www.usnews.com/news/ articles/2016-04-27/high-school-seniors-arent-college-ready-naep-data-show.

5. "Employers Globally Struggle to Find Workers with the Right Skills," Staffing Industry Analysts, June 26, 2018, https://www2.staffingindustry.com/site/Editorial/Daily-News/Employers-globally-struggle-to-find-workers-with-the-right-skills-46531.

6. Ben Casselman and Adam Satariano, "Amazon's Latest Experiment: Retraining Its Work Force," New York Times, July 11, 2019, https://www.nytimes.com/2019/07/11/technology/amazon-workers-retraining-automation.html.

7. Council on Foreign Relations, "U.S. Education Reform and National Security," Independent Task Force Report No. 68, 2012, https://cdn.cfr.org/sites/default/files/report_pdf/TFR68_Education_National_Security.pdf.

8. "Literacy Statistics," Begin to Read, http://www.begintoread.com/research/literacystatistics.html.

9. "Excerpts from Bush's Speech on Improving Education, 1999," New York Times, September 3, 1999, https://www.nytimes.com/1999/09/03/us/excerpts-from-bush-s-speech-on-improving-education.html.

10. "Florida Overview," Nation's Report Card, https://www.nationsreportcard.gov/profiles/stateprofile/overview/FL?cti=PgTab_OT&chort=1&sub=RED&sj=FL&fs=Grade&st=MN&year=2017R3&sg=Gender%3A+Male+vs.+Female&sgv=Difference&ts=Single+Year&tss=-2017R3&sfj=NP.

11. "Florida Continues to Lead the Nation in Advanced Placement Exams," Florida Department of Education, February 6, 2019, http://www.fldoe.org/newsroom/latest-news/florida-continues-to-lead-the-nation-in-advanced-placement-exams.stml.

12. Scott Powers, "Florida Students Top Nation in Taking Advanced Placement Tests," Florida Politics, February 6, 2019, https://floridapolitics.com/archives/287594-florida-students-top-nation-in-taking-advanced-placement-tests.

13. Patrick R. Gibbons, "Option on the Rise: 1.7 Million Florida Students Choose," Redefined, January 22, 2018, https://www.redefinedonline.org/2018/01/changing-landscapes-2016-17-school-choice/.

14. Lisa A. Davis, "Tally Rally to #DroptheSuit Draws More Than 10,000 Florida Tax Credit Scholarship Supporters from across the State," Step Up for Students, February 16, 2016, https://blog.stepupforstudents.org/tally-rally-to-dropthesuit-draws-more-than-10000-florida-tax-credit-scholarship-supporters-from-across-the-state/.

15. "Tampa Tribune: Denisha Merriweather: 'Living Proof' That Tax Credit Scholarships Work," Save Our Scholarships, August 20, 2015, http://saveourscholarships.com/2015/08/.

16. Leslie Postal, "Nation's Report Card: 'Something Very Good Is Happening in Florida,'" Orlando Sentinel, April 10, 2018, https://www.orlandosentinel.com/news/education/os-0s-florida-naep-test-scores-20180409-story.html.

17. "Florida Students Get Certified!" Florida Department of Education, http://www.fldoe.org/core/fileparse.php/8904/urlt/LetsGetCertified-sec.pdf.

18. ExcelinEd, "#EIE18 Highlights—Opening Keynote: U.S. Senator Ben Sasse," YouTube, December 18, 2018, https://www.youtube.com/watch?v=tjSTpUt2ENQ&t=1s.

RESTORING PUBLIC UNIVERSITIES AS THE MARKETPLACE OF IDEAS

1. "Students for Life at Colorado State University v. Mosher," Alliance Defending Freedom, adf.pub/ColoradoState.
2. "Fresno State Students for Life v. Thatcher," Alliance Defending Freedom, adf.pub/FresnoState.
3. Lisa Feldman Barrett, "When Is Speech Violence?" *New York Times*, July 14, 2017, https://www.nytimes.com/2017/07/14/opinion/sunday/when-is-speech-violence.html.
4. Jonathan Haidt and Greg Lukianoff, *The Coddling of the American Mind* (New York: Penguin Press, 2018).
5. Nisa Dang, "Check Your Privilege When Speaking of Protests," *Daily Californian*, February 7, 2017, https://www.dailycal.org/2017/02/07/check-privilege-speaking-protests/.
6. "Liberalism," Dictionary.com, https://www.dictionary.com/browse/liberalism.
7. Jonathan Haidt, "Why Universities Must Choose One Telos: Truth or Social Justice," Heterodox Academy, October 21, 2016, https://heterodoxacademy.org/one-telos-truth-or-social-justice-2/.
8. "Josephson v. Bendapudi," Alliance Defending Freedom, adf.pub/Josephson.
9. David Lehan and Nicolas Badra, "Conflicting Psychiatric Agendas in Our Polarized World," Clinical Psychiatry News, November 4, 2019, https://www.mdedge.com/psychiatry/article/211493/mixed-topics/conflicting-psychiatric-agendas-our-polarized-world.
10. Bradley Campbell and Jason Manning, "Purity and Tolerance: The Contradictory Morality of College Campuses," Quillette, May 2, 2016, https://quillette.com/2016/05/02/purity-and-tolerance-the-contradictory-morality-of-college-campuses/.
11. Cass R. Sunstein, "Conformity and the Dangers of Group Polarization," Quillette, May 17, 2019, https://quillette.com/2019/05/17/conformity-and-the-dangers-of-group-polarization/.
12. Yuval Levin, *A Time to Build: From Family and Community to Congress and the Campus, How Recommitting to Our Institutions Can Revive the American Dream* (New York: Basic Books, 2020).

GETTING RIGHT ON CRIME

1. This is actually a false dichotomy. Many environmental factors, including exposure to violence and growing up without positive role models (especially fathers for boys), undoubtedly make it more likely someone will subsequently engage in criminal activity. However, this does not remove the need for

accountability. While such mitigating factors can inform the part of a sentence attributable to punishment, if incarceration is necessary for the incapacitation function of protecting the public, that does not change regardless of the factors that contributed to the offending.

2. Ryan S. King et al., *Incarceration and Crime: A Complex Relationship*, Washington, D.C.: The Sentencing Project, 2005, https://www. sentencingproject.org/wp-content/uploads/2016/01/Incarceration-and-Crime-A-Complex-Relationship.pdf.

3. "United States Crime Rates 1960–2018," Disaster Center, http://www. disastercenter.com/crime/uscrime.htm.

4. William J. Stuntz, *The Collapse of American Criminal Justice* (Cambridge, Massachusetts: Harvard University Press, 2011), 46.

5. See Marc A. Levin and Vikrant P. Reddy, "The Verdict on Federal Prison Reform: State Successes Offer Keys to Reducing Crime & Costs," Texas Public Policy Foundation, July 2013, 1, http://www.texaspolicy.com/sites/default/files/ documents/2013-07-PP24-VerdictOnFederalPrisonReform-CEJ-LevinReddy. pdf [hereinafter "The Verdict"]. Moreover, in the last few years, while some state prison populations have begun to decline, the federal prison population has continued to grow. Erica Goode, "U.S. Prison Populations Decline, Reflecting New Approach to Crime," *New York Times*, July 25, 2013, http://www. nytimes.com/2013/07/26/us/us-prison-populations-decline-reflecting-new-approach-to-crime.html?pagewanted=all&_r=0 http://perma.cc/

6. UDP5-VHUN. In 2012, one year after the Texas legislature authorized the closure of a prison in the city of Sugar Land, the federal government purchased a new prison facility in northwestern Illinois. Brandi Grissom, "Prison Closing Pleases City and Helps State Budget," *New York Times*, August 19, 2011, http:// www.nytimes.com/2011/08/19/us/19ttprison.html (discussing the closing of the Sugar Land prison); Rick Pearson, "U.S. Buys Thomson Prison from State for $165 Million," *Chicago Tribune*, October 3, 2012, http://articles. chicagotribune.com/2012-10-03/news/ct-met-durbin-quinn-thompson-prison-1003-20121003_1_thomson-prison-guantanamo-bay-wolf (discussing the new prison facility in northwestern Illinois).

7. "The Verdict," supra note 45, at 1.

8. Todd R. Clear and Natasha A. Frost, *The Punishment Imperative* (New York: New York University Press, 2014), 33. ("Scholars have demonstrated that virtually all growth in prison populations over several decades could be attributed to the two sanctioning phases of the system: commitments to prison once convicted and length of stay once admitted. Eighty-eight percent of the growth in prison populations between 1980 and 1996 has been attributed to increasing commitments to prison and increasing lengths of stay"); see also Stuntz, *The Collapse of American Criminal Justice*, 247 (showing that the imprisonment rate per 100,000 population increased from 96 in 1973 to 179 in 1983 to 359 in 1993 and prison-years per murder conviction increased from 10 in 1973 to 21 in 1983 to 38 in 1993). Roy Walmsley, "World Prison Population

List, 10th ed.," International Centre for Prison Studies, http://www.
prisonstudies.org/sites/prisonstudies.org/files/resources/downloads/wppl_10.
pdf. The International Centre for Prison Studies reports that the United States
has the highest prison population rate in the world. We use the limiting language
"in the democratic world" because we are concerned that undemocratic nations
may underreport their prison statistics.

9. Ibid., 3.
10. Ibid., 5.
11. Ibid., 6.
12. Ibid., 3.
13. Ibid., 5.
14. Ibid., 4.
15. William J. Stuntz, *The Collapse of American Criminal Justice* (Cambridge,
Massachusetts: Harvard University Press, 2011), 50. For international homicide
figures, see United Nations Office on Drugs and Crime, Global Study on
Homicide (2011), available at http://www.unodc.org/documents/data-and-
analysis/statistics/Homicide/Globa_study_on_homicide_2011_web.pdf [http://
perma.cc/SML9-8NLN].
16. Stuntz, *The Collapse of American Criminal Justice*, 50.
17. Mark A. R. Kleiman, *When Brute Force Fails: How to Have Less Crime and
Less Punishment* (Princeton, New Jersey: Princeton University Press, 2009),
8–15.
18. Steven Pinker, *The Better Angels of Our Nature: Why Violence Has Declined*
(London: Penguin Books, 2011), 107.
19. Thomas J. Lueck, "Low Murder Rate Brings New York Back to '63," *New York
Times*, December 31, 2007, http://www.nytimes.com/2007/12/31/
nyregion/31murder.html?_r=0.
20. "New York City September 17, 1990 Cover," *Time*, September 17, 1990, http://
content.time.com/time/covers/0,16641,19900917,00.html. For the
accompanying article, see Joelle Attinger, "The Decline of New York," *Time*,
September 17, 1990, 36.
21. See generally Suzanne Daley, "Man Tells Police He Shot Youths in Subway
Train," *New York Times*, January 1, 1985, http://www.nytimes.
com/1985/01/01/nyregion/man-tells-police-he-shot-youths-in-subway-train.
html.
22. *Serpico* (Paramount Pictures, 1973); *Taxi Driver* (Columbia Pictures, 1976);
Dirty Harry (Warner Bros., 1971).
23. James Q. Wilson, "Hard Times, Fewer Crimes," *Wall Street Journal*, May 28,
2011, http://online.wsj.com/news/articles/SB10001424052702304066504576345553135009870.
24. Pinker, *The Better Angels of Our Nature*, 110.
25. David Dagan and Steven Teles, "The Conservative War on Prisons,"
Washington Monthly, November/December 2012, https://nationinside.org/
wp-content/uploads/2016/05/Read-the-Report-Here.pdf. ("[Conservative

policies on crime during this period] worked political magic by tapping into a key liberal weakness. Urban violent crime was rising sharply during the 1960s and liberals had no persuasive response beyond vague promises that economic uplift and social programs would curb delinquency."); Michael W. Flamm, *Law and Order: Street Crime, Civil Unrest, and the Crisis of Liberalism in the 1960s* (New York: Columbia University Press, 2005), 2. ("In the face of the rise in crime [the murder rate alone almost doubled between 1963 and 1968], [liberals] initially maintained that the statistics were faulty—a response that if not incorrect was insensitive to the victims of crime as well as their friends and family, co-workers and neighbors. They also tended to dismiss those who pleaded for law and order as racists, ignoring blacks who were victimized more often than any other group and insulting Jews who had steadfastly supported the civil rights movement.")

26. Flamm, *Law and Order*, 2.

27. Norman Mailer, *The Faith of Graffiti* (New York: HarperCollins, 1974). ("There was always art in a criminal act—no crime could ever be as automatic as a production process—but graffiti writers were somewhat opposite to criminals since they were living through the stages of the crime in order to commit an artistic act—what a doubling of the intensity of the artist's choice when you steal not only the cans but try for the colors you want, not only the marker and the color but the width of the tip or the spout, and steal them in double amounts so you don't run out in the middle of a masterpiece.")

28. Kleiman, *When Brute Force Fails*, 13–14.

29. See generally Judith Greene, "Getting Tough on Crime: The History and Political Context of Sentencing Reform Developments Leading to the Passage of the 1994 Crime Act," in *Sentencing and Society: International Perspectives*, ed. by Cyrus Tata and Neil Hutton (New York: Ashgate Publishing, 2002), 43–64.

30. Dagan and Teles, "The Conservative War on Prisons," 10; see also "1968 Nixon vs. Humphrey vs. Wallace," The Living Room Candidate, http://www. livingroomcandidate.org/commercials/1968 (providing a video recording of Nixon's 1968 campaign commercial, "Crime").

31. See "1988 Bush vs. Dukakis," The Living Room Candidate, http://www. livingroomcandidate.org/commercials/1988 (providing a video recording of Bush's 1988 campaign commercial, "Willie Horton").

32. Ibid.

33. See Eric Benson, "Dukakis's Regret: What the Onetime Democratic Nominee Learned from the Willie Horton Ad," *New York*, June 17, 2012, http://nymag. com/news/frank-rich/michael-dukakis-2012-6/ (providing an interview of Dukakis in which he describes the decision not to respond to the Willie Horton campaign commercial "the biggest mistake of my political career").

34. See Flamm, *Law and Order*, 183. ("The Dukakis debacle and the return of law and order to national politics convinced many Democrats that they would have to find a candidate with the record and rhetoric to challenge the Republicans on the issue. In 1992 he appeared and his name was Bill Clinton. . . . On the

campaign trail against President Bush, Clinton made it clear that he was a 'New Democrat' who would not coddle criminals.")

35. Ibid., 184. ("In 1991, the Republicans had a 37–16 percent advantage on law and order according to a Time/CNN poll; by 1994, the Democrats had a 42–34 percent edge according to a CNN/USA Today Poll.")

36. See "Ann Richards," *The Economist*, September 28, 2006, http://www.economist.com/node/7963556 (noting that Richards "oversaw the biggest prison-building programme in American history").

37. Richard L. Berke, "The 1992 Campaign: Political Week; in 1992, Willie Horton Is Democrats' Weapon," *New York Times*, August 25, 1992, http://www.nytimes.com/1992/08/25/us/the-1992-campaign-political-week-in-1992-willie-horton-is-democrats-weapon.html.

38. John Leo and Jack E. White, "Low Profile for a Legend: Bernhard Goetz, the Subway Gunman, Spurns Aid and Celebrity," *Time*, January 21, 1985, 54.

39. See Daniel DiSalvo, "The Trouble with Public Sector Unions," *National Affairs*, Fall 2010, 11–12, https://www.nationalaffairs.com/publications/detail/the-trouble-with-public-sector-unions; see generally Joshua Page, *The Toughest Beat: Politics, Punishment, and the Prison Officers Union in California* (New York: Oxford University Press, 2011), 44–80 (discussing the California Correctional Peace Officers Association and its political activities generally).

40. DiSalvo, "The Trouble with Public Sector Unions," 12; see generally Page, *The Toughest Beat*, 117–33 (discussing the efforts of the California Correctional Peace Officers Association to enact and defend California's "three strikes" law).

41. Gwen Ifill, "White House Offers Version of Three-Strikes Crime Bill," *New York Times*, March 2, 1994, http://www.nytimes.com/1994/03/02/us/white-house-offers-version-of-three-strikes-crime-bill.html.

42. *Brown v. Plata*, 131 S. Ct. 1910, 1923, 1947 (2011).

43. See, e.g., Christopher Hartney and Caroline Glesmann, "Prison Bed Profiteers: How Corporations Are Reshaping Criminal Justice in the U.S.," National Council on Crime & Delinquency, May 2012, 12–14, http://nccdglobal.org/sites/default/files/publication_pdf/prison-bed-profiteers.pdf.

44. See Antje Deckert and William R. Wood, "Prison Privatization and Contract Facilities," in *Corrections*, ed. by William J. Chambliss (Thousand Oaks, California: Sage Publications, 2011), 219, 224, http://www.academia.edu/2911049/Prison_Privatization_and_Contract_Facilities.

45. Governor Ronald Reagan, "Second Inaugural Address," Governors' Gallery, delivered January 4, 1971, transcript available at http://governors.library.ca.gov/addresses/33-Reagan02.html.

46. Bobby White, "San Quentin Seen as a Hot Property," *Wall Street Journal*, March 18, 2009, http://online.wsj.com/news/articles/SB123732681929562101.

47. Jerome G. Miller, "The Debate on Rehabilitating Criminals: Is It True That Nothing Works?" Prison Policy, https://www.prisonpolicy.org/scans/rehab.html.

48. See Neil King Jr., "As Prisons Squeeze Budgets, GOP Rethinks Crime Focus," Wall Street Journal, June 21, 2013, http://online.wsj.com/news/articles/SB10001 424127887323836504578551902602217018.

49. See, e.g., Radley Balko, "More Democracy, More Incarceration," Reason, October 25, 2010, http://reason.com/archives/2010/10/25/ more-democracy-more-incarcerat.

50. See, e.g., Mitch Pearlstein, "Crime, Punishment, and Rehabilitation," National Review, October 3, 2011, http://www.nationalreview.com/nrd/articles/296415/ crime-punishment-and-rehabilitation. Mike Pearlstein, a social conservative and founder and president of Center of the American Experiment, points out that incarcerated men "are less attractive marriage partners, not just because they may be incarcerated, but because rap sheets are not conducive to good-paying, family-supporting jobs." It is common sense that neighborhoods suffering from high incarceration rates also suffer a plague of single-parent homes and troubled children. This, in turn, leads to dysfunctional communities that are mistrustful of law enforcement. Most American children are taught they may always ask the police for help. In some American neighborhoods, however, children are taught never to engage with the police. See generally Jamie L. Flexon et al., "Exploring the Dimensions of Trust in the Police among Chicago Juveniles," Journal of Criminal Justice 37, no. 2 (March–April 2009): 180–89, http://www. sciencedirect.com/science/article/pii/S0047235209000208.

51. Jeremy Travis et al., From Prison to Home: The Dimensions and Consequences of Prisoner Reentry, Washington, D.C., Urban Institute, June 2001, http:// research.urban.org/UploadedPDF/from_prison_to_home.pdf.

52. E.g., Shankar Vedantam, "When Crime Pays: Prison Can Teach Some to Be Better Criminals," NPR, February 1, 2013, http://www.npr. org/2013/02/01/169732840/when-crime-pays-prison-can-teach-some-to-be- better-criminals (providing audio recording in which Shankar Vedantam and Donald Hutcherson discuss Hutcherson's research on the impact of prison on criminality).

53. See Harry J. Holzer, What Employers Want: Job Prospects for Less-Educated Workers (New York: Russell Sage Foundation, 1996), 58 (reporting that a survey of employers in four major metropolitan cities revealed that two-thirds of employers would not hire someone with a criminal record).

54. Pew Center on the States, State of Recidivism: The Revolving Door of America's Prisons, Washington, D.C., Pew Charitable Trusts, April 2011, 10–11, https://www.pewtrusts.org/~/media/legacy/uploadedfiles/ wwwpewtrustsorg/reports/sentencing_and_corrections/ staterecidivismrevolvingdooramericaprisons20pdf.pdf.

55. Newt Gingrich and Mark Earley, "Cutting Recidivism Saves Money and Lives," Atlanta Journal-Constitution, March 23, 2010, https://perma.cc/6994-3LP2.

56. Council of State Governments, "Justice Reinvestment in Texas: Assessing the Impact of the 2007 Justice Reinvestment Initiative," Justice Center, April 2009, 3, http://www.ncsl.org/portals/1/Documents/cj/texas.pdf.

57. John Buntin, "John Whitmire and Jerry Madden," Governing, http://www. governing.com/poy/jerry-madden-john-whitmire.html.
58. Ibid.
59. Ibid.
60. See Vikrant P. Reddy and Marc A. Levin, "The Conservative Case against More Prisons," *American Conservative*, March 6, 2013, http://www. theamericanconservative.com/articles/the-conservative-case-against-more-prisons/; see also "Levin: Whitmire, Madden Lay Out Viable Alternative to More Prisons," Texas Public Policy Foundation, January 30, 2007, http://www. texaspolicy.com/press/ levin-whitmire-madden-lay-out-viable-alternative-more-prisons.
61. Dagan and Teles, "The Conservative War on Prisons," 10.
62. Governor Rick Perry, State of the State Address, February 7, 2007.
63. Marc Levin, "Adult Corrections Reform: Lower Crime, Lower Costs," Texas Model, September 20110, http://rightoncrime.com/wp-content/ uploads/2011/09/Texas-Model-Adult.pdf.
64. Texas Department of Criminal Justice, Report to the Governor and Legislative Budget Board on the Monitoring of Community Supervision Diversion Funds, December 1, 2016, https://www.tdcj.texas.gov/documents/cjad/CJAD_ Monitoring_of_DP_Reports_2016_Report_To_Governor.pdf.
65. Marc Levin and Vikrant P. Reddy, "The Role of Parole in Texas: Achieving Public Safety and Efficiency," Policy Perspective, Texas Public Policy Foundation, May 2011, https://files.texaspolicy.com/ uploads/2018/08/16094259/2011-05-PP09-Parole-mlevin-vreddy.pdf.
66. "Texas Crime Rates 1960–2018," Disaster Center, http://www.disastercenter. com/crime/txcrime.htm.
67. "United States Crime Rates 1960–2018," Disaster Center.
68. Texas Department of Criminal Justice, *Report to the Governor and the Legislative Budget Board on Monitoring of Community Supervision Diversion Funds*, December 1, 2006, https://www.tdcj.texas.gov/documents/cjad/CJAD_ Diversion_Fund_Report_to_Governor_2006.pdf.
69. Texas Department of Criminal Justice, *Report to the Governor and Legislative Budget Board on the Monitoring of Community Supervision Diversion Funds*, December 1, 2019, https://www.tdcj.texas.gov/documents/cjad/CJAD_ Monitoring_of_DP_Reports_2019_Report_To_Governor.pdf.
70. Texas Board of Pardons and Paroles, *Annual Statistical Report FY 2018*, https:// www.tdcj.texas.gov/bpp/publications/FY%202018%20AnnualStatistical%20 Report.pdf.
71. Texas Department of Criminal Justice, *Statistical Report Fiscal Year 2005*, March 2006, https://www.tdcj.texas.gov/documents/Statistical_Report_ FY2005.pdf.
72. Texas Department of Criminal Justice, *FY 2018 Statistical Report*, February 2019, https://www.tdcj.texas.gov/documents/Statistical_Report_FY2018.pdf.

73. See Right on Crime, "Statement of Principles," 1, http://www.rightoncrime. com/wp-content/uploads/2010/11/ROC-Statement-of-Principles9.pdf.

74. "35 States Reform Criminal Justice Policies through Justice Reinvestment," Pew Charitable Trusts, https://www.pewtrusts.org/en/research-and-analysis/ fact-sheets/2018/07/35-states-reform-criminal-justice-policies-through-justice-reinvestment.

75. H.B. 1176, 151st General Assembly, Regular Session, (Georgia, 2012). For a brief summary of the reforms, see Pew Center on the States, "2012 Georgia Public Safety Reform: Legislation to Reduce Recidivism and Cut Corrections Costs," July 2012, 6–9, http://www.pewstates.org/uploadedFiles/PCS_ Assets/2012/Pew_Georgia_Safety_Reform.pdf.

76. "Governor Deal's State of the State Address: Charting the Course to Prosperity," Governor Nathan Deal Office of the Governor website, January 10, 2012, https://nathandeal.georgia.gov/press-releases/2012-01-10/ gov-deals-state-state-address-charting-course-prosperity/.

77. S.B. 1476, 48th Legislature, 2nd General Assembly (Arizona, 2008).

78. Pew Center on the States, "The Impact of Arizona's Probation Reforms," March 2011, 2, http://www.pewstates.org/uploadedFiles/PCS_Assets/2011/PSPP_ Arizona_probation_brief_web.pdf.

79. Ibid., 1.

80. Pew Charitable Trusts, "State-Local Partnership in Ohio Cuts Juvenile Recidivism, Costs," 2013, https://www.pewtrusts.org/-/media/legacy/ uploadedfiles/pcs_assets/2013/ psppstatelocalpartnershipinohiocutsjuvenilerecidivismcostspdf.pdf.

81. Christopher T. Lowenkamp and Edward J. Latessa, *Evaluation of Ohio's RECLAIM Funded Programs, Community Corrections Facilities, and DYS Facilities*, University of Cincinnati, August 17, 2005, 25, table 10, http://www. uc.edu/content/dam/uc/ccjr/docs/reports/project_reports/Final_DYS_ RECLAIM_Report_2005.pdf.

82. Kleiman, *When Brute Force Fails*, 34-48.

83. Robert A. Ferguson, *Inferno: An Anatomy of American Punishment* (Cambridge, Massachusetts: Harvard University Press, 2014), 39–45.

84. Ibid., 39.

85. Ibid.

86. See Cesare Beccaria, *On Crimes and Punishments*, ed. Richard Bellamy (Cambridge: Cambridge University Press, 1995), 63.

87. Kleiman, *When Brute Force Fails*, 40.

88. Ibid.

89. Ibid.

90. Ibid., 39.

91. Ibid., 37.

92. Ibid.

93. Angela Hawken and Mark Kleiman, *Managing Drug Involved Probationers with Swift and Certain Sanctions: Evaluating Hawaii's HOPE*, December 2009, 18, http://www.ncjrs.gov/pdffiles1/nij/grants/229023.pdf
94. Ibid., 33.
95. Eric Martin, "A Hopeful Approach—Understanding the Implications for the HOPE Program," National Institute of Justice, September 20, 3017, https://nij.ojp.gov/topics/articles/hopeful-approach-understanding-implications-hope-program.
96. Ibid.
97. "To Safely Cut Incarceration, States Rethink Responses to Supervision Violations," Pew Charitable Trusts, July 16, 2019, https://www.pewtrusts.org/en/research-and-analysis/issue-briefs/2019/07/to-safely-cut-incarceration-states-rethink-responses-to-supervision-violations.
98. Texas Legislative Budget Board, *Texas Community Supervision Revocation Project: Fiscal Year 2006 Follow-Up Study*, January 2007, http://www.lbb.state.tx.us/documents/publications/policy_report/texas%20community%20supervision%20revocation%20project%20follow%20up%20study.pdf.
99. See generally Greg Berman and John Feinblatt, "Problem-Solving Courts: A Brief Primer," *Law and Policy* 23, no. 2 (April 2001): 125–40 (providing background information on problem-solving courts).
100. See generally Henry J. Steadman et al., "Mental Health Courts: Their Promise and Unanswered Questions," *Law & Psychiatry* 52 (April 2001): 457–58 (providing background information on mental-health courts).
101. Marc A. Levin and Vikrant P. Reddy, "Peach State Criminal Justice: Controlling Costs, Protecting the Public," Georgia Public Policy Foundation, February 16, 2012, http://www.georgiapolicy.org/peach-state-criminal-justice-controlling-costs-protecting-the-public-2/#ff_s=fKu1Z (citing interview with Merrill Rotter, medical director, Bronx Mental Health Court, January 13, 2009).
102. M. Susan Ridgely et al., "Justice, Treatment, and Cost: An Evaluation of the Fiscal Impact of Allegheny County Mental Health Court," RAND Corporation, 2007, xi.
103. Interview with Julie Clements, pretrial services officer, Washoe County Mental Health Court, January 13, 2009.
104. Ibid.
105. Merith Cosden et al., *Evaluation of the Santa Barbara County Mental Health Treatment Court with Intensive Case Management* (2004), 4.
106. Dale E. McNiel and Renée L. Binder, "Effectiveness of a Mental Health Court in Reducing Criminal Recidivism and Violence," *American Journal of Psychiatry* 164 (September 2007): 1395–1403.
107. Kleiman, *When Brute Force Fails*, 39–40.
108. "Do Drug Courts Work?" Superior Court of California Drug Court Services, http://www.alameda.courts.ca.gov/dcs/facts2.html.
109. Ibid.

110. U.S. Government Accountability Office, *Adult Drug Courts: Evidence Indicates Recidivism Reductions and Mixed Results for Other Outcomes*, GAO 05-219, February 2005, 45, http://www.gao.gov/new.items/d05219.pdf.

111. California Administrative Office of the Courts, "California Drug Court Cost Analysis Study," Center for Families, Children, and the Courts, May 2006, 3, http://www.courts.ca.gov/documents/cost_study_research_summary.pdf.

112. See generally Marc A. Levin, "Veterans' Courts," Texas Public Policy Foundation Policy Brief, November 2009, https://justiceforvets.org/wp-content/uploads/A%20Veterans%27%20Courts%20Policy%20Brief_Marc%20Levin.pdf.

113. See generally Tristan Hallman, "Texas Bill on Prostitution Diversion Modeled on Dallas County," *Dallas Morning News*, June 5, 2013, https://www.dallasnews.com/news/politics/2013/06/06/texas-bill-on-prostitution-diversion-modeled-on-dallas-county/.

114. S.B. No. 1611, https://capitol.texas.gov/tlodocs/83R/billtext/html/SB01611F.htm.

115. "Client Choice Program in Comal County, Texas," Justice Management Institute, https://www.jmijustice.org/blog/client-choice/.

116. "How Lubbock Became the Model for Indigent Defense in Texas," *San Antonio Express News*, December 18, 2018, https://www.mysanantonio.com/opinion/editorials/article/How-Lubbock-became-the-model-for-indigent-defense-13467686.php.

117. James M. Anderson et al., "Holistic Representation: An Innovative Approach to Defending Poor Clients Can Reduce Incarceration and Save Taxpayer Dollars—without Harm to Public Safety," RAND Corporation, 2019, https://www.rand.org/pubs/research_briefs/RB10050.html.

118. "Overcriminalization," Heritage Foundation, https://www.heritage.org/crime-and-justice/heritage-explains/overcriminalization.

119. Dick Thornburgh, "Overcriminalization: Sacrificing the Rule of Law in Pursuit of 'Justice,'" Heritage Foundation, March 1, 2011, https://www.heritage.org/crime-and-justice/report/overcriminalization-sacrificing-the-rule-law-pursuit-justice.

120. James R. Copland and Rafael A. Mangual, "Overcriminalizing America: An Overview and Model Legislation for States," Manhattan Institute, August 8, 2018, https://www.manhattan-institute.org/html/overcriminalizing-america-overview-and-model-legislation-states-11399.html.

121. "Criminal Intent Protection Act," American Legislative Exchange Council, June 7, 2011, https://www.alec.org/model-policy/criminal-intent-protection-act/.

122. Nick Sibilla, "Cops in Texas Seize Millions by 'Policing for Profit,'" *Forbes*, June 5, 2014, https://www.forbes.com/sites/instituteforjustice/2014/06/05/cops-in-texas-seize-millions-by-policing-for-profit/#90545631a815.

123. "Asset Forfeiture Process and Private Property Protection Act—SNPS 2016 Edits in PDF Version," American Legislative Exchange Council, https://www.

alec.org/model-policy/
asset-forfeiture-process-and-private-property-protection-act/.
124. Nathaniel Hawthorne, *The Scarlet Letter* (New York: Dover Publications, 1994), reprint, 33.

THE CONSERVATIVE PATH TO IMMIGRATION AND BORDER SECURITY REFORM

1. Portions of this essay are adapted from James Jay Carafano et. al., "An Agenda for American Immigration Reform," February 20, 2019, Heritage Foundation, Special Report, February 20, 2019, https://www.heritage.org/immigration/report/Agenda-american-immigration-reform.
2. Edwin Meese III and Matthew Spalding, "The Principles of Immigration," Heritage Foundation Backgrounder No. 1807, October 19, 2004, 1, https://www.heritage.org/report/the-principles-immigration.
3. In a 2017 poll conducted by the Associated Press-NORC Center for Public Affairs Research, 71 percent said the U.S. is losing its national identity—that is, the beliefs and values the country represents. Seventy-three percent said the shared use of the English language is extremely or very important. Fifty-seven percent said the U.S. should be a country with an essential culture that immigrants adopt when they arrive. "The American Identity: Points of Pride, Conflicting Views, and a Distinct Culture," Associated Press-NORC Center for Public Affairs Research, March 2017.

FROM SERVING THE NATION TO COMING HOME: HOW STATE AND LOCAL GOVERNMENTS CAN ASSIST IN VETERAN TRANSITION

1. United States Census Bureau Quick Facts (July 1, 2019, estimates) https://www.census.gov/quickfacts/fact/table/US/PST045218.
2. "Veterans 2000," Census 2000 Brief, May 2003, https://www.census.gov/prod/2003pubs/c2kbr-22.pdf.
3. "DoD Personnel, Workforce Reports & Publications," Defense Manpower Data Center, https://www.dmdc.osd.mil/appj/dwp/dwp%5Freports.jsp; 2018 Demographics, Profile of the Military Community, http://download.militaryonesource.mil/12038/MOS/Reports/2018-demographics-report.pdf.
4. "U.S. Military Size 1985–2020," MacroTrends, https://www.macrotrends.net/countries/USA/united-states/military-army-size.
5. Office of Mental Health and Suicide Prevention, 2019 National Veteran Suicide Prevention Annual Report, U.S. Department of Veterans Affairs, September 2019, https://www.mentalhealth.va.gov/docs/data-sheets/2019/2019_National_Veteran_Suicide_Prevention_Annual_Report_508.pdf.
6. "Hazelwood Act," Texas Veterans Commission, https://www.tvc.texas.gov/education/hazlewood-act/.

7. "Employment Situation of Veterans News Release," U.S. Bureau of Labor Statistics, https://www.bls.gov/news.release/vet.htm.
8. National Center for Veterans Analysis and Statistics, *Statistical Trends: Veterans with a Service-Connected Disability, 1990 to 2018*, United States Department of Veterans Affairs, May 2019, https://www.va.gov/vetdata/docs/Quickfacts/ SCD_trends_FINAL_2018.pdf.
9. "HERS – Suicide and Homeless Veterans," U.S. Department of Veterans Affairs, February 27, 2018, https://www.va.gov/HOMELESS/nchav/research/HERS6_ Suicide.asp

DEFENDING THE SECOND AMENDMENT

1. David French, "The Biblical and Natural Right of Self-Defense," *National Review*, January 25, 2013, https://www.nationalreview.com/corner/ biblical-and-natural-right-self-defense-david-french/.
2. "Firearms," Heritage Foundation Special Issue, https://www.heritage.org/ firearms.
3. WLWT Digital Staff, "Police: No Charges for Woman Who Shot Ex-Boyfriend as He Broke into Her East Price Hill Home," WLWT News, June 6, 2019, https://www.wlwt.com/article/police-woman-shoots-ex-boyfriend-as-he- breaks-into-her-house-in-east-price-hill/27780450.
4. Ibid.
5. Joshua Feinzig and Joshua Zoffer, "A Constitutional Case for Gun Control," *The Atlantic*, October 28, 2019, https://www.theatlantic.com/ideas/ archive/2019/10/constitutional-case-gun-control/600694/.
6. Lawrence W. Reed, "Guns Prevent Thousands of Crimes Every Day, Research Shows," FEE, August 23, 2019, https://fee.org/articles/ guns-prevent-thousands-of-crimes-every-day-research-show/.
7. Ibid.
8. Holly Matkin, "Officer Gets Shot, Then Armed Citizen Comes to Her Rescue," Police Tribune, June 18, 2019, https://bluelivesmatter.blue/ officer-gets-shot-then-armed-citizen-comes-to-her-rescue/.
9. Brandon Curtis, "Bloomberg on Texas Church Shooting: Average Citizens Shouldn't Carry Guns 'in a Crowded Place', Only Police Should Have Guns (Video)," Concealed Nation, January 1, 2020, https://concealednation. org/2020/01/ bloomberg-on-texas-church-shooting-average-citizens-shouldnt-carry-guns-in- a-crowded-place-only-police-should-have-guns-video/.
10. Jake Bleiberg and Jamie Stengle, "Firearms Instructor Took Out Gunman at Texas Church Service," AP News, December 31, 2019, https://apnews.com/ de8a2aebc6d95b9131a08975a5d881f9.
11. Elvia Diaz, "Armed, Even in Church: Texas Shooting Is about a Lot More Than Jack Wilson's Heroism," *USA Today*, January 1, 2020, https://www.usatoday.

com/story/opinion/2020/01/01/
jack-wilson-white-settlement-shooting-hero-column/2784355001/.

12. Jason Kravarik and Stephanie Elam, "Good Samaritan with a Gun Saves Wounded Cop," CNN, April 6, 2017, https://www.cnn.com/2017/03/17/us/ beyond-the-call-of-duty-arizona/index.html.

13. Dave Jordan, "Victim of Violent Home Invasion Speaks; Credits Wife with Saving His Life with AR-15," Bay News 9, November 1, 2019, https://www. baynews9.com/fl/tampa/news/2019/11/01/ victim-of-violent-home-invasion-speaks—credits-wife-with-saving-his-life.

14. Patrick Mondaca, "You Don't Need an AR-15," US News, March 2, 2018, https://www.usnews.com/opinion/civil-wars/articles/2018-03-02/ citizens-dont-need-ar-15s.

15. David Heath et al., "How an 'Ugly,' Unwanted Weapon Became the Most Popular Rifle in America,' CNN, December 14, 2017, https://www.cnn. com/2017/12/14/health/ar15-rifle-history-trnd/index.html.

16. Jordan, "Victim of Violent Home Invasion Speaks," Bay News 9.

17. Jeff Daniels, "Definition of What's Actually an 'Assault Weapon' Is a Highly Contentious Issue," CNBC News, February 21, 2018, https://www.cnbc. com/2018/02/21/definition-of-whats-an-assault-weapon-is-a-very-contentious-issue.html.

18. Robert Tracinski, "How the Second Amendment Prevents Tyranny," The Federalist, March 22, 2018, https://thefederalist.com/2018/03/22/ how-the-second-amendment-prevents-tyranny/.

19. Daniel Friend, "More Counties Pass 'Second Amendment Sanctuary' Resolutions, Collin County Reaffirms Constitutional Oath," The Texan, November 26, 2019, https://thetexan.news/ more-counties-pass-second-amendment-sanctuary-resolutions-collin-county-reaffirms-constitutional-oath/.

AMERICA'S GREATEST ASSET: THE FAMILY

1. Lindsay Whitehurst and Jonathan J. Cooper, "A Growing Number of States Call Porn a Public Health Crisis," AP News, May 9, 2019, https://apnews.com/9 c91cfd28a7b461b87948f36117a432e.

2. National marriage and divorce rate trends for 2000–2018, Centers for Disease Control and Prevention, https://www.cdc.gov/nchs/data/dvs/national-marriage-divorce-rates-00-18.pdf; Gretchen Livingston, "Is U.S. Fertility at an All-Time Low? Two of Three Measures Point to Yes," Pew Research Center, May 22, 2019, https://www.pewresearch.org/ fact-tank/2019/05/22/u-s-fertility-rate-explained/.

3. Stephanie Kramer, "U.S. Has World's Highest Rate of Children Living in Single-Parent Households," Pew Research Center, December 12, 2019, https://www. pewresearch.org/

fact-tank/2019/12/12/u-s-children-more-likely-than-children-in-other-countries-to-live-with-just-one-parent/.

4. Michael Schulson, "The Culture War and the Benedict Option: An Interview with Rod Dreher," Religion and Politics, March 7, 2017, https://religionandpolitics.org/2017/03/07/the-culture-war-and-the-benedict-option-an-interview-with-rod-dreher/.

5. Jo Craven McGinty, "The Divorce Rate Is at a 40-Year Low, Unless You're 55 or Older," Wall Street Journal, June 21, 2019, https://www.wsj.com/articles/the-divorce-rate-is-at-a-40-year-low-unless-youre-55-or-older-11561116601.

6. Rachel K. Jones et al., "Abortion Incidence and Service Availability in the United States, 2017," Guttmacher Institute, 2019, https://www.guttmacher.org/report/abortion-incidence-service-availability-us-2017; Michael J. New, "Mainstream Media Continues to Miss Story on America's Abortion Decline," National Review, December 5, 2018, https://www.nationalreview.com/corner/mainstream-media-continues-to-miss-story-on-americas-abortion-decline/; Melanie Israel, "A New Report Shows the U.S. Abortion Rate Is Declining. Here Are 4 Things You Need to Know," Heritage Foundation, September 19, 2019, https://www.heritage.org/life/commentary/new-report-shows-the-us-abortion-rate-declining-here-are-4-things-you-need-know.

7. W. Bradford Wilcox et al., "Mobility and Money in U.S. States: The Marriage Effect," Brookings Institution, December 7, 2015, https://www.brookings.edu/research/mobility-and-money-in-u-s-states-the-marriage-effect/.

8. Kim Parker and Renee Stepler, "As U.S. Marriage Rate Hovers at 50%, Education Gap in Marital Status Widens," Pew Research Center, September 14, 2017, https://www.pewresearch.org/fact-tank/2017/09/14/as-u-s-marriage-rate-hovers-at-50-education-gap-in-marital-status-widens/.

9. Livingston, "Is U.S. Fertility at an All-Time Low?"

10. "Unmarried Childbearing," Centers for Disease Control and Prevention, https://www.cdc.gov/nchs/fastats/unmarried-childbearing.htm; Kramer, "U.S. Has World's Highest Rate of Children Living in Single-Parent Households."

11. "Fragile Families and Child Wellbeing Study," Robert Wood Johnson Foundation, January 28, 2014, https://fragilefamilies.princeton.edu/sites/fragilefamilies/files/rwjf_program_results_report.pdf.

12. Mark Mather, "U.S. Children in Single-Mother Families," Population Reference Bureau, May 2010, https://assets.prb.org/pdf10/single-motherfamilies.pdf; Sophia Addy, Will Engelhardt, and Curtis Skinner, "Basic Facts About Low-Income Children: Children under 18 Years, 2011," National Center for Children in Poverty, January 2013, http://www.nccp.org/publications/pub_1074.html.

13. Addy, Engelhardt, and Skinner, "Basic Facts about Low-Income Children."

14. "Facts on Poverty and Opportunity That Progressives and Conservatives Can Agree On," Brookings Institution, December 3, 2015, https://www.brookings.edu/research/facts-on-poverty-and-opportunity-that-progressives-and-conservatives-can-agree-on/.

15. Wendy D. Manning, "Cohabitation and Child Wellbeing," National Institutes of Health, October 1, 2016, https://www.ncbi.nlm.nih.gov/pmc/articles/PMC4768758/.
16. Ibid.
17. Ibid.
18. "Fragile Families and Child Wellbeing Study Fact Sheet," Princeton University, https://fragilefamilies.princeton.edu/sites/fragilefamilies/files/ff_fact_sheet.pdf.
19. David Popenoe, *Life Without Father: Compelling New Evidence that Fatherhood and Marriage Are Indispensable for the Good of Children and Society* (New York: The Free Press, 1996), 163.
20. Jeffrey Rosenberg and W. Bradford Wilcox, "The Importance of Fathers in the Healthy Development of Children," U.S. Department of Health and Human Services Office on Child Abuse and Neglect, 2006: 12–13, 15–16, https://www.childwelfare.gov/pubpdfs/fatherhood.pdf; "Appreciating How Fathers Give Children a Head Start," Early Childhood Learning & Knowledge Center, https://eclkc.ohs.acf.hhs.gov/family-engagement/article/appreciating-how-fathers-give-children-head-start#father.
21. Rosenberg and Wilcox, "The Importance of Fathers in the Healthy Development of Children," 15–16.
22. Ibid., 11.
23. Parker and Stepler, "As U.S. Marriage Rate Hovers at 50%"; Anna Louie Sussman, "The End of Babies," *New York Times*, November 16, 2019, https://www.nytimes.com/interactive/2019/11/16/opinion/Sunday/capitalism-children.html.
24. Claire Cain Miller, "Americans Are Having Fewer Babies. They Told Us Why," *New York Times*, July 5, 2018, https://www.nytimes.com/2018/07/05/upshot/americans-are-having-fewer-babies-they-told-us-why.html.
25. Ibid.
26. Ibid.
27. Roni Caryn Rabin, "Put a Ring on It? Millennial Couples Are in No Hurry," *New York Times*, May 29, 2018, https://www.nytimes.com/2018/05/29/well/mind/millennials-love-marriage-sex-relationships-dating.html.
28. Ibid.
29. Helen Fisher, "Casual Sex May Be Improving America's Marriages," *Nautilus*, March 5, 2015, http://nautil.us/issue/22/slow/casual-sex-is-improving-americas-marriages.
30. Ibid.
31. Ibid.
32. Ibid.; Helen Fisher, "Fast Sex; Slow Love—Courtship in the Digital Age," *fifteeneightyfour* (blog), Cambridge University Press, February 27, 2019, http://www.cambridgeblog.org/2019/02/fast-sex-slow-love-courtship-in-the-digital-age/.
33. Lindsey Kilbride, "Researchers Say Something 'Significant' Happening in Duval with Dropping Divorce Rate," WJCT News, September 21, 2018, https://news.

wjct.org/post/
researchers-say-something-significant-happening-duval-dropping-divorce-rate.
34. W. Bradford Wilcox et al., "Declining Divorce in Jacksonville: Did the Culture of Freedom Initiative Make a Difference?" Institute for Family Studies, https:// ifstudies.org/ifs-admin/resources/ifscofjacksonvillereportfinal.pdf.
35. Scott Helzer, "Divorce Is Down in Jacksonville," Florida Center for Prevention Research, April 2018, 23, http://mediad.publicbroadcasting.net/p/wjct/ files/201809/fsu_research_report_-_divorce_is_down_in_jacksonville_fl.pdf.
36. In 2018, the Culture of Freedom Initiative was spun off as an independent nonprofit organization called "Communio."
37. Wilcox, "Declining Divorce in Jacksonville," 1; Communio, "Communio at Work: Divorce Drops 24% in Jacksonville," https://communio.org/impact/ aheimer-at-work-divorce-drops-28-in-jacksonville/.
38. Wendy D. Manning et al., "Healthy Marriage Initiative Spending and U.S. Marriage & Divorce Rates, a State-level Analysis," National Center for Family & Marriage Research, February 2014, http://www.bgsu.edu/content/dam/ BGSU/college-of-arts-and-sciences/NCFMR/documents/FP/FP-14-02_ HMIInitiative.pdf.
39. Ibid.
40. Anupa Bir et al., "Impacts of a Community Healthy Marriage Initiative," OPRE Report # 2012-34A, Washington, D.C.: Office of Planning, Research and Evaluation, Administration for Children and Families, U.S. Department of Health and Human Services, November 2012: ES-1–ES-2, https://www.acf.hhs. gov/sites/default/files/opre/chmi_impactreport.pdf; Wilcox, "Declining Divorce in Jacksonville," 8.
41. Wilcox, "Declining Divorce in Jacksonville," 9.
42. David P. King, "How Religion Motivates People to Give and Serve," IUPUI Lilly Family School of Philanthropy, August 22, 2017, https://philanthropy.iupui.edu/ news-events/insights-newsletter/2017-issues/august-2017-issue2.html.
43. Aspen Institute, "State of Play: Trends and Developments in Youth Sports," 2019, https://assets.aspeninstitute.org/content/uploads/2019/10/2019_SOP_ National_Final.pdf.
44. Sean Gregory, "How Kids' Sports Became a $15 Billion Industry," *Time*, August 24, 2017, https://time.com/magazine/us/4913681/ aheimer-4th-2017-vol-190-no-9-u-s/.
45. Gerry Hamilton, "Alabama, Ole Miss, Mississippi State Offer Scholarships to 286-Pound Eighth-Grader Jaheim Oatis," ESPN, July 24, 2017, https://www. espn.com/college-sports/recruiting/football/story/_/id/20145633/aheim-oatis-286-pound-eighth-grader-gets-scholarship-offers-alabama-crimson-tide-ole-miss-rebels-mississippi-state-bulldogs; Michelle R. Martinelli, "6 Times Jim Harbaugh, Michigan Offered a Scholarship to a Middle Schooler," ForTheWin, January 16, 2019, https://ftw.usatoday. com/2019/01/6-times-jim-harbaugh-offered-a-scholarship-to-a-middle-schooler.

46. NCAA, "NCAA Launches Latest Public Service Announcements, Introduces New Student-Focused Website," press release, March 13, 2007, http://fs.ncaa. org/Docs/PressArchive/2007/Announcements/NCAA%2Blaunches%2Blatest% 2Bpublic%2Bservice%2Bannouncements%2Bintroduces%2Bnew%2Bstudent-Focused%2Bwebsite.html.

47. Robert J. Araujo, "Natural Law and the Rights of the Family," *International Journal of the Jurisprudence of the Family* 1 (2010): 200, https://lawecommons. luc.edu/cgi/viewcontent.cgi?article=1498&context=facpubs.

48. Ibid.

49. John Locke, *Two Treatises of Government*, vol. 5, *The Works of John Locke*, (London: 1823), 180, http://www.yorku.ca/comninel/courses/3025pdf/Locke. pdf.

50. Ibid., 135.

51. Ibid.

52. *Meyer v. Nebraska*, 262 U.S. 390, 399 (1923) [emphasis added].

53. *Troxel v. Granville*, 530 U.S. 57, 65 (2000).

54. *Smith v. Organization of Foster Families for Equality & Reform*, 431 U.S. 816, 844 (1977).

55. Locke, *Two Treatises*, 128; *Pierce v. Society of Sisters*, 268 U.S. 510, 535 (1925).

56. *Parham v. J.R.*, 442 U.S. 584, 602 (1979).

57. Ibid.

58. Ibid, 603.

59. James G. Dwyer, "No Place for Children: Addressing Urban Blight and Its Impact on Children through Child Protection Law, Domestic Relations Law, and 'Adult-Only' Residential Zoning," *Alabama Law Review* 62, no. 5 (2011): 892, https://www.law.ua.edu/resources/pubs/lrarticles/Volume%2062/ Issue%205/Dwyer.pdf.

60. James G. Dwyer, "A Constitutional Birthright: The State, Parentage, and the Rights of Newborn Persons," *UCLA Law Review* 56, (2009): 831–35, https:// www.uclalawreview.org/pdf/56-4-1.pdf.

61. See, for example, Naomi Schaefer Riley, "Cuomo Needs to Veto This Bill That Puts Kids at Risk," American Enterprise Institute, August 9, 2019, https://www. aei.org/articles/cuomo-needs-to-veto-this-bill-that-puts-kids-at-risk/.

62. Naomi Schaefer Riley, "Can Big Data Help Save Abused Kids?" *Reason*, February 2018, https://reason.com/2018/01/22/can-big-data-help-save-abused/.

63. See, for example, *Santosky v. Kramer*, 455 U.S. 745, 753 (1982).

64. Jerry Milner and David Kelly, "It's Time to Stop Confusing Poverty with Neglect," Chronicle of Social Change, January 17, 2020, https:// chronicleofsocialchange.org/child-welfare-2/ time-for-child-welfare-system-to-stop-confusing-poverty-with-neglect/40222.

65. Ibid.

66. Scheef & Stone, LLP, "Petition for Writ of Mandamus," Texas Supreme Court, http://www.search.txcourts.gov/SearchMedia.aspx?MediaVersionID=74e18aa5-fd15-4293-b59f-8157660e7196&coa=cossup&DT=BRIEFS&MediaID=f6a61

d8d-44dc-45f3-b4f3-4497836fec78 (See "Statement of Facts" beginning on page 9); Daniel Friend, "Pardo Family Wins Dismissal by Kaufman County Court, Controversial CPS Case Effectively Ended," The Texan, December 3, 2019, https://thetexan.news/ pardo-family-wins-dismissal-by-kaufman-county-court-controversial-cps-case-effectively-ended/.

67. Supreme Court of Texas No. 19-0760, http://www.search.txcourts.gov/ SearchMedia.aspx?MediaVersionID=c91ab2d0-fda8-464f-8ecc-bfddd85f8481&coa=cossup&DT=STAY%20ORDER%20 ISSUED&MediaID=f2e977c5-0a8e-44d9-b52f-d524fdf26ac4.

68. Texas Public Policy Foundation, "Families First: Protecting Parental Rights in the Court Room," YouTube, January 23, 2020, 48:52, https://youtu.be/ BvuKtiE4mbk?t=2932.

69. David Gates, "History of the Orphanage," Newsweek, December 11, 1994, https://www.newsweek.com/history-orphanage-185444.

70. "Toward Stricter Child Abuse Statutes," American Bar Association, https:// www.americanbar.org/content/dam/aba/publishing/insights_law_society/ ChildProtectionHistory.authcheckdam.pdf.

71. Ibid.

72. Social Security Act of 1935, 42 U.S.C.§521 (1935).

73. "Child Maltreatment 2018," U.S. Department of Health and Human Services, Administration for Children and Families, Children's Bureau, 2020: 456, https:// www.acf.hhs.gov/sites/default/files/cb/cm2018.pdf; "Toward Stricter Child Abuse Statutes," American Bar Association.

74. Ibid., xiii, Exhibit S-2.

75. Ibid.

76. Ibid.

77. Ibid.

78. "Adoption Foster Care Analysis Reporting System (AFCARS), FY 2009–2018)," U.S. Department of Health and Human Services, Administration for Children and Families, Children's Bureau, August 22, 2019, https://www.acf.hhs.gov/cb/ resource/trends-in-foster-care-and-adoption; "Child Maltreatment," Children's Bureau, U.S. Department of Health and Human Services, https://www.acf.hhs. gov/cb/research-data-technology/statistics-research/child-maltreatment.

79. "AFCARS, FY 2009–2018," Children's Bureau, August 22, 2019, https://www. acf.hhs.gov/cb/resource/trends-in-foster-care-and-adoption.

80. "The AFCARS Report," U.S. Department of Health and Human Services, Administration for Children and Families, Children's Bureau, August 22, 2019: 3, https://www.acf.hhs.gov/sites/default/files/cb/afcarsreport26.pdf.

81. Ibid.

82. Amy J. Baker, et al., "Mental Health and Behavioral Problems of Youth in the Child Welfare System: Residential Treatment Centers Compared to Therapeutic Foster Care in the Odyssey Project Population," Child Welfare 86, no. 3 (2007): 97–123; Anne-Marie Conn et al., "Youth in Out-of-Home Care: Relation of

Engagement in Structured Group Activities with Social and Mental Health Measures," *Children and Youth Services Review* 36 (2014): 201–5; Amy Dworsky et al., "Midwest Evaluation of the Adult Functioning of Former Foster Youth," Chapin Hall, University of Chicago, 2011; Joanne Riebschleger et al., "Foster Care Youth Share Stories of Trauma before, during, and after Placement: Youth Voices for Building Trauma-Informed Systems of Care," *Journal of Aggression, Maltreatment & Trauma* 24, no. 4 (2015): 341–51; Michael G. Vaughn, "Substance Use and Abuse among Older Youth in Foster Care," *Addictive Behaviors* 32, no. 9 (2006): 1929–35.

83. *M.D., et al. v. Abbott, et al.*, No. 2:11-cv-00084, Document 368 (S.D. Tex. 2015), https://www.childrensrights.org/wp-content/uploads/2015/12/2015-12-17-Memo-opinion-and-verdict-of-the-court-2.pdf.

84. Florida's Center for Child Welfare, 2, http://centerforchildwelfare.org/kb/LegislativeMandatedRpts/Statewide%20Evaluation%20of%20Florida%27s%20Community%20Based%20Care%20June%202005.pdf.

85. Ibid.; Andrew Brown et al., "Right for Kids Ranking," Texas Public Policy Foundation, January 2020, https://files.texaspolicy.com/uploads/2020/01/24143647/Brown-Pressley-huntzinger-CFC-Right-for-Kids-Ranking.pdf.

86. Brown, "Right for Kids Ranking," 18; Greg Angel, "How Is Florida's Cash-Strapped Foster System Finding Success?" Spectrum News 13 Report, May 24, 2018, https://www.mynews13.com/fl/orlando/news/2018/05/24/how-is-florida-s-cash-strapped-foster-system-finding-success-.

87. Jessie Degollado, "Gov. Abbott Calls for Child Welfare Reform in State Address," KSAT News, January 31, 2017, https://www.ksat.com/news/2017/02/01/gov-abbott-calls-for-child-welfare-reform-in-state-address/.

88. SB 11. 2017. Enrolled. 85th Texas Legislature (R).

89. "DFPS Rider 21 Report for Community Based Care," Texas Department of Family and Protective Services, August 2019, https://www.dfps.state.tx.us/About_DFPS/Reports_and_Presentations/Rider_Reports/documents/2019/2019-08-01_Rider_21_Community_Based_Care.pdf; "DFPS Rider 21 Report for Community Based Care," Texas Department of Family and Protective Services, February 2019, https://www.dfps.state.tx.us/About_DFPS/Reports_and_Presentations/Rider_Reports/documents/2019/2019-02-01_Rider_21_Community_Based_Care.pdf; Andrew C. Brown, "Testimony before the Texas Senate Finance Committee on Community-Based Care," Texas Public Policy Foundation Testimony, February 6, 2019, https://files.texaspolicy.com/uploads/2019/02/25092637/2019-02-T-CFC-Brown-Community-Based-Care.pdf; "Community Based Care: Bringing Kids Home," Our Community Our Kids, February 2019, https://simplebooklet.com/ocokfeb2019update#page=0.

90. Robert Putnam, *Bowling Alone: The Collapse and Revival of American Community* (New York: Simon & Schuster, 2000), 287–88.

91. Putnam, *Bowling Alone*, 300, 309, 329–30.

92. Brian A. Primack et al., "Social Media Use and Perceived Social Isolation among Young Adults in the U.S.," *American Journal of Preventive Medicine* 53, no. 1 (2017): 1–8, https://www.ncbi.nlm.nih.gov/pmc/articles/PMC5722463/.
93. Ibid., 2.
94. Ibid., 6.
95. Jeffrey M. Jones, "U.S. Church Membership Down Sharply in Past Two Decades," Gallup News, April 18, 2019, https://news.gallup.com/poll/248837/church-membership-down-sharply-past-two-decades.aspx.
96. Ibid.
97. Ibid.
98. "Religion," In Depth: Topics A to Z, Gallup, last updated 2019, https://news.gallup.com/poll/1690/Religion.aspx; "In U.S., Decline of Christianity Continues at Rapid Pace: An Update on America's Changing Religious Landscape," Religion and Public Life, Pew Research Center, October 17, 2019, https://www.pewforum.org/2019/10/17/in-u-s-decline-of-christianity-continues-at-rapid-pace/.
99. Tim Carney, *Alienated America: Why Some Places Thrive While Others Collapse* (New York: HarperCollins, 2019), 124–25.
100. Ibid., 125–27.
101. Karl Zinsmeister, "Less God, Less Giving: Religion and Generosity Feed Each Other in Fascinating Ways," Philanthropy Roundtable, Winter 2019, https://www.philanthropyroundtable.org/philanthropy-magazine/less-god-less-giving
102. "5 Things You Need to Know about Adoption," Barna Group, November 4, 2013, https://www.barna.com/research/5-things-you-need-to-know-about-adoption/.
103. Hayat Norimine and Obed Manuel, "Dallas' Ban on Churches Sheltering Homeless Won't be Lifted in Time for Winter," *Dallas Morning News*, November 11, 2019, https://www.dallasnews.com/news/2019/11/11/dallas-ban-on-churches-sheltering-homeless-wont-be-lifted-in-time-for-winter/.
104. Ibid.
105. Julia Terruso, "Catholic Foster Care Agency Loses Federal Appeal over LGBTQ Policy," *Philadelphia Inquirer*, April 22, 2019, https://www.inquirer.com/news/foster-care-lgbtq-catholic-social-services-religious-freedom-philadelphia-dhs-20190422.html.
106. Julia Terruso, "Philly Puts out 'Urgent' Call—300 Families Needed for Fostering," *Philadelphia Inquirer*, March 8, 2018, https://www.inquirer.com/philly/news/foster-parents-dhs-philly-child-welfare-adoptions-20180308.html.
107. Kathleen Parker, "Philadelphia's Unnecessary War on Catholics," *Washington Post*, May 22, 2018, https://www.washingtonpost.com/opinions/philadelphias-unnecessary-war-on-catholics/2018/05/22/0b6b1bd6-5e0e-11e8-9ee3-49d6d4814c4c_story.html; Susan Pearlstein, "Philly's Humanitarian Crisis: Too Many Kids in Foster Care," *Philadelphia Inquirer*, August 5, 2018, https://www.inquirer.com/philly/opinion/commentary/philadelphia-foster-care-deep-generational-poverty-dhs-20180805.html.

108. "HHS Issues Proposed Rule to Align Grants Regulation with New Legislation, Nondiscrimination Laws, and Supreme Court Decisions," Press Releases, U.S. Department of Health and Human Services, November 1, 2019, https://www.hhs.gov/about/news/2019/11/01/hhs-issues-proposed-rule-to-align-grants-regulation.html.
109. Michael R. Strain, "Beto O'Rourke's Bad Idea to Punish Conservative Churches," Bloomberg Opinion, October 16, 2019, https://www.bloomberg.com/opinion/articles/2019-10-16/beto-o-rourke-s-bid-to-end-tax-exemptions-for-churches.
110. Alexis de Tocqueville, *Democracy in America*, trans. James T. Schleifer (Indianapolis: Liberty Fund, 2010), 475.
111. Ibid., 472–73

EVERY LIFE MATTERS

1. "Abortion Is a Common Experience for U.S. Women, despite Dramatic Declines in Rates," Guttmacher Institute news release, October 19, 2017, https://www.guttmacher.org/news-release/2017/abortion-common-experience-us-women-despite-dramatic-declines-rates.
2. "Infertility and Fertility," Eunice Kennedy Shriver National Institute of Child Health and Human Development, https://www.nichd.nih.gov/health/topics/infertility.
3. "How Many Couples Are Waiting to Adopt?" American Adoptions, https://www.americanadoptions.com/pregnant/waiting_adoptive_families.
4. Lisa Cannon Green, "New Survey: Women Go Silently from Church to Abortion Clinic," Care Net, November 23, 2015, https://www.care-net.org/churches-blog/new-survey-women-go-silently-from-church-to-abortion-clinic.
5. "Reported Legal Abortions by Race of Woman Who Obtained Abortion by the State of Occurrence," Kaiser Family Foundation, 2015, https://www.kff.org/womens-health-policy/state-indicator/abortions-by-race/?currentTimeframe=0&sortModel=%7B%22colId%22:%22Location%22,%22sort%22:%22asc%22%7D.
6. Alana Varley, "Margaret Sanger: More Eugenic Than Fellow Eugenicists," Care Net, January 16, 2018, https://www.care-net.org/abundant-life-blog/margaret-sanger-more-eugenic-than-fellow-eugenicists.

ADDRESSING THE SOCIAL FABRIC OF OUR SOCIETY

1. Ronald Reagan, "A Time for Choosing (aka 'The Speech')," American Rhetoric, https://www.americanrhetoric.com/speeches/ronaldreaganatimeforchoosing.htm.
2. "Child Abuse, Neglect Data Released," Administration for Children and Families, January 28, 2019, https://www.acf.hhs.gov/media/press/2019/child-abuse-neglect-data-released.

3. "More Than 90% of Sexually Abused Children Know Their Abuser," KDRV ABC 12, November 27, 2017, https://www.kdrv.com/content/news/Most-Sexually-Abused-Children-Know-Their-Abuser-460399633.html.

4. Lyndon Haviland, "Protecting Children from Sexual Abuse: Texas Serves as a Model," Youth Today, March 1, 2016, https://youthtoday.org/2016/03/protecting-children-from-sexual-abuse-texas-serves-as-a-model/.

5. Carmen Niethammer, "Cracking the $150 Billion Business of Human Trafficking," Forbes, February 2, 2020, https://www.forbes.com/sites/carmenniethammer/2020/02/02/cracking-the-150-billion-business-of-human-trafficking/.

6. Chris Swecker, Commission on Security and Cooperation in Europe United States, Helsinki Commision, FBI, Washington, D.C., June 7, 2005, https://archives.fbi.gov/archives/news/testimony/exploiting-americans-on-american-soil-domestic-trafficking-exposed.

7. "Human Trafficking Statistics by State 2020," World Population Review, https://worldpopulationreview.com/states/human-trafficking-statistics-by-state/.

8. Ellen Wulfhorst, "Without Family, U.S. Children in Foster Care Easy Prey for Human Traffickers," Reuters, May 3, 2018, https://www.reuters.com/article/us-usa-trafficking-fostercare/without-family-u-s-children-in-foster-care-easy-prey-for-human-traffickers-idUSKBN1I40OM.

9. Allie Malloy, "Trump Signs 'Right to Try Act' Aimed at Helping Terminally Ill Patients Seek Drug Treatments," CNN, May 30, 2018, https://www.cnn.com/2018/05/30/politics/right-to-try-donald-trump/index.html.

10. Joce Sterman and Alex Brauer, "Right to Try Was Supposed to Help Terminal Patients. Here's Why Experts Say It Didn't Work," Fox San Antonio, July 1, 2019, https://foxsanantonio.com/news/spotlight-on-america/right-to-try-was-supposed-to-help-terminal-patients-heres-why-experts-say-it-didnt-work.

11. Allison Lee, "Texas' New Adult Stem Cell Law Underway," Houston Public Media, October 28, 2017, https://www.houstonpublicmedia.org/articles/news/2017/10/28/244813/texas-new-adult-stem-cell-law-underway-almost/.

12. "Stem Cells: What They Are and What They Do," Mayo Clinic, https://www.mayoclinic.org/tests-procedures/bone-marrow-transplant/in-depth/stem-cells/art-20048117.

13. "Impact on Families," National Survey of Children with Special Health Care Needs," 2004, https://mchb.hrsa.gov/chscn/pages/impact.htm.

14. Joseph Shapiro, "Katie Beckett: Patient Turned Home-Care Advocate," NPR, November 8, 2010, https://www.npr.org/templates/story/story.php?storyId=131145687.

15. Linda Marsa, "Improving Care of the Medically Fragile Child," U.S. News & World Report, September 29, 2017, https://www.usnews.com/news/healthcare-of-tomorrow/articles/2017-09-29/improving-care-of-the-medically-fragile-child.

16. Matthew Herr, "The Conservative Case for Saving Medicaid," *The Hill*, July 5, 2017, https://thehill.com/blogs/pundits-blog/healthcare/340715-the-conservative-case-for-saving-medicaid.
17. Tennessee Justice Center, https://www.tnjustice.org/.
18. Lazarex Cancer Foundation, https://lazarex.org/.
19. Alex Gangitano, "11-Year-Old Cancer Survivor Sees Her Bill Signed into Law," *Roll Call*, June 8, 2018, https://www.rollcall.com/2018/06/08/11-year-old-cancer-survivor-sees-her-bill-signed-into-law/.

THE MEDIA: "GOODBYE, IPHIGENE"

1. Owen Dyer, "Wakefield Admits Fabricating Events When He Took Children's Blood Samples," *BMJ* 336 (April 19, 2008): 850, https://www.ncbi.nlm.nih.gov/pmc/articles/PMC2323045/.
2. Lisa A. Rickard, "The Anti-Vaccine Movement and a Trial Lawyer–Funded Climate of Fear," *Forbes*, April 28, 2014, https://www.forbes.com/sites/theapothecary/2014/04/28/the-anti-vaccine-movement-and-a-trial-lawyer-funded-climate-of-fear/#5100ae0c62bd.
3. Grace Hauck, "3 Migrant Children Have Died from Flu in Custody, but US Won't Provide Vaccines," *USA Today*, August 21, 2019, https://www.usatoday.com/story/news/nation/2019/08/21/undocumented-children-wont-receive-flu-vaccine-us-custody/2070386001/.
4. Lars Willnat et al., "The American Journalist in the Digital Age," *Journalism Studies* (2017), https://www.academia.edu/35631066/The_American_Journalist_in_the_Digital_Age_How_Journalists_and_The_Public_Think_About_Journalism_in_the_United_States_2017_._Journalism_Studies._doi_10.1080_1461670X.2017.1387071.
5. Hiroko Tabuchi, "Inside Conservative Groups' Efforts to 'Make Dishwashers Great Again,'" *New York Times*, September 17, 2019, https://www.nytimes.com/2019/09/17/climate/trump-dishwasher-regulatory-rollback.html.
6. James Freeman, "Yale Prof Estimates Faculty Political Diversity at '0%,'" *Wall Street Journal*, December 9, 2019, https://www.wsj.com/articles/yale-prof-estimates-faculty-political-diversity-at-0-11575926185.
7. Ibid.
8. James Freeman, "Faculty Lounge Is Sanders County," *Wall Street Journal*, December 11, 2019, https://www.wsj.com/articles/faculty-lounge-is-sanders-country-11576012617?mod=djemBestOfTheWeb.
9. "Iphigene Ochs Sulzberger Is Dead; Central Figure in Times' History," *New York Times*, February 27, 1990, https://www.nytimes.com/1990/02/27/obituaries/iphigene-ochs-sulzberger-is-dead-central-figure-in-times-s-history.html.
10. Byron York, "New York Times Chief Outlines Coverage Shift: From Trump-Russia to Trump Racism," *Washington Examiner*, August 15, 2019, https://www.washingtonexaminer.com/opinion/columnists/

new-york-times-chief-outlines-coverage-shift-from-trump-russia-to-trump-racism.

11. Benjamin Hart, "Times Makes Major Correction That Undermines Its Big Brett Kavanaugh Story," Intelligencer, *New York*, https://nymag.com/intelligencer/2019/09/nyt-correction-kavanaugh-story.html.

12. Austin Ramzy and Chris Buckley, "'Absolutely No Mercy': Files Expose How China Organized Mass Detentions of Muslims," *New York Times*, November 16, 2019, https://www.nytimes.com/interactive/2019/11/16/world/asia/china-xinjiang-documents.html.

13. Ken Rudin, "Assessing Ronald Reagan at 100," NPR, February 4, 2011, https://www.npr.org/sections/itsallpolitics/2011/02/06/133448787/assessing-ronald-reagan-at-100.